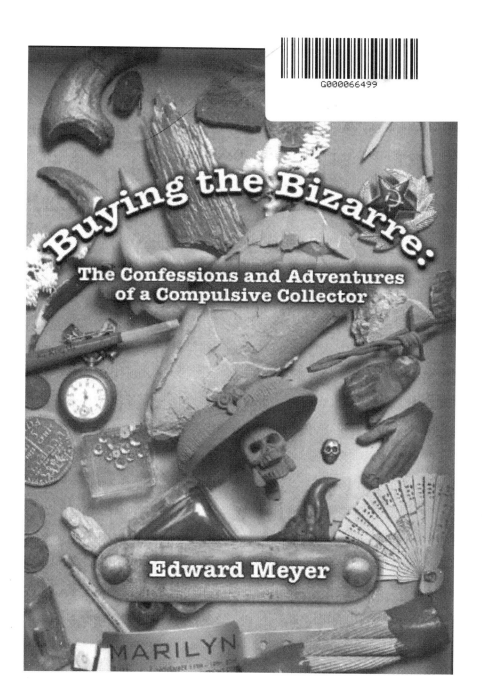

Buying the Bizarre:

The Confessions and Adventures of a Compulsive Collector

Edward Meyer

MARILYN

Buying the Bizarre:

The Confessions and Adventures
of a Compulsive Collector

Edward Meyer

Table of Contents

Part Three: Travels & Adventures –
A Tough Job but Someone Had to Do It

Part Four: Heads I Bought, Tales I Tell

To my mother and father
who put me on the right path,
and to my wife Giliane,
who kept me on it for 40 years.

© Lifetouch Portraits

Part One

Setting the Stage

1

Foreword

This book is definitely a vanity project, a challenge to myself to prove I could do it, but also an answer to the dozens of people who for years told me "you should write a book", but probably didn't believe me when I said: "I plan to, but not until I retire. I don't have time right now."

Writing was always a critical part of my job at Ripley's, everything from museum show card text for thousands of exhibits, to presentations, to reports, to meeting minutes, to answering endless fan mail. So despite preferring to verbally tell stories rather than write them, I was sure I could write them if motivated.

Within two weeks of retiring in June of 2018 I put my money where my mouth had always been and sat down determined to beat the keys for as long as it would take to reminisce about 40 wonderful years as the "buyer" — Vice President of Exhibits & Archives — for Ripley Entertainment Inc., makers of all things "Ripley's Believe it or Not!"

I spent a couple of days thinking about it, but in truth I had been doing that for years, then I made an eleven-page list of everything I thought was worth writing about. The first six chapters were more or less written sequentially but the rest were quite random. I figured sequencing would be the second stage job of a good editor. The plan would be to look at the list daily and pick a line that I felt like weaving that day. On my first day of writing I did 2,800 words and figured that as long as I was disciplined enough to look at the list and the computer every day, and wrote about that much every day, the tale would unravel like a long radio interview, the list being the interviewer prompting the next chapter.

For years I have kept diaries, calendars, and travel journals, so where specific names, dates and places are mentioned they are accurate, and based on my own earlier scribblings. Where things sound a bit more generic, I have written more from memory than from source material. I have always prided myself on my memory though, and haven't fabricated anything. There are dozens of eye witnesses to this history, so if any readers find something they feel is in error or are sure is just downright inaccurate, I hope they will make me aware of it, but also forgive me for being fallible.

2

A Prelude to My Ripley Adventures

It initially seemed to me that this book should start at the beginning of my Ripley career when I was age twenty-two. I wrote a few chapters and sent them to various friends for feedback and was surprised that the biggest complaint was why didn't I say anything about my upbringing, the years before Ripley: "What happened in the first twenty-one years"? Obviously quite a lot: hockey, school, blues music, romance, family deaths, and most significantly, marriage to the love of my life for forty-one years, Giliane Clare Aviet just to name a few important things. At least on the surface, however, I don't think there are more than three relevant linking moments to the before and the after. In Chapter Five I do discuss, knowing Ripley's via the cartoon and my Aunt Ivy's newspaper before landing the job, but this seems to me more coincidence than a life altering epiphany. In Chapter 47 I mention seeing my first Fiji Island Mermaid in a trading post store on the main street of Banff, Alberta at age fifteen. This definitely affected me, and proved beneficial to my Ripley future, but, still it is only a footnote that got dredged up from the furthest corner of my brain years after it happened.

So where does that leave me?

Upon reflection it boils down to family, and specifically family vacations. My father Robert was a working class hero, thirty-plus years at the same mindless, and somewhat dangerous job, poorly educated, but the salt of the earth. A guy who would help anybody without being asked, and expect nothing in return. At our wedding he kept more than 160 people waiting for twenty minutes while he helped an old woman who was not a guest at the wedding, park her car in a hotel underground lot. We thought at best he was lost, or at worse, gotten into an accident. Rain or shine, and for years in bad undependable cars, dad always took us on a road trip summer vacation. I saw a lot of Canada by the time I was seventeen.

My mother Sylvia had only a high school diploma, a three-year secretarial business degree, but she was an avid reader, and a keen observer. No vacation lacked a heavy element of learning. We went to museums, tacky roadside nature displays (we once fed a chained bear a blueberry pie), welcome centers — I still remember the monstrous snapping turtle in the little nature museum in Algonquin Provincial Park, a place we went to religiously many years in a row

forts, churches, monuments and graveyards. We were by most people's standards, poor; we camped, we didn't ever stay in a motel or hotel.

I learned a lot from the backseat of a car, on those family vacations including when to fight my two sisters, and when to surrender to their majority wishes. It seems the seeds of my adventures may have been sewn somewhere on Highway #11 going to Huntsville, Ontario, or maybe in the deep woods along the Trans-Canada Highway traveling to parts further flung.

My mother definitely taught me about birds, flowers, insects, trees all the things around me, as well as dinosaurs, mummies, English history, poetry, God and formal religion, and years later after my father had passed, baseball. From the earliest age she instilled me with the passion for learning, from reciting my math times-tables, to writing and rewriting the words of my weekly spelling lists, to typing college essays. At some point she even convinced me to throw down the hockey stick once in a while and read. I don't recall my mother ever buying books, but from an early age my sisters and I had our own library cards and were expected to take out three books from the local Dorset Park, Scarborough library every Monday night. With a little help from the public grade school librarian, a Mrs. Taffe, mom also pushed me to get a university education — a first in my father's family-and a career in library science. Sorry mom, but the path forked, and I took the road less traveled.

3

Introduction
What is your house like?
Is it like your office was? Is it a museum?

Over a lifetime of collecting and travel I have amassed a lot of "stuff", and being a pack rat I haven't exactly expunged too much of it.

None of my six different offices, or for that matter four different archives, were ever what anyone would call "orderly", though anyone who ever ventured into these domains can attest that I knew where everything was, and had a pretty good track record of putting my fingers on things that no one else could have located.

My last office, at 7576 Kingspointe Parkway #188, Orlando, Florida, the one I was in the longest (fifteen years), was particularly cluttered and chaotic. From the start, it was smaller than at least three of the previous ones, so the odds of keeping it "neat" were a million to one. One whole wall was full to bursting with built-in book shelves. A work ledge built to be used by an assistant wasn't used "for work" in fourteen years, and I refused (for forty years) to get a bigger desk, so there was always a lot of stuff on the floor. Early in my career I had been inspired by a television show about a magazine whose editor-publisher, played by Bebé Neuwirth, who laid all her pages on the floor "to see the whole pictures at once". The desk, and one other exactly like it (1) had come from the original 1930s Ripley offices in New York, and at least one of the two had been used by the founder himself. They were perfect for an archivist with a love of Ripley history. They are over 100 years old, solid wood, beautifully made and quite practical in their drawer arrangement. They even have a secret lock. By modern "executive" standards, however, they are less than ½ size, being a mere six-foot by three-foot, and there was never more than a few inches of work space beyond the lap top. There were people in the Ripley office who claimed that they had never seen my desk's wood top.

In addition to a lot of paper, and books, sample historic licensing goods, and small articles related to Robert Ripley, like his reading glasses, on any given day there were also the occasional exhibit either on a chair, or the "work" shelf. The office was never what one could call "inviting", but it did always turn heads, especially if the passerby noticed the replica Maori mokimokai tattooed head on the window sill staring over my shoulder, or the legs of the Wicked Witch of the West in her ruby red slippers peeking out from under a glass book case. Most people thought my office was a Ripley museum in miniature.

Every journalist – and a few other people too — who ever interviewed me, inevitably asked if my house looked like this too? Was my office an extension of my home, or possibly, was my home an extension of my office? Did my home look like a museum? Typically I would laugh and not answer. At best I would admit my house was a little full too.

I have no "special display lighting" in my home, nor do I have descriptive text for anything, so technically it is not a museum by modern definition, but I do have fourteen chock-full glass display cases, African statuary, tribal masks, exotic rugs, including a full length Tibetan tiger rug made from yak hair, a vial of dust from a Martian meteorite, a few old valuable coins and stamps, over two-hundred framed pieces of art — more than forty-pieces in one room alone — including a collection or original water colors by my wife's father, a selection of original Caribbean Island scenes, and an antique map of Iceland. Then there are the personal "bits", a pocket watch collection, a book shelf shrine to baseball, and my two biggest collections: thirteen racks of a few thousand record albums and CD's, and more than a dozen large bookshelves filled with everything I have ever read, and then some. I do give away the occasional book, but I have never sold one. In my first home — pre-children — I had a proper library, complete with a step ladder — but, today the books are everywhere.

I have no trouble admitting my house is full to bursting, but it wasn't until I retired and moved a good deal of my office to my home's television room, did I realize that by a lot of people's standards, my home

probably does resemble a museum, not necessarily a Ripley odditorium, but more like a 19th century wunderkam-
mer — a cabinet of curiosities filled with a lot of unrelated personal "stuff".

In June of 2018 I retired from Ripley Entertainment
(hereafter referred to as Ripley's Believe It or Not!),
and plunked myself down amongst all the above said
treasures to write a memoir, a book of adventures, behind the scenes revelations full of mirth and mishap,
and a record of an extraordinary unusual well spent
life. Using co-pious personal diaries and travelogues
dating back to the very be-ginning, annotated annual
calendars, a photographic memory

the real reason Ripley's kept me employed for so long —
and the recollections of a host of characters who will
make appearances in this book, I started writing immediately. The result is now in your hands. I hope you
will enjoy.

4

The Origin Story

It was a lovely early Thursday afternoon May spring day in downtown Toronto with blue skies, chirping birds and the promise of an unknown future.

I had just finished writing my last four-hour college exam — on the field of an outdoor football stadium called Varsity. What subject the exam was is not important. What was important was that it was my last exam, my official last day of school. I was finished my undergraduate degree, unemployed for the summer, and not yet sure I would be accepted into the post-graduate Library Science program I had applied for in the fall semester. I wanted to celebrate, but already being married, with rent to pay, and all sorts of the other financial burdens of adulthood, the reality was I was unemployed, and worried about the future. I needed at least a summer job — asap.

A short walk from the stadium was the federal government sponsored office of student employment: "Canada Manpower". I had been in this office dozens of times in the last few weeks and had never seen a job listing that suited me in the least. Nothing even close, so it certainly wasn't my intention to go there today though I would have to walk quite close to it to catch the subway home. A few paces away from their door I met one of my dearest and oldest friends, Noreen Crawford (1), whom I had known as a neighbor and school mate at least back to Grade Three, age eight. I saw Noreen regularly socially — she was even a bridesmaid at my wedding — but I very seldom saw her on the campus of the University as the school, the University of Toronto, was huge, and we were not enrolled in the same college. Meeting her on the street was cause for celebration, but she turned down lunch and a drink in preference for a trip to Canada Manpower. I had no good excuse to abandon her, and frankly she was quite forceful in dragging me in. I owe a successful adventure-filled lifetime to her determination.

In a moment seemingly out of a cartoon, sunlight cast a glow on a particular 3" by 5" card on the wall, drawing

17

me straight to it. "Wanted Library Science Student to catalog cartoons for Ripley International, 10 Price Street, Downtown, Toronto". As strange as it may sound I loved cataloging, as I assume most would-be librarians do, and I loved cartoons (did then and still do), so it sounded like the perfect job. I was content to write the information down and call later, but again Noreen forcefully took control. I may be exaggerating, but I think she actually dialed the number and handed me the receiver before I could say no….

I spoke with a young woman named Marge Damon. She asked generic questions to which I gave generic answers, lying that I was already a library science student. I figured having worked part-time in the University's medical library for over a year was somewhat the same thing. To my surprise she wanted me to come for an interview right then and there; the office apparently was only four subway stops, roughly five minutes, away. I stated emphatically that I was not dressed appropriately. She said that they had no dress code, they were a very casual office. No matter how hard I tried to wiggle out, Marge, and Noreen, kept pushing until I finally agreed and said I would be there in a few minutes. I crossed my fingers, kissed Noreen goodbye and boarded the eastbound Bloor Street subway train.

I had been traveling the Toronto subway system for about eight years at that point and every day for the last three, so I had no trouble finding the office. It was a four-floor small brick building with no exterior signage, and a trick elevator as I was about to find out. I needed to be on the second floor, but the elevator didn't stop on the second floor. After at least three failed attempts, I walked down from the third floor. The receptionist, named Alannah Singh, was a gorgeous, vivacious Brazilian; things were quickly looking up. The waiting area, was not a room, but merely a couch in a hall next to her desk. Clearly the office was small.

Ms. Damon appeared from the back of the building a few short minutes later, but by which time I had already been well interviewed by Ms. Singh. Marge, having asked everything she really needed to know on the phone, only spent a couple of minutes with me. The only question I remember was whether I could start the following Monday, May 8th, 1978, to which I shrugged confusedly, "sure". I was then led into the office of Rita Copperthwaite (2), who was Marge's boss and the department head. The interview was again very brief, with the immediacy of the starting date seemingly the only thing of real importance. I was totally befuddled at the ease it appeared I was getting this job. Rita then excused herself for a moment and returned with a man named Alec Rigby. He shook my hand, turned to Rita, and said "he'll do," then turned and walked away. Four days later I would learn Alec — Mr. Rigby to me until the day he died thirty-five years later — was the president and owner of the company. Rita confirmed I had the job, and told me to report to Marge Monday morning. After months of looking I had gotten a summer job in less than fifteen minutes. I still didn't know what the job was, or more significantly, who the company was, but I was employed. Hallelujah. Now I really had something to celebrate on my last day of school.

Part Two

The Formative Years:
Chief Cook
& Bottle Washer

5

The Formative Years

There is a lot I could say about my first seven years with Ripley's, and some of it will be revealed later in this book, or maybe in a second book, but for now there are just a few keys things to know.

On Monday May 8th I quickly discovered that Ripley International equaled **Ripley's Believe It or Not!**, and the cartoons I was to catalog were forty-nine years-worth of comic strips published daily around the world in the "funnies" section of newspapers. At that time, Toronto had three daily papers, the Globe which was a morning business oriented paper (no one I knew read this one), the Telegram, an evening conservative newspaper (the one my family read), and the Toronto Star, a nightly liberal paper that my favorite Aunt Ivy subscribed to. I mention this detail because from an early age I discovered the comics in her paper were different than my family's paper, and one of the differences was something called Ripley's Believe It or Not! which always caught my attention when we were at her home. I don't remember if I believed them or not, but they certainly intrigued me and spurred my curiosity, the one human characteristic that guided me for my entire Ripley career.

My desk was in the archive vault, and my exposure to others was very limited. I seldom saw the brass, and virtually never saw Mr. Rigby. What was then called the design department consisted of six people including myself. Before the summer was over Derek Copperthwaite retired, leaving Rita in charge of Marge, myself, and two design-construction guys: Jimmy Doyle and Terry Hull (1). Marge would be fired before the year's end — leaving me in some resemblance of purgatory-chaos — but she was soon replaced by a secretary. Jimmy and Terry would be let go in 1982 because of a national economic recession beyond their control, and Rita would retire in 1984. I went from gopher-peon, to archivist, to VP of Exhibits & Archives (head of a newly formed small department of two), in a short seven years.

But I get ahead of myself.

The first thing I did was read every cartoon, all forty-nine-plus years-worth, memorizing the best ones as I went along. Then I devised a library style catalog system based on roughly 325 reoccurring categories. Then working backwards from the most recent releases I started hand writing descriptive catalog cards. My typing was never great, so in order to get as much accomplished in the short summer I had, writing seemed to be the answer. I always could write small and fast. After the first few weeks I loved the people and the place, but knew the job was impossible to complete, and to be truthful, somewhat dull. I was somewhat relived when my grad school acceptance arrived, and with it, the offer to continue working at the medical library. By summer's end I was ready to return to the halls of academia. Alec Rigby, however, had a different idea. Out of the blue one day late in August he asked me if what I was doing was a real job. I explained to him the importance of cataloging the cartoon in order to know exactly what the archive room held. The reason for doing so, was to be able to grow the fledgling licensing department that had been a small part of Ripley's since the early 1930s when Ripley himself had sold the rights to a board game called Disk-0-Knowldege. My premise being that – for example — if we knew we had a 1,000 cat cartoons, we could sell these to cat food companies to make calendars, or food labels, or printed ads, for their products.

Alec was a very smart man, and combined with John Withers, his VP of Finance, and future Ripley president, he understood third party licensing much better than I did. Literally he was sitting on an untapped gold mine that just needed to be organized in order to be exploited. I repeat, the company had always done some licensing and even had a high-powered New York City super salesman named Bob Whiteman as an exclusive agent, but Bob was mired down in smallish deals, like giant vegetable seeds and sea monkeys, unable to crack the big deal without "organized "content at his fingertips to sell. In the years to come Bob and I would work on dozens of projects, capitalizing on the system I developed that summer. Bob would become a very rich man off of Ripley's and continued to work the brand into his nineties, well after his official retirement. As the only Ripley employee I worked with that had ever actually met Robert Ripley, there will always be a warm spot in my heart for Bob Whiteman.

Much to my surprise Alec offered me a part-time job, to continue what I was doing as many hours as possible after I went back to school. I was very flattered and had no trouble accepting his offer, although I had no idea what my school class hours or my library job hours would be. For the first couple weeks that September I worked four pm until six pm, five days a week. The most memorable event in that time was Alec stealing my brown paper "dinner" from the kitchen fridge. He figured because it was still in the fridge long after lunch time, and anything in the fridge by some crazy logic belonged to him, he ate the contents of the bag without any remorse. Having to work another four hours at the library, then take a subway and a bus home close to midnight, without having eaten a speck of food since noon, was a real hardship. The following day I happened to comment to Claudia Kent, Alec's administrative assistant (read "secretary", as the other term didn't come into "popular", or at least Ripley jargon, for several years after this event), the case of my disappearing lunch red, and her eyes bugged out of her head, but she said nothing as if nothing had happened. I went back to the archives. Moments later Claudia comes in holding Rigby by the collar, demanding him to apologize. To this day I have never seen a more forceful, woman controlling her "boss". Alec apologized, and offered me $1.00 recompense (keep in mind this man was a multi - millionaire). I was too awestruck to say a word, but perhaps frowned, as he then picked up a copy of the company's latest book, a small paperback called **Ripley's Undersea Oddities** (Simon & Schuster 1976, value $2.25) which he handed me. He said he was sorry — but cautioned never to leave anything in the fridge past 3pm tea time again — and sheepishly walked away with Claudia bellowing "You ought to be ashamed of yourself. A dollar?! What were you thinking" (2).

Within a month I knew it wasn't going to work. I simply couldn't do all three activities and stay married and sane at the same time. Early in October I went into the Ripley office prepared to quit. I told Marge and Rita what I was thinking and they said "hold that thought". Moments later Alec appeared. He sat on the corner of my desk and basically reiterated the conversation from a month ago asking me was I sure cataloging the cartoon was important, and a real job. I assured him it was. He then out of the blue offered me a full time job. Without a moment's hesitation I accepted. He confessed that up to this point the government — Canada Manpower — had actually been paying most of my salary, but if I would take a raise to $150 a week, $600 a month, $7,200 a year, I could start full time the next day, October 11, 1978.

Now all I had to do was tell my wife and mother, both of whom cried, screamed and cried some more for days to come. As I had never even hinted that I was struggling at school, and had been on a trajectory to be a librarian for at least six years, this was the most uncharacteristic shocking thing I was ever to do in my life. God bless Alec for seeing something no one else, even myself, had seen. When my father died suddenly in 1980, Alec would become my surrogate father, my mentor and my biggest advocate.

6

A Taste of the Limelight

I started the previous chapter with the notion that I wouldn't say much — if anything — about the first seven years of my career. The following thirty-three years when as the VP of Exhibits & Archives when I would travel the world spending lots of money on some very strange stuff were infinitely more life changing, but important things did happen in those formative years, such as my introduction to prime time television, and book publishing. So be patient, I will get to the shrunken heads, mummies, Mars rocks, and lady's undergarments, but for now, a lengthy tangent digression.

Jack Haley Jr., Gloria Haley (Parnassus), his sister, and Jack and Holly Palance — Ripley's Believe It or Not! ABC TV 1979-1985

Though never spoken, or even hinted at, I suspect talks, if not actual negotiations, for a network TV show were underway before I was hired full time, and perhaps even before my initial summer student stint. Certainly within a few months of my new career my "catalog system" was being tested, and was working magic. John Withers and Bob Whiteman in 1979 signed a deal with Sony and ABC to do a pilot for a weekly television show, and my archives were expected to supply segment ideas. The first one-hour pilot aired in May 1980. A second thirty-minute pilot ran later that Fall, then a second one-hour version ran a year later in May 1981. Each of these three shows and the subsequent seventy-nine one-hour shows would feature at least seven stories. The archives were the starting point for about 80% of the segments, and in many cases our files provided virtually everything but host Jack Palance's voice. Every week I watched the show with family members and smiled with ecstatic joy to see my name mentioned in the credits.

In terms of hardcore research this was the best work I ever did, with so much of it being done by hand. Our office at this time only had one enormous computer shared by sixteen people, and only about two years of cartoons were in the system, so the job required memory, a lot of reading, and tireless hours oblivious of the three-hour time zone differences. I've always been a morning person, so it was easy to get a head start on my friends on the coast, but when they were still calling me at nine at night it took endurance, desire, and a real passion to keep up with the demand for amazing content.

I am proud of dozens of the ideas I provided and I loved virtually everything Jack did on the show, but my two favorites were the very first segment on a Danish bog man, a story featured in a Ripley cartoon circa 1972, that I remembered from a sixth-grade school book-let, and had haunted me for years. The Tollund Bog Man as he was known, was a centuries old mummy that had been so perfectly preserved in a Danish bog that police hunted for his ritualistic murderer in the late 1950s, as if the crime had just happened. To date, I still have not ever seen him, but pictures are worth a thousand words, and the pictures of this guy still haunt me. Jack of course went to Copenhagen and got up close and personal with the corpse, close enough to see the nose hairs. Unforgettably creepy.

The other story was about a Pyrenees Mountains werewolf. Werewolves were a little outside of our newspaper cartoon content — everything we printed had to be 100% true, and to date I don't think anyone has absolutely proven the existence of werewolves. The story, however, had been used in a comic book series we published in the late 1960s — early 70s, called **True Ghost Stories.**

With minimalist background images, Jack simply sat on a sofa in a Victorian-era looking sitting room, and "read" the story of a man who shot a wolf, dismembering one of its paws, returned to his home, noticed limping wolf tracks in his garden, and then found a "friend" in bed with his wife who was nursing a bloody stump of his missing hand. He shot the wolf man dead this time, and Jack closed the book softly, stared straight into the camera and in his eeriest voice said: "Believe It or Not!"

It was by far the most shocking piece of storytelling ever shown on Sunday night prime time television, and I have to confess, it changed my thinking on werewolves forever.

Jack would visit just one of our company museums, St. Augustine, Florida, in the show's four years, but he did also visit the Church of One Tree Ripley Memorial Museum, in the town of Ripley's birth, Santa Rosa, California. This museum was opened nearly thirty years, with exhibits borrowed from our collection, but it was owned and operated by the city, and was virtually ignored by Ripley employees for all the years it existed. I visited it only once when it was under operation, and then once more years later when I was searching for Ripley's grave site in the same town for a television project (see chapter 79). The company's only Jack Palance souvenir from the show is a green painted wooden chair he sat on in St. Augustine. In what may have been my very first "vulture" move, I had the chair bound in canvas straps and wrote: "JACK PALANCE SAT HERE 2/16/81", and removed it to the archives where it still sits like a hallowed throne nearly 40 years later.

I only actually spent quality time with Jack once, and it was also the first time I met Jack Haley Jr, son of **The Wizard of Oz**'s Tin Man, and Oscar winning director in his own right. The show was a huge success in its first year, and when it was renewed for a second season, Jack Haley Jr. threw a huge Hollywood-style party in the legendary Chasen's of Beverly Hills restaurant. The guest list would include Jack Palance and his daughter Holly (who would take over as co-host of the show in seasons two and three), **The Wizard of Oz** Straw Man, Ray Bolger, Henry Mancini who wrote the show's Emmy winning theme song, Liza Minnelli, daughter of **"Oz's"** Dorothy, a star in her own right, not to mention former wife of Jack Haley Jr., basketball legend Wilt Chamberlain, Lucille Ball (a real favorite of my wife Giliane), a midget horse, Gloria Haley (Parnassus), daughter of the Tin Man, Jack's older sister, and my main daily contact with the show, and Giliane and I! A dream come true.

In addition to being an honored guest sitting at the head table with the before mentioned stars (an honor even Alec Rigby and John Withers weren't granted), I had to create a mini-museum of classic exhibits to display in the restaurant. To help me with this, I got my good friend Ian Iljas, the Ripley museum manager in San

27

Francisco, invited with the proviso he came in a truck with a few choice items from his show. One of these exhibits was an eight-foot long quarter-mile style dragster made by Ken Applegate completely of matchsticks. A thing of real beauty, bought before my time, it was featured in the front window of the San Francisco odditorium for many years. When I was first introduced to Jack Haley I was laying sprawled out on the floor of Chasen's just hours before the dinner, with a bottle of Elmer's white glue trying desperately to repair a broken wheel of the dragster. Jack for whatever reason thought an archivist had to be seventy years old; I was twenty-six. His four-letter exclamation greeting of shock would be a topic of conversation all evening.

I didn't carry a camera in those days, and I only have a couple images of the night's activities. I wasn't really star struck, I didn't care for Liza, and I didn't watch basketball. The miniature horse — and Chamberlain's comic size juxtaposition posing with it, were mildly amusing. Ray Bolger entertained the crowd delightfully, but I never got past a handshake with him, so the high point of the evening probably was the food — Chasens' famous mini-hamburgers (1). I think I had at least a dozen of them. I had of course been expecting caviar, and something French that I wouldn't know what it was. Who knew that Hollywood stars ate normal food? Certainly not I.

The low point was that Lucy didn't show — she was sick. This is one of the greatest disappointments of my life, the only star I have ever really wanted to get my picture taken with was a no-show. I wasn't a huge fan, but Giliane was, and like everyone else, I did at least "Love Lucy".

A very hot looking actress named Catherine Shirriff had been the hostess in Season One, but for Seasons Two and Three, Jack's daughter, Holly would have the honor (2). I don't think I met her at Chas-ends but not too much afterwards Ian and I would have a second trip to Hollywood for our show. This time I needed Ian to bring one of the most famous pieces of our collection, the lifelike statue of Japanese artist Hananuma Masakichi to Jack Haley's house in the Hollywood Hills for a filming. Ian's role in the Chasens' gig was rather subdued, so I don't think he was particularly excited by this

28

mission. The exhibit was insured for a million dollars and the drive from San Francisco was at least five-six hours in the best traffic. We were also needing to be there before 9am.

This would prove to be one of the most boring days of our lives. Jack's house was spectacular. The view from his combination bedroom-studio (perhaps a whole new meaning on the legendary "casting couch"?) was breath-taking. The furnishings were ultra-modern. The full-wall stone fireplace was to die for (does it really ever get cold enough in the Hills to have a fire at night, or was this just to utilize the natural cliff the house was built on into the architecture? I will never know), and the swimming pool, seemingly floating over the cliff, couldn't have looked much better, even if Cathe-rine Shirriff had been lounging pool side.

Unfortunately, we would stare at these views way too long. Holly was more than an hour late, then took an-other hour for hair and make-up, and then about three hours to do the five-minute film piece. I kid you not, there was more than sixty takes. She simply could not say Hana-nu-ma Mas-a-kit-chi, to save her life. We feasted on donuts and craft services — red licorice be-ing my go-to-snack — and I tried desperately to avoid Ian's menacing stares. I wasn't sure my film crew ca-reer was over, but I was pretty sure his was. As I re-call, he ended up staying the night in some hotel the day before and the day after, making it not just one day, but three days of living hell for him.

I would never see Holly again, but I would have one more soirée with the Haley family. Late in season four, spring 1985, Gil and I, with our less than a year-old baby, Curtis, would vacation in nearby Laguna Beach, California where Gil's father lived. We would have a day in Beverly Hills with Gloria Haley, as "old Holly-wood" as anyone could be. She had never been a "star" but she had been in films in the 1950s and a Ziegfeld Follies chorus girl at one point in her earlier days. She lived in a mansion comparable to the 1960s **Beverly Hillbillies** television show home, just a couple houses away on the same street. For a couple hours it was the biggest house I had ever been in.

With Gloria driving a late 1950s pink Cadillac with

fins, we drove around 'town" and visited Jack. Gil took about two seconds to fall in love with his house, and even got a command seating on the master's bed to watch future clips of the Ripley show. From a bedside table, buttons were pushed, a large television came out of the ceiling, and curtains rolled down over the 180-degree view front window. Could it get any better? We doubted it, but we were wrong.

From Jack's we went back down the hill into the "old" neighborhood again, to Mrs. Jack Haley's (wife of the late **Tin Man**) monstrous gated mansion. The first thing we saw beyond the gate was a white Rolls Royce, an absolute gorgeous car, the next thing was a doorman followed by a maid. Real people apparently really did live like TV's Jed, Ma, Grannie, Ellie Mae and Jethro.

The plan was for Mrs. Haley to baby sit our son while we went out for dinner and a show. This was super hard to fathom. Yes, it was Mrs. Haley's house, and she would be home, and she provided not just a room with a view of the pool, and a rented crib too, but the boy would be under the direction of the maid. Mrs. Haley definitely didn't change a diaper or hold a milk bottle that evening.

The room was at least as large as our whole 1,200 square foot home and had thousands of 8" by 10" studio photos adorning the walls

a virtual museum. It is unfortunate that Curtis was too young to re-member a thing, but he was gifted a child's oak rocking chair with his name painted on it for a lasting memento.

After a short debate whether we would take the caddy or the Rolls, Gloria, Gil and I were off to the venerable Brown Derby in the twenty-five-foot long pink paradise. Gloria was a reel hoot, made up to the nines and reminding everyone of one of the Gabor sisters, big boobs, and even bigger blonde bouffant hair. Arriving at the restaurant she almost drove over the valet parking guy refusing to let anyone drive her car. She then promenaded to the best table in the house, name calling to other tables as she went. Seemingly she knew everyone, and everyone knew her, including a reporter for the **Hollywood Reporter** who just had to know who Gloria's guests were. We were suitably fussed over and actually made the next morning's gossip column. I was very glad we met the reporter here and not at our next stop!

I don't remember what we ate, but suffice to say we spent the time like "Lucy Ricardo" on her first trip to Hollywood, staring at the drawings of hundreds of famous people that adorned the walls in those days. Another dream come true for a young couple from the burbs of Toronto.

Our last stop of the day was Louis Pacioccos's **La Gage Aux Folles** drag show, men dressed as famous celebrity women, singing hit songs and flirting with the men in the audience. It was a high-end classy show, not tawdry at all, but still nothing I ever saw myself experiencing. I had my picture taken with my hand on "Tina Turner's" upper thigh. He may not have looked exactly like Tina, but he sure didn't look like a man!

It was nearly 2 am when we returned to Mrs. Haley's house to pick up our sleeping beauty. We had a quick nightcap and listened to Mrs. Haley talk about the people in her photo gallery before getting in our humble, rented, Toyota Corolla, and driving the ninety minutes south to Giliane's dad's home. The next few days on the beach were very anticlimactic.

Holly and Jack Palance were gone from my life almost as quick as they had entered, but Gloria Haley would remain for a few more years, and through her I would retain a most bizarre connection to Jack Haley. Try to picture in your mind opulent wealth, then imagine a man who could buy anything he wanted, and a loving sister who would always want to give him a present for his birthday or Christmas, that no one else would give him. Now imagine a cheap Canadian-English men's cologne not available in California. Believe It or Not, for the next several years I would get a call from Gloria once or twice a year, asking me to go the Eaton's department store on Toronto's downtown Yonge Street to buy Jack a bottle of Yardley's "Lotus" lavender scented cologne. She never wanted more than one bottle at a time — God only knows why — until 1993, when I was to move from Toronto to Florida, at which time she ordered a case. I imagine he was still using those bottles until he passed away in 2001. Gloria died nine years later at the age of 83. God rest both their souls.

7

My First Foray into Publishing

Simultaneously with our television show, came our first foray into "self-publishing" — the birth of Ripley books. As a company we had been producing small cartoon compilation pocket books (30 numbered volumes in total) since Robert Ripley's best seller in 1929. Most were published by Simon & Schuster — the original two gents were personal friends of Ripley's in New York in the 1920s — but there had been a few experiments, with Bantam, Gold Key, and Warner as well. None had any photos, and only a few had distinct subjects, most of which were published between 1976 and 1978 — the afore mentioned **"Undersea Oddities"; Ripley's Believe It or Not! Book of Women; Ripley's Believe It or Not! Book of American History; Stars, Space & UFOs; Ghosts, Witches & ESP; and Great Disasters** (1).

I had been marginally involved with "Series #29 and 30", and the three subject books that came out in 1978, but in 1982 with the Ripley property hotter than it had been in years thanks to the ABC Palance television show, I was made editor and compiler of our cartoon series — I would produce numbers 31 through-34 over the next two years — as well as serving as archive-researcher for six other books we would self-publish: **The Book of Chance; The Book of Australia & New Zealand; Magic & Magicians; Accidents & Disasters, Stunts & Stuntmen;** and **Space Travel & Colonies.**

Only the first two numbered **Believe It or Not!** series books, the two written and compiled by Ripley himself, probably ever sold a large number of copies, but the Ripley numbered series were evergreen products that kept our name in the market place, and were truly instrumental in a lot of young people, boys in particular, learning to read. I myself had read a few as a youngster; they made excellent summer cottage reading. They could be started and stopped on any given page, and they fit in your back pocket if you were wanting to carry them with you to the outhouse, or to the dock. The number of people requesting specific cartoons they remembered from these books kept me busy for years, and drove the necessity to computerize my catalog system as quickly as possible. (It would take a couple decades to get "caught up", and of course the job will never be truly finished as long as new cartoons continue to be published every day, and technological changes influence how research searches are made. The system has changed pretty dramatically from the one I first created, and is radically changing again as I write this line today, but the heart of the system I created is still intact).

To do the other six titled books we hired three new full-time employees: Allen Stormont (sales and marketing), Patrick Crean (editor and publisher), Laurie Freedman (photo researcher), and three contract writers. In one form or another they had all worked together before and were very much a package deal. None of them knew much about Ripley's, but Patrick and the writers all had decent credentials with the huge publishing giant Harlequin Romance, and Allen could talk up a storm, charm the proverbial knickers off a nun, or sell icebergs to Eskimos. He did get our books printed and published, but he certainly didn't sell too many, and I suspect he earned more in his two years at the helm than the company made on those six books.

The writers never had offices in our building so our contact was minimal, Patrick, however, was my first real close friend in the company. He was only a few years older than myself, and I saw myself wanting to be him. He was smart, well read, successful, and passionate about what he did. How he ever got hooked up with Stormont remains a mystery. Patrick worked very hard and deserved better, but he was not a salesperson, and without one that could be trusted, Ripley Books was doomed from the start.

On one of my first ever trips to New York City, Allen and John Withers went to see our distributors, while I met Bob Whiteman on his home turf for the first time. Bob Masterson, the then VP of Operations, was also with us, though he was off looking for plush toys to give as prizes at our Myrtle Beach, South Carolina, bingo parlor, for most of the day. We all met up at a strip club on Broadway (there were lots of them back then before Mayor Giuliani's later cleanup the neighborhood project). Drinks flowed incessantly, and John kept repeating "64, 64-copies, 64! I can't believe they can actually track numbers that small".

Allen disappeared pretty quickly after that night, and Laurie didn't have enough work to justify her existence. Patrick hung around long enough to finish the other two titles and for me to open his ears to Bobby Blue Bland [2], but when we got the first quarterly report on the four "juvenile" book titles (books designed to be read by teenagers, but unfortunately marketed to look like they were for ages five through eight) — and saw in black and white the grand total of just sixty-four copies sold (note: not sixty-four each, but sixty-four collectively!),his future writing for Ripley's was likewise more on the wall than on paper.

Patrick stayed in touch for a couple years, and did become quite an accomplished Torontonian editor making a lot of money with a little kid's book deal — real small books inside a plastic box that was to be used to keep specimens (bugs, seashells, rocks, etc.). Bob and I loved him as a pure Ripley character, but either he, or more likely Allen, absconded with a series of 1930s photos of nude ladies at a Robert Ripley house party featuring a torture device called the Iron Maiden of Nuremburg, and was eventually excommunicated from our alumni club. If anyone reading this ever comes across those images, please call me! I consider them the only thing I ever **personally** lost from our archives, and one of only two things that totally disappeared under my watch, never to be seen again. More on the larger second disaster a little later.

Ripley Books, died after three years and just ten books total, and wouldn't be resurrected for another thirteen years, but I had a good taste of the publishing world, and knew this was something I would want not just for me, but for Ripley's to try again.

8

Cataclysmic Change, and My Coming of Age

By 1984 Alec Rigby had remarried for the third time, and was spending more time on his yacht traveling the North Sea and the Caribbean, than at his big office desk. For all intent and purposes, John Withers was in control, and as President his biggest job was to find a buyer for the company; Alec wanted to "retire". John probably didn't, after all he was only about forty years old, but as an equity partner in the company, selling it made economic sense to him.

I helped write a history of the company and I compiled some images to illustrate the sales package, but otherwise I had nothing to do with the sale, but to sit and worry about would I still have a job under a new owner, and what would that job entail since publishing had flopped and television was nearing its end? (1). There was also the fear: Would I have to move, and if so, to where?

Probably to everyone's surprise the company was purchased by an-other Canadian, Jimmy Pattison, from Vancouver, Canada. No one would be fired, we wouldn't be moving, and there would be no personnel changes at least for the foreseeable future (2). It would be business as usual, and I in fact would be made a Vice President. The official changing of the guard happened in January 1985. I first met Jimmy the next month, and my life, and Ripley's, would never be the same.

Simultaneous to the sale of the company two important things were going on. We had a best-selling board game, produced by Milton Bradley, that I was the lead employee on, and was duly rewarded for. It had sold over a million copies its first year (thanks to my catalog system), three-quarters of a million its second year (no doubt having an influence on Jimmy and the sale), but then tanked off the map in its third year, a year after Jimmy had bought us. With the television show and

36

the board game having raised the awareness of the brand, it seemed like a good time to build a new odditorium, the first in eight years. The location was Bourbon Street, New Orleans. Bob Master-son would be in charge of building it, Jimmy Doyle would design it, and I would choose the exhibits to fill it. By the time we finished it in 1986, our exhibit warehouse was bare.

In one of our first conversations with Jimmy we were told he expected the company to grow. In order for the company to grow we would have to build more museums. He wanted to build lots more museums, including, potentially, franchised locations [3]. In order to build more museums, we would have to buy more artifacts. The Robert Ripley collection was large, but not infinite. Someone would have to start shopping. I was chosen to be that someone — "the new Robert Ripley".

In 1980 we had acquired twelve new exhibits, in 1981, thirty-four, in 1982, eleven, in 1983, four, and in 1984, thirteen. It is probably safe to say that the majority, if not all of these 74 items came from H.M Lissauer (see Chapter 10).

In 1985 the total would rise to 450 new items. From 1985 through 1999, I [4] added more than 9,900, averaging 660 per year, or 1.89 per day, and peaking in 1994 with 1,619 items, or more than four every day of that year. The first exhibit(s) I bought on my own were two decks of hand painted sandal wood Indian playing cards, in lovely hand crafted wooden boxes. These would be used in our first franchise museum in Las Vegas, in 1986, as part of a display on gam- bling, and the history of playing cards. The first really significant piece I bought in 1985, was a small strip of human skin, belonging to an English murderer named John Horwood (circa 1821). Horwood was convicted of murdering a young girl named Eliza by hitting her in the head with a rock, sentenced to be the first person hung in the Bristol (England) Gaol, then dissected to see why he was so evil and disturbed — something the officials of course never actually ascertained. A book was actually covered with his back skin, and the doc- tor who did the dissection signed the small strip we obtained. The story was found in a local Toronto paper by Norm Deska, one of the company's accountants at the time, and the piece of skin it turned out, was in a shop on Vancouver

Island. Using the newspaper article and having no fears of cold calling anyone, I found the owner and offered $100 for the skin. They asked for $500. I rebutted at $300 and won the prize. Measuring about one-inch by three-inches, it certainly isn't a show-stopper. I hazard to say most patrons walk right by it without even noticing it, but it is still one of my personal favorites. I haven't seen it in more than ten years now. It was displayed in Australia from 1988 until 2008, then in India for the next several years until that location closed. I trust it is now safely stored waiting for reassignment.

The first New Orleans Ripley odditorium was a thing of beauty. I had only been to a couple other odditoriums at that point, but New Orleans, perhaps because it was new and shiny, was by far the best, the new gold standard. There was a real red truck in the lobby that had special effects and looked like it had just crashed through the entrance, tossing out crates full of exhibits. Upstairs there was a real train car, in a recreation train station; the car was full of wax figures of some of the odd and unusual people Ripley had met on his real travels. There was also a diorama with two wax figures retelling the Believe It or Not! cartoon story of how a boy fishing in the Mississippi had accidentally hooked his father,' Capt. Michero a riverboat captain, who unbeknownst to his family, had died in a boat explosion up river the day before. A painted mirrored floor gave a realistic illusion of real water. Another gallery featuring New Orleans stories had a café theme, with a wax figure of a guy who could eat more oysters in a sitting than anyone should; Jay Gwaltney, a guy who diced up a small tree and ate every bit of it as salad over a number of days; and the city's number one citizen, Louis Armstrong with a trumpet, as if he was entertaining them. The Armstrong figure was one of the best the company ever did. For a brief time after the grand opening we even had Buddy Bolden's actual 19th century trumpet on display. On loan from the local jazz museum, Bolden was one of the founders of New Orleans jazz and blues, and was reportedly so strong a player that you could hear him play across the river in Algiers. Touching it was for me an early Holy Grail moment.

The highlight of the museum for me was the wax figures

and costumes of two Mardi Gras Indians, Chief Tootie Montana of the Yellow Pocahontas, and Chief Bo Dollis of the Wild Magnolias. Ripley's acquiring these two suits was a first, and cause for a near riot in the Treme neighborhood of the 9th Ward across Basin Street outside the French Quarter. No Indians had ever sold their costumes — -there is a good chance no one had ever before asked to buy one. No Mardi Gras Indian had ever posed for a wax figure either, and most importantly, no one outside of New Orleans probably had ever heard of the tradition of African Americans "masquing Indian" in order to parade on Mardi Gras Day (blacks were traditionally outlawed from Mardi Gras, but Indians weren't). This was a Ripley exclusive pushed by me, but consummated by John Withers and Bob Masterson in some neighborhood bar over lots of alcohol. Most of the tribes were furious that these two chiefs had sold out to tourism, but when word got out how much we had paid, we soon had plenty more tribesmen of all ranks, spy boys, flag boys, trail chiefs, second chiefs, and big chiefs alike, trying to cash in.

Ripley's was the first place in New Orleans to display these artistic masterpieces, huge heavy feather and beaded costumes that look vaguely like Plains Indians' dance outfits, but with more elaborate beading, dyed colorful feathers of every hue, and a lot heavier, sometimes weighing over a hundred pounds. Each costume took a year to make (at least), and then was only worn twice, on St. Joseph's Day (March 19th, a religious holiday observed by Sicilians in New Orleans), and Mardi Gras. The different tribes of Indians, and there are probably more than thirty different tribes,confront each other in the streets, and have mock dance-battles accompanied by wild rhythmic drumming and chanting. In days long ago, the battles could involve bloodshed, but by the 1980s, winners were decided on the beauty of the costumes, and the stamina of the dancers wearing them.

What little I knew about them before-hand was from two wonderful music albums recorded in the mid-1970s by Bo Dollis and the Wild Magnolias, and The Wild Tchoupitoulas with the future Neville Brothers band, under the recording auspices of the great Allen Toussaint. What I soon learned was they had two important local white advocates, Michael P. Smith a fabulously talented photographer of all kinds of New Orleans music, and Jules

39

Cahn, a documentary film maker who had spent more than twenty years filming them. Both these men would play a huge part in the visuals we used in the museum. Smith took photos not just of the Indians, but also of a Cajun family who made flowers from the scales of giant alligator gar fish, and another family that made sculptures of New Orleans street characters from Mississippi river mud, both of whom we had samples of their works in the museum proper, and for sale in the gift shop. Jules' contribution was even more significant.

Elsewhere I have mentioned the loss of naked lady Iron Maiden photos that were probably stolen from our archives. Here I must confess to my all-time biggest f*ck-up, the accidental loss and subsequent burning, of one man's life work. While the museum was under construction Bob Masterson lived in a rented apartment in the city,coming into the office only a day or two per month. In the months he was in the Vieux Carré he certainly spent his share of time among the real underbelly characters of the city. Jules probably was the only full time employed real businessman-artist of the menagerie. Jules had reels and reels of film of the Indians — at least one for every Mardi Gras he had attended, going back I believe twenty-three or twenty-seven years, and he had plans to someday make the authoritative documentary film about them. He knew them all by name and was critical in the negotiations to buy our costumes. Bob had somehow convinced him to ship all of his films care of me to a small studio we used in Toronto. Our video producer, Rick Taylor really didn't know what to do with them all and if the truth be known, probably only watched one or two of them, then said he had enough to make a short museum clip. We got what we needed, and used the five-minute film in many other museums for at least fifteen years. Jules, however, would never see his films again.

Our office at the time, the third in our history, was a very open concept space high up in a nondescript business tower on Eglington Avenue, just off Yonge Street, one of the busiest corners in "uptown" Toronto. I had a small corner office (two sides of glass, but with a view of brick walls in both directions), the wide-open archives shelves were directly in front of me, and my assistant Kathy Vader, sat in an "open office" to my left. The cardboard boxed films took up more space than

I had in my office, but could be lined up along the adjoining wall between my office and Kathy's space. At the end of a long Friday afternoon we lined them up along the wall thinking nothing of their being right next to a garbage bin, and went home for the weekend.

Come Monday morning it was hard not to notice the boxes were not where we had left them. They had totally disappeared. Panic and chaos ensued. Oh my God, could they have been thrown out by the weekend janitor? Apparently yes, and even worse, they had been incinerated.

I never saw Jules again. He probably avoided me, and I definitely avoided him. I regret, however, that I never looked him in the eye and personally said "I am so sorry", and I am still ashamed and remorseful thirty-three years later. Ripley's paid him one thousand dollars for each reel lost in addition to whatever our deal was for the original loan and the five-minutes-worth we used — a pittance for one's life's work, but at least something to acknowledge my guilt.

Bob Masterson and John Withers would never let me forget this, and I would never have an open archives area again. Going forward, film would always be locked away.

I've been to New Orleans about ten times in my life, the last time only a couple weeks before I retired. It is my favorite city in the United States, if not the entire world. I love the people, the music, the food, and the **Mardi Gras Indians.** Where else but in New Orleans could I repeatedly buy vampire kits, or a late 18th century portable Louisiana guillotine? When I bought the guillotine I thought it would be the very last piece I would buy, bringing a dramatic and symbolic end to a long shopping spree that had started with a murderer. New Orleans as the city where my first curated Believe It or Not! museum was built, seemed a very logical place to end my years of travel, but someone in a galaxy far, far away had a different idea.

9

First Impressions of Jimmy Pattison

The Ripley company Jimmy Pattison bought in 1985, was small, with less than twenty employees in corporate office, and just twelve attractions. The employees involved were fiercely loyal to owner Alec Rigby, and President John Withers. The business was run despotically, but within a fun "like family" environment. We all dreaded being bought by someone in some "God-forsaken" place like Butte, Montana, or Detroit, we understood Alec would be leaving us, and we feared John would too [1].

We were somewhat surprised when it was announced we had been bought by another Canadian, and very pleasantly surprised when were told no one would be losing their job, or having to move. Jimmy Pattison flew to Key West, Florida, for a couple hours that February and introduced himself to the management team. We were all impressed and relieved. A month later five of us from Toronto had our first taste of Jimmy in action; we were the new kids on the block at his annual corporate conference. I had the honor and privilege to attend seventeen of these conventions, and they were all amazing functions, but that first one was really special. Jimmy had just reached one billion dollars in sales, and was in a celebratory mood. The meetings always featured (so we were to learn) a high profile guest speaker, frequently a former US President [2], but in 1985, Jimmy went Hollywood. He staged a musical production and his guest was comedian, legend Bob Hope. I remember his opening joke was something about having more people in his living room than were in the present room (the actual number of people was around 100). He proceeded to make jokes about how he met Jimmy, and how much he liked him. It was instantly apparent we now worked for a real mover and shaker.

I always loved Bob Hope and having my picture taken with him that night and spending about ten minutes with him, giving him a personal tour of our one-room mini Ripley museum display, was an early high point of my life. I cherish the photo, and to this day consider Bob Hope the most important celebrity I ever had the honor to meet… Jimmy, and Bob, thanks for the memories!

What a great first impression the new boss had made, and about two months later it somehow even got better. On my third time meeting Jimmy, out of the blue he asked me if I liked the Beatles. Without hesitation I said yes. By this time, I was a hard-core blues fan, but I had indeed once been a big Beatles fan, so I wasn't stretching the truth too far. He asked me if I knew anything about John Lennon's Phantom V, yellow floral psychedelically painted, Rolls Royce car. To his surprise, I did, and I preceded to tell him everything I knew about it (I had a bad case of verbal diarrhea if ever there was one). He listened to me intently while people in the background gave me the cut throat signal to stop. Eventually I got the message. When I finally stopped, he asked me if I thought it would make a good exhibit in a Ripley's museum. I am not sure what demon was possessing me, but I calmly said "no". Personally, I liked it because I was a Beatles fan, and I was sure some car people would like it for its unique carness, but frankly, I didn't see it as a being unbelievable. In a car, or a music museum, I could see it being a big success, but probably not at a Ripley's attraction. Jimmy looked me straight in the eyes, and said, "I am going to buy it next month (June 1985), how much should I pay for it?" He then showed me a picture with an auction house estimate of $200-$300,000. I nearly fell off my chair. This was considerably more than I would spend on exhibits in a whole year during the 1980s.

Jimmy then explained to the room, that as Chairman of **Expo 86**, the World's Fair to be held the following year in Vancouver, Canada, he thought this would be a big draw if displayed at the fair's English pavilion. He then asked me if I thought it was worth $300,000. Still being an idiot, I flat out told him I didn't think it was worth it. He asked John Withers to provide him with a wax figure of John Lennon that could be displayed with the car, and invited John to the Sotheby's auction in New York the following month.

Jimmy, John, and a large entourage attended the auction in NYC, and Jimmy without ever putting his auction paddle down, bought the car for the then record price of $2.3 million dollars — ten times the estimated price. I learned that day if Jimmy wanted something, Jimmy was going to get it. This would prove to be the highest price paid for an individual car for more than thirty years. Jimmy left a very big first impression on me that day — and on John Withers too, who now had to worry about what "we" were going to do with the car.

Jimmy didn't need it for almost another full year when **Expo** would open, and he wanted Ripley's to use it — try to make some money from it — in the meantime. John looks suicidal in the photos and film shot that day. The wheels were spinning in his head trying to figure out the ROIC (return on invested capital) on a $2.3 million exhibit.

It was determined that we would move the car to Myrtle Beach, South Carolina, the closest location to New York City at the time. In addition to the moving and insurance costs, we had to tear down some walls of the museum to get the car inside. We would also have to provide security for the car for the six months we would display it.

The car was initially displayed as an add-on with a separate entrance fee. As the summer rolled on, and almost no one came to see the car, the extra admission cost was eliminated. When we gave the car back that December, we had actually lost money with it, rather than having earned any extra. We were glad to see it go.

Jimmy was right, however, and the car and the Lennon wax figure were major hits at his fair. Thousands of people had their picture taken with it, and it became one of the iconic images of EXPO '86. Why it didn't work for us is anybody's guess, but when the fair was over and Jimmy asked us if we wanted the car back, we politely declined. Once bit, twice shy.

I had the invoice framed and displayed it in my office for thirty-three years with a photo of the team with the car that was taken in the back alley behind Sotheby's on purchase day. It was a permanent reminder of my fallibility, and a remembrance of the importance of first impressions [3].

10

Quite Possibly the World's Most Interesting Man, Certainly the Most Traveled

Ripley exhibit acquisitions didn't totally stop after Rip's death, but for the most part the odditoriums built in the 1960s by Alec Rigby

Niagara Falls, Chicago, San Francisco-utilized items acquired personally by Ripley, with the addition of a just a few location-centric topical additions. By the time Alec was sole owner of the company in 1969, and he wanted to build two more museums, Gatlinburg (1970), and Estes Park, Colorado (1972), there was a need to acquire some additional ethnographic items, the kinds of cultural artifacts Ripley had acquired on his most exotic trips between 1922 and 1948.

I don't know how, or where, Alec, or more likely his VP of Design & Development, Derek Copperthwaite, first discovered Hermann Mark Lissauer — Mr. Lissauer to me (I knew him for over thirty years before I found out what his initials H.M. stood for), but as far as I can tell they started buying tribal artifacts from him as early as 1970. For the next eight years with Derek, then under my guidance, for nearly thirty-eight years more, Ripley's would acquire over twenty-five hundred artifacts from this wondrous man (1).

Every May and again in November, for forty-six years, Mr. Lissauer visited Ripley's, be it in Toronto, or Orlando, with three huge hardshell suitcases containing seventeen four-inch ring binders, full of snapshots that he took himself of the highest quality and most exotic cultural items he personally collected six months of every year, in the world's most off the beaten track locations. His typical year, starting in January through March — summer in the Southern Hemisphere was spent traveling the South Pacific on a buying trip. He would then go home to Melbourne, Australia for one month to catalog his new acquisitions. He knew exactly how many things he had bought in his career and photographed every one, giving them a sequential purchase number, then filing them into their relevant binder, fifteen of which were organized by country or region, and the remaining two being of high-end jewelry, primarily from India, but with the occasional pieces from other foreign shores too. He would then fly to several spots to visit museum curators in Europe and North America for the next two months to sell his wares out of the binders and suitcases. Ripley meetings typically took place in our corporate office boardroom, but occasionally in hotel rooms and once pool-side in Las Vegas. To go through all seventeen binders typically took me about six hours. Upon returning to Melbourne by the end of June, he would spend the next month shipping around the world the items he had sold.

By August he would head further North to the Far East: China, Japan, Korea, to shop for another two months, occasionally changing the agenda with trips to the Middle East, and or Africa. Home again in October, he would do more cataloging and photo taking, then set off to America in November, followed by Europe and his motherland Germany for Christmas, and then home again to Melbourne for New Years. To my knowledge, he traveled in excess of 70,000 miles, including two circumnavigations of the globe, every year for at least forty-five years. During the era of paper plane tickets, he would practically need a separate case just to hold his hotel and plane reservation documents.

Mr. Lissauer was a bit of a curmudgeon with me, but always got along easy and well with my wife, and my various female assistants over the years. He seemed to be ancient from the first time I met him — detainment in a German concentration camp in World War II probably did that to him. Despite having slept in hammocks in jungles, being able to paddle a canoe for miles, and regularly toting nearly two hundred pounds of luggage, he was as thin as a rail, and seemingly very frail. He usually wore a cardigan, or a tweed jacket, no matter what the temperature. He was also one of the pickiest eaters I have ever met. Eating only kosher and for the most part vegetarian, dining with him was always an adventure. No matter how hard I tried to find the perfect place, something always went wrong. The tomatoes were raw, or the table light was too dark, or God forbid, his drink was the wrong temperature. In later years — he was still traveling past his 90th birthday — he took multiple pills. I did have to take him to an emergency doctor one time when he had run out of a certain blood pressure med, and was stunned to learn his one none-binder suitcase had more meds in it than clothing. He read voraciously, buying books from airport stores as needed, then giving them away so as not to have to carry them further than necessary. His memory and knowledge of tribal cultures was encyclopedic, and he spoke more than a dozen native languages to go along with the eight European ones he knew.

I twice visited Mr. Lissauer in his home in Melbourne, which looked like a cross between a Japanese Zen rock garden complete with a short waterfall, and the Pitt Rivers Museum in Oxford, England. Everything in those massive catalogs was used to decorate his house until they were sold.

The actual buying process with Mr. Lissauer was ritualistic, but simple. We would have a croissant and coffee or tea, and orange juice together at about 8:30 am, and by 9 am be into binder #1. I can't speak for any of his other hundreds of customers, museums and private collectors alike, but my attack was always the same. I didn't go in his numerical binder order, but rather in the order of the ones I was most likely to buy from, always starting with New Guinea, and ending with the jewelry, which I never bought from but always enjoyed perusing; some of his Rajasthani ruby, pearl and diamond pieces were priced at a king's ransom!

We would never stop for lunch, but would have a salad brought in. Employees would poke their head in occasionally, some from pure curiosity, but some from recognizing him as a friendly uncle or grandfather type whose manners and charm simply demanded a brief hello. As mentioned above, it would take about six hours to go through the binders. Each item would have a photo and a couple lines of description. If they caught my eye, I asked questions and he, Buddha-like, elucidated, knowing every object's value, purpose and origin. If it was already sold a colorful dot sticker was placed over the price. If it was still available I would add a removable "post-it-note", and continue on page flipping. No money was typically discussed until "round two"

After going through and marking all items of potential interest, I would start again from the beginning, removing some "stickies" because of similarity to other

47

items seen elsewhere, or because the price was too high, or simply because I thought I didn't need it that day and would take the chance that he would still have it six months later. I lost a few things due to this kind of indecision, but nothing I recall that was heartbreaking. It was an unwritten rule, but I tried to stay under $40, 000 per visit, which usually meant purchasing between twenty and thirty items. If I had tagged a hundred, a lot had to be weaned out. He would at this point become talkative, scorning and chiding me, and always assuring me his prices couldn't be beat. Once the list had been decimated to a reasonable number of items, he would put sold stickers on my new acquisitions, then make a hand-written (in the worst unreadable handwriting imaginable) tissue paper carbon copy of the invoice, each of us to retain a copy. We would then shake hands, and he would pack away the binders in the exact same order he had been doing all his life. I would then drive him back to his hotel, or return to my office as the case may be, promising to return for dinner in two or three hours. Dinner would be attended by me, sometimes my wife, and sometimes my children. Conversation was never on the day's purchases, but rather on where he was going next, with hints of his varied past thrown in for good measure. It took years to put it all in order, but his mother and he had been prisoners in Bergen-Belsen, his father had escaped to South America, they later joined him on the Orinoco, where H.M. learned to trade with the natives, they moved to a property in New Guinea (a coffee plantation), and eventually wound up in Melbourne, Australia. His father had been a "trading merchant" long before H.M. got the fever, specializing in animal bone fancy buttons in Hamburg and Amsterdam in the 1920s and 1930s.

A list of what I bought from Mr. Lissauer would fill a book of its own, everything from New Guinea widow's finger choppers, to bird feather money, to shrunken heads (the two best ones Ripley's owns), to bamboo opera suits, to ancient Samurai armor, to hundreds of masks and totems. The largest most elaborate piece was a mirrored and jeweled Indian Lord Krishna swing that came in about fifty pieces and required a day to assemble. The largest piece he ever offered — which I wish we had of bought — was a Melanesian forty-foot long ocean - going war canoe. Over the years he offered us just about everything but the kitchen sink. The closest thing to that was a thousand-year old Roman stone bath-tub.

When I saw Mr. Lissauer in Melbourne in 2010 I gave him an emerald-studded, eighteen-karat gold Ripley twenty-year service pin. He deserved it. His nephew later told me he wore it proudly in his retirement, and I am led to believe he was buried wearing it. He retired a couple years before me, and died almost instantly afterwards — presumably from boredom. He did, however, leave behind a wonderful oral history that was later transcribed into a very enjoyable read

titled **"A 20th Century Jewish Life"**. Remnants of his collection can be viewed in the Jewish Museum of Australia in Melbourne, and every Ripley odditorium around the globe.

A well spent life indeed.

11

Norbert Pearlroth & A Ripley Biography

Robert Ripley was a fascinating man, and I wish I had of written his biography, but his long serving behind the scenes researcher Norbert Pearlroth may have been just as interesting, albeit, not as flamboyant.

Robert Ripley died in May of 1949 and I wasn't even born until 1956, so meeting him was out of the question, but when I started in 1978, his four closest associates and confidants were all still alive. I talked and exchanged correspondence with all of them: Doug Storer (Rip's VP, publicist and successor), Hazel Storer (wife of Doug and radio show script writer), Li Ling Ai, (Rip's closest female companion (1940-49)), and Norbert Pearlroth (his head of research (1923-1975). From interviews with these four people I figured I learned more about Robert Ripley than anyone else on earth knew. They qualified me as the official Ripley historian for most of my forty-years' service.

The Storer's collaborated with New York journalist Bob Considine in 1961 in writing a Ripley biography called **Ripley: The Modern Marco Polo**. It's an easy, fun read, but the reader can tell that Considine himself was not intimate with his subject, personally I doubt they had ever met, though it is certainly possible. Considine's book was basically an interview with Doug Storer. All the high points were covered, but the depth of the man wasn't fathomed. Nearly from my Ripley day one, I made notes, and contemplated how I could write an updated, more in-depth version. In the late 1990s I made outlines and even wrote two lengthy essays that I saw as introductions to bigger works. They remain unpublished to date, though they have been widely circulated and quoted by other writers. Long before that, however, I went in search of Norbert Pearlroth, the man behind the Ripley legend.

Pictures of Norbert Pearlroth are almost non-existent. He appears only in the forefront of one Ripley archive photo, in the background in a couple others, and literally with his face hidden by volumes of mail in a handful more. His name, however, is everywhere, both as the guy who answered much of Ripley's mail — queries regarding any of his researched published items — and with footnotes on the research of every single piece he was the responsible source of. For fifty-two years — yes you read that correctly, fifty-two years, half of which were after Ripley had died, Norbert spent six days a week in the New York Public Library, reading thousands of books in more than a dozen languages. A conservative estimate would be that he found the source stories for more than 80% of all the items Ripley's published during his fifty-two year tenure — let's call it 60,000 items for the sake of argument since no one has ever actually done the math (1). Clearly the man was amazing, a walking encyclopedia, and an inspiration for any researcher in any field who came after him. He has been honored both by the main branch of the New York Public Library on 42nd Street, and the **Jeopardy** television show library, and he is also the subject of a moving short story by author Melissa Pritchard, called, **"The Odditorium"** (2011). That he was a Polish Jew and a bank teller when Ripley first met him is about all anyone really knows about him beyond the volume of work he did behind the scenes at Ripley's.

For many of the most unbelievable cartoons, dare I say the "best" items in the Ripley archives, there would be scant back-up information on file beyond a book title, maybe a page reference, a series of numbers followed by "N. P.", and a date referring to when he submitted the item to his editors (Robert Ripley, Doug Storer, and later a King Features Syndicate employee named Lester Byck whom I know virtually nothing about). For someone, myself, trying to answer fan mail queries regarding the origin of the company's published stories based on these partial hieroglyphs, it was often an impossible nightmare. Sometime in 1979-80, I found the retired Pearlroth's phone number, cold-called him, and asked for an explanation. He told me the notations referred to his private notes, fifty-two booklets, one per year of employment, which he still had, written in shorthand forms of his own creation for where the source books could be found within the NYC Central library. They sounded like the Rosetta Stone to me!

In 1980 I begged Ripley's then President and owner, Alec Rigby to send me to New York to meet Norbert. It was my very first "business trip".

I met Norbert, then approximately eighty-six/eighty-
seven years old, his wife, and his two adult children
(both older than me) in a small immaculately tidy
Brooklyn brownstone. He was happy to be remembered, and
very willing to talk. I learned that Ripley had paid
for his kid's college tuitions, and was generally regarded as kind and charitable, but had only ever had
Norbert travel with him once. Norbert, like Ripley,
claimed he had never had a holiday.

From day one, Norbert had accepted the role of behind
the scenes ghost writer. Until his final days with King
Features, he had loved his job, but he was now bitter
at having been fired at age 80. He felt he could still
do the job at least as good as the man who had inherited his position.

I was a little surprised that he considered his notes
his private property, and not the company's, but I
wasn't prepared to argue with him about anything, and
considered him not just my mentor, but my hero. He
teased me with just a couple volumes, and outlined exactly what his notations meant. Not having ever been to
the NYCPL I took him at his word. He told me he
wouldn't give me the books, but he was willing to sell
them. His asking price was $1,000 per book.

I was skeptical they were worth anything near that price
to Ripley's, and told him I would have to see all fifty-two books before I would even think about it. He
said they were locked away in off-site stor-age, and I
would have to give him a few days to retrieve them. I
left having had a very memorable day, but doubtful that
anything would come of it.

In Toronto I pleaded my case with Alec and John Withers, but essentially agreed that $52,000 was an unreal-
istic crazy number. I was given the okay to go back to
New York to see all the books as soon as Norbert was
ready to show them, but the approval to only offer $100
to $200 maximum for each volume.

My second visit with Norbert, with just his son in attendance this time, was short, and not amiable. Not only did he find my offer offensive, but in the interim
he had reconsidered his price and now wanted more, not

less. I had no real trouble walking away that day, but often thought back whether I made the right decision. At least at the time, I couldn't see ever spending the time to write out everything in legible longhand, and cross checking it with the library's catalog system. At best I would probably only use the files a handful of times a year. For me it came down to being a completest, a hoarder just believing we should have them whether we used them or not. The computer age came along very shortly after, however, and made it all a moot-point. I never really missed them.

Once or twice years later rumors of them being in circulation and for sale by a grandson would crop up, but I never physically saw them again past 1980. Pearlroth died in 1983 a few days short of his 90th birthday. A nice obit was widely circulated, but it raised more questions than it answered. The accompanying photo was not very flattering.

Even if I had never met Norbert, or known Doug, or Li Ling Ai, or Hazel, my years amongst the files seemed to point to me as the obvious person to write a new Ripley biography. When a different employee was first considered for the job, I balked very loudly. I won that immediate battle, but not the war. Somehow, I wasn't even considered; the project would be farmed out to a professional writer, so that it would not appear to be a blatant piece of self-promotion by the company and our burgeoning publishing department.

The first outside man chosen for the job, was named Sidney Kirkpatrick, an established author and screenplay writer. He visited the archives in Orlando a couple times, with his wife Nancy, and I enjoyed working with them very much. He was organized and clearly loved both what he knew about Robert Ripley, and Ripley's Believe It or Not! (the company). I felt there was some magic between us, and had no jealousies.

Unfortunately, the project went sideways and didn't progress as Ripley's desired it. Sidney seemed bogged down in Ripley's Santa Rosa years (1890-1912), and after months, hadn't even gotten to the meat of the subject (1918-1949). At the rate he was going it was feared it would take years. We were hoping for something in two-three years maximum, and preferably less. I am sure

Sidney can better tell what went down than I can, but suffice to say, the project was aborted. Lucky for writer Neal Thompson, Sidney didn't burn his research, and in 2010 was honorable enough to pass it along to Neal who would use it as a launching point for his Ripley biography, **A Curious Man** (2013).

I don't consider Neal's book the definitive word on the subject of Robert Ripley, but read in tandem with the earlier Considine book, a reader will get a pretty clear and complete picture of the marvelous Mr. Ripley. Thompson's book definitely filled a huge need, and in that it was the initial inspiration for the successful PBS television documentary of 2015, Robert Ripley: Believe It or Not! by Catherine McConnel, I suspect the company got its money's worth. I no longer feel compelled to write my own version of Ripley's story, but I could probably be easily swayed if the need for another version ever arose. In some ways this current book is my form of healing for a perceived wound.

12

The Ripley Cartoon in My Time

From day one the cartoon was an important part of my job and my psyche. For my first ten years I was the only liaison between Ripley's in Toronto and the syndicator, King Features Syndicate (KFS), in New York, who were initially responsible for every aspect of the cartoon. The cartoon had our name on it, but really wasn't our creation. By the mid-1980's I was supplying the content for about half the published cartoons, literally forcing the KFS staff to expand their vision of what should be in the cartoon. For example, Ripley had started as a sports cartoonist exclusively. As he got more famous, he introduced other topics of personal interest and the sports con-tent dwindled somewhat. After his death "professional" sports all but disappeared from the cartoon, because no one on the KFS staff was personally interested. Little Bobby Smith, age ten, who threw a no-hitter might get in the cartoon, but Mickey Mantle never did. My goal was to do as much research and content selection as possible to try and infuse a more universal flavor into the cartoon, while leaving KFS to concen-trate on drawing and syndicating the final product.

It was an uphill battle all the way, their salesman was not even trying to get new clients, readership was down, and the staff was very set in their ways. The four main players, three men and a woman, all who had over thirty years experience, didn't know who to follow — their heart, or some kid a thousand miles away. It had to have been tough on them to take direction from a twenty-something that they saw at best twice a year.

Our biggest battle was over typeset captions versus hand written ones. I gave in for a time, but thought this sucked the uniqueness and homey charm out of the cartoon. As the artist Walter Frehm got older, he wanted to draw only two items a day rather than three or four. This too was a drastic change for the worse

in my mind. When in 1988 Ripley's got a new president—Bjarne Christensen — my first suggestion to him was that we should not renew our contract as it existed with KFS, take over the creation of the cartoon totally, and if necessary, go shopping for another syndicator. I had full support from Bob Whiteman our New York licensing agent who felt he couldn't get another television show or any other big licensing deal unless we went for drastic change in the cartoon. We had been with KFS since July 1929. A sixty-year relationship was about to end.

This was a huge, tough decision, but to our surprise KFS didn't even try to keep us. Ten years earlier they had retired researcher Norbert Pearlroth — a fifty-two-year veteran — against his wishes, based on age (and presumably pension benefits). All four of the cartoon staff were pension age eligible. If Ripley wasn't prepared to pay their salaries and pensions, as well as the rent for office space in the KFS building, then KFS was prepared to retire them all, and **we** would have to start a new. We felt under that threat, it was best to break away completely, and not only leave KFS, but New York as well.

Starting in November 1989, the production would be done by the new Ripley publisher, and editor in chief — me — in Toronto, and the cartoon would be syndicated by KFS' biggest competitor, United Media, who handled the two biggest syndicated cartoons at the time: **Peanuts** and **Garfield.**

I was ambitious, but naive. I knew nothing about newspaper production and cartooning, but was sure I could do a better job than KFS had been doing for the last ten years. I had a lot to learn. In sixty-years we had never missed a day of publication, so the first giant problem was to make sure we didn't miss one now. I had to hire a researcher and a cartoonist PDQ.

Hiring Karen Kemlo to be the researcher was relatively simple. It was a dream come true gig for any writer wannabe, and as I had been doing the job myself for the better part of nine years, I understood what the job required — a love for research, the ability to read fast, often, and anything, and be disciplined enough to go to the library as often and for as long as it took to find a minimum of thirty unbelievable stories every week, come hell or high water, without daily contact and reinforcement from "the boss". Karen submitted an intriguing story about Toronto tattoo parlors as part of her interview portfolio. It screamed Ripley's, and I knew she was the right person for the job.

The more stories fans (our readers) provided the better, but Karen was expected to fill seven days-worth of toons each week in case no fan submissions were good enough to be published. At bare minimum we would publish twenty-four stories a week, three each week- day, six on Sunday. If she ever hoped for a day off, or a proper vacation, she needed to do much more than the minimum; she needed to always be six to eight weeks ahead of publication day, and having a surplus was the only way to do it without having a nervous breakdown. The schedule didn't allow for illness or fatigue.

Together we would meet each Monday and pick the twenty-four stories to be drawn the next week. Karen would then write them up, each story to be a maximum of thirty-words in length, submit them by Wednesday for my final editing, and deliver them to the artist. Her research for each used item became part of the permanent Ripley archives. For four years we were a dynamic team. Her job got infinitely harder once I moved to Orlando, but with zero human con-tact she forged on for another eleven years. She was a first-class re-searcher and a great rock-like foundation for the cartoon for fifteen years in total.

Hiring the artist was much more difficult. Knowing that the job was critical to the company, I had a decent budget to advertise for the position, but since I can't draw anything, and I had no real layout design experience at the time, I didn't really know what to ask in an interview, and I certainly couldn't train or show anyone any ideas I might have. All I could really do was offer an educated opinion and hope I could articulate my visions. The artist would need to be good already, because no one was going to be able to teach them to draw better.

I advertised the position across the entire country of Canada and received nearly 300 applicants. I don't recall how I narrowed it down to a workable size, but from the 300 I chose twenty and gave them six stories to choose from in order to make one daily cartoon. I was generous and gave them two-full days to complete the assignment. From those twenty I had no trouble picking the best, and had him in for a face to face interview smugly feeling he would start the next day. His work was exemplary, head and shoulders above the rest.

His main drawing was a depiction of Peter Minuit trading beads to Indians for the purchase of Manhattan. Before we even got to salary discussions, I thought to ask him how long it had taken him to com-plete his sample drawing. When he said over twenty hours I knew I was in trouble. At his pace he would be hard pressed to complete two out of seven pieces required per week. He quit before he was hired.

My second choice, Kelly Brine, drew in a very angular commercial art style. It was a drastic difference to what we had been doing for most of our seventy-year existence, but I liked it and was willing to change the overall look if we didn't lose readership. Thinking positive I thought the new look would increase, not decrease circulation. Unfortunately, he didn't last long enough to tell. He drew the panel for about one month before having an artistic difference of opinion with Karen. I sided with her, and he quit.

My third choice, Randy Timms, was a very young, fresh out of art school student. He wasn't in the same league as either of the first two, but was willing to work for much less money, and seemingly would take direction from two non-artists. It was now December and we had no surplus built up. He got sick over Christmas and fell behind. I had no choice but to fire him and beg Kelly to come back to work at least until I could hire someone else. This took several weeks, but Don Wimmer eventually drew his first cartoon of fifteen years-worth of Ripley cartoons, in March of 1990.

Don lived in New Jersey and was not one of my 300 initial applicants. He was suggested to us by Bob Whiteman who had met him in New York doing freelance work for United Media. I liked his style, though very different from our traditional one. Again, I was too desperate at the time to argue, and felt I would be able to mold him once he was on the job. Don and I never fought in fifteen years. He always took my editorial suggestions without hesitation, and never complained when I changed the text at the last minute, or even after the fact, but

he seldom backed down when it came to his actual drawings.

Over the years his drawings got more caricaturist than
realistic, and he went out of favor with a few people
at Ripley headquarters. I defended him sometimes to my
own detriment, but knew he was eventually going to have
to change, or leave. He took me completely by surprise
one day announcing he was leaving to fulfill his life-
long dream of having his own feature panel. Since leaving Ripley's Don has successfully drawn the **Rose is
Rose** cartoon. I read it every day in my paper, and I
hazard to guess its circulation exceeds Ripley's at
this point in history.

With a new researcher and a new artist coming on board
in 2006, it was wise for me to step down (or at least
back) at the same time. For the next nine years, as
long as our book publishers and the cartoonist were not
physically in our office, I was still involved in editing, and assuring the content was Ripley-worthy, but
more and more the content was provided by our London
book researcher. When publishing finally moved to Orlando, from London, in 2015, when publisher Anne Marshall retired, I became more of a consultant than a
hands-on editor. The artist John Graziano still asked
my opinion regularly, but the new editors and researchers made it clear they didn't need or want my opinion —
too many cooks spoil the broth. In my last year with the
company I had no idea if they took my suggestions in
draft form or not, and I actually stopped reading the
cartoon in its finished form unless someone specifically showed it to me.

I have only seen Karen once in the last twenty-five
years, and I haven't seen Don for twenty years, but he
and I still exchange a small Christmas gift each year.
With just a hint of competitiveness, we try to outdo
each other by sending the most obscure CD of Christmas
music we can find. I confess that many of his gifts only get played once each year, but Willie K's **Willie
Kalikimaka**, Joey Ramone's **Christmas Spirit**, and Lucy
Clark's **Jersey "Bada Bing" Christmas** have become Meyer
family Christmas traditions.

I was in total control of the cartoon for sixteen years
(1989-2005), and like to think I left a lasting impres-

sion on it and its place within the company's bigger entertainment picture. I read the archival car-toons for one reason or another — answering fan mail, doing book, television show, or museum research, fulfilling licensing needs, — virtually every day I was at work for nearly forty years. I can quote hundreds of them nearly verbatim as they are forever stored in the recesses of my mind, but my local paper doesn't carry Ripley's, so I no longer see it (1). I still read my newspaper comics every single day, seven days a week, 365 days of the year. I find it is the best way to start every day with a smile and a laugh. I do miss Ripley's panel though.

13

A Short Tribute

I am not sure I ever truly understood Bob Whiteman's position in the company. Officially he was the company's licensing agent. He wasn't paid a salary, accepting rather a retainer against a share of the busi- ness he brought in. At times he was listed in our corporate directories, but not always. He never had an office in a Ripley building, and he always had other businesses aside from Ripley's on his agenda. He was a very special person in the company's history, and as the only one who had ever actually met Robert Ripley, was regarded as somewhat of a mythical potentate. I personally loved the man — though he often drove me nuts with his special requests and his unrealistic urgencies — and trust that the feeling was mutual based on respect. I acknowledge him here because I worked with him longer than with any other Ripley associate.

Bob was stationed in New York, first just off Central Park, about two blocks from where Ripley once lived and had an office, but then later from his home in Rye, NY, in Westchester County. He had been a child prodigy violinist in his teens and first met Ripley while trying to raise money for a Broadway musical. He described Ripley's Manhattan apartment as being like a museum. It was the first place he had ever visited that the elevator stopped inside, rather than out-side in a hallway. The doors opened and you were immediately overwhelmed.

I believed Bob dabbled with Ripley's in the 1950s, but it wasn't until the 1960s that he became really active, marketing everything from Ripley sea monkeys, to plastic monster model building kits, to ka-leidoscopes, to coloring books, to sure fire giant growing vegetable seeds, and the very popular Simon & Schuster paperback Ripley cartoon books. His batting average was consistently high for at least twenty years, and in the late 1970s, early 1980's he finally hit two home runs with the very successful Milton Bradley board game, and the ABC-Jack Palance television show. Later he would be instrumental in getting Ripley's back on television with Dean Cain and TBS, and he also played an important role in getting the company physically back in

New York with the current Time's Square Odditorium. People in the Ripley office, including myself, typically did the grunt work for Bob's projects, but it was Bob that created and closed the deals. He was a great success, and a real "Ripley character." Should either of the following stories cause him to roll over in his grave, I beg and pray for his forgiveness.

Bob didn't attend too many of the company's full-managerial meetings, typically preferring to stay behind the scenes, and only deal with the presidents, Norm Deska, and myself. Part of the reason may have been because he was a real talker — keeping him to a schedule was nigh impossible. If you gave him an hour for a presentation he inevitably took two. One year at least, however, he gave a half-day presentation to the museum managers in some nice southern resort town. After his presentation, and at the end of the day he was lounging pool side while a group of employees played water volleyball. I was standing in the position next to the net right below him. Officially he was supposed to be the referee-score keeper, but I suspect he was not too diligent at his job. A ball was served, it hit him on the head, he spilled his drink on me, and fell off the chair landing part on the side, part in the pool. He was too big for me to lift him out of the pool alone, but several people hurried to his rescue. When back in his chair and seemingly okay, the first words out of his mouth were: "Out of bounds, foul, point to the receivers". We all laughed and were relieved he wasn't hurt. The next day, however, he confessed to be in pain, and was visibly bruised. He flew home, and never came back to another manager's meeting.

I don't think I can honestly say that Bob ever really retired, I know he was still scheming about a possible Ripley project less than a week before his death, but he did have a big birthday party in 2005 when he turned eighty. I didn't attend the event, but I did pick out his present from Ripley's head office. It was the first time we de-acquisitioned a piece from the Ripley archives for a gift. Bob lived well and was the kind of person that buying a gift for was tough-if he didn't already have it, he certainly could afford to buy it. I am not sure how I became the Ripley gift shopper, but I took the job seriously and I prided myself on "odd" gifts that had a lot of personal meaning. For Bob I chose a matchstick violin. The instrument was made in 1932 by Robert Ratte, of Springfield, Massachusetts, who twice had played it on the Ripley radio show. I knew Bob would be nostalgic and appre-ciative. He wrote me a nice letter, so I know he was, but it was not until he died twelve years later, at his funeral service, when I saw a photo of him playing it, did I understand just how perfect a gift it had been. His wife and daughters told me he would often disappear after dinner, and moments later sweet violin music would waft through his house. He apparently played it regularly, and loved its tone.

If there was ever a man who dreamed bigger than Bob Ripley, it was Bob Whiteman. May he RIP.

14

Publishing — Take 2

Several times during the company's tremendous growth decade of the 1990s, people's jobs and responsibilities changed; as the company grew, new things were often needed of people. As Bob Masterson found himself on the road more than he was in the office, it was often difficult for me to get the okay to proceed with different purchases, and more importantly to get people paid in a timely way. Bob came to me one day and said he was sorry, but he needed me to answer to Norm rather than directly to him. Everyone involved knew this wasn't going to be ideal, and had a slim chance of working. Norm and I were two very different people. Though I respected him — he is very intelligent, intuitive and right more often than not — I simply didn't agree with his management style. Our boss — to staff relationship deteriorated pretty quickly; I had answered directly to the president for nineteen years and it was too late for me to change my habits to suit him. Bob tried to ease my pain by giving me more staff, but they weren't totally comfortable either. They really weren't sure who they worked for. They worked side by side with me, but saw doing what I said could be overruled, and more often than not led to conflicts and even open hostilities. After a year of turmoil Bob offered me a new job. I wasn't going to lose my existing job, but my friend Peter Mac was going to take on some of the day to day activities of the warehouse, so that I could go on what would wind up being a two-year sabbatical. My new job was to re-launch **Ripley Books.**

I more or less lost my staff, I lost my nice office, and I had to move to smaller digs with no windows or view. I had total autonomy though. No Norm in my life. I got a bit more money, and a second business card that said "Vice President and Publisher". It seemed like a promotion; it was certainly a whole new ball game.

After a few "blue sky sessions" my mandate was defined as to travel a couple of the interstate highways researching roadside attractions, and to do a "series" of books on the weird things people could see and do on their travels (**Ripley's Looks at I-95, Ripley Looks at I-75, Ripley Looks at I-10, etc.**). I researched hundreds of location-centric cartoons, and with my family in tow spent the summer of 1998 driving north along I-95. It wasn't a "holiday", but it wasn't hard work either. Despite the AAA organization having shown early interest in teaming up with Ripley's on the project, it was soon apparent that lots of these kinds of books already existed, one called Roadside America, which I loved, was actually already a best-seller.

I worked hard on this project for about four months. I interviewed writers, I cold-called agencies, government officials, printers, and designers, I learned about ISBN numbers and how do copyright products, and I learned to type. Up until this point in my career I had always had a secretarial administrative assistant, but now as a department of one, I had to do everything myself. Thank God for having learned the basics in grade nine typing class with the gorgeous Miss Angie. Without knowing I had been given a sizable raise, the general public figured I had been demoted.

I still believe the travel books were a good idea, and that I could have done it, but in 1997 we had opened our first aquarium (Myrtle Beach, S.C.), and by 1998 we were on schedule to open a second one. (Gatlinburg, Tn.). In the first six months of operating Myrtle Beach we had quickly learned aquariums could make a lot of money in the gift shop (considerably more than was made in a typical Believe It or Not! odditorium gift shop). Books in particular were in demand. Everyone asked agreed that if we were going to sell loads of books, they should be Ripley books. Bob asked me once again to change my direction, put the travel books on the back burner, and create some Ripley "fish" books.

On the surface this would be easier, photos were readily available (at a price), we had experts on staff that could help with research and writing, I could do most of the work from my office (virtually no travel would be necessary) and we had more than a thousand cartoon stories that could be utilized as is, or updated to another format (new art, captions, primary text). I tackled the new challenge full steam ahead.

I planned six books (1), thinking I could do two a year for the next three years. I contacted dozens of photograph libraries, I hired three different writers, and I convinced Joe Choromanski, the company's VP of Husbandry to write "forewords". Through a small Orlando newspaper story about local "Women in Business" I found myself a small firm called "Infinite Ideas & Designs" (IID) that could do all my visual design work, and they in turn introduced me to my future printer. JoAnn Polley, the owner of IID, and her two associates, first Laurie Briggs, then later Candace Register, would become valued outside members of the Ripley family doing multiple design projects for the company, and many of our franchises as well, for more than a decade. In fact, they even designed and produced this book.

Four hardcover sixty-four page books were created, and published in two years. Each had a cutesy gimmick, a piece of shark skin-like sandpaper in the first, a disc of whale noises in the second, complete with a singing Elvis faced whale drawing on the cover sleeve, and lenticular book marks in the third and fourth books. It took a while, and some deep discounting, but eventually the print runs of 10,000 of each sold out through our two aquariums. I am very proud of these books. I can truthfully without hesitation call them mine, from start to finish. They even spawned a later Ripley soft cover series, using the same format, produced by Scholastic books (2).

I had been making books for two and a half years when Ripley's Aquarium of the Smokies, in Gatlinburg, Tennessee, opened just before Christmas 2000. On December 29, 2000, Bob Masterson called me at home and asked if I would come to Gatlinburg as soon as pos-sible. I said I would be there the following week on January 4th. Gatlinburg is not the easiest place to get to. In those days it required two planes and an hour's car drive. It was freezing cold.

Bob proudly showed me every inch of the new aquarium, inside and out, and asked me to arrange a photo shoot, which I happily agreed to do and accomplished later that month (3). There was no sense of emergency in anything he did, or said, however; I couldn't help but wonder why I had been called at home over the Christmas holidays and asked to meet asap. We spent about six hours together that day talking about everything under the sun, except what ultimately was on his mind.

In the process of saying my goodbyes — I was flying back to Orlando that same night — standing in the cold twilight darkness, he blurted out he wanted me to go back to my former job, and fold up publishing. I was surprised, there had been no indication he was "unhappy", but I didn't feel like a failure. I was sure he had no fault with what I had, or had not, accomplished. I was actually glad he had noticed the archives and exhibits department had suffered quite a bit in the last two years, and I was happy he wanted me to return to it full time to fix it. In Peter's defense he had never really wanted the job, and he had never fully embraced it. In fact, he had delegated much of the job to a person who was totally wrong for the job. I agreed to do what Bob was asking under the proviso I could fire this person, I would not be subject to Norm, and that Bob would personally clear the path with Peter. As it turned out Bob was already considering sending Peter to Myrtle Beach, where he had been the odditorium manager for many years before moving to Orlando, to become the manager of the Myrtle Beach Aquarium. My physical reinstatement was accomplished the same week. I even got a personal letter from Jimmy Pattison, saying I had been missed, and he was glad I was back where I belonged.

I didn't immediately fold up Ripley books, however. I would write and produce souvenir guidebooks for all Ripley museums and the two aquariums over the next year that would be used for more than a decade, selling hundreds of thousands of copies, and Bob had one more surprise big mission for me. He asked would I work with attractions legend Harrison "Buzz" Price to edit, print and publish his memoirs? I knew Buzz only from a seminar I had attended at which he was a keynote speaker. I loved his personal style and sense of humor, but I didn't know him, didn't know if he could write a book, and certainly knew nothing about **"Rollercoaster Math"**, the proposed title of his opus (4). It would be one of the most rewarding projects of my life for which I am ever grateful to Bob, Buzz, and his wife Anne for having faith in me that I was the right person for the job and could do it in a timely and economically sound manner.

For the next two years I would have daily phone conversations with Buzz, and the occasional in-person meeting — Musso & Frank's Grill on Hollywood Blvd. was Buzz's favorite rendezvous spot. Turns out Buzz had already written a first draft manuscript long before he met me, and it didn't need too much tweaking. I'll confess I didn't really feel qualified to rewrite anything for him, but I did severely reorganize the order of the chapters, and eventually I convinced him to change the title to **Walt's Revolution**. I was sure no one would ever buy a book with the word "math" in the title no matter how good it might be. His title did in fact describe much of the book, but not all of it. The book is really about Walt Disney as much as it is about Buzz, and Walt's name on the cover, used by permission of his brother Roy, assured at least a few sales.

I carried Buzz's manuscript, printed and in a giant white binder, everywhere I went for two years. I slept with it. I absorbed it, I saw numbers in my dreams, but I can't say I really ever grasped it beyond the basic premise of "location, location, location."

Buzz was to receive a lifetime achievement award at a November IAAPA (International Association of Amusement Parks and Attractions), conference so we launched the book to coincide with his day of glory. We expected big sales from the event, but were sadly mistaken. Buzz was a little disappointed, but proud that it was done, and being in his 80s, very content that he had seen it through to completion.

The book sold on-line for years. It became "the Bible" on the subject of strategic planning of attractions, and even a school textbook at the Rosen School of Hospitality in Orlando where his archive papers now reside. Buzz loved our chats those two years and gave me a lot more credit that I deserved.

I like to think that I made a difference to this important book, and   I am definitely proud to have worked with Buzz on it, but it was not my crowning achievement as a publisher and an editor. There is one other thing that as time goes by I now think I am even more proud of.

Going back to those "fish books" of 1998-99…

I didn't have much of a budget to commission new art for those books, but I knew I needed more "color" to bring the books to life, and I wanted to include some original artwork in each of the books. I really hadn't seen much of Corena Ricks' (5) art at that point, and in truth she was more sculptural and multi-media oriented than a painter, but I really believed she could do what I needed, and though she didn't owe me a thing, as an underemployed new mother, I figured she could use some cash. I have always found bribery does work as a last resort, and after much whining and begging, I was able to cajole her into doing ten original oil paintings — based on earlier Ripley cartoons — for each volume — sixty in total — a truly massive output for any artist.

All of her paintings for the four published books were used; nothing of the first forty was left on the editorial cutting board. Most were only used once, for the book in question, but some became artwork in our museums, specifically the ten done for our shark book. Corena was proud of them at the time, but would probably consider them too "simple" today. Turns out I was amongst the very first people to encourage her to follow a career in art. She is now a world-class artist of some renown, and in 2018, with a tear in her eye, she thanked me for believing in her, long before she believed in herself. I may not have sold many books, but as the Ripley VP of Publishing, I did make a difference in at least a couple people's lives.

Five published books and a handful of guidebooks don't make for much of a publishing career. More copies of each of my 1998-2003 books were sold than my attempts of fifteen years earlier, but after two very marginal attempts at publishing **Ripley Books**, it was clear I should stick to editing and writing. My role in the third resurrection of **Ripley Books**, **which** would start in 2005 under Norm's auspices, would be financially more rewarding for all involved.

15

Birth of a Media Slut

Limerick for my Father

When traversing the world of the weird throughout
all the exhibits you've cleared none outshine the
sight

Half-red and half white:

The boss with the duplicitous beard!

© Curtis Meyer, April 30, 2005

I'm not too proud to admit it. I love being interviewed. Maybe I love hearing my own voice. I certainly
love seeing myself in the paper, or in a magazine, or
on an important website, and I especially love being on
television. Prostitution is defined as selling one's
self, for money. I seldom got paid extra cash for my
services, so I was never an out and out whore — just a
slut. For over thirty years I was ready to give myself
at a moment's notice, anytime, virtually any place,
back alleys, and washrooms included.

Print Media

I am pretty sure my media career started with an article titled **"Executive has an "unbelievable" job."**
printed on page C-19 of the Toronto Star newspaper, on
December 24, 1987. I had been with the company nearly
ten years by that time, but the story related how I got
my job through Canada Manpower, and listed a couple
things I had recently acquired: dressed fleas from Mexico, a shrunken head from South America, life-size paper bag sculptures from Pennsylvania, and a 19th century French head measuring device used by hat makers.
Even at this early stage my office was described as
"cluttered", though to me it looks pretty sterile in
the printed photo. The photo shows me looking very casual, with collar open, and cuffs rolled up — definitely
not a standard businessman photo. The article was syndicated in papers all across Canada. It was a quarter-

page, above the fold. I was famous. It was a very nice Christmas present.

There may have been other articles with Meyer quotes in them, but the only other full article I remember from my home town paper appeared September 15, 1992, in section – B, page 6, one third page size, above the fold, with a large photo, and a second page continuation. Once again, the title was **"Unbelievable job"**, expanded on the second page to: **"His job is absolutely unbelievable"**.

This article was significant for several reasons:

1) The story was teased on the page one banner — above the masthead — a position I think l only ever got once more in my life.

2) The picture documents that I was well on my way to baldness by age thirty-six.

3) The office is again described as "cluttered" — oh if these people could have seen it thirty years later!

4) I predict that I may never work anywhere else.

5) I state that I will never buy anything in formaldehyde, a rule that though I would break it one time, I used as a significant mantra for the next twenty-six years.

6) I claim not to have a "favorite", exhibit, that my favorite changes regularly depending on what the last acquisition was, or the next one will be — - another mantra for the rest of my career.

7) I describe my mission as finding the next **Holy Grail** — my most oft repeated favorite mantra, and two other **really** important things:

8) The casual mention that the company was going to move to Florida ten months later, and

9) The first public acknowledgment of my future legendary two-toned beard.

Number 8 would get me in instant trouble. Number 9 would have a lingering effect for years.

71

As a company, Ripley's hadn't been talking too much about the big move, it wasn't common knowledge, and certainly my wife's bosses didn't know anything about it. Reading it in the morning paper caused quite the kafuffle. They were upset, she was mortified. The last year of her nineteen-year tenure as a Canadian government civil servant was not the most comfortable for her.

Off and on during my life I have grown a beard. In Canada it started as a seasonal winter thing, but at some point it became part of my persona — "larger than life" one might say — , and I grew it whenever I got tired of shaving. People, including President Jimmy Carter (1), would randomly ask: "Is that beard real?" I assured them all that it was, but most didn't believe me, and those who did, assumed it was how I got my job at Ripley's. The beard **was** (past tense as it has been white for many years now), two-toned, split right down the middle, half red, have dark brown (blackish). My mother's side of the family has several redheads; my father's side all has black dark hair. Until I grew my beard the first time, I had no red hair on my head, and considered myself blessed.

I'll talk more about the beard's fame later, but getting back to the article and photo….

Newspaper photos in those days were almost always black and white. Pity as the light and angle in this photo show the beard off really well. What bugs me to this day was that the writer, one Bill Taylor — bless and curse him — spent over an hour interviewing me, not including the outdoor photo shoot, and only asked about the beard in the last minute as he shook my hand goodbye. I was actually quite pleased that it had not been a topic of discussion, or a distraction, during our time together. I coolly answered his question and parting stare with: "it just grows like this".

So imagine my surprise when the article came out and I see the first four paragraphs about the beard! To make matters worse, he clearly didn't believe me that it was real. The rest of the article was quite good, but I was mortified, my beard was more important and famous than I was.

Over the next few days everyone I met, including a com-

72

plete stranger, smart-ass teenage waiter in a Pizza Hut restaurant, mocked and teased me: "Oh it can't be real, you're lying", or "Who painted that beard on you?" (It was split perfectly in half, and did look like someone had created a dividing line right down the middle between the two colors). The article was published on a Tuesday and the beard was gone the following Saturday. It would not appear live again in its most glorious color combo in Toronto ever again (2).

It would take a couple years for the American press to find Ripley's after the move to Orlando in July 1993, but eventually it would become easy to get media coverage for my activities, our newest exhibit acquisitions, our annual contests, public events, my travels, in general, whatever was new that could be exploited as a local story. The big differences in the interest in Ripley's were, Orlando is smaller than Toronto, so there is less hard news to compete with, and more importantly our warehouse was in Florida, we now had something besides my beard to show. The potential for photo ops was almost infinite. Major magazines, like **People, The National Enquirer, National Geographic Traveler** and **The Smithsonian**, would all soon find us.

Starting on December 27th, 1995 with an article in the **Wall Street Journal**, after the **National Enquirer** turned the story down, my most talked about, written about, and televised, exhibit interviews concerned two African fertility statues from the Coté d' Ivorie: Ripley's African Fertility Statues. They have toured Ripley odditoriums around the world four or five times (I have lost count), but I was only along for the ride on the first two tours. That was enough for me. At some point I got very tired of saying things like: "There is no scientific explanation, but they do seem to work" — as demonstrated by the dozens, then hundreds, then thousands of testimonials to their "powers" that we continued to get for the next twenty-three years. "Touch them and you too (or your wife/girlfriend) may get pregnant." I produced a small souvenir book that sold very well, and we had printed logo-ed baby blankets, postcards and keychain "merch". They were the company's first foray into "traveling exhibitions" without trailers. Our first generation website in the 1990s was developed primarily to publish their tour schedule. It remains the most popular Ripley museum exhibit ever.

Over the years I heard so many sad stories, and so many heartwarming "thank you" stories too, that it makes it difficult to be anything but sympathetic, but if they worked for you, please thank your spouse, and GOD. I assure you I had nothing to do with your pregnancy, and the birth of your child(ren). I am not a magician, a scientist, or a doctor. All I did was buy the statues.

On a lighter note, but still speaking of "fertility"….

My personal, **yes I really did say that**, all-time favorite newspaper quote appeared in the **Los Angeles Times** in an article about buying dinosaur bones at auctions. I had just bought the world's largest pre-historic walrus oozik (penial bone) — nearly five feet long. The quote — and the article's two-inch high headline was: "**When it comes to fossils, size matters** — bigger is better." Somewhere else years later when talking about New Guinea penis sheaths I quipped, "One size does not fit all". The two quotes can go together on my tombstone.

It would be remiss of me to not say something about Dewayne Bevil of the **Orlando Sentinel**. He did so many stories with and about me that some of my neighbors were sure I must be paying him — they actually thought he was the company's (read "my") press agent. It did, however, take years to get his interest. I used to cringe at how much he wrote about Disney and not a word about Ripley's. It was like we were invisible. "Just what did Ripley's (me) have to do to get his attention"? I would ask anyone who would listen. It was very frustrating for a long time, but he more than made up for it when he finally did find us (me) through our actual publicist, Frank Woolf.

I estimate Dewayne wrote about thirty articles quoting me, most with a photo, some even in color, some above the fold, and some even on page one. In addition, he frequently wrote about our books and Florida odditoriums once we got his attention. All of his articles were very positive; he never attacked us like some other writers sometimes did (London writers in particular didn't seem to like us too much). One large, page one, business section article was even specifically about my "**unbelievable job**" — a title that seems to have followed me all over the world. A couple magazine articles came out after the fact, but it was also Dewayne who broke the story about my retirement with a long lengthy illustrated article that was seen and commented upon by people in Orlando for several weeks. He even did a thirty-minute podcast version. He was very nice and kind. I hope he will write my obit when the time comes.

On the Radio

I was definitely doing radio interviews by 1987, but I really don't know for sure when the first one was, and I didn't start keeping track of how many I did until around 2005, when at least twice a year, I would do a blitz of radio interviews regarding new Ripley books. For a few years I did over 100 interviews in a calendar year, most in the months of September through December. Some days I did as many as five in a day. These heavy days were typically in September when the annual new book was first released. I never found radio hard. All I had to do was talk, and I could always do that as I had a story to tell. I got so good at it, certain radio stations would interview me two-three times a year, just to see what was new in my life. One station even had me do a regular weekly gig for several years.

The first couple shows I remember doing were late night things, usually an interview, followed by an audience call-in segment. These were always at least an hour long, and sometimes as much as three hours. They don't have much of a format, and literally anything can happen. I remember one night, long past 1am someone asked did I know about a guy who ate an airplane? No prologue, no set-up, the caller just assumed I knew everything that had ever been published by Ripley's. In this case I miraculously did know the story he was talking about. The gourmand was French, his name was Michel Lolito, and he had, piece by piece, over several months, eaten an airplane as if it was a salad. We had featured him on an early Jack Palance television show. I knew only enough to talk about him for about two minutes. That two-minute speech rolled into over forty calls and three hours of people telling me all the weird things they, or their friends, had eaten in their lives. It was surreal. It was the longest show I ever did.

The after-midnight crowd always tended to want to talk

about aliens or cryptozoological creatures like chupa-cabra, or sasquatches. I used to wonder what drugs these people might be on that talking to a stranger about these kinds of things at 2 am was more important that sleep. Around about 1975-76 I truly believe I saw a UFO. Understand that I am making a distinction, I am saying an **unidentified flying object**, I am not saying an alien space ship...although..... who knows? Mistakenly I told listeners this on the air one night. The show was so popular I had to come back a week later for a round two.

I once even did an interview about belly button lint — yes there are people out there that collect the fluff from their navels (one person even sent me a sample of his collection from Hong Kong — one of the funniest letters I ever received; another, from Australia, had enough to fill four large glass bottles — thirty-plus years' worth!). If no one has done a PhD study on "innies and outies", and why some navels collect fluff while others don't, perhaps I should. Trust me, people are willing to talk about this kind of thing on the radio — at least after dark.

The hardest interviews I ever did were vaguely book related. Our "annual" book always had a chapter on "animals", a combination of both pets and wild creatures. I love animals. I currently have a cat, and most of my life I have had a dog. I've also have had snakes, rabbits, birds, salamanders and several other animals as pets. My son is an animal expert (read "know-it-all"), and we have visited zoos all over the USA, and a few in other countries too. I love animals and have no trouble talking about them, but, doing a one-hour Saturday after-noon 4pm show hosted by veterinarians and sponsored by dog food, is as close to radio hell as I've ever gotten. This was a twice a year regular gig for several years. We talked about everything from slugs to elephants. We may have even talked about "Norwegian Blues", but I suspect the hosts were unfamiliar with John Cleese's famous pet shop comedy sketch. I am sure this radio station had posted reminders in the studio: 'No frivolity allowed."

I've had the honor to be interviewed in many countries aside from America, Australia, Ireland, England, Canada, New Zealand, Guam, South Africa to name just a few.

76

I don't speak a second language, so all of my interviews have always been in English except on a two-week
tour of Colombia, South America, where I had Mateo
Blanco, a Colombian born artist, opera singer, full of
life, translator glued to my hip. The tours of Bogota,
Medellin and Cartagena were organized by him, and included newspaper, radio and television interviews, for
the most part, held in Spanish. I spoke English, he
translated, and the deejay replied either in Spanish or
English depending on their fluency, but even if the
host spoke English it was assumed the audience didn't.
Mateo needed to translate every word that was said. He
had no professional experience as a translator, but he
was fantastic. There were several highlights to this
tour, but my favorite interview occurred in a studio in
Bogota within an hour of my first having arrived.

The deejay towards the end of the interview asked what
was the one thing — not work related — that I wanted to
see, or do, in Bogota. I didn't know too much about Bogota, and didn't have any real expectations. I recalled
that when Robert Ripley had visited Bogota in 1925 he
had written about people eating guinea pigs. I didn't
know if they still did this, or how common it may have
been back in the twenties, but it was the first thing
that came into my head. I blurted out: "I want to eat a
guinea pig". Mateo and the host fell off their chairs
laughing. The host asked "Really?" about five times.
Through Mateo I assured him I wasn't joking. With no
English translation he then told his listeners where
and when I was appearing that evening for a meet and
greet, and offered a prize for the first person to
bring me guinea pig to taste. The locals call it "coo-
ey".

Less than an hour later, I was eating guinea pig, plan-
tains and rice made by a woman for her own dinner, but
brought to the shopping mall where I was. In front of
about fifty people I ate roast guinea pig. I liked the
meat — very much like any barbecued pulled pork, but
with lots of little bones-but I wasn't keen on the
"mini-pork rinds." Another guest that night told me
where I could see guinea pig racing the next day. We of
course did go to the races, and it was a sight to behold. I lost money on each race we saw. Turns out I
can't tell a good runner from a sleeper. I couldn't
help wondering what happened to the losers. For the

next three days every interview started with questions about guinea pigs.

Most of my "foreign" radio interviews were done in nice studios. On the other hand, most of my "domestic" interviews were done sitting somewhere on the phone. A few were done on location — at a Ripley odditorium. These typically were "event" oriented, me promoting a public appearance of someone other than myself. The best of these was from the parking lot of the Orlando odditorium on the first day we displayed the African Fertility Statues in January 1996. The show was hosted by two Orlando morning show legends "Doc & Johnny" who interviewed me several times over the span of their morning show. They talked with women who had already become pregnant via the statues while they were in our office (for 13 months starting in November 1994), or were there that day to touch them in the hopes of becoming pregnant. The deejays, not quite shock jocks, but irreverent to say the least, had a field day. One particular guest who had driven all the way from Key West, approximately an eight-hour drive, was the object of much attention. Her name was Hope. We were glad it was radio and not television when she hoisted up her skirt, and started to mate with the male statue in the entrance foyer of the museum.

I have never met John Carney of St. Louis, but he has talked to me so many times on his radio shows (originally 11pm EST Thursday nights, then later 3:30pm Wednesday afternoons) that he calls me "Eddie Baby" like we are brothers. Usually he would give me at least a twenty-minute spotlight, sometimes as much as thirty minutes. The topic was always "what's new", usually referring to new exhibit acquisitions, but also encompassing shameless advertising for new books, new displays, new museum openings, etc. Even before I talked to him the first time, I was already enamored. I have an old record album called **Cruisin' 58**. It is a recreation of a St. Louis radio show from 1958 — classic rock n' roll hosted by Jack Carney, the man who launched Chuck Berry's career. It's a fabulous record. I thought I was going to be interviewed by Jack Carney — rock n' roll radio royalty. I was ecstatic. No such luck. John's his son. Close but no cigar.

Many a week I would not be in Orlando at interview

hour, but this never stopped John; he would talk to me from wherever I was, in a bar, in a car, with a Wiccan, or a chicken…it didn't matter, the show must go on. He would often open the show with the question: "Where in the world is Eddy Baby tonight?" My favorite was one from my car, while illegally parked in the driveway of a nuclear plant in Southern Ontario, just outside of Toronto, off the side of the 401 freeway. The call came as scheduled, and I pulled over, oblivious to where I was. Next thing I knew two heavily armed guards were asking me what was I doing. I was officially in "no man's land", move now or else…. John found this very funny, I didn't then, but do now.

Our best interview – at least from my "point of view" — happened on a Wednesday night. I was about to leave for a long trip on the Thursday and had told John I couldn't do our regular spot. John asked on the Wednesday afternoon if we could do it that night instead. I said "no problem" then immediately forgot all about it. I went to bed early that night knowing I needed to get up before the crack of dawn for the flight.

Over the years I had often told my wife I could do a radio interview in my sleep. That night I did, and naked too. At about 11:05 my wife was screaming in my ear, "Get Up! St. Louis is on the phone". I knew I wasn't dreaming, but I figured she was — Carney phones on Thursdays, not Wednesdays. She assured me in no uncertain terms Carney was on the phone. The phone was in the next room — the kitchen. She propped me up in the closest chair, stuck the phone in my hand, looked at me, and burst out laughing. Luckily she did not take my photo. I apologized for being late, but didn't let on why. I spoke extemporaneously for thirty minutes, most of which were with my eyes still closed. I had proven my prowess — I really could do an interview in my sleep.

When John's show moved from night time to mid-afternoon, a lot of his spontaneity got swallowed up. When they gave him a co-host, I knew my time was up. The interviews got shorter and I was never allowed to freewheel it; they now needed to know in advance what I was going to talk about. Trouble was I seldom knew myself.

79

I once gave John a present, a large white taxidermy chicken, made into a lamp. He assures me it is still in his office/studio. One day I hope to actually meet John and talk in his studio, live on the air, not somnambular from a kitchen high top. Hopefully the chicken-lamp will still be there. John is the best deejay I ever worked with.

The Web and On-Air Podcasts

I know I am old because I can remember car-sized computers, phones with cords and a time when not everyone (read "anyone") had a web page. Though these things may seem more fantastic to a young reader than the tales from the **1,001 Arabian Nights**, they are in fact all true, the 1980s and 90s did really exist and I was there. Even more phantasmal is the fact that I was in charge of Ripley's first web site in 1999.

In charge might be too strong a phrase. Norm Deska pushed the company into the web era, foreseeing the need for us to have our own site before the Dean Cain – TBS TV show was to air (the show started in January 2000, we first went on-line in May 1999). All I had to do was simply hire a third-party consulting firm to develop, produce, host, design, and ultimately, grow our site. Once a quarter I would produce a chart to report our number of hits, users, page views and kilobytes used. I did have to vaguely understand the terms, but I didn't need to know how to make a website, that would be done for me. I did have a few good ideas over the years (1999-2005) that I was in charge, but I never did learn a line of code, or what the hell "Flash" meant. I saw our single page grow to about forty, including pages of games (a couple of which became staples of our museums as well), and links to movies (that needed "flash"), and I saw the number of monthly hits grow from 48,803 in May 1999 to a high of 7,418,954 in June 2005. I am proud to say our site even won a significant CLIO advertising award for content and style at one point.

When Steve Glum joined Ripley's in 2005 (see Chapter 22), he took over the development of **Ripleys.com** and the pages thereafter were created in-house. I had a good run. My new job under Steve's auspices was to be a video star. Steve brought with him, Todd Day, a programmer and videographer. It would no longer be enough to show movies, we had to make a few of our own. Steve called the series **"Inside the Vault"** with Edward Meyer. We made eighteen of these, mainly in the exhibit warehouse with single specific exhibits, an Iron Maiden episode and a Babe Ruth baseball uniform episode being amongst the best (3), but we also ventured outside occasionally. Footage of me chasing an iguana in the Caribbean, with the thoughts of eating it if I were able to catch one, was particularly funny. The films were purposely unscripted and manic. The company's first live streams and blogs followed much the same style. We were breaking new ground, and learning as we went.

Todd had learned his electronic skills in the Marines. He was always on the brink of chaos, that was his style, but he was a joy to work with. He stuck around for several years after Steve left the company and created several great museum films for the company, including the definitive film piece on Hananuma Masakichi (see Chapters 6 & 77). Todd's premature death, still only in his 40s, in December 2016, was a hard pill for me to swallow. Steve gave him a memorable wake; I and several others eulogized him befittingly.

Steve and Todd also introduced the company to Podcasts. Steve and I would just talk, a little like an interview, but more like friends just chatting on the front porch. We did about twenty of these. Podcasts, or as we would call them, "Oddcasts", are not too different from real commercial radio, the main difference being you really don't know if anyone is listening or not.

In 2009 our new in-house publicist, Tim O'Brien, with Todd as engineer, reinvented the Ripley oddcast. Going forward, they would now be a regular once a week thirty-minute timed, and scheduled production. Typically, we would record four at a time, back to back. Some were recorded "on-location' in venues as diverse as a haunted house in Cassadaga, Florida, to the world's busiest McDonalds restaurant, but most were done in a makeshift studio in the back of our corporate office in the former president's office.

The first handful of shows featured Tim, Todd, myself and for the female viewpoint, Marcie Pikel, a long-standing employee with varied Ripley experiences including being Steve's right hand for five years and the president's administrative assistant for many more. Tim who had some college era background as a deejay would write and read some actual weird news stories, and Marcie and I would comment on them, off the cuff and unrehearsed. The show seriously lacked pizazz so we added a real sports-background deejay, Ralf Ingwerson, who at the time was doing ghost tours full time for our company in St. Augustine, Florida — featuring our very own haunted building. I had the face for radio, Ralf had the voice. There was some good chemistry between us.

Occasionally Tim brought guests live into the studio — numerous different Ripley employees — and he and Ralf did pre-recorded phone interviews. Tim eventually let Ralf take the lead on the "unscripted" portion or the show and pushed Todd out after he learned to run the machines himself, becoming more the producer than an on air participant. He did keep one main component for himself, called "Spot the Not", a game show like quiz given to the members in the studio.

In total 200 shows, over a period of five years, were broadcast. After about thirty shows Marcie was replaced by my assistant, Angela Johnson. It was her first taste of the spotlight. Tim was on all 200 shows. I was on 192 of them, but to date I have never heard a single one. People did write me the occasional letter asking questions about things I had said, and I know a few hard-core fans did listen to every single episode, and knew them by heart, but the medium was never alive for me. There was no immediate feedback or feeling of accomplishment. Once the monthly taping was finished, so was I.

Television

I don't recall the definite date, or the show, of my first television appearance, but it may have been an interview in Penticton, British Columbia in March 1989, for the national Canadian CBC news. Jimmy Pattison was hosting United States President Ronald Reagan at a private event. After the event he had allowed some press to enter the hotel (the President had already secretly left the building). There were about 120 people the news team could have picked to interview. I have no idea why they picked me; it might possibly have been that I was the youngest person in sight. I know they interviewed several people, including Jimmy, but it was my babble that they highlighted the next night across the entire country on the 11pm news. John Withers' (the then president of Ripley's) wife Bibi saw it in Toronto, and called John in B.C. She wondered if I, and more importantly he, still had jobs. It really wasn't that bad if you deleted the section where I stupidly discussed not knowing why we all wore a uniform at the conference. I obviously had a lot to learn about branding; hope-fully with experience, I did.

The first shows I remember doing were in the early 1990s. Up until the time they left, either Alec Rigby, or John had done whatever media needed to be done. Both of them were certainly qualified, but I am not sure either "enjoyed" it, and there wasn't actually a lot done. I do recall the entire office having a group lunch at the nearby **Ports of Call** (our favorite nearby watering hole at the time), to watch John on a local lunchtime talk show. He scared the host by pulling a shrunken head out from under his jacket and got more squeals than laughs. We thought he had done great, but he had made the host look bad, and that's a big media "no-no".

When John left the company in 1988, he passed the media firmly to me, and I got to do a couple New York second-tier morning talk shows. On one, the host set me up and pretended to have sat on my matchstick violin. I was as gullible as can be, and the host, crew, and live audience had a huge laugh at my expense. On another, hosted by Johnny Carson's then favorite comedian, David Brenner, I had the pleasure to meet three people worth having on a talk show (how I got this gig God only knows): Celine Dion, Steve Irwin, and Jeanette Lee, aka. The Black Widow.

Of the three, the Black Widow, a female pool champion, was probably the most famous at the time. Her demonstration of pool tricks was amazing, and she looked really good too in a black leather Cat Woman style outfit. Brenner didn't have a chance.

I knew who Steve Irwin was, and was pleased to meet him, and his pet monitor lizard, in the green room. He

83

did a great routine with the lizard and the host where both parties got applause and laughs — the way it is supposed to go.

People in the greenroom were fussing over Celine Dion, and she clearly was the star of the show (she went on right after me!), but I didn't know who she was, and didn't stay to see her act. The next day I was a hero at the office, and especially with my young children who apparently were big Dion fans. My wife reminded me that I had paid good money to see her just a couple years earlier at a winter ski resort called Hidden Valley, in Huntsville, Ontario. Everybody has to start somewhere, but I can with a straight face, claim to have once opened for one of the biggest pop stars in Canadian music history.

I was feeling pretty good about myself after that show and was ready for the big time. Bob Masterson, the new president as of 1990, however, wanted and needed to get some exposure, so while I wall-lowed in the wings, he got two or three plums, the most memorable being a long two-part spot on **The Joan Rivers Show**. Bob did great and we were all very proud of him. I had coached him on the exhibits he took on the show, including a replica of the Mona Lisa made from toast, and a portrait of John Wayne made from laundry lint. Joan was patient, attentive and kind, but did make Bob blush pretty red when she put a chastity belt on her head. He had to explain to her that was not where it was worn. She was extremely funny. I consider it the best television spot anyone at Ripley's ever did.

By 1996 I had done several local news spots and had been interviewed briefly more than once by CNN regarding significant auction purchases. We were a client of Dan Klores Inc. out of New York and they did a decent job at keeping our name in the news. I had learned to be quick on my feet, I was totally comfortable, and I was ready for the big boys. I just needed a story that was national news worthy.

Enter the African Fertility statues into my life. Their fame would last years, with countless radio and print stories, but in their first month of exposure — January 1996 — it was all about television. The big news boys — **Inside Edition, Good Morning America, Current Affair,**

84

The Today Show, and CNN Live, all came calling, as did teams from Germany, Austria and Japan. My office, and the Orlando odditorium became Fertility Statue Ground Zero. I did over twenty television shows that month, including four in one day. **The Good Morning America** segment at about 7:20 am live at the odditorium on January 18th was the highest profile. I was to introduce myself and four mothers and their newborns "fertility babies". The earplugs didn't work so well and I missed my cue. I never fully recovered, and once I was through speaking the intros of the moms, the camera never came back to me — I was in limbo on an uncomfortable high stool for what seemed like an eternity. All the excited, proud moms did much better than I did. A star was born, but it wasn't me. One of the moms had no trouble telling the whole of America that she really believed the statues had made her pregnant. She was on the pill. It had to be a miracle. She was so lovable; she instantly became Ripley's poster girl. If I hadn't had been the guy that bought the statues, I would have become totally superfluous right then and there. Fortunately, I did much better on other shows — including **"Unsolved Mysteries"**.

Four months after the initial flurry of activity, a crew from the mega-popular nighttime drama, **Unsolved Mysteries** descended on me, the mothers, the babies, and our warehouse. This wasn't just to be an interview, it was a going to be a full-scale dramatic presentation, with a recreated main set, off-site visits to the homes of the babies, a real actor for one of the main parts, costumes, make-up, hair stylists, craft services, and even professional nannies to baby sit. It was to be my first real "acting role" as we pretended I was in a market in deepest darkest Africa buying the statues from a costumed actor whom I had never met before (4). My African-American assistant Lisa McCalla was typecast as a market shopper. My other assistant Margaret Halpert, who was single and a few years past prime child - bearing age, played a woman who wouldn't touch the statues in case they worked. She had "lines" that she improvised, and displayed moments of great English style wit and sarcasm.

On day one of a five-day shoot, I spent my entire day taking people shopping for props, and decorating our warehouse to look like an African market place. Not a single word was said about my infamous two-toned beard, relatively long and luxurious at the time. After the director said "that's a wrap" (yes, they really do say that) and dismissed his large crew, he asked me to stay a few moments longer. I had no inkling of what was about to happen. In a hushed private tone, he told me that the big wigs back in LA didn't like my beard. They found it distracting. Would I please shave it off? I was flabbergasted. I told him loud and boldly: "Are you kidding me. A distraction? This beard got me this job — sorry, no F*&%ing way am I shaving it for a fake television show". The actors union would have been proud of me.

I went home in a very big huff, but sure I had made my point.

Seven am the next morning the producer says to me: "Edward, I thought you were going to shave the beard off"? This time I went ballistic. I told him the whole thing was off if they weren't going to shoot me with my beard. I called Bob Masterson and he gave me the okay to stand my ground. The crew asked for some alone time and had a powwow. They came back with the compromise: "Could they dye it all black." I couldn't believe their gall, but reluctantly I agreed. I of course didn't know I would have to wear thick black shoe polish for the next four days. It was very uncomfortable (dry and itchy), looked stupid (my real beard not only had never been one color, it had never been jet black. I looked more like Abraham Lincoln than Edward Meyer), and Bob gave me grief for "selling-out".

The show was a roaring success. Over the next year they aired it four times. Over the next few years it may have aired as many as twenty times. Years later I discovered Candy Prizer, one of the mom's interviewed, actually got royalties every time it aired. I certainly never did, and I didn't win an Emmy either. It was the only time in my mind that I acted unnaturally on television. The show was so fake, I felt I should shave the beard so I would never be recognized on the street again. After years of convincing people my two-tone beard was totally authentic, I now had to start all over again. People said: "Oh, we saw you on **Unsolved Mysteries** and your beard was all black. We knew you were lying when you told us it was naturally two-tone".

86

They must have been blind to not see the fraud, but it was pointless to argue. Even my biggest fan — my own mother — had to weigh in on the subject. She knew my beard really was two-toned but she laughed and said: "I didn't even recognize you. That beard was ridiculous. Your sister had to tell me it was you." The only unsolved mystery that remains was why I let them do it to me.

With this acting experience under my belt, I was now finally ready for "prime time", Wednesday nights at 8pm on TBS to be exact. I was a very active crewmember in all of the Dean Cain shows in season's 1-3, but in season 4, I actually got to be on air in eleven episodes. The segment was called **Ripley's Amazing Pets**, and it involved me and a team traveling to a different Ripley odditorium each week (the shows were not aired live so filming was not literally every week) to host the Ripley version of David Letterman's famous **"Stupid Pet Tricks"**. I was a "celebrity" judge.

There was no script as we did not know what animals (with their trainers) would show up, or be used, so ad-libbing and acting were encouraged. After seeing a hundred or so border-collies do more or less the same things (they really are the smartest breed of dog), acting surprised or amazed does become very difficult. In retrospect, I often was bored, and with a voluptuous, scantily dressed female judge sitting immediately beside me, I knew where the camera was going to be focused more often than not, no matter what I said or did. The random placement of a woman with large breasts in the last two years of the Dean Cain shows was so accepted at the time that it even had a nickname: SRP — shameless rating ploy.

My single favorite pet story was a dog story, but not a trick, rather a survival story. It was in San Francisco. The dog, named Dosha, had been hit by a car, put out of its misery by a bullet in the head from a police officer, then placed in a veterinarian's freezer. Three days later it was found to be still alive, and miraculously seemingly "healed" of all three traumas. The dog didn't do much, and lots of people complained that he won the show spot when their animal did legitimate tricks, but it was unanimous amongst the judges that it was the most unbelievable pet story we found during the whole cross-country trip.

The majority of animals we saw were dogs, but we did film a very talented Amazonian macaw, a black panther, an alligator, an ostrich, and even a buffalo. The buffalo came to our Hollywood museum. It lived with a couple inside their home, and had learned a few dog-style tricks: roll over; raise a leg, play dead, etc. On camera he did everything that was asked of him, and the crew loved him. At the end of his session I asked could I touch him? Could I get my picture taken with him? The cowboy-dressed Texan owners assured me it was perfectly safe, just come up to him from behind, not head on. I did exactly as I was told and was able to pet the gentle giant. After a couple strokes, the bison started to move its head, nudging me like a cat or dog might do as a sign of affection. It was PDC (pretty damn cool), and I was loving it….until…the bison's horn got caught under my belt. The nudge became increasing stronger, then there was an angry snort, then a full-fledged head butt, and then I was three feet off the ground screaming for my life.

I was rescued pretty quickly by the owners, but I was quite shaken up, and later when I took off my clothes in the hotel bathroom, I discovered I was pretty bruised, my waist, leg and groin were all black and blue. Try to explain that to your wife.

I was told one of the cameramen got the near death experience on film, but for obvious reasons it was never aired, and I never saw it. The next time I met this bison, four years later in San Antonio, Texas, I stayed as far away from him as possible.

CBS Sunday Morning (originally with Charles Kuralt) has been on the air for forty years, and I am told it has been one of the biggest television shows in the country that whole time. I, however, have never seen a single (complete) episode. I don't watch a lot of daytime television ever, but never on a Sunday — I'm in church, religiously — every week. So telling me I was going to be on the show had about as much effect on my demeanor as telling me I am bald. Sure I had heard the name, but I was thinking it was "just another show". Turns out it was a pretty big deal. Judging by my mail and phone calls, it probably was the most watched show I was ever on. I gave segment host Bill Geist a lengthy tour of the warehouse, and the Orlando odditorium (5). My golden rule for television was give the host and crew one hour of my time for each minute of expected airtime. I gave them about seven hours, and was rewarded with a full twenty minute segment of prime time — a publicists' dream, something they could brag about for a long time.

I never did see the whole show, and it wasn't until quite a while later after it aired that I even saw my segment. I don't have a copy, so I don't remember it very well, but I did think it was very good at the time. It was easy to admire Geist. He was a consummate professional who made me feel totally at ease — just two friends talking. I am sure he got paid as much per word as I did monthly, maybe even annually, but he made me feel like a star.

The heart of the program was a long discussion on "lint art" — pictures made from laundry lint. The collection's largest one – a depiction of Da Vinci's **Last Supper**, measuring thirteen-foot wide by six-foot high, that took 200 hours over a span of six months to make, was on display in the museum (Geist would later interview the artist, Laura Ball of Michigan, to fully corroborate my story). It was something Geist had never seen or heard of. He was astounded to know that we had more than just this one lint art masterpiece. In fact, at the time we had about twenty pieces of lint art, by three different artists. The collection nearly doubled in size a few years later when I found a fourth very prolific female artist in Pennsylvania who happened to have seen this show.

2015 was my single most rewarding year on television. I was discovered by PBS in a big way, first on a national award-winning show — **The American Experience**, then on two episodes of a local Orlando WUCF-PBS production. The one-hour **American Experience** documentary style look at the life of Robert Ripley that would air January 6, 2015 across the continent started as a "what if" possibility for Mark Samels, a producer, who in turn handed it over to Cathleen O'Connell, an independent writer, director, producer out of the Boston area, who made it her personal passion project. By the time I met her she had read the then new **A Curious Man** biography of Robert Ripley by Neal Thompson and knew pretty much what she wanted to do. She already had a team together, but needed the Ripley Company's blessings to proceed. Over a long languid lunch lakeside in South Orlando, Cathleen, Norm Deska, myself, and Cathleen's future executive producer, Mark Samels, agreed that she would have full access to the archives, myself, and my assistant Angela Johnson, and that we would cast our lot with PBS television.

Angela, myself, Cathleen, and her associate producer Melissa Pollard, would work on every aspect of this show for nearly two years. It was all consuming, but fun, and the final result was much better than Neal's book version.

In July 2014 PBS wined and dined Angela and I at a swishy sneak preview release function at the Beverly Hills Hilton in California. We got to mingle with PBS stars Ken Burns and Louis Gates Jr., and many of the ultra-rich contributors who God bless them keep public television alive. I was a guest speaker with a Q&A panel discussion, was interviewed by television reporters from around the country (one was from my old high school who was visiting from Toronto), and I gave the VIPs a tour of our nearby Hollywood odditorium at a cocktail function that Ripley's footed the bill for.

Angela, Cathleen and I were a big hit; the attention given to our little show was very encouraging. We had everything we wanted except a limo, instead it was the first time we used Uber which we thought was just an LA thing. Angela probably hasn't been in a real cab since.

A couple of months later I was filmed in our warehouse for a tease commercial that aired repeatedly in the month of December. I was also asked if I would do a web Reddit -AMA (Ask me Anything) promo. This was ground breaking stuff for all involved, American Experience, Ripley's and me. It was described to me as being like call-in talk radio, except no one really talks, every one types on a web site. I knew I could handle the "ask me anything" questions, but I also knew I couldn't type well enough, or fast enough, to make it interesting. I would end up doing it with a very talented team of three women, Angela Johnson would type my off-the-cuff responses, while Lauren Hubbard would scan the internet for photos that related to what I was talking about, and Suzanne Smagala would cut and paste content from our cartoon and exhibit databases to match my text.

As a team, set up in the Ripley office boardroom, we performed live for ninety minutes just before the television broadcast aired nationwide. We had over a hundred questions and answered as many as we could in the allowed time frame. It was a huge emotional rush. The only tough question — read stupid — concerned the shape and size of my turds. Who knew, but there is actually a scatological chart describing types of "shit", complete with descriptive names. I dodged the question by saying I was unfamiliar with the chart (by this time Lauren was already showing it to me and we were all in hysterics), but I satisfied the writer's curiosity by talking about artwork I had bought painted on cow patties. Real deep shit, eh?

The PBS show itself was an even bigger success, viewed by a record five million viewers that night, and re-aired at least three more times that year. My on-air segment was filmed in a historic Winter Park, Florida, mansion called Casa Feliz, and looked suitably dark, and reverential. PBS really are the masters at making people look smart and important. It was my finest media hour, and the single thing I am most proud of when it comes to listing personal Ripley achievements. It also led me to two other wonderful, but not quite so extravagant, productions.

Orlando is blessed to have its own local PBS television station, produced in conjunction with the local University of Central Florida. I had a cameo on at least one show before, but they liked what they saw on the **American Experience** and asked me to do a whole thirty-minute episode of a weekly show called **"Artisodes"** concerning the strangest pieces of art in our warehouse, and the Orlando museum. To me, they did the best warehouse shoot anyone ever did — and there are lots to choose from. One of the items they filmed was by a local artist named Mateo Blanco (see above — he was born in Miami and bred in Colombia, but has lived in Orlando for many years). They liked it so much they did another episode just on him, which I was also featured in.

Anyone who watches PBS knows they rerun shows a lot. In the case of these two **"Artisodes"**, one or the other of them was run every Sunday afternoon and every Thursday night at 8:45 for over a year. I am sure they both were seen by every person in Central Florida at least twice. A weekend never went by where someone didn't greet me with "Oh, I saw you on TV the other night". It was very hard to tell them that the show was not exactly new. If only I had gotten residuals from this and **Unsolved Mysteries**, I might have been living in Jamaica or Antigua by now.

So how do I end this chapter and my remarkable fling with fame? How about with a regret? Yes, there is one real big one…pun intended — as it is a story about a twenty-four-foot tall Easter Bunny.

For my whole career, **"The David Letterman Show"**, under all of its different titles and network changes, was my media Holy Grail. If I could get on Dave, I could retire, maybe even die, happy. In my early years, being a total slut, I would give his talent coordinator free stories and especially the names of performers, thinking I could bribe them: "Take me and I will give you Siamese twins joined at the head". The answer was always the same — "But what can you do Edward, Dave won't let you just talk." For years I had a newspaper cartoon posted in my office. It showed a "one dog band", a dog playing a dozen or so musical instruments. The voice bubble-caption being spoken by someone looking vaguely like Dave, said, "But can he dance at the same time?" (6).

I knew I was never going to get on Dave, but I didn't hold a grudge and always gave them a story every time they called. They loved the sound of a twenty-four-foot tall chocolate Easter bunny. Could I get it to the show that Thursday night for the pre-taping of Friday night's show? I busted my proverbial balls to make it happen. I still wouldn't be me on the show, but at least it would be a totally Ripley story.

A couple thousand dollars later, the bunny arrived in plenty of time for the mid-afternoon taping. Unfortunately, it wouldn't fit through the stage door. The Ripley driver, Irv Wurst, had to leave it in the studio driveway. Dave's people assured me it would still get on the show and Dave would go outside to see it. Trouble is, it started to rain — hard.

Dave did not go outside in the rain. The rabbit, melting and looking disgusting, was shown for about ten seconds during the closing goodnight credits. Ripley's wasn't mentioned. I was defeated by Mother Nature. We abandoned the melted bunny.

I think every Ripleyesque performer I know has been on Letterman, even my son the only time he was ever in New York City got on the show, but not me (7). Shutout, disappointed and full of a giant regret. Dave, where are you? Without you, I am incomplete. I am still ready when you are. 6

Publishing: Third Time's a Charm

I previously said that Ripley Publishing came to an abrupt end on January 4th, 2000. Though technically true, this doesn't mean the company stopped releasing books, just not ones under our own name. As early as 1924, Ripley had teamed with other publishers to create product. For most of our pre-21st century volumes, the partner was **Simon and Shuster**, out of New York. In 2001, as part of the company's ongoing licensing program, we teamed up with two other New York giants, Black Dog & Leventhal, and Scholastic Books in conjunction with Nancy Hall Inc. In 2004, we added a third party, Miles Kelly Publishing Inc., out of England.

Black Dog & Leventhal produced two oversized Ripley coffee table stylebooks. The first one relied primarily on color Ripley cartoons, something we had only utilized once before (1). It also had some complimentary text, and some Ripley archival photos. It was an okay book, but the design was too simple and the book was physically too big — libraries, stores and buyers couldn't fit it on their shelves. Black Dog's second book, **Ripley's Encyclopedia of the Bizarre**, with text by Julie Mooney, was considerably better. It had a great lenticular cover of Alexander Patty, an early 20th century acrobat, bouncing down stairs on his head, lots of cartoons, more photos too, and some quality text. I enjoyed working with Julie and the Black Dog team compiling the book, and really enjoyed my first book tour when it was finished. I did some television and radio spots, and did some bookstore lectures on Ripley, Ripley odditoriums, and the book. I also did autograph sessions in large department stores across the country, including in Houston, Los Angeles, Chicago and New York. These two books relied solely on the Ripley archives for content, so my contribution as archivist was substantial.

Starting in 2001 Nancy Hall, and her associate Mary Packard created books for Scholastic that would be sold in school traveling book fairs as well as stores. They created several small products, but the cornerstone of their program was a 144-page hardcover book, called the **Ripley's Believe It or Not! Special Edition** filled with

94

Ripley archive photos and new color illustrations (not drawn by the traditional Ripley cartoon artist, but by a commissioned illustrator). Like with the Black Dog books, my involvement as complier of the Ripley content, both stories and photos, was critical. The style of the book changed over time and Nancy and Mary were eventually replaced with Anne Marshall and her delightful British team. As more and more third-party photo library images were introduced, my involvement became more proof-reader-fact checker, and my name disappeared from the masthead. I con-sider my biggest contribution to this line the insistence of including an index. As a one-time would-be librarian I knew the importance of an index to get libraries and teachers to consider any book a must have classroom reference book. I did the indexes for our fish books (see Chapter 14) and know that no one in their right mind likes this job, but in my opinion the indexer is one of the most important members of the team, highly under-appreciated, yet critical.

I first met Anne Marshall in a fancy hotel over a Poly-nesian-Asian Fusion Disneyesque dinner in Orlando, Florida. Her boss Gerrard Kelly was with her, as was Norm Deska, our then VP in charge of licensing (later Senior VP of Intellectual Property). She was already a respected and seasoned editorial director. She flew into our lives like a gentle breeze out of the east; being British she may have even been carrying an umbrella. I fell in love with Anne instantly and couldn't wait to work with her.

England has a long tradition of "annuals" — gift books of all sizes, shapes, and types, that are published every fall to be sold primarily at Christmas time. The most famous sample being the **Guinness Book of World Records,** a product Anne had some experience with. Her Ripley "annual" would be substantial in physical size and represent the most amazing stories that could be found in any given calendar year. It would be sold in stores, and though there would be content suitable for grade-school children, the target audience would be teenagers and young twenty-somethings. It would have a few cartoons to start with, but these would be weeded out over time until the book would be exclusively photographs, mostly in color. Once again, my main job would be to suggest and compile Ripley archival content. As Anne's staff grew from two to a dozen, including researchers and photo editors, I would be less a compiler, and more a proofreader, fact checker, opinionated moral voice, and public spokesperson when each volume was complete.

The first three volumes were chock full of Ripley archive material, and are markedly different than the twelve that followed. At some point Norm wooed Anne away from Miles Kelly, and Ripley Books, version #3 was officially launched. Over the next ten years Anne developed a marvelous crackerjack team and produced several lines of books, in addition to her annual, including children's novels, children's science books (called **Ripley's Twists**), a couple **New York Times** best sellers, and along the way sold over one million books per season. Numbers a little easier to be proud of than sixty-four or even 10,000.

Her legacy is huge, and I am overjoyed to still call her a dear friend after several years of her retirement. To date my wife and I have vacationed with her and her charming partner Chris Seaber three times, once in the States and twice in England. She has taught me a lot about writing and has taken me to many places I had once only dreamed of. With her help I took a shrunken head on a book tour of London and Ireland, punted on the river Cam, climbed the clock tower of Oxford University, and was featured not just in the **London Times**, the most important newspaper in the world, but also in the distinguished **Fortean Times**, perhaps the best interview of my print media career.

Did you know that in the 1960s you could actually picnic on the monolithic fallen stones of Stonehenge? No? Well, Anne can prove it. She's been my guru, and my Mary Poppins. She made my publishing life so grand for nearly fifteen years, and in addition to her effect on me, she has inspired a whole generation of Ripley fans and readers.

17

Brushes with the Law – Part #1

When one imports and exports exotic "things" across international borders, one must expect to have brushes with the law, at least occasionally. I count myself lucky that I have never been in jail. I have however, had some border issues, a strip search (with prying fingers), and a handcuffing. The following escapades are listed in sequential order, not in levels of seriousness.

When I first started with Ripley's the corporate warehouse was in Niagara Falls, on the American side. Ripley's was a Canadian company with headquarters in Toronto and an odditorium in Niagara Falls, Ontario, Canada, but otherwise, all the museums and other businesses, were in the USA. It made sense to have the warehouse near the border, but on the American side. In those days, before September 11, 2001 changed international travel forever, going across the Niagara River from one side to the other was not a big deal; our employees did it regularly without incidence. I had done it a couple of times as a tourist, but the first time I did it for work, I was too naive, too green, and way too sure of myself, not to get into trouble.

In addition to a Believe It or Not! odditorium we had a Louis Tussaud's wax museum in Niagara Falls, Canada. Upstairs in the museum was where our sculptor-Ron Booker then, later Anton Gosley — worked their magic. The studio looked like something out of a horror movie, and had body parts on every table. It was very narrow, and space was at a premium….so finished pieces before museum installation, were stored across the river. I was going to the warehouse mainly just to see it, and maybe do a little exploratory inventory work, but I was asked to bring back Liz Taylor's head to Tussaud's. Not meaning to be a smart ass when asked what I had in the box, I told the customs agent I had Liz Taylor's head. Faster than I could blink I had a gun in my face and was being pulled from the car. First lesson learned: border patrol people do not have a sense of humor. Nothing is funny, especially not a famous beautiful actress' head in a box. They lightened up when they opened the box and discovered a wax head, and not a real head, and I was able to talk my way out of any real trouble, but I certainly was never volunteering to go to the warehouse again. I suspect it was a Bob Masterson set-up practical joke, which I fell flat on my face into.

As the 1980s wore on I began to travel more often by plane, not yet to anywhere real exotic, but I made frequent trips to Los Angeles, St. Augustine and New York. In New York I always found time to do some personal music record shopping. There was huge HMV record store right on Broadway that had a bigger and better blues section than just about anywhere in America; I could always find something to buy. On one particular two-day trip with John Withers and Bob Masterson, I was returning to Toronto with a suitcase full of film that we had picked up from Bob Whiteman, our New York licensing agent. Both John and Bob assured me I didn't have to declare them in the airport, so I didn't. I did, however, declare three blues albums I had bought (one was Johnny Littlejohn's first album (1968) on Arhoolie Records, price $6.00 US, $8,00 Cdn.) for a "declared" total value total of $20. The allowed duty-free amount for a twenty-four-hour trip was $25. I couldn't see anyone raising an eyebrow over three blues records, and I assumed that if I declared them no one would have reason to open my suitcase with thousands of dollars of undocumented film in it. For the record, I did cover the film with dirty clothing making the inside of the suitcase as disgusting looking as possible. Bob and John breezed through the line. I handed in my declaration slip and was briskly pulled out of line. "What do you have that you are declaring worth $2,000?", asked the armed gentleman. "Nothing", I said quizzically. "This slip says you have records valued at $2,000", he said argumentatively, and with intimidation. Lesson two, also learned the hard way: border people can't read. While John and Bob sat across the way laughing insanely at my misfortune, I passionately tried to convince the officer I had music records worth

$20.00, not $2,000. I was now sweating profusely. It was evident I was going to have to open my bag to prove my innocence, and his mistake. If I did that, he may discover the films. Too late, he opened the bag before I could. The records were on top. He handled them quite roughly, even opening the plastic wrap to make sure there were only records inside the sleeves. He then turned back to the open case. The mess must have disgusted him. He threw the records back on top without touching or looking at the contents, snarled at me, and said "next". Miracle of miracles, I was now a successful professional smuggler. After this event, and my associates retelling of it several times, people would become very afraid to travel with me.

Jimmy Pattison annually threw a big business meeting called **Partners in Pride** attended by his top executives from his over forty companies. Typically, about five Ripley people, including myself, were invited to this soirée. For many years the event was held in the beautiful little mountain town of Penticton, British Columbia.

Ripley's corporate office also held an annual shindig for our museum managers. In those days we simply called it the annual manager's meeting. Our locations were always in the warm south, and typically in places a lot more fun than Penticton.

In 1987, by some strange perverse act of God, the two meetings were to be held consecutive weeks in early March, and if that wasn't bad enough, our meeting was in New Orleans — during Mardi Gras. Surely the powers that be must have known this was a recipe for disaster. It was to be my fourth Ripley manager's meeting, my first Mardi Gras, and my second Partners in Pride. Highlights in New Orleans would include a drunken accountant missing the first day of meetings after a night spent sleeping in a gutter on Bourbon Street outside of our museum (1); an architect being pick-pocketed on a dance floor by a seemingly very sexually aggressive woman; lots of women, "showing their tits" for plastic beads; and a stolen watch and near death by stabbing. A good time was had by all. That is at least until we had to leave and fly from New Orleans to Houston, Texas, to Calgary, Alberta (Canada), to Penticton, a route that would take the better part of a day.

The first flight was very early. I remember being baffled how clean and quiet the streets looked on Ash Wednesday, the morning after the Bacchanalia of Mardi Gras. I seriously thought I must have been dreaming. Surely they couldn't have cleaned up so fast? The last thing I had seen before going to bed were cops on horseback blasting fire hoses at the streets, moving the crowds out of the French Quarter and cleaning the streets at the same time. The streets were now much cleaner than normal and the smell of stale urine and beer had disappeared.

I traveled to the airport alone. I made it in plenty of time. Norm Deska on the other hand was the last person to get on, racing down the gateway at the very last moment. The flight to Houston was without incidence. The flight to Calgary wasn't full, and Norm and I were the only two people who had started in New Orleans. We didn't look like the typical-Houston to Calgary route oil businessmen, and dressed in winter clothes, and being slightly hung-over, we did maybe look like potential criminals. That is to say, at least I did.

In Calgary, Norm was asked more than the usual questions, but ultimately was let through. I was asked no questions, but directed straight to a little "conference" room. It would be a long time before I would see Norm again. Planning to be away from home for two full weeks, I had more than the usual number of suitcases. One of them was completely full of plastic Mardi Gras beads which I was planning to bring home to my then four-month old daughter. Maybe finding beads instead of drugs or guns, or whatever, in the biggest case pissed them off, because the friendly interrogation suddenly took a turn for the unexpected, and the worst. They took apart my cap, then they took the lining out of my coat, then they told me to strip. A finger was then inserted where the sun don't shine — and still they found nothing to incriminate me. The "meeting" ended abruptly, no apologies, no repairs to my damaged clothing, no "sorry", just "Get dressed, you can go now. Welcome to Calgary."

Norm was sound asleep on a bench when I found him. He wasn't quite sure where he was, or how he got there, or how long I had been held up. We still had a flight to catch and a long ways to go, but luckily we had not missed our flight. **The Partners in Pride** meeting in Penticton was definitely a little more subdued. We would never have the two meetings back to back again, and in fact we would eventually move the Ripley meeting from Feb-March to October. Once bit, twice shy.

In addition to customs agents, I did also have one little issue with highway state patrol officers. It happened in June 1990. My plane had landed in Madison, Wisconsin, and I had a rented a car to drive to the newest Ripley odditorium in Wisconsin Dells. I wasn't going directly to the museum, however, as I had a little side trip planned to see a Frank Lloyd Wright home, and the tourist attraction known as the **"House on the Rock"**. I hadn't been on the road too long when I spotted signs saying: "Farmer's market today" in the idyllic pastoral setting of "Mt. Horeb". Everything around there reminded me of the Mennonite area of Southern Ontario, and the town of St. Jacob's where my family visited every autumn to stock up on the bounties of the harvest. I couldn't just drive by.

The market was wonderful, and to my great surprise, I actually found some potential Ripley museum exhibits: a collection of 19th century human hair jewelry, a perennial Ripley classic, and a half dozen five-foot long "Zaire Iron Money Swords". All the same size and shape, this unusual type of currency wasn't a "must buy", but the novelty of finding it at a flea market in southern Wisconsin made it too good to pass up. My trunk was full of luggage, so I threw the swords into the back seat of the car.

Having spent a little too long at the market, I was now running a little late for my agenda. It was quite likely I was going to have to forfeit the Wright house, unless I could make up some time. I wasn't back on the highway two minutes when I saw a flashing light and was being pulled over for speeding. I had no excuse, and was caught red-hand-ed, but I was still going to try and talk myself into a lesser fine. Un-fortunately, the more I talked the more the officer peered into the car. Clearly paying no attention to my lame excuses, he suddenly asked: "What are those things?", pointing to my little mountain of money swords. I am sure I said "money swords", but he only heard "swords". I just made his day: he had caught a Canadian weapons runner in the backwaters of Wisconsin. I explained that I had just bought them in Mt. Horeb, but of course I had no receipt to prove it. Somewhere along the line, I mentioned I was going to take them to the new Ripley's museum in the Dells.

"You work for Ripley's Believe It or Not!?" "Yes officer I do". "Do you know Jack Palance?"

"Well not exactly, but I did work on the television show when it was on (five years previously), and I have met him".

Now sounding like Jim Nabors from the **Andy Griffith Show**, he said:

"Well golly, you have to meet the mayor, he is a huge fan of the show and Jack."

"Can't I just write a check, pay my fine and get back on the road, I really should been in the Dells by now".

"Are you filming in the Dells? Is Jack Palance going to be there?!"

It seemed pointless to remind him the show had stopped airing five years ago. The concept of reruns might not have been fully understood.

"Officer, can I please just pay my fine." "Well sir, you can pay it at the station". "Where's that?"

A couple miles back down the road, in Mt. Horeb". Of course.

So now on my second visit to beautiful downtown "Mt. Horeb", I was entering with a police escort. I suspect my new officer friend must have been on the walkie-talkie for the whole ride back into town. The police station was in the same building as the mayor's office, and I was greeted on the stairs as a celebrity by the mayor -maybe the number one Ripley TV show fan in the entire state it turned out. It seemed like the whole police force, government administrators, and significant others — everyone who wasn't at the market, was there to meet the guy from Ripley's — who was a television celebrity, and knew Jack Palance! They made me talk at length about Jack, how television shows were made, and Hollywood in general. I posed for pictures, was given something to eat, and was given the second best small town reception I ever had. I was now four hours behind time, however, with no chance of seeing the Wright house, or **The House on the Rock** that day —

they would have to wait a few days until after the Dells — and I did still get a speeding ticket.

Lesson three: shut up and play dumb when dealing with authority figures.

Not long after this affair I had my worst run in with the law of my career. I didn't go to jail — luckily — so it could have been much worse, but it was very scary at the time, and once again, I was guilty, and I was caught – in this case — "blue" handed.

I personally was in Mexico, a few thousand miles away from the scene of the crime when it happened, but my name was on some important documents, and I had bought the illegal endangered hyacinth macaw parrot feather headdress from the Yanomamo Indians of Brazil in the first place. The trouble occurred at the bridge cross- ing at Niagara Falls — again. This time, the museum manager, under my direction, was taking the headdress from Canada to the USA. He declared the bird feather headdress, but neglected to say what kind of feathers they were. The sharp-eyed border patrol officer cor- rectly identified them as hyacinth macaw feathers, and without a Cities Permit, despite the artifact clearly not being "new", the manager was under arrest for smug- gling. Taken into custody, his briefcase was inspected. Inside the briefcase were very incriminating papers with my name on them. So the man in custody had an ac- complice, who just happened to live in the States, and even worse, just happened to be currently out of the country in Mexico. By the time I was notified by Ripley officials, a warrant was out for my arrest. I was told by the company lawyers to get out of Mexico asap, but to fly directly to Canada, do not stop in Houston (per my existing plane ticket). This would mean changing my existing ticket and waiting at least another full day.

By this point, I was sure I was going to jail, and deeply afraid of being imprisoned in Mexico. Houston sounded like a lot better place to be handcuffed if that was to be the outcome. Call it bad luck, or karma, but there wasn't a single empty plane seat on a flight going from Acapulco to Toronto for several days. Won- dering how the hell do I explain a couple extra days in Acapulco to my wife, I was much too scared to enjoy my extended stay.

The lawyers got to work very quickly, however, and discovered "we" could plead guilty, and pay a big fine, without any court proceedings. It definitely was the right thing to do. I was able to go home to Florida after just two extra days.

The stain was on my record for a number of years. It didn't prevent me from going anywhere, but it did make every plane trip — not just international — an adventure. A blip would appear on the agent's computer screen, whenever, I flew. Some agents would just ask a couple extra questions, but more often than not I would be ushered into the back room for a longer series of questions, or a suitcase inspection.

I was never "knowingly" guilty again, but I did hang a papier mâché blue parrot in my house as a reminder "not to do that again".

The problem with all "artifacts", but animals in particular, is they don't always come with records of provenance, and pinpoint dating when an animal was killed is virtually impossible with anything of any age. In the case of the parrot feathers it would have been my word against theirs, I knew the item was approximately forty-years old, but that wasn't old enough to make it an antique, and it wasn't precise enough to argue that it was not made for me specifically as a tourist souvenir. I had not bought the headdress myself from the original maker (there was a middle man whom I did not want to implicate) and I could not say with any conviction whether the bird had been killed then, or earlier. It was a battle I couldn't win. Two other episodes, however, I fought till I was blue in the face.

In both cases I knew the artifacts were thousands of years old — dare I say even a blind man could tell that, one being a mummified Egyptian falcon, the other being a fossilized walrus penial bone, known in the languages of the Inuit as an "oozik", and used as a club to kill seals.

I had all the proper paperwork in line to ship the falcon to Germany, but it was confiscated anyway. I was dumbfounded. The reason given was not because it was illegal, or that they disputed the stated age, but that

104

falcons – even 4,000-year-old ones apparently — carried dangerous Asiatic bird flu, and therefore could not be brought into Germany. I fought the absurdity of this tooth and nail, but in the end lost the battle and the bird. It was confiscated, and not returned. God only knows what they did with it; presumably they burned it.

The oozik was just as bizarre. I was aware that walrus were endangered and no new ivory could be exported (or imported), but this was a gnarly old bone, not ivory, and have American origin in the first place. Again I had the proper papers, which were successful in shipping it from the USA to Canada for a temporary three-month exhibition in Surrey, British Columbia, so why couldn't I bring it back into America? The border patrol agent argued that it had been let in by mistake; it shouldn't have been allowed to leave the USA.

I argued "Fine, we will keep it in Canada".

They said, "No sir, sorry, but we must confiscate it".

Five hours later, after much ranting and raving, and after they had investigated every single item on our truck, we were allowed to pull out, with "no harm, no foul", but without the oozik. I assume they used it somewhere as a paperweight, or perhaps to club some sense into someone.

For years people asked me "how do you transport a human shrunken head?" Well, believe it or not, it's a lot easier than birds or walrus parts. In fact, it has never really been an issue for me. I do know people who would disagree, having had problems themselves, but when I had one in my bag, I always traveled with a letter of authenticity on corporate letterhead explaining what it was, how I came to obtain it, its approximate age, and what I intended to do with it. Identifying it as an old museum display item, typically did the trick.

In Dublin, Ireland, while on a book tour for a book called **"Ripley's In Search of the Shrunken Heads"**, I did, however, have to show the head off to several disbelieving officials. It was like Mt. Horeb all over again. I wasn't in trouble, but no one in that airport had ever seen one, so everyone wanted to see it, or touch it, and a few even took pictures to show their families. Over the years, and through previous negative experiences, I had learned to be quiet, smile, nod and be patient. I got through with no repercussions. That night on a local telly show, I retold the story and became an instant Irish celebrity. I was treated like royalty everywhere I went in Ireland for the next several days, and showed the head off repeatedly to oohs and ahs.

In 2008, my wife, Giliane, and I, went to India. I will discuss this monumental trip in greater detail elsewhere, but for here the story is about my trying to get back home to America — without a passport, or a permanent USA resident green card. We had been in India for twenty-six days, and though the documents (my passport and both of our green cards) had been stolen from our room the first week, it had never occurred to us to try and get them replaced while in India. Being a seasoned traveler, and generally quite well organized, I had made duplicates of all my important papers and credit cards before we had left Florida. I wasn't worried about re-entering the states one bit because I had a photocopy of everything agents would need to see. The flight home from Calcutta — Gil's place of birth — through Frankfurt, Germany, took about twenty hours. We arrived at about 8 pm in Orlando. Imagine how exhausted we were as we approached the counter. I was asked for my passport and green card, and I apologetically plunked down two photocopied pages. It was as if I had tried to carry a bomb through customs. Pure panic ensued, Gil was taken one way, and I was taken another. Her being of Indian origin may have helped her. Her interrogation lasted only about twenty-minutes. Mine would go on for four hours. Contrary to my logic, having the photocopies was a bad thing. I was suspected of having made them in India, and of having sold my originals. Apparently no one in the history of air transport had ever submitted photocopy documents. I must be a liar, and some kind of international criminal seeking to sneak into the country. The fact that I had no American money in my possession was another strike against me.

We were of course eventually freed, but I would have to get new documents made, and pay a substantial $790.00 application fee. Strangely, if we would have had cash on hand, we could have paid a much smaller fine and been done with it. Without the cash, however, we were now in the bigger system. We were granted temporary papers, but had to wait several weeks to get the new official documents, and now once again, I would cause a blip on the radar screens at every border for another three years.

"Sir, the computer says this is not your original green card number. Where is your original card, and how did you get a new one?"

"It was stolen in India." "Three years ago".

"Sir, please step out of line, and go to the room over there". A criminal again, or should I say, still?

These multiple second level investigations though were much shorter than the post-parrot feather ones. A few seconds on a machine, a new photo taken, an apology given, and I was let go. I got so used to the program I virtually volunteered for it going forward: Immigration Agent "Do you have your green card?"

Self: "Yes sir, I do, but you are not going to like it." Perhaps you could point me to the interrogation room right away and save us both some time." In 2011 the computer blip finally went away, just in time for a long trip to New Zealand, Australia, Thailand and Japan. My troubles with the law were behind me, and I was excited to be going to three countries I had never been to before (2). I was also excited at least to a degree about being scheduled to guest on two non-talk show format shows in New Zealand. By this time, I had been on several television shows in Canada, the USA, and Ireland, typically being inter-viewed about specific exhibits, but occasionally being asked to act. I do watch my share of television, but having seen how it happens from behind the scenes, I am not too often impressed, especially by so-called "reality shows", which in reality are the fakest of all pro-grams. My first filming in New Zealand was to occur in the airport upon arrival in New Zealand on the country's number one reality show, called **Border Patrol.**

It was about a sixteen-hour flight from Orlando, to New Zealand, across many time zones. I was just a wee-bit exhausted when I disembarked, but pulled together quickly when I found a four-piece film crew waiting at the plane gateway. They started filming me from the second I stepped off the plane, no rehearsal, no direction, no hello, just "look into the camera as you walk". I descended a series of stairs and followed a PA (production assistant) with signs, pointing me in a specific direction to a specific area. Apparently, my bags were to be expedited and I wouldn't have to wait with my fellow passengers, who by this time wondered what the hell was going on even more than I did. Once I had my bags, I was again directed to a more intimate area and line, the camera still rolling. Here I was finally met by a producer and a director, and was told what to expect. Up to then I really had no idea what the show was about as I had not seen an episode, nor – intentionally — had I been prepped. The television show people knew I was traveling with some exotic exhibits, including a four-winged, two-headed raven, a shrunken head, and a rare vampire killing kit. Everything had been pre-approved by the New Zealand customs department, and I had papers for everything, everything except the flintlock pistol that was part of the vampire killing kit.

The customs agents, whom, I was not sure if they were real, or actors, quizzed me hard, and made me open both my suitcases of exhibits, and unwrap each and every item within. I spoke politely and officially in my best acting voice, looking straight at the camera when told to, or at the officer if not otherwise redirected. Each artifact was explained in detail, especially the shrunken head, which as long as it wasn't a Maori native, was fine to import. The vampire killing kit was saved for last.

These kits, Ripley's own more than twenty-five different ones, are reportedly from the mid -19th century, and were made in Boston, and sold to wealthy Americans planning to go to Eastern Europe, specifically Transylvania, the notorious, mysterious, home territory of all vampires. Some of the kits are housed in beautiful wooden boxes, oak, cherry wood or mahogany. Others look much more makeshift. Virtually all contain some garlic, a rosary, silver bullets, a cross or crucifix (usually of ivory), a wooden stake and mallet, a Bible or Psalter, and a period flintlock pistol. The pistol and the books can be dated, but that doesn't really prove the age of the whole kit. There is some dispute on whether vampire kits are real antiques or compiled fakes. Admittedly I had never seen or heard of one until the 1990s, but I do believe there are some real ones, which have a certain high quality of craftsmanship to the cases, and the objects inside of them, which distinguish them from the obvious fakes. The first one I ever heard of was in an article in **Guns & Ammo Magazine**, not exactly a distinguished historical reference guide. Several were bought in New Orleans, some with obvious late-model pistols. Only two were from Europe, one from France, shaped like a book and meant to be hidden on a book shelf, the other, the most basic looking of the lot, was from Romania. I often wondered if rather than it being a fake whether it was the real progenitor of all the rest. Several, but not all, included a list of enclosures, and credited a Prof. Blomberg for their assembly. The authenticity of Professor Blomberg is also disputed, though there seems to have been a like-named gunsmith in Belgium and France in the right time period. At some point I stopped buying all but the best-looking kits, unsure of their authenticity, a debate I leave to the doubters on the web who seem to have way too much time on their hands.

The officials inspected my kit, and specifically the gun, seemingly afraid that it might go off at any minute, whether by magic, or some carelessness of their handling. It was determined that because it had no apparent serial number it couldn't be allowed in the country, and I, as the exporter, was under arrest for trying to bring an illegal firearm into the country. As I was still unclear what was "real", and what was Hollywood (Kiwi style), this came as a shock to me. Everything had been pre-approved, what the heck was going on? My going off the "script", and questioning the authorities, resulted in my being handcuffed, and marched off camera, the officer carrying the kit in his hands. Once off camera, I was instantly released, but the kit was to be held for three days in case the real authorities had questions. Losing it for three days would affect my book tour, but there seemed to be nothing I could do about this unpredicted turn of events.

I suspect from comments I have heard over the years, that I looked genuinely scared and confused; more than one person has asked me what a New Zealand jail was like? My "acting" seems to have thoroughly convinced people that I was arrested and the kit was confiscated.

I have still personally never seen the episode, but I know it has been aired in England, Australia, Canada and South Africa in addition to New Zealand, and my own sister thought I had spent time behind bars in New Zealand. My most serious criminal activity lives on in legend. It was a good thing I didn't confront any vampires during my stay in New Zealand, but despite some questionable decisions over the years, I still have never been jailed.

18

Brushes with the Law – Part 2

Even scarier than grumpy custom and immigration agents, are FBI agents. Their guns are very visible, and if they are making house calls then something is definitely wrong. The FBI came to my door in Florida on two different occasions in the 1990s. In the first incident, they were actually looking for Bob Masterson. In the second, they weren't specifically looking for me, but in both cases, however, I was "guilty" by association, and the "best" man to deal with the situations, one very serious, one somewhat comical, at least for Ripley's and myself.

Probably the most controversial item I ever acquired were North American Indian scalps. The last one I bought convinced me not to ever consider them again, no matter how good the condition, or how low the price. Once bitten, twice shy.

With a touch of irony, however, it wasn't the scalp that was the legal problem.

The offending item was sold by Butterfield & Butterfield Auction house out of San Francisco, at a "Western memorabilia" auction. The scalp had good provenance, and even came in a small original box addressed to the owner from a US frontier soldier, circa the 1870s. It was also in immaculate condition. Trouble was, it had an eagle feather attached to it. The buying and selling of the scalp were not illegal at least at the time – but the selling of the feather, and the possession of an illegally obtained eagle feather was strictly prohibited. I had bought the item not knowing of the law. It was Bob Masterson's name on the payment check, however. Two agents came to the office front door. They asked for Bob. Bob wasn't in. They weren't happy. I am not sure how our receptionist determined that I may be the best person able to help them —I assume there was some conversation that identified the issue as being "exhibit" based – but I was paged on the intercom. When I didn't respond the first time, the second page, spoken with a certain scared sounding urgency, announced there were agents from the FBI anxiously waiting for me in the front lobby. Come immediately, do not pass go, run if necessary. She was obviously terrified.

The questioning started with: Where was Mr. Masterson? I don't re-member where he was, but I assured them he was not in the building. "Could I help"? Did I know anything about an Indian scalp Mr. Masterson had bought some months ago at an auction in San Francisco? My casual answer that it was in fact me who had bought it, Bob had just signed the payment for it, didn't exactly relieve the tension. With still no real knowledge of what the problem was, but understanding clearly there was a problem, the next set of questions heightened my anxiety:

"Is the scalp here?"

"No officer, it is in our nearby warehouse." "We need it here, immediately".

"I can call someone and have it brought here in about thirty minutes."

"Call now, and tell them to get it here right away". "Does it have a feather attached to it?"

"No officer, as a matter of fact, it doesn't" "Did it, when you bought it?"

"Yes, it did officer"

(Angrily) "Where is the feather now?

"It is around the corner, down the hall, in my office in the original box it came in, sitting on my book-shelf".

I suspect this last detail wasn't received too well as I was instantly escorted down the hall, passing other offices, and several startled employees. Even at Ripley's you don't see armed FBI agents every day. Inside my office, away from any other people for the first time, they finally told me what the problem was. The scalp would be confiscated and used as evidence against Butterfield's auctions. It might possibly be returned in the future but the eagle feather would be confiscated, and definitely not returned. Neither I, nor, Mr. Masterson would be prosecuted if we "willingly" forfeited the objects in question. It sounded like a deal to me.

They watched me make the call, and stayed silently, menacingly, sitting in my office until the warehouse manager delivered the scalp. They took a copy of my business card, and left. I never saw them again. After a couple years, the box was returned. The scalp was too. The feather wasn't.

The box remained on the same shelf behind my desk in my office for the duration of my career visible to anyone who looked. The scalp has never been displayed, and remains in a safe hidden place in case anyone ever comes looking for it again.

I hinted earlier that the second incident was somewhat humorous. It made me laugh then — after the initial fear of having the FBI return to my front door – and it still makes me laugh. I have to assume, however, the agents never saw anything funny in the case whatsoever.

I'm guessing the initial questions went something like this:

"Afternoon ma'am. Is this the headquarters of Ripley's Believe It or Not!? Does an Edward Meyer work here?"

(Receptionist stuttering with fear): "Yes, it is, and yes he does!" "Can we please see him — right now".

Whispered softly via our new and improved phone style intercom:

"Edward, please come quickly to the front lobby — there are two armed FBI agents asking for you that are scaring the S*it out of me!"

No coffee was offered, no seats were taken, no formal introductions occurred.

"Are you Edward Meyer?"

(Spoken timidly) "Yes officer…Can I…"

"Do you own a gold Lincoln stretch limousine".

"No officer, but **our company** does own a gold-coin covered-Lincoln stretch limousine."

"Is it registered in your name?" — shoving a photocopy of a vehicle registration slip in my face that clearly had my name on it.

Now trying desperately to remove myself from whatever and where ever this was leading: "Officer that is my signature, and I did buy the car, and I did register it at the Winter Park, Florida office of Vehicle Registration, but it isn't **MY** car. It belongs to the company."

Stone faced, as if he didn't hear the last bit: "Were you driving it south on I-4 on the afternoon of August 29, 2002….

Now even more desperate than before: "No sir, I have never driven the car".

The words were barely out of my mouth, however, when I realized the date he had given was the only date the car had ever been driven in Orlando — the date we drove it first from the Winter Park licensing office to the Ripley office, then from our office to our museum — with me as a passenger both times. I still was looking to prove my innocence:

"Officer, I was in the car, but I was not driving it."

It was quickly established, that neither owning it, nor driving it was the issue at hand.

"Did you drive by such and such address" on I-4. Hesitatingly: "I suppose soooooo,,,,,"

"Did you witness a shooting?" "Definitely NOT!"

Even during a shoot-out, a couple hundred yards away, on another street, my gold-coin covered limousine had made a lasting permanent impression. The injured party in the process of being shot recalled the car in enough detail for the investigating officers to trace the most unusual and beautiful car the injured had ever seen to Ripley's. Believe It or Not!

Turns out I was not wanted for anything other than possibly being a witness to a crime. I was sure I had seen nothing, and they believed me. They said thanks, and were on their way. I had escaped the long arm of the law once again and it boded well for my having bought a car that people would definitely pay to see.

114

19

America's Pastime

I grew up playing hockey. I was skating by age three, and in a league at age five. For me the 1960s were the Golden Age of Hockey — Jean Beliveau, Bernie "Boom Boom" Geoffrion, Jacques Plante (the first goalie to wear a mask), Stan Mikita, Bobby Hull, Gordie Howe, Frank Mahovlich, Johnny Bower, and Tim Horton were my heroes [1]. By the time I married in 1977 — coincidentally the year the Toronto Blue Jays entered the National Baseball League — I had stopped playing hockey, and didn't even watch the game on television much. In 1984 I totally switched alliances and became a big fan of America's National Pastime — baseball.

I had played softball as a kid, and my father had played first base in an industrial league when I was very young (I still have his glove), so I understood the game, but until my mother started listening to the Jays on the radio shortly after my father died in 1980, I had shown no real interest. So, I missed many of the greats: Williams, Maris, Mantle, Mays, Gibson, Koufax and Aaron, and had a lot of catching up to do.

Through Ripley's I got to meet Mays and Aaron, and Dom DiMaggio too (our landlord in San Francisco!), and I got to regularly sit in great first base line season tickets seats in both Toronto stadiums (Exhibition and Sky Dome) for thirteen years. I got to see the 1991 All-Star game in which Baltimore Oriole Cal Ripkin put on a great home run hitting display, a no-hitter by Oakland's Dave Stewart, a one-hitter by the great Nolan Ryan (the best game I have ever seen), and I even got to see two World Series games in 1992 before we moved to Florida. For Ripley's I got to buy the occasional baseball-oriented exhibits for the collection, a few balls, some stadium seats from several old parks around the league, and even a bat…or ten.

My big bat purchase was rather a sad story for those involved, but for me it was a highlight of my life. In one of the most bizarre trades of all time, the Calgary (Alberta, Canada) Vipers, a Western Division professional team, traded ten-Canadian made maple black bats for John Odum, a right-handed pitcher who had wanted to be traded to a Canadian team for legal reasons. No one really wanted him, and no one had offered his San Francisco team anyone they wanted in return.

Reading a small news clip on this story, I swung at it immediately. Turned out the manager was more than willing to sell the ten bats for a "donation" to the team's children's baseball league. For a donation of $10,000, we would get the bats, have an official Ripley Day at the ball park, with Ripley cartoons and trivia flashing on the electronic scoreboard between every inning, and I would get to throw out the first pitch at a home game! Not quite the Jays, but still a dream come true.

After presenting the proverbial giant over-sized check at the mound, the crowd cheered, I wound-up — conscious not to "overthrow" and wreck my arm (better to throw a slow-ball strike than a fast ball wild pitch), and threw a "perfect" one-hop fifty-five foot strike. One more thing off my bucket list.

Tim O'Brien, our publicist at the time, and I, got to call the play by play for a couple batters, and shoot Ripley t-shirts out of bazookas during the seventh inning stretch. I was also given a team pitcher's warm-up jacket. After the game we met the players in the locker room, and discovered why I would never be a professional baseball player — these guys had arms bigger than my neck! Where to put my eyes in a room of very buff naked men was a disturbing predicament.

It was a great evening in Canada's far north. Today the bats are on display in Ripley's Baltimore odditorium (2).

20

Oddball —

One of the Best Weeks of My Life

I have never played "baseball", softball yes, but hardball no, and I really had no interest in the game at all until 1984. For the last thirty-five years though, I have loved the game, every aspect of it. I have thrown out a first pitch, and I have been to Cooperstown. I'm not a "stats" guy but I have studied the history of the game, and appreciate the pantheon of the greats. At least from my vantage point in Florida, football is now way more popular than baseball, and some might argue basketball is too, but for me baseball is still America's sport. Creating a display in 2016 for the Louisville Slugger Factory & Museum, quaintly called "**Oddball**", was a dream come true.

It was a dream for John Corcoran too. John is a hardcore baseball fan, ten or twenty times more intense than I am, and he happened to have a job at Ripley's trying to sell "traveling shows" to third party independent museums. John has a long-storied career with Ripley's, dating back nearly as long as mine. Whereas my whole career was focused on one or two areas, and always based out of corporate office, John worked in various Ripley locations, and seems to have changed titles about every five years. He brought the deal with Anne Jewel, Executive Director, and her people at the Slugger Museum, to the table and set it on its path, but through an unkind (to him) twist of fate, it was Angela Johnson and I that got to run it around the bases all the way to home plate.

Towards the end of 2014, just as planning for the Slugger project was starting, John had his job changed. As a team we had only met with Anne once. We selected the name of the exhibition — **Oddball** — but that was just about all that was settled when John was asked to change jobs and graciously handed the project over to me. I couldn't have been more thrilled. Coincidentally Angela was born in Louisville, and had a driving passion to bring Ripley's to her hometown. Her knowledge of the town was a perfect complement to my knowledge of baseball, specifically the Ripley baseball collection.

The initial plan called for two galleries, one to be "a best of Ripley's", including a shrunken head, a two-headed calf, a dinosaur skeleton, etc. The exhibits in the larger second gallery would all be somehow tied to baseball, a matchstick baseball stadium, Ripley's connection to Babe Ruth and Lou Gehrig, a couple of uniforms, bats and balls, whatever I could come up with. To fill this room we had to get very creative, but I'll come back to this in a moment. In addition to these two rooms, we ended up placing a few exhibits in the museum's main permanent gallery room, and we decorated the adjoining hallways with Ripley baseball cartoons and one extremely large postcard mural for the entranceway rotunda. In total we had nearly 200 exhibits that were displayed from March 2016 through January 2017. It was by far the best "little" show we had ever done.

The single best exhibit we displayed was actually about boxing, not baseball, a micro-miniature sculpture of Louisville's favorite son, "The Greatest", Muhammad Ali. The best baseball exhibit was something we had commissioned from Orlando artist, Mateo Blanco. It was, a two-sided, bigger than life-size, bust of "Hammering" Hank Aaron, for many years the Home Run King, and listed by "Sporting News" as the fifth greatest player of all time. One side was made from **Oh Henry** chocolate bar wrappers, the other with actual **Oh Henry** chocolate bars [1]. Both these exhibits were in the permanent collections gallery, not in the "Ripley Rooms".

The core display room was wonderfully decorated to look like different parts of a ballpark, the manager's office, with Ripley as the manager, a concession stand, the field, and a locker room. The three lockers displayed were labeled Johnson, Corcoran, and Meyer. Not exactly "murderer's row", but I sure felt honored. The concession stand featured art made from "ball park food", a life-sized woman made from licorice, a Wrigley's gum wrapper chain, a portrait of Tom Cruise made from ketchup and mustard, and a giant portrait of Louisville's own Jennifer Lawrence, made from over 12,000 shelled peanuts.

The plan for the majority of the exhibits in this room was to have something that somehow represented each individual team in the pro leagues. We had a matchstick model of Yankee Stadium for the Yanks, a world record taxidermy marlin for Tampa Bay, a Johnny Depp – Captain Jack Sparrow statue made from seashells for the Pirates, and a giant bear made from pine needles for the Cubs, to name just the larger pieces. Mid-size pieces included a knitted tiger illusion for Detroit, an autographed Charlie Sheen Hollywood movie prop Phillies jersey, and some vintage Ripley owned beer steins for the Brewers. Small exhibits included a spider web painting of a Cardinal for St. Louis, a pair of white socks, worn by a man for his whole life for the Chicago White Sox, and my favorite, a bird's nest with a golf ball in it, made by a real Baltimore Oriole. Some were more obvious than others, but kids loved the "treasure hunt" questionnaire they got upon entering, and would as a result spend time with every single exhibit no matter how big or small.

The hardest team to represent turned out to be my Toronto Blue Jays. The Ripley collection had absolutely nothing, but luckily, I had my own personal collection! Displayed inside the locker with my name across the top, we placed a pair of used World Series tickets, from the first World Series game ever played outside of the USA, which also featured Joe Carter's first home run in a World Series in Canada, a pair of used tickets for the first all-star game ever held in a foreign country (with a close-up photo I took of Willie Mays and Hank Aaron, who just happened to be sitting two rows behind me at the game!) and a scruffy twenty-five year old t-shirt commemorating that the Blue Jays were the first team ever to have an annual attendance in excess of four million fans (I was there the day they did it). This is a Believe It or Not! fact that astonishes me. The Jays did this in 1991, just fourteen years into their history. They went on to do it three times in a row, before any other team did it once, and to date there is still only three other teams that have done it once, two of them being in NYC that has a population more than twice Toronto's.

The display opened in March 2016, and was an immediate success. I did some media events, and some speechifying, and Angela officially opened the doors by unveiling two bigger than life-size superhero statues — Iron Man and Captain America — outside on the sidewalk by driving by in a Peel P-50 mini car (the world's smallest) that the covering sheets were attached to the bumper. She then drove the car through the entire museum and factory, while the press stood by in dumbfounded awe.

Two months later, we came back for an even bigger event: Kentucky Derby week.

I had never been to a horse race before in my life, and Angela despite having lived most of her life in Louisville, had never been to the Derby. The Derby, however, is not just a two-minute race, it is a two-week long event, and some could rightfully argue, a whole way of life. I would have to buy my own race tickets, but if Angela and I were willing to "work" a bit, the Slugger team would make a visit well worth our while.

On the Tuesday before race day, we set up a mini-museum display for an event called "Pegasus", in the convention center where locals get a sneak preview of everything that will be in the parade on Thursday. On Wednesday, we would get to ride in the steamboat river race, a very hard ticket to get because of limited space, and free bourbon — and on Thursday, we would get a backstage tour of the Slugger museum and factory, and be in the parade with our friends from the Slugger museum. This is probably the third biggest parade in the country, not far behind Macy's in New York, and the Rose Bowl in Pasadena, California. Talk about being treated like Royalty. I had a ball all week long.

Angela and I were experienced convention booth people and knocked Pegasus out of the park. With probably at least a hundred booths to compete against, we were by far the most popular. Our exhibits were a huge magnet, and we gave away a lot of books. We made all the local news stations, and the next day's papers.

Wednesday was "my" day. Angela was there, and so was my wife Giliane, but it was all about pleasing me. I got to bat in a cage with a Hank Aaron bat (it didn't help me none, I hit two singles and two pop-ups and missed the other six pitches altogether), a photo op with a Paul Molitor bat (the MVP of the 93 World Champion Blue Jays), and a private walk into the bat vault.

I was initially told Angela could take my picture holding any one-vault bat I chose. I assume choosing just one bat would be impossible for most baseball fans, but it took me less time to decide than it did to say "Jackie Robinson". Chris Mieman our extremely knowledgeable guide, explained the filing system, disappeared momentarily, then returned, and with white gloves, and royal reverence, presented me with the Robinson signature bat. Every player in the history of the game who plays with a Louisville Slugger bat has his first bat, autographed by the player, in the Slugger museum vault. I could have chosen literally anyone of thousands of players, but I chose my hero Mr. Jackie Robinson......but there was more.

Chris, appreciating the thrill holding this one bat caused, had a huge surprise in hand. He was willing to fetch me six more bats from the vault. In order, I chose Babe Ruth, the greatest player of all time;

Ted Williams, the last man to bat .400 in a season, and arguably the greatest hitter of all time; Joltin' Joe DiMaggio, holder of the greatest sports record of all time — the fifty-six game streak of 1941 (2); Lou Gehrig, the RBI and Iron Man demigod; Willie Mays, the second all-time greatest player, whom I had once met; and Mickey Mantle, the original Mr. October, and pride of the Yankees. Angela captured some of the best pictures ever taken of me. I have a smile as big as a ballpark in every one. It was an even greater baseball day than in Calgary, and I knew my mother was looking down on me with a smile

(3) .

As previously noted, I had already handled a replica Aaron bat earlier that day. Two months earlier, I had held the signature Honus Wagner bat. Put the nine together, and you have my personal world's greatest nineman baseball team.

Later that afternoon accompanied by Anne Jewell and Angela, Giliane and I were to board **The Belle of Louisville**, and be passengers on the annual riverboat race down the Ohio River against **The River Queen** paddle wheeler from Cincinnati. For me, this was going to be a much bigger thrill than the actual Derby. Being a student of the Civil War, a lover of Mark Twain (his **Life on the Mississippi** is one of my very favorite books), and a life-long fan of Mississippi Delta blues music,

taking a river trip on an authentic paddle-wheeler (4),
was a real bucket list item. To be in an actual steamboat race, was going to be way better than a day at the
horse races, or even a trip to the moon for that matter.

What I didn't know was that Anne had previously worked
for the riverboat company, and had even written a book
about the ship. She not only got us the hard to get
tickets free, she got us a personal tour with a local
historian, Kadie Engstrom — the authority on the city's
glorious history, a television spot on the local news,
and a seat in Master Kevin Mullen and Captain Mark
Doty's pilot house for the second-half of the race. The
view of the river from the pilot's house was priceless,
and I got a souvenir captain's cap, and a brief touch
of the wheel. It doesn't get much better than that.

Our boat lost the race, but I suspect the race was
"thrown". We had a huge lead going into the return leg
that I do not believe the other boat could have caught
up to if we didn't let him. I suspect the winner is pre-
ordained, and changes every year, but that didn't take
away from the thrill of the sprint to the finish line.

Coming down from the pilot house, with the captain's
hat on my head, I was greeted by several well-wishers,
saying "better luck next year" — they had mistaken me
for the real captain — and two people even handed me
shots of bourbon to drown my sorrows on the loss. It
was a great night to end a great day.

Thursday was Angela's big day at the plate. I got to
walk in the parade (more than two miles) holding an
enormous baseball glove, but she got to lead the Museum's parade entry, driving the miniature Peel P-50 car.
It was the Museum's first time ever having an entry,
and needless to say Angela's first time in the parade
too. It was unseasonably cold and long for me, whereas
she was warm, probably even hot, based on the poor ventilation of the Peel car, and she got to do tricks in
the car. She got on the news, I didn't. I am sure it
was better than being prom queen for her. It was a definite triumphant public return to her hometown. All her
Louisville friends watched from curbside, and cheered
their approval. Friday we — Angela, her local friend

Beki, Giliane and I, drove out of town, and checked another two things off my bucket list — we toured three different bourbon distilleries, and we went inside the Mammoth Caves. Not in that order. I have drunk whiskey, and primarily bourbon, almost exclusively for all my adult life. I certainly knew there was good ones and bad ones, but until that day, I didn't know there was any real good ones! I had been in underground caves before (Bermuda and Santo Domingo), but nothing had prepared me for Mammoth Caves. We seemingly walked for hours, yet didn't even dint one of the several chambers. Caves are not for everyone, but they really are more beautiful than creepy. Beki was a great cave guide, and she also knew the best bourbon places to stop at. The weather was beautiful, literally the calm before the storm.

People in New Orleans celebrate the first Saturday in May every year as part of Jazz Fest. For years I thought it was the second biggest party in the country, but coincidentally, the Kentucky Derby is held the exact same day (maybe someone should declare it a national holiday and let the rest of the country celebrate too). I imagine it depends on who you ask, but the Derby is definitely bigger than Jazz Fest, and might be bigger than Mardi Gras too. The track holds over 165,000 revelers (5), not to mention the gatherings of people all over the rest of the city. Other than drinking, everything in Louisville stops for **the race.**

There is of course more than just one race. The Derby Race is the emotional climax of a long full card of races that starts at 10am and goes until about 8pm. As the main event, it happens around 6:30 pm. The fashion statements, particularly the women's hats, are legendary, and I did spend a lot more time looking at them that at horses, but what I was unprepared for was the level of drinking, dare I say alcohol poisoning. We saw people that couldn't walk by 10 am, and I swear even Boy Scouts had bourbon booths on the field — the best fundraiser any troop in the country could ask for. Our little party of six (Beki, her husband Tony, and son Evan, Angela, Gil, and I), sat on the field on folding lawn chairs that we carried ourselves — the cheap seats. The craziness might not be so wild up in the stands amongst the elite, but on the field, where for the most part you can't even see the horses (most people watch giant video screens), the main event was definitely drinking. We avoided straight bourbon, but we did have a few obligatory mint juleps. I did not gamble on a single horse until **the race**.

All day the weather was pleasant, near perfect for a day at the races, but rain was in the forecast, and it did come down in buckets just before the big race. We did have umbrellas, and ponchos, but only Gil had the fore-sight to put hers on before the skies caved in. The rain didn't last long — the first time — but we were like proverbial drowned rats by the time it was over.

Getting out of the track is pure hell. It took us two hours to get to the free bus, about 119 minutes of which it was pouring rain. I am pretty sure I have never been so wet, despite the rain gear. I know for sure I have never stood longer in a rainstorm. FYI, big fun hats don't count as rain gear, and typically don't look so good once wet.

Angela stayed with her friends Beki and Tony a couple more days, but Gil and I went home bright and early the next morning (it had stopped raining, after about ten solid hours). I probably don't need to go to a horse race ever again, after all it's all downhill after the Derby, but a week in Louisville during Derby season is equal to a lifetime of memories, and like Mardi Gras, something I believe everyone should experience at least once. I wear my captain's hat now when I go canoeing.

I love Louisville. I love baseball, and I love Anne Jewel and her team at the Slugger Factory & Museum. I have a warm fuzzy feeling they love me too. On two separate occasions they presented me with a couple of the best gifts I have ever received. One is a black Slugger bat; the other is a white bat. The black bat is autographed by Dave Winfield, and is a limited edition #92 of 200, vault signature bat, 1992 being the year Winfield hit the World Series winning run for the To-ronto Blue Jays. The white bat is an authentic signa-ture vault "Edward Meyer" LS bat, and is my ultimate baseball treasure. I don't know any reason why anyone would go to the Slugger factory and order an "Edward Meyer" bat, instead of say a Ruth or a Robinson, but knowing they could if they wanted to, brings a huge smile to my face every time I walk by it in my trophy room (5).

21

Another Short Tribute

There are lots of Ripley fans around the world, and even some true fanatics, people who live and breathe all things Ripley's. I have always had a big place in my heart for these people. I don't pretend to understand them, but I used to bless them every day. It is no exaggeration to say that fans pay the bills; without them I wouldn't have been employed for forty years.

The list is way too long to name them all, but the following are a handful of the most special ones, the ones whose love of Ripley's extended over many, many years.

Based on archival mail, Robert Ripley in his time, had at least two hardcore regular fanatics that submitted cartoon suggestions frequently. I never met either of these gentlemen and only know them through their letters and Ripley's publication of their contributions. The first is Ben Laposky of Iowa, the second, Robert Dalee of Mississippi. I wish I had of known these two guys because they didn't just submit ideas, they submitted finished products.

Laposky was a math wizard. Three or four times a year, for more than twenty years, he sent Ripley elaborate number puzzles, typically in "Magic Squares", but sometimes star-shaped, triangular, circular, etc. My admiration for Ben is partially because I could never figure the puzzles out; that he could regularly come up with new ones, was almost heroic.

Dalee's submissions were not themed, they literally covered every imaginable subject, from natural formed oddities, to hurricanes. What made him unique, was that he drew the stories as well as wrote them, and his cartoon artwork was good enough that Ripley didn't redraw them, publishing them exactly as Bob drew them. I often wondered if he ever applied to Ripley for a job. His content was always worth printing, and his art though purposely caricaturist and simple, was witty and fun — perfect for the stories he submitted.

In the 1960s-through the 1980s Ripley's #1 fan was Tom

Higgins of San Diego, California. He was the first person to have 100 of his submissions drawn and published. If memory serves me correctly, I believe he went on to have more than 250 submitted items used. I never met Tom, but I regularly corresponded with him in the days of actual mailed letters, and I was invited by his wife to eulogize him at his full military honors funeral in San Diego. It was the first military funeral I ever went to. The guns and flags, and rows of identical crosses in the military cemetery, had a huge effect on me. It was an early glimpse at understanding patriotism. That his family wanted me to talk about his contribution to Ripley's at such a solemn occasion, was a real honor to me and the company.

After Tom, Richard Gibson of Louisiana, took up the gauntlet. I don't think he has yet caught up to Tom, but I am sure he is the second all-time biggest contributor, and by far the longest serving. His good friend Dan Paulun of Ohio, would be a close third. Dan is a former librarian, and must read a dozen newspapers a day. His submissions tended to have a Pennsylvania-Ohio angle, and weren't as worldly as Tom or Richard's, but he was certainly prolific, and in the game for the long haul. He also probably has the biggest collection of Ripley memorabilia on the planet.

Three other gentlemen became my constant companions in my last ten years, one or the other of them contacting me at least weekly, and even daily through some stretches. Paul D'Ambosia of Massachusetts holds the world's record for achieving the most "diplomas", most of them relating to karate and other martial arts. Paul called me every time he won a new one. He also often called just to say hello. John Carpenter of Kentucky, collects sports memorabilia, and called regularly to tell me about some unbelievable accomplishment, or addition to his collection. Usually these were stories related to high school and youth league teams, but he had a good understanding of horse racing, basketball, football and his favorite, baseball, at all levels of competition. Nate Westbury of Minnesota, during my last years of service, not only submitted cartoon ideas every day, but also combed the internet for auction items, and for possible copyright infringements against Ripley's. He visited at least one Ripley odditorium every year, and even took two vacations to visit me in Orlando. His mother drew a portrait of Ripley and me as a retirement gift for my home. She said Nate loved me like a brother, and would forever remember my kindnesses to him.

I hope these people, and hundreds more like them, will continue to support Ripley's for many years to come. I have always felt that Ripley's readers found the best cartoon items, and often the best museum exhibits too. Everyone needs fans.

There is one more super fan who needs to be mentioned, and that is Wayne Harbour of Bedford, Iowa. He was truly in a class by himself.

Wayne did submit a couple items for publication, but his mission was very different from any other Ripley fan. For twenty-nine years (1943-1972), every day, he would randomly pick at least one item from the Ripley daily cartoon and write to someone related to it   to verify if it was true. He didn't write to Ripley's, but to complete strangers, often with incomplete addresses (care of the local post office or tourist bureau). It really isn't clear if he wanted to find Ripley at fault, or whether he just liked writing letters. Either way, it was a really weird hobby. Not everyone answered him, but thousands did, and not a single answer he received ever refuted Ripley's drawn claim. Wayne may have set out to disprove Ripley's, but in the process became the company's all-time best fact checker.

Wayne wasn't just a fan, or even a super fan, he was a real obsessed fanatic. When he died, his widow leftthe company with fifty-plus boxes of scrapbooks, filled with over 10,000 letters. Samples of these letters are displayed in virtually every Ripley museum around the world, under the title: "The Man Who Refused to Believe". God bless him.

Part Three

Travels & Adventures:
A Tough Job but
Someone Had to Do It

22

Odditorium Openings — Showbiz Ripley's Style

Robert Ripley was a lot of things — cartoonist, educator, entrepreneur, movie star, writer, radio star, but first and foremost, he was a showman, in the tradition of P. T. Barnum. It was always about "the show". A lot of this pizazz, however, was the work of his right-hand man, Doug Storer, because Ripley was by nature, shy. Doug was a brilliant PR man.

There are just enough print ads still in existence for anyone to get a glimpse of the pair's genius. Radio copy, actual radio shows, television and film performances, and of course advertisements, are readily available in a number of places. For the sake of this chapter, I am only interested in one little known piece; it hung in my office for years, and I've never seen a second copy of it in all my research and travels. As it dates from July 12, 1939, its rarity is not surprising. Its text explains why I never reprinted it anywhere. In bold type it exclaims: "Blow Yourself to a Good Time"…then announces the opening of Ripley's new odditorium on Broadway. The poster is a personal invitation to a party like no other. I have no idea how many were printed, but I do know there was a lot of people at the party. To be fair, this invitation did have a logoed balloon attached that you needed to bring with you to obtain entrance, thus the catch phrase — pure marketing brilliance.

The company probably never did anything quite so bold and audacious as that again, but we did always do museum openings in a big way, and especially under the direction of Steve Glum (2004-2009), an invitation to a Ripley opening was the hottest ticket in town.

I had not been to a Ripley odditorium opening until 1985 — the opening of the company's first museum in New Orleans, Louisiana. The company had just been bought by the Jim Pattison Group, and this was the first new Ripley museum to open in seven years; I am sure we were overdoing the opening to make a big impression on the new owner. The archives as I have suggested, do reveal that Ripley himself, and Alec Rigby in the 1960s and 1970s also knew how to throw a party. Alec's parties mainly involved food and drink, and maybe magician Ron Conley doing a few tricks while circulating through the audience. Ron was a personal friend of Alec's who was involved in the company's Magic Shops in San Francisco, Gatlinburg, and Myrtle Beach for several years. He was a nice guy, and a good magician, but not flashy in the Hollywood style. For Myrtle Beach in 1976, there was a high school marching band in full regalia, but these were small time events compared to what we did in Nawlin's.

New Orleans means Mardi Gras, and Mardi Gras involves a lot of masks — people hiding their true identity. Our award-winning party invitation was a four-fold card shaped like a mask, each fold revealing a different traditional Mardi Gras style mask, until the last fold which showed a Jivaro shrunken head with the caption: "Meet the New Face in Town." It was pretty clever.

New Orleans is also the parade capital of America — maybe the world so no brainer, we had to have a parade. It couldn't be any old parade, however, it had to be "unbelievable". Enter two Mardi Gras Indian tribes (1). The people of New Orleans, at least most of them, know about the tribes and the Mardi Gras tradition of "masqueing" Indian (wearing a disguise to appear to be an Indian, concealing the fact they were Afro-American), but only one in ten tourists have ever heard of it...and thirty years ago, the percentage would have been more like one in a thousand — me being that one.

Getting a permit to close Bourbon Street for a private party – with a parade — was unheard of. Getting the Mardi Gas Indians to wear their costumes, which traditionally are worn only twice a year, then discarded, was an even bigger coup, one that literally had never been done before. There was of course, food, drink, speechifying by Ripley brass as well as political nabobs, even a jazz band, but to have about twenty costumed Indian dancers facing off in a mock battle with wild drumming, and the uproariously loud chanting of Mardi Gras anthems like "Meet Me on the Battle Ground" and "Big Chief" on Bourbon Street, deep inside the

French Quarter, was epic. No one there will ever forget it. It was a grand entrance, literally and figuratively.

Dressed in a black tux, my job was to be a museum tour guide for the press. Several people thought I was with the band, and wanted to know when the next set would be. It was the first time I ever wore a tux (2).

Over the next twenty years there were several openings, each very different, but until the Steve Glum era, only three others – that I was at (3) – need to be noted here. In 1987 we fully renovated the then twenty-four year old attraction in Niagara Falls. This was the first time I had a "private conversation" with Jimmy Pattison. Dressed in a casual jacket, he was the guest of honor, the keynote speaker. Dressed in a tuxedo, I was a helping hand. The crux of the conversation went something like this:

Jimmy: "The food's good, but they should have had ice cream. Do you like ice cream?"

Me: "Yes sir, I love ice cream, but it is probably too hot out here in the sun to have any."

Jimmy: "Well there must be somewhere around here that sells ice cream. I feel like having ice cream."

Me: – somewhat puzzled: "Well there is a Dairy Queen about halfway down the hill."

Jimmy: Great. Let's go.

Me – in total shock – Sir I am not sure we can do that, people will be looking for you."

Jimmy – "We have plenty of time, let's go." And so off we went.

For the next ten minutes Jimmy quizzed me about everything under the sun while we ate an ice cream cone, on the street, watching the tourists go by. He learned more about me in that short time than my fellow employees had in seven years, and I don't think he forgot any of it. Luckily, I didn't dribble ice cream on my tux, or my hands.

Needless to say, he – not me – was missed in our time

away.

One year later, we had a similar event in Myrtle Beach. It was a grand re-opening after a total renovation. The museum had originally opened in 1976. I had driven about 1500 kms. from Toronto in a Toyota Corolla station wagon, my first company car, that had no air conditioning, but four passengers, two being my under four years old children, the others, my wife, and a lovely senior citizen "auntie" from India, named Queenie Peterson.

I arrived late afternoon the day before the unveiling, totally frazzled. The first thing I saw was the new president of the company, Bjarne Christensen, working a jackhammer! The next thing I saw was an undressed exhibit display case front and center in the lobby. The third thing I saw, was mine to be worn the next day, stark white tuxedo, with pink bow tie and matching cummerbund. Seeing our new president getting down and dirty was a revelation, and inspiring. Seeing the empty display case, and no one seemingly caring, was cause for a meltdown conniption. As for the clothing, suffice to say it was the first and last time I wore any of these garments in those hues.

With no prior experience, I spent the next several hours dressing the showcase with a six-legged chicken, a wax bust of a four-eyed Chinese man, a torture piece — possibly a chastity belt — and a piece of wood with over 5,000 coats of paint on it. A smörgåsbord of "pure Ripley's". It was well into the night before any of the crew went home. The next day, we all looked splendiferous in white and pink — including our bloodshot eyes.

By 1989, when we renovated San Francisco (originally opened in 1966) I had become "the voice of Ripley's" doing radio interviews for all occasions. This was one of two renovations that were being done simultaneously and everyone was glad the end of the projects were within sight (Jimmy had given us money to renovate all of our shows within five years of his having purchased the company, a task that would be done in four). Everyone wanted to kick off their shoes and celebrate. There had been a press only ribbon cutting in the afternoon, at which I drank a little wine, to be followed by an invitation only party in the early evening. In between, I had a one-hour in studio, radio interview on one of the major local stations.

I arrived on time with a bottle of local champagne. The idea was to give it to the host of the show as a present. I suggested we could have a toast to the new Ripley's during the interview. He told me he couldn't possibly drink on the job. For some impulsive reason I told him I could, opened the bottle and over the next hour, drained it. The listening audience had no clue that I was drunk, nor did most of my associates, and the interview went off without a hitch. It was the only time I ever did that, but not the only time I did something a little off the cuff, and outside the box, while on air.

By the time I got back to the party about 8 pm it was in full swing. The last thing I remember was walking through our lobby water fountain with another bottle of champagne.

Steve Glum was a breath of fresh air when he joined Ripley's in 2004. He was the first VP of Marketing we had ever had, and the first marketing expert in all the time I had been with the company. Steve was bold, brash, flamboyant in vocabulary and style, in short pure Hollywood. Bob Masterson had hired him to bring some razzle dazzle to the company, knowing that in the next few years, Ripley's would be undertaking some of the biggest jobs of the company's — and his personal — history.

For the 2007 opening of the company's triumphant return to the Big Apple (4), Steve hired A-list Hollywood glamor girls Jennifer McCarthy and Carmen Electra, a sword swallower who would cut the opening ribbon with a sword — freshly removed from his esophagus (the ribbon was adorned with rubber toy shrunken heads), several "human oddities" (including Lizard Man Erik Sprague and Larry Gomez, Werewolf Boy — see Chapter 23 & 26), cartoonist John Graziano to draw a cartoon of any guest who wanted an original Ripley cartoon drawing of themselves, and at least 500 people. To enter you had to walk across a simulated flaming bed of coals! One table of hors d'oeuvres featured edible bugs.

It seemed like the entire city showed-up. Traffic on 42nd Street was virtually at a standstill, the building was full, and Steve was a great host, and bon vivant. He wore a white jacket, but no tie. With the help of his right hand man, videographer and electrical whiz, Todd Day, he live-streamed the event to over 10,000 viewers on the Ripley web page — a Ripley first.

I missed a good deal of the party. I was the on the street doorman-greeter. I did have my longest ever conversation with Jimmy Patti-son who was anxiously awaiting some important guest and didn't go inside until they arrived (fashionably late), so it wasn't a total blow-out, but I never got inside the building until nearly midnight. There is no picture of me with Carmen, or Jennifer.

It was hard to imagine Steve could top this evening in any way. The London Odditorium opening a year later was, however, in the same league; it was much a repeat of New York in programming, but with different special guests. Music by mini-Kiss, a group of "little people" in Kiss band make-up in New York, was replaced by a Mini-Elvis. The bed of coals was replaced with a guy lying on a bed of nails —

seeing him wince every time a hi-heeled lady delicately stood on his stomach was the night's best photo op. The biggest difference in the two events, was the invitation. For London, Steve wanted something no one else could think of, or be able to copy, and most importantly, something that would generate press.

Jeremy Bentham was an 18th century philosopher-philanthropist. He had been featured in Robert Ripley's cartoon in the mid-1920s, and again in Rip's first book in 1929. He left a fortune in an ongoing legacy donation to University College London, provided they displayed his mummified head on a wax body at the college's annual board meeting. Jack Palance had visited Jeremy for one of our first television shows, and we showed the story via a wax figure tableau in a couple of our museums. It was an iconic signature Ripley story that I pointed out to Steve occurred within walking distance of our new Odditorium (5). With the help of Barry Anderson and Bruce Miller, the primary sculptors in the Ripley wax figure art department, 175 replica

135

Bentham mummy heads were made, packaged in branded custom wood boxes, with a pretty blue ribbon, then mailed to every significant media person in the United Kingdom. One can only imagine the facial expressions as 175 life-like resin mummy heads were opened at desks around the country. I suspect a few secretaries fainted the morning they were received.

For at least two weeks all of Great Britain was a buzz about Jeremy Bentham, and the opening of Ripley's Piccadilly Square odditorium. The campaign was a monster success, and for the coup d'grace, one head was sent to University College. It was widely reported that Jeremy had declined the invitation to the party, feigning ill health. Steve was my hero.

The third card in Steve's triumphant royal flush was the opening of the Great Wolf Lodge Resort and Water Park in Niagara Falls, Canada. I was very involved in the production of both New York and London, but they really were Steve's finest hours, I was just along for the ride. With the Great Wolf Lodge, it was a little different. Steve still arranged the band (Smash Mouth, then one of Canada's top pop groups, who miraculously played pool-side without getting electrocuted), and the major photo-op, Bob Masterson and Jimmy Pattison, in expensive business suits, being showered by 4,000 liters of water from the Water Park's signature giant bucket; their face in the photo that appeared in papers all over the country was priceless, but I like to think, I topped even this.

For many years my wife Giliane worked for the Canadian Federal government arm of Native Affairs. One of the best-known Indian reserves (original home of Canadian-Bob Dylan's legendary guitarist, Robbie Robertson), was located not too far away in Brantford, Ontario. My wife knew the chief, and a group of ceremonial dancers. In a 360-degree turn back to 1985 we organized a procession (small parade) with costumed indigenous dancers and drummers. The chief himself would appear and do a sacred smudge pot ceremony instead of a ribbon cutting. It was a masterpiece of theatre, history, religion and spectacle, all in one. Unforgettable and unbelievable, it was a once in a lifetime show. The smudge pot still has a place of honor in the lodge's lobby as does a carved moose antler, a gift from the tribe. An original

136

Robert Ripley 1930s totem pole from Seattle, is displayed elsewhere on the property.

I of course still couldn't have pulled it off without the masterful direction of Steve, my favorite producer, and the good woman behind me too.

Before he went on to other pastures Steve produced two more shows of epic proportions: Bob Masterson's inauguration as Chairman of IAAPA (International Association of Amusement Parks and Attractions) in 2008, and his end of term, passing of that baton, in 2009. Bob had been an active IAAPA committee member since the mid-1970s. He was a legend in the organization and was a natural to eventually lead them. When his time came, he wanted a showbiz extravaganza that would never be forgotten. Steve and his team (including myself) gave it to him.

The hall was decorated with about twenty of Ripley's very best exhibits — a full size mastodon skeleton, a giant gorilla made out of car bumpers, and our then-most valuable exhibit, an English Austin Mini covered in one million Swarovski crystals. There was also a cabinet with genuine Jivaro shrunken heads.

There were dancers, musicians, acts of all kinds and of Las Vegas showroom quality, but the hit of the night was the announcement that one person at each of the packed tables would win a door prize. The prize — a replica shrunken head made by the illustrious Ripley art department — was hidden under one chair at each table, and like London's Jeremy heads, concealed in a custom box with a regal blue ribbon. People thought they had won something from Tiffany's. Women who won gasped when they opened theirs. Men laughed uproariously.

It was classic Bob humor, and classic Steve "wow factor" (7).

The position of IAAPA board chairman is a one-year elected position. Bob's "resignation" gala was similar to his inauguration, and the definitive event of the 2009 IAAPA fall convention. For the in-coming chairman the highlight was Bob presenting him with a lock of Elvis Presley's hair cut in 1958 when Elvis went into the army (a little something I had picked up) — worth slightly more than the traditional gift of an expensive bottle of booze. (Bob did give him one of those too). For me, the thrill was a full size ceremonial Japanese drum ensemble — more than fifty pieces. They were fantastic; where Steve found them I can only imagine. They didn't top our Great Wolf Lodge Indians, but came damn close.

Steve left an indelible mark of "Hollywood showbiz" on the company, never to be matched again. His last museum opening in San Antonio included a multi-act "freak show" starring **TSD (Traumatic Stress Discipline)**, a group of people suspended like a mobile on meat hooks, a guy who let you staple money to his chest, and a live buffalo. Ripley's Baltimore odditorium, a post-Steve era opening, had a world-famous tightrope walker, John Astin of the **Addams Family** television show fame (a local Baltimore legend well past his prime), and a "ribbon" made of the tightrope walker's steel cable steel that was cut with a hand-held band saw metal grinder. It clearly followed Steve's pattern, as did Bob's retirement party from Ripley's in 2010 (Steve had taught us well), but no one at Ripley's could come close to Steve's chutzpah, his charisma, and his big picture Hollywood vision. Certainly not me.

His star was bright, but with Bob's gradual exit from the company, Steve crashed and burned. He was an accountant's worst nightmare, and the new regime didn't quite understand him. For me, it was an honor to work with him and to call him friend.

23

Presentations:
Writer, Director, Producer, Star

Each year for thirty-three years I had the unenviable tasks of writing, compiling images, directing, producing, and starring in a significant corporate presentation to Pattison Group dignitaries. The stakes were high, and many in the audience were complete strangers. Having to impress 100-150 Type-A businessmen is not an easy task. Certain business parameters were always the same, but the presentation had to be different each time, and with increased technology, the expectations were for bigger, better, and glitzier, each year. It was always a big challenge, and would take four to ten weeks of my life each January through March. For those whom I drove crazy each year expecting long hours and total devotion to the task at hand, my devoted assistants: Kathy Vader, Jan Florio, Kim Birch, Margaret Arnez, Lisa McCalla, Viviana Ray, Anthony Scipio, and Angela Johnson, and outside helpers, Marcia Pikel, Candy Prizer, John Dussling, Steve Campbell, and especially Todd Day, I owe you every scrap of commendation I ever received. The people behind the scenes always came through to make the people on the stage look a lot better than we really ever were.

I could say something about each presentation, they were so much a part of my business life, but I will limit my words here to just four, two early ones and two later ones. It should be duly noted that many of the other Pattison companies hired outside professional writers and producers to do their presentations, whereas Ripley did almost everything in-house. Depending on whom you were to ask, our presentations may not have been the very best each year, but they were consistently, year after year, in the top two or three. Our unusual visual content always gave us a pretty big leg up on much of the com-petition.

The goal was to tell how the company had performed in the last calendar year. The presentation would be made mid-March in a neutral hotel location. The invitations and instructions most years were received between

Christmas and New Year's. Typically, there was a loose theme and a couple specific questions that had to be addressed. The format of the presentation was wide open however, the only hard rule being that everyone from each invited company had to have stage time, a part in the presentation. Ripley's for years sent five people, but this number grew to a maximum of nine in some years.

Back in 1985, I made the "mistake" of saying I had written two plays before, one in grade school, and one in high school. With these as my credentials, I was given the job of scriptwriter for the rest of my Rip-ley life. As time went on the whole production became my albatross, even when I wasn't invited to the actual convention.

The first year we were brand new to the Group, literally only a couple weeks old when the conference rolled around. We played it straight and conservative and did what came to be called within the office: "dueling podiums". One person speaking from one side of the stage, at a podium, followed immediately by someone from the other side, back and forth until all participants had spoken. This was perfectly acceptable, but as the "entertainment" company in the group of forty-plus companies, the expectations from us were considerably higher. For our next one, we had costumes, sound effects, lots of visuals, partial nudity, and wigs. We were a huge hit, and created the mold for all others to follow for years to come. I wrote a play in which Robert Ripley discovered the fierce Pattison tribe on some far-off island. I played the role of Chief Jimmy-Pat, wearing just a grass skirt, and a bright red curly wig. Lots of groups mocked other company's bosses, but it was the first time anyone had risked making jokes at Jimmy's expense. Once a rebel, always a rebel. We set the bar extremely high.

Literally hurdle high in 1989.

That year the theme was corporate "hurdle" rates. I again went topless portraying a diver tumbling over Niagara Falls, while two members of our little group dressed as female cheerleaders, and our fearless leader, Bjarne Christensen, dressed in a track suit, jumped over ever increasingly higher hurdles, until he had a near heart attack on stage. Good clean fun gone a little sideways.

For about the first ten years, we had sound effects, but no soundtrack, and visuals were 35mm slides. The first big innovation was the introduction of "Power Point", a visual technology that allowed us to have multiple images on the screen at the same time. We went from a typical show of sixty slides to several hundred, almost overnight. Next, we introduced the use of theme songs, and video. Timing became an issue, and I no longer could do it all by myself. For one show, featuring our mini-Peel cars, I had an eight-man film crew under Todd Day's direction, splicing video and stills together to match my written words. That year I delivered the final product just after midnight, the morning the attendees were flying out five hours later. There was no rehearsal until they got on site, and no one performing had actually seen the final production they were to act in. It seemed like a recipe for disaster, but I think it was our best ever.

Our next revolutionary step was to bring an uninvited guest per-former with us. This had to be cleared by Jimmy and his assistant Maureen Chant, but was kept a secret from just about everyone else. We had shown pictures of Erik Sprague the Lizard Man before, but to actually have him appear, live as part of our presentation, was even riskier than me performing as Jimmy back in 1987.

Dressed in a custom-made Olga Irizzary (1) original stars and stripe, red, white and blue sequined vest, with top hat, I pretended to be a carnival barker. It was the closest I ever got to being a circus ringmaster. The set up was that I unveiled our company's latest wax figure, a very good life-like figure of Eric. The build-up was much greater than the reveal, and the puzzled looks in the audience suggested that they thought we had finally lost our senses……but when the figure came to life, and Eric took center stage, it was an instant WOW factor hit. People nearly fainted when he put a corkscrew up his nose, through his mouth and into is ear, and they lined-up for over a half hour to have their picture taken with him.

After Todd left the company — and later passed away — -

video production fell to Steve Campbell. As he and I often didn't see eye to eye, Marcia Pikel got more involved as a mediator between us. Eventually, I became just the writer, and the production became their project. Costumes and special effects became the norm, and the text grew less and less important. My last live appearance was in 2017 when I unveiled the infamous five million-dollar Marilyn Monroe dress (see chapter 74). My last on-screen role was as Yoda from **Star Wars**. The make-up and costume were so real, I suspect no one even knew it was me.

The annual Pattison Group presentation in my mind, was the single most important thing I did every year, but I did do a lot of other less "produced" productions that I am equally proud of as well.

For all but one of thirty-five Ripley museum managers' meetings (now called **RipCon**) I attended, I did "a state of the union" exhibits presentation. A few times I had seconds with me, but generally these were solo events, lasting anywhere from twenty minutes to an hour in which I told the audience what was newly acquired, what I was currently looking for, and what I hoped to buy within the next calendar year. They more or less were the same format every year, but with new content each time. I struggled to keep them fresh, but somehow managed to always score high on exit surveys. Angela Johnson and I did one year's show with our look-alikes on screen as marionettes. It was clever, but probably too cerebral for the majority of the audience. Edgar Bergen and Charlie McCarthy, we weren't. The presentations I am most proud of typically involved me talking, and Angela working the visuals. Together we did science fairs, museum conventions, kid's summer camps, publishing events, libraries, and school classrooms, about forty presentations in total. Mid-November in Florida is **"Teach-In"** a couple days when schools beg adults to come to classes and teach students something about the real (work) world. I did every year since my kids were little. I was a master at "Show and Tell". Blessed with enthusiasm, and the gift of the gab, policemen, and firemen, and especially accountants, didn't have a chance against me. I usually was invited back for the following year before I even left the building. I have a file full of hand-drawn thank you cards that I deeply cherish, as well as photos of small kids posed with everything from dinosaur bones, to anaconda skins, to the ever-popular two-headed cows. In my next life I will be a teacher, or at least a storybook reader. Nothing can make me happier than seeing a child smile when they learn something brand new — especially if I was the one that taught it to them.

24

Flogging Books in Seven Different Countries

From 2000 through the end of 2017, flogging new Ripley books was a significant part of my job. I did countless radio interviews, the occasional local Orlando television news shows, and lecture appearances at conventions, schools, and libraries in the Spring and Fall every year. On four separate occasions I even did full-fledged book tours, involving radio and television appearances, and book signings in book and department stores. In 2002 I did the USA; in 2007, England and Ireland; in 2010, Australia, New Zealand and Thailand; and in 2015, Canada. Safe to say, they all were full of adventures and mishaps.

My first tour in 2002 was to promote a book called **"Ripley's Encyclopedia of the Bizarre"**. It was before we had our own publishing company, and the tour was not organized by Ripley's. I did appearances in Orlando, New York, Chicago, Los Angeles and Houston. The only television was in Chicago where I appeared with a man who could turn his feet around 180 degrees, yet walk normally. The Hotel Monaco I stayed at was a considerable upgrade from my "usual", and when they greeted me by name before I had even checked in, I was feeling pretty special.

In New York and Los Angeles, my ego received pretty big bashings. I appeared in large glamorous chain book stores, typically three a day, but not too many people attended. If there were fifty in the audience for a presentation it was a good day. If I sold twenty books per gig it was a great day [1].

In Orlando — my home turf, I got some television and radio spots, and was able to promote the bookstore appearances. The stores were smaller, inside malls rather than stand-alones, but the crowds were a bit bigger, and the actual sales were much greater, helped by a little exhibit show and tell with displays from the local odditorium and warehouse. For the subsequent tours, "show and tell" would be a regular feature in addition to just hearing me speak about the book and Mr. Ripley's personal amazing story.

The tour ended in Houston where I appeared at huge Sam's Club box stores. They had large multi-colored posters all over the stores, and they used the book as a loss leader to get customers in, selling the book for less than half-price. This tactic worked well. The size of my audience at one was over 300, and they almost all bought a book. At another, I shared the bill with a troop of boy scouts. They made a giant chocolate chip cookie in the store's parking lot that attracted over a thousand people. The cookie was a much bigger hit than I was, but with the deep price discount, it was the best single day for number of books sold I ever had.

My next foray in the tour business was five years later to sell **Ripley Publishing's** first "special" book, **Ripley's Search for the Shrunken Heads**. I did singular events in Toronto, Canada and Palm Beach, Florida, then headed to England and Ireland. In England most of the work was print interviews, including a cover story for **The Fortean Times**, a magazine I personally subscribed to (see Chapter 16). On this leg of the trip I gave away more books than I sold, including a whole box full at the BBC London radio studios, but I was warmly received everywhere I went as the guy with a shrunken head in his pocket. The head was borrowed from the Ripley London odditorium, and was a huge sensation.

In Ireland I had the best PR agent imaginable. She had me booked all over Dublin, six and seven gigs a day: print, bookstores, radio and national television. On one nationally televised afternoon talk show they kept me on the entire hour so I could show every other guest my famous shrunken head.

The head had been somewhat of a gamble. We did not know much in advance whether I could fly out of England to Ireland with it, and despite informative letters of introduction, and provenance (written by myself), it caused quite a ruckus at customs. It is quite possible I only got it through because the ABC-Jack Palance television show was still airing in twenty-five-year-old reruns. People knew what Ripley's was, and seemingly loved the show, and because I let everyone in the whole customs office have their picture taken with it, I made the day for quite a lot of people.

Highlights in Dublin, included a private audience with the **Book of Kells**, an illustrated book of the Gospels dating from the 9th century that is one of the corner stones of European Christianity, and a new-found love for **Jameson Irish Whiskey**. I have never been much of a beer drinker, and I was actually nervous about having to drink **Guinness** in Dublin, but in a pub that was a converted train car, I dis-covered more people drinking **Budweiser** beer than **Guinness**. Not being a fan of that either, I took up a shot of Jameson's. I had drunk Jameson's before, but from that trip on it replaced **Jack Daniels** as my "usual". My favorite interview was in another pub: a centuries old Catholic church that had been converted into a drinking establishment during the English Reformation of the late 1600s.

I love Ireland. The climate sucks, but Dublin is truly a magical place. In 2010 I had been picked to do a tour in Iceland for the latest "annual" with my friend Erik Sprague, The Lizard Man. To my chagrin it didn't happen. Iceland stayed on my bucket list until 2017 when I finally got there for a couple days of vacation post a European trip involving Ripley's odditoriums in London, Copenhagen and Amsterdam. It was well worth the wait, and I am sure I enjoyed sharing a geothermal pool with my wife infinitely more than I would have with a tattooed green man.

The Iceland trade-off was that I did get to go to Australia, New Zealand and Thailand the following year. I had been to Australia twice before, so my excitement level was for visiting two countries that I

had never been to before and had always wanted to visit. The tour, my longest, started in New Zealand, (Auckland, Wellington, Christ-church) then went to Australia (Sydney, Melbourne, Adelaide and Surfer's Paradise), then to Thailand (Bangkok and Pattaya).

In New Zealand I had a handler who was a dynamo. I barely had a minute to myself, and when I did have a gap in appearances, I was wined and dined at cocktail parties and shown the tourist sites: the ruins of the Canterbury earthquake where I saw people living and shopping in forty-foot long by eight-foot wide, metal shipping containers that had been turned into emergency dwellings; Maori historic sites and botanical gardens;

and the famed WETA film studios where I met Sir Peter Jackson, and many of the behind the scenes heroes of **The Lord of the Rings** film trilogy (2).It being Halloween, I witnessed many ghouls and goblins, and was even treated to a choreographed midnight flash mob performance of Michael Jackson's song "**Thriller**" on a nearby hilltop by a costumed group of unearthly zombies. The highlights were two television shows, one described in detail in Chapter 17, where I was arrested for smuggling, and the other, a full one-hour Sunday morning kid's activity show, in which I was subjected to physical abuse, a scavenger hunt, athletic competitions, and non-flattering costumes.

I'd like to compare it to **Sesame Street**, but it was more like the kid's show **Nickelodeon** produced at Universal Studios in Orlando. As it was filmed live, I was able to advertise a bookstore appearance I was making the same day. It was one of my best ever-sales days, with a one-hour appearance stretching into three. I couldn't believe how many people said they had seen me on television that morning. Clearly television in New Zealand is not quite up to American standards, or perhaps no one goes to church on Sunday mornings?

Ripley Publishing had a strong distributor in Australia, and as Ripley's had an odditorium for over twenty years in Surfer's Paradise (3), they were able to get me interviews everywhere; people knew what to expect and I could borrow museum exhibits to spice up my appearances. My most unusual interview was with an adult gentlemen's magazine called, Penthouse (owned by American Penthouse, but with local content). The interview subsequently appeared on their website, but not in the monthly magazine. I guess I wasn't racy enough.

In Thailand, presumably because of the language barrier, I didn't work quite so hard trying to sell books. The book wasn't even available at that time in Thailand — outside of a couple stores in Bangkok

but I did, however, find the "werewolf" girl I was looking for; pet a tiger; ride an elephant around the world's largest wooden building; get caught in a monsoon; sleep in a bed normally reserved for the residing Queen; eat the best street food (steamed fish cooked in a banana leaf); take a river cruise; visit temple sites

Ripley had been at in 1932; and buy two twenty-two foot tall giant car part sculptures deep in the jungle, all in the name of work (3).

My flight home from this nearly three-week trip was via Japan. From Tokyo to Washington, DC., is one of the longest non-stop flights I ever took. Add on the time from Bangkok to Tokyo, a ten-hour layover in Japan, and a further two-hour flight from Washington to Orlando, and it was a nearly 40-hour in the air flight home, and that says nothing to time zone changes. I think it took me about a month to fully recover.

In comparison, my 2015 four-city cross-Canada, 3,000-mile trek in bitter November cold, was a walk in the park. The tour was unlike any other book promotion I ever did. I wasn't alone, I now had two travel companions. I didn't need to work quite so hard, but I now was more ringleader than circus star. W. C. Fields once famously quipped "never work with dogs, or children". My "child" was a young man on his first ever big gig, who was a professional clown. My dog, with female trainer, was a diva. Almost immediately, I knew my new place in the grand scheme of things: Sherpa, bus boy, stagehand, shopper, and dog watcher and sitter. I would get a minute to introduce myself and the book, Jorge Lattore, aka "Chicle", would get two-three minutes to do his very funny act as seen in the book, and the dog, also featured in the book, would get anywhere from four minutes to ten, depending on its cute factor and temperament on any given show.

The tour included television and radio spots in Toronto, Calgary, Edmonton and Vancouver, with additional book signings in Toronto. My mother and friends in Toronto, and nearby Barrie, Ontario, got to see me in action, live for the first time, but weren't impressed; selling a thirty-dollar book is definitely not easy, especially when you are only an editor and not the author.

I loved Jorge both as a person and for his act. I would enter the field of view with a large suitcase, put it on the ground, then ignore it while I talked to the hosts. When finished my blurb, I would direct their attention to the case, say some pre-determined magic word, and out would come Jorge having been folded-up inside the case for several minutes by that time. He would then blow up a giant pink balloon, climb inside it, and bounce around the stage. Accompanied by extraordinary facial contortions it was hilarious. With a patented outfit of suspenders, a striped shirt and funny hat, clown make-up, and fire-engine red sneakers, he was always a hit, but on one particular late-night show in frigid twenty-seven degree below zero Fahrenheit weather, in Calgary, Alberta, he stole the show with his comic-improvisation. The balloon would roll, but not bounce, and he couldn't get out of it. In Edmonton, the next day when it was even colder -minus forty degrees - we had to buy a new balloon, and we had to add gloves to his costume.

The dog act was a whole different scenario. Male hosts were bored stiff, but female hosts couldn't get enough of the cute little Boston Bull terrier. The dog skipped, skateboarded and walked across two parallel tightropes. In addition to a female trainer, he had about ten pieces of luggage. Assembling his tightropes would typically take longer than the three of us had per show, and of course there was never any guarantee she would perform as advertised. Some days she would not skateboard on cue, or on camera, preferring to go out into the audience. Some days she would jump into her trainer's arms rather than around the skipping rope, and at her best, the act only took a few seconds, leaving the trainer to talk about how clever her puppy was, and to promote her dog training school until the allotted time was up. There were times I wanted to gag, and of course there was always the fear of an "accident". I dreaded holding the little devil, and loathed having to carry her gear. I see on the internet that she now has her own traveling show. God forbid I and Ripley's helped make her a star.

I would be hard pressed to guess how many books I could take credit for having sold on these four trips, probably not as many as I sold via radio interviews from the comfort of my office or home, but I got to see some great places, meet some intriguing people, and in general, have a lot of fun. I am very grateful for the people who trusted me and gave me the opportunity to add "traveling salesman" to my resume, and especially to my foreign guides and publicists.

25

Stalking the Stars (TV Part 2)

With the Ripley-ABC-Jack Palance television show, the majority of my contributions were done from the comfort of my office. There were a few trips to Los Angeles, but other than sessions with ABC's "Standards & Practices" watchdogs (they didn't like to be called censors, but that is what they were), the trips were more like rewards, rather than work. No one knew the cartoon database or the exhibit collection as well as I did, so I was consulted on virtually every story. I got a weekly on-screen credit, but I was only ever on set once.

In the fifteen years that passed before Ripley's returned to television, I had been made a vice president, acquired a few thousand additional exhibits, written the definitive short version Ripley biography, consulted on a prime-time major documentary about Ripley on TBS (1993), and basically made myself indispensable to any third-party needing access to the vault and its treasures. So, for the Ripley-TBS-Dean Cain show I would be both a fact checker, and a segment ideas man. I chose exhibits for the closing **"Inside the Vault"** segments, I was on the set whenever filming was done at a Ripley location and as mentioned in Chapter 15, in Season four, I even got my own acting role in eleven episodes, and by the second season, having proven myself, I got my own, full-screen, not shared, screen credit. I definitely felt, and believed, I was a significant player with an important role.

In the early 1990s I had been a big fan of the **Lois & Clark, The New Adventures of Superman** television show, more for Teri Hatcher (Lois Lane) than for Dean-Superman-Cain, but my wife liked him, and thought he would do a good job as the host of the new **Ripley's Believe It or Not! Show.** His good looks, and his muscle-bound, football player-build certainly helped him look like the Superman of my youth — George Reeve's, whom I watched every day as a kid on **The Commander Tom Show,** on Buffalo's Channel 7 ABC affiliate (1).

Cain wasn't the first choice for our host, nor even the second. Somewhat in desperation, he was chosen after an open cattle call audition where over a couple hundred people appeared, and after first-choice actor, John Corbett, turned us down at the last minute. Corbett had just had a good five-year run on a quirky show called **"Northern Exposure"**, and was a hot commodity. Within a year or two after our show started airing, however, he was all but forgotten, the voice on a series of American Express Commercials, but otherwise gone. We were not sad he had turned down our final offer — which was substantially lower than his initial asking price.

Dean's start, therefore, was a little auspicious, but he was following in good footsteps. Jack Palance had also been choice number three, behind Peter Ustinov, and Vincent Price. Sometimes it is so interesting to fathom "what ifs".

I had met most of the key players for the show in Florida during the summer and Fall of 1999, but it was December of that year before I met the star in the newly created "permanent stage" in Burbank, California. We at Ripley's corporate were a little disappointed that they had decided not to film in Florida, utilizing both the Orlando office, and the St. Augustine odditorium as de facto Ripley headquarters, but in retrospect it was a blessing that after seeing our warehouse they had decided they could recreate the feel in a better lit and sound controlled real studio. It would mean a few more trips to California for me, but I didn't mind: a tough job but someone had to do it.

The studio was as big as a football field. It was divided into areas that would be used on all episodes: a warehouse full of exhibits on shelves (which were changed each season); a medical lab; a dark tunnel; and a generic sofa room for the occasional interview sequence. This was to be Dean's home for the next four years; he would not do any location traveling for the show. When Kelly Packard was hired for Sea-sons Three and Four, she got to do all the on-location segments as the show's "field correspondent".

Several episode segments were filmed on the same long twelve-hour days. When Dean was available the director made good use of everyone's time, and filmed him for hours, knowing it might be weeks be-fore they would get him again. If you watch several of the shows back to back, you will notice Dean's costume didn't change much. This is a telltale sign of when the show was filmed as opposed to when it aired. Knowing a big part of Jack Palance's budget had been on costumes,

I think it may have been written into Dean's contract that he had to wear the same clothes at least three times.

The date of my first shoot with Dean, was December 16, 1999, my daughter Celeste's thirteenth birthday. (The first show aired three weeks later on January 6, 2000). Two things happened that December day that I still remember clearly. The first was seeing Dean bare-chested.

Approximately ten people, including myself, were perched in director's chairs watching the filming. Everyone was older than me, and the oldest person, a woman, was clearly the queen bee. I have no idea who she was, or what she did, but the director, the producer, Dean, and the head guy from TBS, all kowtowed to her every whim and word. When the filming of a scene ended, a still-photographer asked Dean if he would mind posing for some publicity stills before the set up for the next scene. He was willing, and the flashes started to go just a few feet in front of his audience of VIPS. Not more than a couple minutes into the session, he complained he was hot, could he have a wardrobe change? An underling rushed in with a white shirt to replace his bulky turtleneck. Unpretentiously, he removed the turtleneck right there for all to see his abs of steel. There was a giant audible gasp from every woman in the seats. The elderly lady actually fell off her chair. People rushed to her rescue, and were able to re-seat her on her throne without incident. She exhaled, and said in a loud and clear commanding voice: "He should do that in every episode".

Everyone howled, and the tension was broke. Though I don't believe you ever see Dean shirtless in a sequence, his clothes did get considerably tighter over the duration of the series. Beefcake in the first two seasons, may have bought as many ratings as cheesecake did in the third and fourth.

Dean was surrounded all day, and his manager in particular made it difficult to get anywhere near him, but I was on a mission, and would not be foiled. I didn't

152

like missing my daughter's birthday (the second time I had done so), and I was determined to get her Dean's autograph for a "sorry, but hope you forgive me" present. At thirteen she had a mad crush on Dean; something from him would be worth mega-brownie points. I at first tried politely, asking the manager to be a go between, but when he obviously lied to me, then proceeded to ignore my further ventures, I decided to take matters into my own hands. I certainly wasn't above being a slimy pestering jerk. I was going to meet Dean if it took me all day.

I did several silly things to get noticed, but all to no avail. After repeated failures, I finely just seized the moment, pushed my way through the crowd, and presented myself in Dean's face before he could return to his trailer. To my surprise, he not only didn't shun me, or have me dragged away in chains, he was actually nice — probably the warmest celebrity I had ever confronted. I told him about how much Celeste liked him, and that it was her birthday. I put a pen and a scrap of paper in his hand and begged. He said an autograph wasn't enough. If I wanted to make a statement, I had to have real physical evidence I had met him. He called for the humbled, and disgraced, manager to get an eight by ten-inch promo photo. He then autographed it personally to Celeste. He then asked where she was. I said in Orlando, at home, having a birthday party with a dozen giggly girlfriends. He then asked did I have a phone. I said yes. He said call her. I did. She of course just thought I was calling to wish her happy birthday. When Dean took my phone and started to talk to her she nearly fainted. I could hear all thirteen girls squeal. He asked her how the party was going, did she miss her dad, etcetera, keeping her engaged for nearly ten minutes. It was the best birthday present she ever got from me. My wife later said the girls didn't stop talking about Superman until well into the middle of the night's sleep over. The picture became a holy icon a few days later, and was often carried to school for verification and bragging rights. It is still ensconced in her childhood bedroom in our home.

Dean was no Jack Palance when it came to acting and creating a Ripley persona, but he's okay in my books — a real Superman.

Years later, I bought Superman outfits worn by George Reeves, Christopher Reeves and Dean Cain. The first came with considerable underbody armor. The second was too tall for me, but was not a terrible fit. I was too embarrassed to even think about trying on Dean's. Even my belly is not as big as Dean's chest.

Petite blonds are not my type. I might concede Kelly Packard was cute, but she definitely wasn't my type. I had no anxiety, or hot flashes, regarding meeting her, but I may have been the only male in our office that could say that and mean it. At least two of my associates were seriously enamored by her.

I not only got to meet her, but for the good part of a day I was her handler for an episode she was going to narrate, and host, filmed in our then brand-new Gatlinburg, Tennessee Aquarium of the Smokies. Afterwards, I would escort her up the street to the Believe It or Not! Odditorium where she would do an autograph and photo session for an hour. Then in the evening she would return to the aquarium, and film an outdoor segment on the patio with a guy who was going to be buried in earthworms and attempt to eat his way out in an hour. I had to deal with Kelly's time, her clothes, her food, her stylist, and her fans.

The morning segment at the aquarium involved a diver who held the record for staying underwater the longest, something in the neighborhood of ten or twelve minutes (2). Our staff chief diver, Frank Bulman, could do more than five minutes, which we thought was quite impressive, so for the segment both men would enter the aquarium's Ray Bay tank and sit on the bottom as long as they could, subject to rays and small sharks inspecting, and bumping them as often as they pleased, in an appearance of aggression. Kelly meanwhile, in a "custom" extra skimpy wet suit would wade in knee deep amongst the fishes and provide eye candy for an otherwise dull segment.

The divers both set personal bests, and the expert set a then world record. Kelly, however, did not co-operate. She refused to wear the wet suit we provided, apparently indignant over its blatant sexism, despite having appeared in considerably less in a gentlemen's magazine just a month earlier, and having regularly appeared as

154

a Bay Watch babe in a very revealing famous red bathing suit throughout a whole season of shows. She blamed me for not having warned her what the suit looked like. We were off to a bad start. In addition to getting her to wear the suit, the single biggest part of my mission was to get her to autograph it for future aquarium promo and display purposes, and now she not only wouldn't wear it, she wouldn't even look at it. I was left holding it for most of the rest of the day.

The photo shoot was not without drama either. I did manage to get my associate Scott Brody the cheesecake shot of him and Kelly he want-ed, but she played diva and didn't win any friends that afternoon. She was the polar-opposite of Dean. The line was long -a big success in my book — but she left many people standing, refusing to do a minute more than her contract demanded. The suit was still not signed.

The evening session was much as could be expected — cold, not well attended, and very gross. The worm-eater stood up inside a plexiglass rectangle, open at the top, and buckets full of earthworms were poured in up to his chin by Ryan DeSear and his wife Suzanne, the Ripley odditorium managers. The worms were pre-weighed so a record could be recorded as to how many pounds of worms he ate in one hour. On air he would be the first segment, then they would revisit him at half time, and again at the end of the show. For my money, he didn't do too well. He barely dinted his earthworm torture chamber, but definitely ate more than I, or anyone else I know, could or would have. Kelly didn't have a whole lot to do, and I approached her once again about signing the suit. She eventually broke down, and said she would sign it after the filming. I could appreciate her not wanting to do it publicly and backed off, but I was not going to let her off the hook now that she had verbally agreed to do it. I put it back in its case and waited.

There weren't too many places that stayed open late and served alcohol in Gatlinburg back then (Gatlinburg had been "dry" only a few years previous), but it was my job to find one for an after-party. The place of choice was a loud second story country bar near the Ripley's odditorium and across the street from where everyone was staying the night. Everyone was expected to be there — including Kelly.

155

It was nearly 1:30 in the morning but she finally signed the wet suit. Mission accomplished.

The suit was never displayed. It laid around inside our warehouse, then our wardrobe department, unceremoniously, for years. In 2013 it was put inside a time capsule with some other relics of Ripley history, and buried. It now lies underground beneath the lobby of the Ripley odditorium in San Francisco, gone but not forgotten.

26

Some Dear Friends

It goes without saying that I met many unusual people over the years, some who performed unusual stunts, some who underwent body modifications, and some who were born "different" from the norm. Ripley himself avoided the word "freaks" as much as possible, and collectively called them all "Special people". So-called political correctness pushed these people out of the Ripley limelight for many years, but the Ripley's-TBS-Dean Cain television show (2000-2004) brought them back to the front of the stage in an unprecedented way. The company did a full 360-degree turnabout back to the days of the Ripley's odditoriums of the early 1930s, featuring "human oddities" at museum openings, book launches, television interviews, and as wax figures in various locations. The list of people is nearly endless, and ranges from an armless baseball player to a man who ate earthworms, to a man who let his wife drop bowling balls on his head. The following are just a handful of the ones who most impressed me.

Up until about 1990, the unusual people I met were limited to a Wiccan Priest who I sold some Dr. Gardner witchcraft books to (see Chapter 36), and Hollywood celebrities: Groucho Marx's son Arthur, who was going to write a book about Ripley (he only completed about thirty pages, but my week with him was great), the Haleys, the Palances, Ray Bolger, and Jerry Belson, the screen-writer who had worked on my all-time favorite television show, **The Dick Van Dyke Show** (1961-66). Belson was the guy who wrote the classic Ripleyesque episode "Odd but True" (Season 5, show # 134) concerning a dog that didn't eat, a man who had walked from Buffalo to New York City on his hands, a potato shaped like a duck, and Rob's "Liberty Bell" patterned moles …with Alan Brady (Carl Reiner) acting as Robert Ripley. If you have never seen it, or somehow have for-gotten it, look it up, I don't want to spoil it for you.

By 1990, however, we had started to make videos for our museums and were actively seeking "talent". The initial inspiration was a Californian man by the name of **Fakir Musafar** who was introduced to us by two gallery operators named Mark Sloan and Roger Manley, who did two book projects with Ripley's, including my favorite Ripley book, **Dear Mr. Ripley,** a collection of unique archival black and white photographs. At a gallery opening in San Francisco that featured about ten photos from the Ripley's archives amongst thirty or forty other unusual photos from several archives around the country, Musafar sat dressed in business attire, typing at a desk in the middle of the room. At a given time he got up, made his presence known, then left the room. He came back, stripped of all clothing but a Speedo-like pair of shorts, and carrying a big rope. He then threw the rope over the ceiling beams, tied one end to the typewriter, and threaded the other end through piercings in his nipples. He then proceeded to walk backwards, lifting the typewriter off the desk and in to the air using only his nipples. Look ma, no hands! The stunt was inspired by a Mandan Indian ritual called the **o-kee-pa** known to the white world via a painting called **"The Last Race"** by George Kaitlin (1832) and a depiction by Richard Harris in a Hollywood film called **"A Man Called Horse"** in 1970 (2).

I was so impressed by this little show and my conversation with Musafar the next day at our odditorium, that I went back to Toronto with the new idea to tape live performers. In Toronto, we hired a talented filmmaker named Rick Taylor, and set to work. With some technical help from an independent designer, named Anton Gosley, we made three very memorable movies in one week. The first being a "Pepper's Ghost" illusion using an actor playing Robert Ripley. The Pepper's Ghost illusion is a centuries old magic trick — literally "smoke and mirrors"-altered by the attractions business to work with film. Ours was groundbreaking in that we used bigger than life size mirrors to project full-scale people and objects, not the typical miniaturizations that were being used in science museums at the time (1). The other two films were our first live performer ventures. Stevie Starr, the Human Regurgitator and Brad Byers, Champion Sword Swallower

I lump these two performers together because we filmed them in the same studio, on two consecutive days. I don't recall who went first, but both were very special performers, and the films we made were used for well over twenty years. Both are still amazing — and shocking, but unfortunately not up to today's "hi-def" standards.

Stevie Starr was from Scotland. I had first seen him perform on the David Letterman late night TV show. He could swallow small objects and regurgitate them moments later. For us, he did coins, a #8 black billiard ball, a regular size light bulb, a goldfish, powdered sugar washed down with water (then brought back up – dry!), and a wedding ring on a padlock. I sat inches away from him, and know for sure the objects went into his mouth; whether he actually swallowed them, is a mystery I cannot solve. I do know that he ate nothing all day, no breakfast, lunch or craft service snacks. I suspect he didn't wish to regurgitate anything unexpected. The ring "trick" was truly baffling. We supplied the lock (brand new, unhampered), the key, and even the wedding ring taken from one of Rick Taylor's female employees. Stevie swallowed the ring, then the key, then the padlock, in the open position, talked a little, then thumped his chest a couple times, and brought up the ring now locked on to the closed padlock. Another chest thump, and up came the key. With a grin a mile-wide, he spit the key into the lady's hand, she opened the lock, and much relieved, reunited her finger with her wedding ring. I have no idea how this "trick" was done.

Brad Byers, from Idaho, was billed as the only man who could put multiple swords down his throat at the same time, twist them around (I can still hear both the sounds of the swords, and the gasp of the onlookers), then actually bow with them in his throat. A show stopping feat if ever there was one. In our interview portion, Brad told a funny story about being a juggler in a circus until he discovered the sword swallower made a lot more money than him. With no practice or warning, he then went into an army surplus store, took a sword off the wall, and proceeded to try to swallow it. He seriously wounded himself on this first attempt, but went on to master all kinds of stunts, including swallowing as many as a dozen swords at once, swallowing large, toothed, saws, and swallowing bent clothes hangers. He also somewhere along the line learned how to put sharp objects up his nose — including an electric drill!

One of the oldest carny sideshow stunts in the books is called the "Human Blockhead". It entails a performer hammering a large spike up his nose. There is a long narrow channel into which the nail fits perfectly. In theory anyone can do this provided they have the courage — or stupidity — to try it. Ripley featured a guy named Melvin Burkhart doing this as early as 1933; I saw Burkhart do it at the very last "freak show" ever to play Toronto's Canadian National Exhibition c. 1970. Since then I have seen at least a dozen other performers do it, and even have a couple of the snot-covered spikes in my personal collection of trinkets. I have not, however, seen another human being put a working drill up his nose. The sound is horrific. Imagine the proverbial dentist drill, just several times louder, coming straight at your face. In the published version of the Ripley film, if you look close you can actually see a drop of blood shoot out from Brad's nostril. The first time we showed the finished film on a big screen at a corporate function, the screams and squeals were even louder than the sound of the drill. The film is hard to watch, but even harder to turn away from — a piece of cinematic brilliance.

Reverend Doctor Kevin Fast

In the fall of 1999 I was in a car with three behind-the-scenes people who would be the core production team of the Ripley-Dean Cain-TBS television show (2000-2004), heading north from Orlando, to St. Augustine, Florida. The purpose of the trip was to access the possibility of using St. Augustine as the "set" for the future series, but they were picking my brain fast and furiously for potential content for the show. One random question was:

"Do you know anyone who can pull an airplane — or hold one back from taking off?"

"No, but I do know a guy who can pull a fire truck", I said.

[With astonished excitement] "Really! Oh, that would make a great first segment! Where is he? Is he in Florida?"

"Well, no, he is in the small town of Cobourg, Ontario, where my mother lives. He works out at the local YMCA and I met him through my stepfather. I am sure he would be willing to travel to any place you want. Oh, and by the way, he is a Lutheran pastor."

The combination of a religious leader and a strong man who could move a 32,000-pound fire truck, was too much for them.

"Can you call him? Right now!?"

Before the two-hour drive was over, Rev. Dr. Kevin Fast had agreed to come to St. Augustine, and be the first person filmed for our show. The filming took place four months prior to the eventual airing in February of 2000 (3). I had barely met Kevin and had probably exaggerated my "knowing" him, but my parents were close friends, and had been telling me about him for a couple years. I was confident he could do what they were hoping for.

Kevin is only about five-foot-five-inches tall, but his body is huge — 260 pounds of solid muscle. In 1999 he was about thirty years old, and had already been Canada's strongest man for five years. Today, he has thirty-plus world strength records, has traveled around the world doing feats of strength, and has been on a countless number of television shows. Ripley's was his first time performing outside of Ontario, and his first television show.

It was a hot steamy night when he and his wife Suzie arrived in St. Augustine. Immediately we had a problem. Our driveway, where the stunt was to be performed was uneven gravel. He doubted he could perform there, and at very least would need different shoes. A PA (production assistant, read "gopher") was selected to take him shoe shopping while the crew set up the "runway" for a rehearsal. High school cheerleaders had been hired to whip the "live audience" of townspeople into an excited frenzy (reality television at its best), and the local fire department had provided the required truck.

After a long wait, everyone was ready for a rehearsal. Kevin tied a rope to his chest, and the director said "action". Kevin proceeded to move the truck the required distance (about 100') in about two seconds. The feat was amazing, but it would not make for very good

TV. It was too quick, and he made it look too easy. He was asked, "Could he pull two trucks?" He had never done it, but he was willing to try. Someone made an emergency phone call, and a second 32,000-pound truck was rushed to the odditorium. The two were tied together — 64,000 pounds in total weight.

Even with two trucks, Kevin made it look fairly easy and the producer and director were worried it wasn't going to make for good TV. They certainly wouldn't need the ambulance, the firemen, or the medics that were on site in case something went wrong.

A few hours later when it came time to do the actual filmed version, the air was electrifying. The crowd, the cheerleaders, and Kevin were pumped. Only Suzie was worried. Unbeknownst to myself, or Kevin, the pull was not going to be a walk in the park. Kevin got strapped in, the director said "action", Kevin roared like a lion, and nothing happened. He tried again, and still nothing. A third effort produced a flood of sweat, Kevin's shirt was soaked through with Florida humidity, but the trucks started to move. "Step by step, inch by inch" magic was occurring. The medics were on alert and the crowd was now cheering wildly. The director, the producer and the cinematographer smiled ear to ear with collective winks.

The distance was marked and counted down with bowling pins (later displayed with the only used once big tread shoes in the St. Augustine odditorium). As Kevin passed each pin the crowd was encouraged to roar. At the finish line they went nuts. Kevin collapsed into the arms of his wife, and a doctor with an oxygen tank. For a moment I thought he was in serious trouble. His collapse definitely made for "good TV." A new world record had been successfully achieved and filmed. Our first episode "was in the can".

Only weeks later was I to learn the brakes had been set on the second truck — my step-father's friend easily could have been killed with the extra strain. I am surprised Kevin ever talked to me again, let alone go on to do much bigger pulls and incredible stunts for Ripley's.

I have now been close friends with Kevin and his family for nearly twenty years. Both his sons, who were quite small when I first met them, are now world champions in different strength competitions, and all three together have literally moved houses for Habitat for Humanity. Kevin has also pulled the world's biggest airplane, a CC-177 Globemaster III, weighing 188.83 tons — an incredible 416, 229 lbs.

Kevin has grown even bigger than he was in 1999, and now has a huge white beard. He regularly plays Santa Claus in shopping malls throughout Southern Ontario, and looks the part to a "t". Dressed as Santa, he once let me beat him in an arm wrestling match for a staged photo-op. Kevin is one of my biggest heroes [4].

Troy Hurtubise and Tim Cridland, the Great Zamora, a Pain-Proof Man

After the Rev. Fast fire truck pull several other television segments were filmed in St. Augustine, typically two different performers on the same night back to back from 7pm until midnight. On July 31, 2018, I read a newspaper obituary of one Troy Hurtubise. I certainly would never have forgotten him, but seeing Ripley's name prominently featured in his obit, made me appreciate the accomplishment we caught on film back in 2000.

Troy was a legitimate scientist and photographer, interested in filming bears — specifically grizzlies. In order to get really close to bears, even climb into their winter hibernation dens with them, he had invented an "indestructible suit". For Ripley's, he put on the suit and let us smash into him at about 100 miles per hour with a car tied to the side of our St. Augustine museum and swung like a giant pendulum. The impact knocked him down, and destroyed a brick wall be-hind him, but miraculously — though noticeably stunned — he did get up and walk away, dizzy but unharmed. It certainly was crazy and unbelievable, but it was only our opening act. Troy was a one- trick pony. Tim Cridland on the other hand, had several tricks up his non-sleeved shirt.

Tim actually appeared on our show twice. The second time, was filmed at the Orlando odditorium, and showed him walking on kitchen hot plates that were frying eggs. His first appearance in St. Augustine featured several jaw-dropping body piercings — skewers through his biceps, calves and tongue — followed by his laying on a bed of nails while having a regular size car driven over his stomach — driven by yours truly. Seemingly impervious to pain, he encouraged me to do it a second time – faster. I chickened out, however, and opted instead to jump on his stomach while he lay on a bed of broken glass. Just another day at the office for both of us (5).

164

Erik Sprague, The Lizard Man, & Maria Cristerna, the Mexican Vampire Woman

Erik and Cristerna are definitely the strangest looking people I ever had to deal with. Both have undergone severe body modifications, starting with full body tattoos, but also including filed pointed teeth, stretched ears, some piercings, implanted horns, and in Erik's case, a bifurcated tongue. I only met Cristerna once over a three-day period. Erik, I met several times over several years. Each time he was greener, his desired transformation into a lizard being one step closer to completion. For nearly fifteen years, he was the visual icon most associated with Ripley's.

Erik was on our very first Ripley-Dean Cain-TBS television show in January 2000, but it was about a year later when I first met him. Based on the audience response from his television appearance, we decided we needed to film him ourselves for an odditorium video. I picked him up at the airport in my small car, and proceeded to drive to a specialty pet shop, where we had arranged to rent a large monitor lizard. We got stuck in traffic, and the lizard got loose in my car. Erik thought it was very funny, and may have actually done it on purpose to gage my response. I wasn't really scared, but I certainly was not comfortable, expecting it to bite my leg at any minute.

At this point in time, Erik was only about 10-15% green tattooed. The horns were already inserted and the tongue was already split, but if he was dressed you might not have noticed him. By the last time I was with him in 2013, he was 90% green, and with the word "Freak" emblazoned across his chest. You certainly couldn't miss him then.

At our first gig, he was actually more about stunt performing than his physical appearance. He allowed me to break cement blocks across his crotch, throw darts at his back — a very disturbing act (he kept encouraging me to throw harder so they would stick into his skin), and for my assistant Lisa McDonald (nee McCalla), to hand feed him grubs. Her reaction, caught on film, was worth the price of admission. In total he did twenty-three strange stunts, each one designed to have people in the audience faint.

The next time I met Erik it was to make a wax figure of him. By this time, he was about 50% green, and now the most popular personality on the sideshow circuit. The Ripley art department did a full body cast and made one of the company's best ever figures. We also filmed the procedure and interviewed Erik at length. The results were featured in Ripley odditoriums for years, and Erik became the company's poster boy. We even broke with all rules and conventions and brought him to a Jimmy Pattison Partners in Pride conference (see Chapter 23).

The last two times I was with Erik involved nipple piercings, and a Peel P-50, small car. At an October **"Oddfest"** carnival at the Orlando Believe It or Not! Odditorium, I got in a fifty-four-inch long, 150-pound Peel car and had Erik pull me around the parking lot, while walking backwards with ropes attached to the car at one end, and to nails through his nipples at the other. Fearing the weight would pull through his skin, it was extremely unnerving watching him face to face through the windshield. Luckily, nothing happened, the stunt went off as hoped for. The second time we weren't so lucky.

I must add that after the Orlando performance, my wife, Giliane, my assistant Angela Johnson, and her friend Stephen Coll, offered to take Erik out for dinner and drinks — I knew from previous experience that he was a big beer drinker. Deciding where to take a green guy for dinner was quite difficult; we were not prepared to take him anywhere we frequented in our small town of Winter Park, Florida. We settled on a drag queen show in Orlando's arts district, at a place called "Bananas". The show was excellent, and the food was decent, but Erik was the real hit of the evening. All the ladies loved him, and an impromptu performance with his two-part tongue around a singer's microphone, brought down the house, prompting cat calls from women, while turning just about every man in the place bright red. It was definitely a show-stopping act.

The very last time I saw Erik, my wife and I met him at the airport in Toronto, about to board a small plane for a short ride to Sudbury, Ontario for the grand opening of a show created in conjunction with the world-famous Sudbury **Science North** museum, called **The Science of Ripley's Believe It or Not!** We knew Erik was going to be there, but hadn't expected to be on the plane with him. The plane was seriously delayed, and we now found ourselves having dinner for the second time with a guy who liked to eat bugs. It was unbearable to witness how difficult it was for him to do anything without being tormented by people — asking if the green was paint, or tattoos, feeling his horns, gasping at the sight of his split tongue, children running away scared, and in general, everyone in the whole airport "gawking". I will never forget the immigration agent asking him if he had any photo identification to verify he was real! It was a very long dinner and evening.

In Sudbury I was to give a speech to a group of teenagers, then Erik would do a speech and some of his acts, then a repeat of our Peel Car stunt would be the big finale. Almost instantly something went wrong. His skin wasn't ripped apart — potentially my worst night-mare — but he literally pulled the steering wheel shaft through the floor of the car! I couldn't steer, and he couldn't move it more than a couple inches without scraping the floor. It was a very disarming end to my circus career.

Erik still tours bars and is a regular at Halloween horror shows across the country. He doesn't do more than two or three stunts anymore, sticking mainly to his giant corkscrew up the nose act, but he is now almost all green and talks of having a tail surgically attached to his butt. I call him the "World's Most Unusual Man" for a lot of reasons.

After our success with Erik, I went actively searching for the "World's Most Unusual Woman". I found Maria Cristerna, **The Mexican Vampire Woman**, in Guadalajara, Mexico. Like Erik, Maria is almost to-tally covered in tattoos. Unlike Erik though, her tattoos are random pictures portraying her children and her life, rather than being all one pattern, and, believe it or not, she did most of them herself!

Maria, a mother of four, at one point had been a lawyer, but by the time I found her she was singing in a punk music band and had become a tattoo artist. She had stretched ears and Teflon horns like Erik, but she also had metal screws implanted in her head, which she could take out in order to go through the metal detectors at the airport, and when sleeping – so as not to rip up her pillows every time she turned her head.

Maria came to our office in Orlando to have a wax figure made, and to star in a short film. The interview process was not as fruitful as Erik's session had been as Maria spoke no English. I used two staff translators and asked all the pertinent questions, but she never re-ally opened up to me. In private, or at least in Spanish, she revealed much more of her troubled life to our art department's manager, Olga Irizarry (who would make her sexy black leather bustier costume and her Goth jewelry for the wax figure). Turns out she was a battered woman, her first tattoos being ways of hiding bruises and scars. The produced film made its way onto our web site, but was never incorporated into a full – fledged museum video, her story not being exactly "family friendly". Her bravery to tell her story, and her ongoing charity work to raise funds for women's shelters, however, is remarkable and inspiring.

Like with Erik, the highlight of her visit was a dinner together. Choosing a place for the meal was a little easier as she only ate Mexican food, and Olga and our team had a regular place we liked to go for margaritas and fish tacos. It was a little off the beaten path (at least for me), and typically not crowded. Dinner couldn't have been more "normal". Having experienced a three-ring circus environment both times I ate with Erik, I expected the same with Maria, but for some reason (she does look pretty scary), she was ignored while we ate. It was almost like she wasn't there, or that she was invisible. Once she finished dinner, however, things changed immediately. I have never seen so many phone cameras magically appear out of nowhere. From the table to the door couldn't have been more than fifty-feet, but it took us more than an hour to get to the exit. Every single person in the restaurant stormed her, touching her, quizzing her, and requesting a photo with her. It was excruciating for me; I could only imagine what it was like for her. Presumably this happens everywhere she goes in public.

Maria already had a title when we met her, the **Mexican**

168

Vampire Woman, because of her sharpened fangs, but we billed her as Erik's counterpart: "The World's Most Unusual Woman". The two wax figures are displayed side by side in Ripley odditoriums, eliciting squeals and screams, and generating "selfies" that via social media are seen all around the world to this day.

Live in New York City — Khagendra Magar, Momentarily the World's Smallest Man

Ripley spent most of his life in New York City. He had a mansion in nearby Mamaroneck, as well as two Manhattan apartment addresses. It was home to his most famous odditoriums (1939, 1940, 1955-1972), and the home of the cartoon from its inception in 1918 to 1989. Our licensing agent Bob Whiteman also operated from the city and nearby Rye, NY. Ripley's and NYC go hand in hand.

Despite Alec Rigby moving the offices out of NYC to Toronto in 1969, NYC was always the company's spiritual home, and I had been going there occasionally since the early 1980s. I had twice visited Ripley's legendary researcher Norbert Pearlroth, and I had met a grand-niece of Robert's who owned several interesting archival family films and company pieces (I bought hundreds of photos and several reels of home movies from her). I had also done book signings in NYC bookstores in 2002, but not until 2007, when the 4th incarnation odditorium opened on 42nd near 7th, did I have a regular reason to visit the "Big Apple".

At the grand opening of the museum we had several unusual people attend, an armless baseball player — I played catch with him on a closed off section of 42nd street — a sword swallower who cut a ceremonial ribbon adorned with rubber shrunken heads to announce the official opening, a Mexican circus acrobat with hypertrichosis (more on him later), conjoined Siamese twin girls — joined at the head (they had totally different personalities and frequently fought with each other; one wanted to be a country western singer) — and Lee Redmond, the woman whom at the time, had the world's longest fingernails. Lee's nails were each about three feet long. Several people, mainly in India, had individual nails much longer, but every nail of hers, on both hands, were at least two-feet long. She walked with four bodyguards around her to prevent people from bumping into her. She baffled everyone. Everyone wanted to know "But why?" and how she did simple tasks, like opening doors, or wiping herself in the bathroom (she would later demonstrate this on the popular daytime TV show "Ellen DeGeneres" in a comic set-up of epic proportions). Ripley's would do a couple things with her over the years, but eventually her nails were broken in a car accident, and Ripley's had to go back to India for a replacement person.

In addition to featuring odd people at the NYC odditorium, we also did press conferences and contests in the lobby, including my judging a toilet paper wedding dress contest (an annual event that Ripley's took part in for several years), and a couple art contests — one winner made an elaborate lady's outfit out of human hair, and another did a portrait of Darth Vader out of staples, but the "biggest" deal we ever did was bringing Khagendra Magar, from Nepal, the world's smallest man, to the city and the odditorium to promote a book launch. Norm Deska, Ripley's Executive VP of Intellectual Property, and his staff, had arranged the tour, but I had been asked to be the spokesman, and to be Khagendra's handler. We also brought our then staff videographer, the late Todd Day, to film the entire weekend's events. Despite Khangendra's minuscule size — twenty-six-inches tall, and weighing a mere nineteen pounds — this was a big job.

Everything was scheduled, but nothing pre-planned could really prepare us for some of the difficulties we would face, the first, and most serious, being his inability to walk for more than a few feet at a time. Norm chastised me repeatedly for not letting him loose on the ground, but I felt compelled to carry him like a baby not just for his comfort, but also for his safety. The first time we let him walk around Times Square he was almost trampled; no one scrambles hurriedly along Broadway looking at the ground! At one point he was actually rescued by a very muscular policeman; it made for a terrific photo op.

The second big problem was we didn't have a high chair or a child's booster chair. No matter where we went to eat, he couldn't reach the table. At one Indian restaurant the owner folded about a dozen tablecloths on his chair to raise him to table level; another great photo

170

op.

Scheduled appearances in addition to the initial press conference at the museum — where Khagendra demonstrated his karate moves and was photographed on my shoulders with the wax figure of 8'11" Robert Wadlow, the world's tallest man — included a trip to the top of the Empire State Building; a visit to a Nepalese Buddhist Temple; a stop at a fire station, where Khagendra got to spray me with the hose, wear an honorary fire hat, and sit in the driver's seat of a fire truck; a carriage ride through Central Park (he hand fed a horse a car-rot, but to everyone's horror, the horse swallowed his arm right up to his shoulder); and a visit to a famous deli.

The deli was a terrible mistake. Seemingly, no one con-sidered the fact that Khagendra was a vegetarian whose daily food intake was only four ounces. Not only would he not eat the half-pound pastrami sandwich, it was too big for him to hold. In the end, he ate the bread, he liked the hot mustard — and he posed standing on the deli's counter with a giant salami with me supporting him. This photo is still on the restaurant's wall — a neighbor of mine in Florida delights in sending me pic-tures of it every time he goes to New York. I have only been up the Empire State Building once since visiting with Khagendra, but I believe they too still display a picture of Khagendra and I on their wall of fame at the top of the building.

Our most touching moment with Khagendra happened in a quiet waiting room when we showed him a photo of the world's smallest woman, Jyoti Amge, from India. The photo was in a Ripley book, and showed her beautifully dressed in traditional Indian clothing, life size at twenty-five inch tall (weighing a mere eleven lbs.). It was love at first sight. The couple would eventually meet, and famously toured together, but the romance never fully blossomed.

Our tour was a great publicity success, and helped sell a lot of books. Our movie was also one of the best Todd ever made, but the story didn't have a happy ending. As a result of all the media attention Khagendra received at our hands, a smaller man, Chandra Bahadur Dangi, on-ly nineteen-inches tall, and also from Nepal, came for-

171

ward, and stole Khagendra's crown as "the world's small-est man" before the second leg of Khagendra's Ripley tour in England had even started.

Hypertrichosis: Larry Gomez and Supatra Sasu-phan

It was at the opening of the Times Square Odditorium where I met my first werewolf -or at least someone suffering from hypertrichosis, aka "werewolf syndrome".

Several members of the Gomez family of Guadalajara, Mexico, are afflicted by this strange disease, the obvious symptom being, excessive body hair, including

full facial hair. The tradition of persons with hyper-tricholsis being called "dogs", "lions", or "wolves", goes back at least as far as P.T. Barnum and the 19th century when "Jo-Jo the Dog Faced Boy", and "Lionel the Lion-Faced Prince", toured with circus sideshows. Both these performers had unbelievable — fabricated-origin stories, but in fact were simply hairy people with this particular genetic disorder hypertrichosis. Two of the Gomez brothers had appeared on a Ripley-Dean Cain Show (twice in fact), so getting Larry to appear in New York was easily arranged. He had never been to the big city, and though excited, he was also very nervous about how he would be received. Speaking no English would be a handicap.

My personal contact with Larry was not extensive. I interviewed him through a translator, my administrative assistant, Viviana Ray (2003-2008), introduced him to the media, and we had a late-night dinner with him. I probably gawked as much as anyone. His body hair was thick, long, and very black; it wasn't much of a stretch to see why he was called a "wolf boy", or were-wolf. He did no circus tricks that day, he simply talked and answered endless questions: "How often do you shave?" "How many bottles of shampoo do you use in a week?" and the most embarrassing, "Is it real?". "Can I feel your face"?

Viviana was a warm, caring person with a heart as big as the sky. She also spoke Spanish. She virtually adopted Larry that day, being more like a sister than a handler. I was never more proud of her. About ten o'clock that night after a twelve-hour media circus, she insisted we take Larry across the street to a second-floor rib joint. There may have been eight or ten of us in total, but otherwise the restaurant was empty. In the first quiet moments of the day, Viviana took charge, and we learned more about Larry and his family than we had all day. He showed us pictures, and explained that the circus was the only job option available for him. He had been miserable all day, and had only taken this gig because he needed the money; normally he did not do press conferences and photo ops. I was ashamed, but never so happy to break bread with someone outside my comfort zone. It was a beautiful meal full of love and laughter. God certainly works in mysterious ways.

In Bangkok, Thailand, three years later, on a book tour, I put the word out that I was eager to meet Supatra Susuphan, a young girl stricken with hypertrichosis — another "werewolf". Supatra had been featured in a Ripley book, and (probably) unbeknownst to her, was quite a celebrity in America thanks to Ripley's. Her hair was even longer than Larry's, and blonde in color. She was reported to be only six years old. I hunted around Bangkok unsuccessfully for her for a couple days, but had given up on the mission by the time I got to the Ripley odditorium in the nearby beach town of Pattaya. The odditorium manager there, Somporn Naksuestrong, however, had also been looking for her on my behalf.

Pattaya is a strange town, full of pornography, and "Ladyboys" sex shows, appealing originally to American soldiers on leave from Vietnam, but later exploding to attract both American and Asian tourists. At least at first glance, it doesn't seem to be a logical place for a family museum attraction. It does have a lengthy beach, but even this is somewhat seedy and dirty. It totally lacks the charm, history, and beauty of Bangkok. It is not some place I would ever want to go back to again.

My five-star hotel was a short walk away from the museum (located in a three-story shopping mall) with a shortcut option along the beach. On my second day there I took the beach route to the odditorium. To my utter

173

surprise, I walked past Supatra and her family having a meager breakfast under a palm tree on the beach; I suspect they may have slept there the night before. I speak only two words of Thai — pad thai — so I was jumping up and down with excitement. I am sure I appeared to be a crazy person as I wildly gestured for them to either stay put, or to follow me, but somehow, they understood, and agreed to stay where they were. I flew down the street, pushed through several people, climbed the escalator to the third floor, and panting and sweating, got out that I needed a staff member to follow me. Somporn, the only person I really knew, and the only person I knew who could speak both fluent English and Thai, was not available. A young lady who knew me only by photo and reputation, understood my urgent babblings, and agreed reluctantly to follow me. I regret I did not get her name, but she was a Godsend.

The Susuphan family luckily was right where I had left them. My young translator was suddenly as excited as I was, and revealed that Somporn had in fact talked to the father the day before and invited them to the odditorium. They, however, had not found the building and were contemplating leaving town. Miracles do happen.

Inside the mall, Somporn managed to get a television crew to come and meet Supatra and myself. We did an impromptu photo shoot and toured the museum together. For such a young person, she was totally poised and unflustered by anything — except for the clowns in Somporn's "dark ride" attraction. Clowns scared her. No one else in her family suffered from hypertrichosis, and they were torn by indecision on what to do regarding "exploitation", but it was clear they accepted her, loved her and lived for her happiness. My photos with Supatra are amongst my most treasured Ripley possessions. This young lady taught me more in one morning about love, respect, and human dignity, than I could ever have imagined.

The Incredible Daredevils: Dave Munday & Stein Hoff

I met a lot of people whom most people would call weird. Benny, a guy who let people staple money to his body — ones to his chest, fives, tens and twenties to

174

his face — I am sure was really crazy by anybody's definition, but people who challenged the elements, as well as themselves, are a different kind of strange. To be honest, I certainly don't understand them, and shudder at their audacity, but I also admire them. Their brain and thought processes are definitely different from the norm, but to call them crazy seems to dismiss the facts that they themselves seem to be perfectly aware of their irrationality, and that they are organized, determined, meticulous and even, I would say, heroic, in their endeavors. Dave Munday, a man who went over Niagara Falls in a barrel, not once, but twice (!), and Stein Hoff a seventy-year old who attempted to row solo across the Atlantic Ocean, are my poster boys for this kind of unexplainable crazy heroic behavior.

Almost immediately after Jimmy Pattison bought Ripley's in 1985, we started to renovate the then existing Ripley odditoriums, Gatlinburg in 1985-86, Niagara Falls in 1987, Myrtle Beach in 1988, San Francisco and St. Augustine in 1989. Bob Masterson piloted the ship through the physical reconstruction of these shows, but my involvement in providing new exhibitory was paramount to the next generation level of improvement Jimmy was demanding. Niagara Falls was the first Ripley's odditorium I had ever been in, and at that time, probably the only one I had been in more than once. It was also the one where my family was most likely to visit, and either praise me or criticize me for. I was totally invested, I wanted it to be the new gold standard.

Working with two designers who would become life-long friends and associates, Norm Rollingson, and Anton Gosley, it was decided the cornerstone gallery would be about the daredevils of Niagara Falls, the historical personages that had gone over the Falls in wooden barrels and other contraptions in the early 20th century — everyone from Blondin, the tightrope walker, to William "Red" Hill Jr, the rapids runner, to Jean Lussier, who went over in a giant rubber ball, and was subsequently interviewed years later by Robert Ripley on one of his live, on-location radio broadcasts, recorded from behind the Falls.

I was able to find dozens of photos and cartoons, and the company already owned some Blondin exhibits — a costume, a bike and a wheelbarrow in which Blondin had pushed a lion across the Falls — but we would need something none of the other local attractions had, something to make our display unique. I found it in a guy named Dave Munday.

Dave was a local engineer by trade, well-educated and well respected in his field. He had studied the history of the daredevils in great detail, and could tell you what each of them had done wrong, or right, in their attempts to conquer the Falls. I first met him, with my wife Giliane, over breakfast in a greasy spoon diner about thirty minutes outside of the Falls area, the day before he was going to go over the Falls in a metal barrel of his construction. He was as calm as a man could be, and had not considered failure — death — as an outcome. In minute detail he described the construction of his barrel, and where and how he was going to enter the river (an illegal process, thus our secret meeting). What was going to make his trip very different from that of his predecessors was that he was going to have a video camera attached to the inside of his barrel. He was going to film the whole trip. If he died, people would be able to see his last moments on Earth. I not only didn't think him crazy, I thought him brilliant. In less than ninety-minutes he convinced me that there was no way he would die, and that I should buy his video. It was a no-brainer.

Dave did indeed survive, and though it didn't quite go as smoothly as he had foretold, he suffered no major injuries. He was fined, and the barrel was confiscated, but Ripley's got the film. To be honest the film isn't very visual. For the most part all you see is white water, a stonewall, the edge, then nothing. It is, however, terrifying, unique, and worth every penny I paid. There is no other film like it in the world, and it is unlikely there ever will be.

Dave went over the Falls a second time a couple years later, but without a camera. He is the only person to ever conquer the Falls twice.

Judge for yourself if he is crazy or not. He clearly knew exactly what he was doing, and rationally planned both trips methodically to beat the odds and assure survival. I wouldn't attempt it for all the money in the world, but he did it twice just for a little glory.

I was first introduced to Norway's Stein Hoff on May
15th, 2016, about fourteen hours before he would get in
a small twenty-four-foot long, by four-foot wide, wood
and metal row boat and start rowing across the Atlantic
Ocean — solo — from New York City to the Isles of Sicily, off the southwest coast of England. I had known
about Stein and his mission for a couple months, but it
wasn't until I saw this seventy-year old, tall, wiry,
muscle-bound man in person, in the bottom of New York's
"Norwegian Sailor's Church" (the Viking Church to me),
surrounded by friends, and other sailing adventurers,
that I believed the mission was humanly possible.

I was at Stein's farewell dinner party at the invitation of another Viking sailor, Victor Samuelsen, a distant relative of Gabriel Samuelsen, who in 1896, along
with George Harbor, had been the first two people to
row a boat across the Atlantic. Their story was featured in the very first Ripley book in 1929 and in the
syndicated newspaper cartoon a couple years earlier. I
had been talking with Victor for a couple months by
this time regarding another boat — Ripley's Chinese
Junk, the Mon Lei, which was owned by a friend of Victor's, but I had only met him a few hours earlier at
his home in Connecticut. We had driven around in a fancy Mercedes, and picked up a giant cake at a favorite
bakery. At one point he gave me the keys to the car — a
virtual stranger — while he got in an even fancier car
(a 1930s Duesenberg), and told me to follow him. Going
much faster than I was comfortable at in an unfamiliar
$200,000 car, we raced the country-style roads of
Greenwich like mad men; Victor was determined not to be
late for Stein's send-off, which I would later realize
he had organized and financed.

Dressed sartorially in yachting blue and white, Stein
looked more or less like any other seventy-year old. It
wasn't until he took off his jacket — and later his
shirt, replacing it with a branded Ripley's Believe It
or Not! rowing shirt — that one could perceive his
rock-hard chest and bulging biceps. In body if not in
face he looked like a Norwegian god. I was astonished
that someone that old could look that strong and fit.
If anybody seventy -years old could row across the

Atlantic Ocean by himself, this was the guy to do it. I
was convinced he wasn't crazy, and would succeed.

The evening was full of speechifying, and a lengthy slide show by Stein detailing his planned route and displaying his food supply, lovingly made and packed by his wife Diana — who had a few years back at the age of fifty-five, rowed across the Atlantic from Africa to South America (the so-called "short" route). There was a Norwegian opera singer named Lis Daehlin, who performed a couple of songs, most notably, a ballad about Harbo and Samuelsen that everyone but me knew the lyrics to and sang along to with great gusto. I really felt I was at a Viking banquet. By the time I presented a framed copy of the original Ripley rowing cartoon to Stein, and outlined that Ripley planned to report the trip daily on the company website, and if Stein was successful, we would acquire the boat and gear, I felt like I was spiritually part of this very unique and special family that was about to embark on a once in a life time unbelievable voyage.

The next morning at 6 am the entire party group met in Battery Park to board a giant sailing ship to escort Stein in his boat, the Fox II, out of the harbor to the Bayonne Bridge. Stein appeared promptly at 7 am already rowing. Several people had told me that because of cross currents and lots of boat traffic — including the Staten Island Ferry — that the harbor would actually be one of the hardest parts of Stein's trip. He didn't expect to get more than about twenty miles this first day.

It was quite cold, and the water was rough. It was impossible not to feel worried as Stein seemed to take one row forward and two rows back, dodging the ferry, and just about being swamped by a ship before he had gone fifteen minutes. At one point, a good friend in a Zodiac boat, actually had to pull Stein away from the rocky shore as we all watched in fear.

The atmosphere on the schooner was strange. Some people were exuberant, and couldn't stop talking about the magnitude of Stein's voyage, others, like me, who had never been on a ship of this size were enjoying the wind, the waves, and the sunrise. Some, specifically Stein's wife, were sullen, aloof, and clearly lost in thought. Would she ever see her husband again?

Eventually Stein got into the central current lane, and

stood up in his boat for a farewell photo as he passed the Statue of Liberty. It was the last anyone would see of him for eighty-four days.

Stein's boat, though simple in construction, was equipped with several life-saving gadgets, including ship to shore radio, flares, a GPS system, and a computer on which Stein wrote a daily diary that he sent to Ripley's and fellow rowers. As promised, we broadcasted his journal around the world via **Ripleys.com.** For the most part, the journal is not exciting reading — not a lot happens. Stein describes in detail the weather, and what, and when he eats, and the occasional siting of whales and albatrosses, but one day is pretty much the same as the rest. One can try to imagine the physical fatigue and the mental boredom he was experiencing, but still it is impossible to really comprehend the lack of comfort and difficulty of every minute of his lonely existence.

Stein went overboard briefly on his second full day (he was able to get back in the boat without too much trouble, but everything was wet for days afterwards), and within the first two weeks was miles off course. He wound up off the Grand Banks of Newfoundland engulfed for days in fog. By the time he got back on track, he had traveled almost twice the original planned distance of the entire trip (roughly 2,000 miles) and it was clear he would not be able to complete the journey in the hoped for ninety days (he had rations for 120 days — his worst-case scenario). On day 80 he realized he was in the path of an oncoming hurricane. The sense of danger in his last journal entries is electric. He was wet, hungry, exhausted and for the first time, scared. When his anchor and one of his oars broke on day 82, he knew he was finished. On day 83, he sent out distress signals that were received in Ireland. On day 84, he was refused by a ship bound for Canada. It was August 10th. On my calendar I had noted months before, I was to meet him in Hugh Town, on St. Mary's, the Isles of Sicily, on August 14th. He eventually got there by plane after recovering in Montreal, Canada, but I didn't.

The story of his rescue and safe return to Canada was shown on every news station across the world. The footage of him being lifted aboard his rescue ship while the Fox II was being beaten by twenty-foot high waves, is hard to watch. His boat could not be rescued. Stein himself appeared rail thin, haggard, and, unrecognizable as the bold determined Viking of three months earlier.

With no boat to display, I was somewhat deflated, and defeated. As a media event we had done well for eighty-four days, and I did get photos, video, and a few pieces of gear (his well-worn rowing gloves, his Ripley branded shirt, and his butt pad), that could be displayed, but without "success" the story lost its gloss (6). It was certainly noteworthy that he had tried, but that he wasn't successful, took out the "un-believable-ness" of the adventure. Anybody could "try" to row across the Atlantic, but unless you succeeded, where was the "wow" factor? We did feature Stein in that year's annual book, but we soon quietly distanced ourselves from the near tragedy. The story was gone, and soon forgotten……until nine months later.

Throughout the remainder of 2016 and for much of 2017, I continued to chat with Victor about the Mon Lei, and was determined to acquire it (see Chapter 78). One day in May he called very excited: Stein's boat the Fox II, after nine months at sea, had been found! Most people had thought, that without an inhabitant, the boat had probably sunk back in August. Stein and Victor had been more optimistic and figured it might still come ashore near Ireland (the nearest coast Stein was headed for when he abandoned ship), at any time. Ironically, it found its way back to its mother country.

The boat was discovered high and dry near seventy-degree latitude north on the shore of the Norwegian Island of Spildra, not too far from Stein's home town, by fourteen-year old Trgve Tideman Bjorklund and his father, while fishing. It was frozen solid, but relatively undamaged. Both Stein and Victor were determined to reclaim it as soon as the weather allowed, and hoped Ripley's would still be interested in buying it. Sadly, we weren't. Stein was heartbroken.

I was invited to join them the following month for their journey by barge-ferry and foot to Spildra. I was scheduled to be nearby in Copenhagen, and could have, should have, made the trip. It would have made a great full circle to this Viking saga. I, however, reluctantly declined.

Victor was fully vested in Stein and the Fox II. He has had a bronze statue of Harbor and Samuelsen in their Fox I erected in his home town in Norway, and paid to preserve and display the Fox II in a shopping mall in Stein's home town.

In forty years at Ripley's, Stein Hoff was the second most amazing individual I had the pleasure of meeting. Someday in his honor I hope to sing a verse or two of the ballad of the great Viking rowers at the base of Victor's two worthy monuments to adventure, stamina, tenacity, and unbelievable courage:

"We'll see you in France or we'll see you in Heaven

Cried Harbo and Samuelsen out on the bay

Two hardy young oystermen after adventure

And no one believed they could row all the way." (7)

(James Bryant -1985).

I Got the Best Mail

I always got the best mail. I loved getting my daily mail, and almost always opened it myself, wanting to be the first to be surprised by the really good stuff, say a shrunken head, or a collection of belly button lint, or the umpteenth letter claiming the writer had made the world's smallest origami crane. I once got a strawberry that the sender thought looked like Mae West, but by the time I got it, it looked exactly like a giant red stain. Some of the things I received were really quite remarkable. I always used Federal Express if I was shipping anything of value, but what can be sent via regular mail is quite extraordinary. The post office has a pretty bad rap, but not from me. They have a tough job, and I loved George Householder (sic), the regular Ripley postman.

For nearly three decades, I held an annual exhibit contest just for company employees, but every now and then I held a contest open to the general public. The goal was always the same — to get new exhibits for the collection — but the style of the contest always varied. I only did the exact same contest twice, in 2013-2014, and this was because it was the best contest I ever devised. I called it **Ripley's Strange Mail Contest**.

Long before me, Robert Ripley had annual contests, and got weird mail, but he never solicited it, his just arrived. I never had a contest that was even remotely comparable to the successes Ripley had, but my prizes weren't quite in the same league either. The idea for my mail contest came directly from my daughter, Celeste, who at the time lived 100 miles away in the town of Gainesville, Florida. Birthdays are a big deal in our family, and because she wouldn't be able to come home to celebrate mine, she made a very realistic fake piece of chocolate birthday cake out of window caulking and a sponge and mailed it to me. It had a piece of cardboard attached to it bearing the address, and a short letter of apology. The stamp was on the cardboard. The cake looked so real that if I displayed it non-sign side forward, people thought it was real. When I showed them I had received it via the mail, they were baffled [1].

For my two mail contests I challenged Ripley fans to send me **any- thing** — absolutely anything, no restrictions as to content, size, age, etc. The only restriction, or rule, was that whatever was sent had to be sent with no packaging of any sort, and had to be sent by regular post — no couriers allowed. The address and the postage had to be directly on the object.

According to the post office, they would guarantee delivery of anything except perishable food. One of the first things I received was a chocolate bar. This was followed a couple days later by a giant zucchini from New Jersey — the Garden State. More food would follow. Clearly there was no real restrictions. I believe the postmen had more fun with this contest than the players, or myself. George who actually brought the stuff into the lobby of Ripley's, loved it so much, he would often request if he could personally come into my office and hand deliver the best of the entries. He wanted to see my expression when he handed me a birdcage, or a fifteen-pound bowling ball.

With the help of an article in **USA Today**, a pair of articles from Dewayne Bevil at the **Orlando Sentinel**, and some radio interviews, the first year was a huge success, over 200 different eligible items received from twenty-seven different states, and three foreign countries. The most oft-repeated item was rolls of toilet paper — light and cheap to mail. I did get some small things, like a toothbrush, and a nametag, but small things ran the risk of being too easily lost. Repeat players soon learned that to guarantee delivery the object needed to cost at least a couple bucks to mail, and the bigger the object, the more likely it would win a prize. I gave regular weekly prizes for my favorite, and at the end of sixteen weeks, I gave one grand prize, and also a prize for the item that had come the furthest.

In Year One the item that came the furthest had come from Copenhagen, Denmark. It was a hardcover book by John Tingey titled: **The Englishman who Posted Himself and Other Curious Objects.** The cover had more than a dozen stamps on it and the address was written both on the cover and along the edge of the exposed pages. It is an excellent book about the exact same thing I was doing. The sender clearly had a sense of humor, and really grasped the spirit of the contest.

So, what could possibly beat that for best overall item? Not an inflatable six-foot tall pink flamingo, not a rubber Halloween skeleton, not even a five-foot tall Raggedy Ann doll that had cost $65.00 to mail from North Carolina. The winner had only traveled a few miles from nearby Kissimmee, Florida, but against all odds, and the official Post Offices rules, I received a McDonalds' hamburger, fries and apple pie glued to a paper plate with the address on the reverse of the plate. It was real food seemingly untouched by postal hands. Somehow it stayed "fresh" for over four years; we displayed it in our Atlantic City odditorium until it finally disintegrated.

The second year of the contest was not quite as successful as the first. We did get more items, and from more states, but the "quality" slipped considerably. Perhaps the prizes weren't enough of an enticement. The biggest item, an effigy of myself tied like a hostage to a chair, was a little unnerving, but was disqualified as it had come by UPS. The item that traveled the furthest was a plastic toy from Ireland. The item that won the prize for "best", however, was exceptional: a large twenty-four inch in diameter slice of a tree with a horseshoe in the middle! The tree had grown up around the horseshoe, which was only found years later when the tree was chopped down.

The iron shoe was embedded so firmly that you could carry the twenty-pound tree slice, like a purse, using the horseshoe as a handle. It had traveled about 500 miles from North Carolina, and was by far the most expensive thing mailed we received.

A couple other items of note from both years that will attest to how much fun this contest was include:

> a large three-foot long hand-painted home décor fan that had the address painted on the handle, and could only be read when the fan was shut. The stamps were on the spines of the fan, and could only be seen if the fan was opened. It also had a personal message painted on the paper folds. The post office had to have been very patient to deter-

184

mine if this one would get delivered.

a deck of cards that was mailed one card at a time. Forty-eight of the fifty-two found their way.

a deer skull

a very large bra

several diapers — thankfully not used

a Casper the Friendly ghost doll with a suspicious bloodstain

a headless mermaid doll — I suspect she was decapitated en route

a plastic lawn flamingo in a birdcage

the aforementioned bowling ball — complete with a face made of stickers

a large inflatable monkey in a coconut tree floating pool toy

and a large yellow metal mailbox with my name painted on the side!

Say what you will, but it seems to me the post office does a pretty **unbelievable** job.

28

Manager's Meeting Expeditions

In Search of the Fountain of Youth.

History books will tell you tell you that Ponce de Leon discovered Florida while searching for the Fountain of Youth. The suspected spot is well designated in St. Augustine, Florida, so imagine my surprise when I was told by "locals" in Baja, California, that the real Fountain of Youth was in the Baja desert about sixty miles north east of Cabo San Lucas. The one in St. Augustine had done nothing for my aging, so I had nothing to lose by going out for an adventure from Cabo in search of the much less known Fountain.

A short digression before I get in the jeep....

Every year since 1970, the management of Ripley's has held a company-wide manager's meeting originally in the winter, but moved to the fall a few years ago. Bob Masterson, I believe attended 37 of these, and was in charge for roughly half of them. He picked the time and place, and who would attend. He faithfully carried on a tradition started by Alec Rigby, then continued by John Withers until his departure in 1988. Of the forty-seven meetings there have now been, only two were in Northern climes, one in Quebec City, and one in Toronto. The other forty-five have been in the Southern States, Mexico, the Caribbean, and once in Hawaii. I attended thirty-four consecutive such meetings, and it was at one of these in the winter of 1992, that I was in Cabo San Lucas with approximately forty other Ripley employees.

The people, at least the tourists, in Cabo drink a lot, and pictorial evidence suggest I held my own. The revelation that there was a local Fountain of Youth, came in a bar called Senor' Frogs, after several tequilas: margaritas, sunrises, and straight up. That I, or my traveling companions were fit for a jeep ride through the desert the next morning is a Mexican miracle. We were told it wasn't far, but that it would take several hours — by most people's definition there was no **road**

once you left town. There would be a few markers, however, and we were advised to ask directions of anyone we
met, just to make sure we were still going the right
direction.

I had three musketeers who were willing to spend their
day-off on a wild goose chase: Anton Gosley from Niagara Falls, Canada, Ian Iljas, from San Francisco, and
Klaus Broge from Copenhagen, Denmark. Klaus spoke only
broken English, but better Spanish. His linguistics
skills came in handy more than once; he rode shotgun.
Anton drove the rented jeep, and Ian and I, sat in the
back "navigating". We had very few supplies, but we did
have a very good bottle of 1978 Gingrich Hills, char-
donnay (from Napa, California), which Ian had brought
to the meeting as a gift for me, knowing it was my then
favorite wine.

We set off before 8 am. Once out of town, and off the
coast, the scenery was very generic: sand, tumbleweed,
saguaro cactus, a couple of the most emaciated cows on
earth — it was very apparent why Mexican beef was not
to be ordered in Cabo — and one or two small adobe
farms. The occasional hand painted signpost pointing to
a town many miles distant, helped us stay on the un-
beaten near in-visible path. Animals may have used this
trail, but there was no sign of tire marks nearly the
entire day. It was hot, and got hotter by the hour. We
had nothing to keep the wine cold.

At about 1 pm, after five hours of brutal heat, and bone
shaking progress, we came to an oasis: a small but modern, building, with a cement patio, a vegetable farm,
and an idyllic calm ocean bay front. It was one of the
most beautiful views I had ever seen, cliffs, blue-
green clear water, and a giant sailboat moored just off
shore. There was no one in sight, on land or in the water. There was, however, comfortable and inviting beach
chairs on the patio. We were exhausted and had no real
sense of how much further we still had to go; we were
definitely discussing giving up and heading back to
Cabo. We decided we would at least take a seat, and
think about our options. Within seconds of our sitting,
a woman — a vision — -appeared out of we don't know
where. In Spanish she asked us if we would like a
drink?

"Si, gracias." We shouted in unison. "Cervesas?" "Si"!

"Cuatro"?

"Si!"

She quietly, shyly, backed away, and disappeared into the house. We were amazed, absolutely astonished.

Moments later she reappeared as quietly and unexpectedly as she had the first time.

She asked us if we wanted lunch, but we didn't understand, beyond hand gestures suggesting food. We again said "Si".

As if afraid to turn her back on us, she again silently backed away.

When she appeared a third time, she was accompanied by an American man not much older than us. He owned the house, and was the woman's husband. He had sailed the boat in the cove by himself from San Francisco two years previously – an escaping "lost" hippy, looking for God, or whatever he might find. The cove appealed to him, so he landed, and never left. His dream was to live right here, and avoid mankind as much as possible. He was self-sufficient with the small garden, and fish. He went to "town" only once every couple of months. His wife would be happy to make us tacos. Would we like meat or fish? Unanimously, we said fish. He said it would take a few minutes, and offered us more beer. We accepted, but told him we would pay for them. He didn't expect our money, but was grateful for it. We asked him if by any chance we could put our wine in his fridge in the hopes we could drink it with our lunch. He said "no problem". As we talked a bit more, the wife went back into the house and produced four more beers. The couple dismissed themselves and left us to enjoy the cold beer and the view. We were in heaven.

Moments later, with fishing rod in one hand, and a bucket in the other, our host strolled down to the beach, perhaps thinking we hadn't seen him. He proceeded to catch our lunch! Within minutes his bucket was full of some unknown long mackerel-like fish, enough for twenty people to feast on. He smiled as he returned to the house, pleased with himself. A few more minutes passed, and he came out and greeted us again. Stating the obvious, he said it was too warm to eat outside, we must come into his house. We did not argue.

His wife was still rolling and cooking tortillas, but the table was beautifully set, complete with wine glasses, and all the ingredients for our feast were chopped and ready: cilantro, onions, tomatoes, chilies, and a bowl of guacamole. The six of us ate and drank together. The wine never tasted better, and the tacos were the best I've ever eaten. We were the first people they had seen in weeks, and the first to be in their house in over a year.

While eating we divulged our mission, and our host laughed uproariously. First, he said, we were quite lost. Second, we had barely dinted our journey despite five hours on the "road" — much of it in the wrong direction. Fundamentally we had gone in a circle, and at an average of less than twenty miles per hour we hadn't gone but about one-fifth of our trail...but he told us not to worry, he could put us on the right path, and we should be able to get there and back to Cabo, in about another four or five hours. He drew us maps much more detailed than ours; he clearly knew the area quite well. He did not tell us the trip was a waste of our time, because he could tell the camaraderie, the trip itself, was more important than the goal. He did, however, laughingly, inform us by way of a real map, that by water we had traveled less than fifteen miles. We were the first guests that they had ever had that had come upon them by land. Tequila drinking boat tours came close to their hidden cove two or three times a day; Klaus mentioned he had already been on one of these. Unbelievable. We drank to his health, and he drank to our sense of adventure. No doubt he thought we shared some of the bravado that had made him leave San Francisco and start his life anew in the wilds of Baja.

Even if I had of kept our maps, I wouldn't have told you dear reader, how to find the Fountain. It is a secret that must be sought, not read about. Our new maps were indeed very helpful as they soon placed us on real roads, not highways, but recognizable as roads, complete with mileage signs. We did still have to stop for directions more than once, but as we got closer, we did come upon more people, most of who were going to the

189

same place.

It was nearly 6 pm when we found the Fountain, that is to say the three-foot by two-foot mosquito infested stagnant cement pond that had been built around the trickle of a natural spring. My three companions howled with laughter, and groaned with disgust. We watched several locals, one at a time, wash their faces and hands, and one woman doused her naked infant all the way into the foot-deep cesspool. It was very apparent my amigos were not going to dare the pond, but I was resolute. In the nearby bush, I exchanged my shorts for my bathing suit, and proceeded to sit down in the mini-swamp. The temperature was soothing and cool. I could understand why someone at one point must have thought it had healing powers, but I didn't dare dab my face in it. Of course, I should never have gone anywhere near it.

The drive home was long and exhausting. Like Gilligan, our three-hour tour, ended up taking fourteen, but like Ulysses, we returned as heroes. Miraculously I did not get sick. I had no side effects of any sort, but the tequilas I drank the rest of the week while retelling the tale multiple times, may have killed any germs I had picked up. I was very lucky.

I am not sure Anton was ever at another Ripley's manager's meeting, but I know he still has photos of this one that can verify my story. Klaus did go to a few more meetings, but we never got close; I am not really sure we ever said more than hello after that trip. Ian and I were already friends, having met years previously, and would remain meeting buddies as long as we both still attended, and past that date too.

The Road to Hana

I doubt a year went by when Ian and I didn't have a manager's meeting adventure of some sort. Most involved world-class restaurants,

and great wine, as Ian is quite the gourmand (and gourmet chef too), but only one other involved a road trip adventure of misery, fun and frivolity.

In 1996 the group, by this time approaching 100 in size, went to Maui, Hawaii. In 1983 there had been no

190

meeting, so Hawaii was a special treat to celebrate the 25th anniversary of the manager's meeting functions. It was the furthest the company ever ventured, and until that time the biggest group ever assembled (1). It was also the first, and maybe only meeting, every franchisee attended.

For our day-off excursion Ian and I, and a few others, specifically the family of Ed Wideman (wife Laura, and three of their young sons), our then franchisee of the Atlantic City, Ripley Odditorium, had decided to scale — by car — the road to Hana, a treacherous, but beautiful six to eight-hour road to the top of Haleakala National Park and volcano (2). The highway is nicknamed both **the Highway to Heaven**, and **the Highway to Hell**. For me it was more hell than heaven.

The road is steep and full of hairpin turns. The scenery is gorgeous, provided you keep your eyes open and actually see it — many people don't. We started as two carloads. I was driving one car, with Ian, a lady named Barbara Wilson (the only year she was invited to the meeting), and a gentleman from Jakarta, Indonesia whose name I have forgotten (conveniently). It was his only meeting, as the Ripley Jakarta odditorium lasted less than six months, no real fault of his, but he probably didn't help things much. In the other car, was the Wideman family.

I don't really believe anyone had fun that day, as all of us had some combination of elevation and motion sickness. I managed not to whoop my cookies,

but recall there were times I thought I would. We made numerous stops, some for scenery, but more just to get fresh air. The higher we went, the more frequent the stops. About half way up the mountain, Ed signaled that he wanted us to pull over. His youngest son had vomited, their car smelled horrible, and his passengers wanted to turn around and go back.

My car was not for quitting — yet — but Ian got out and returned down the mountain with Ed. I took the one healthy Wideman child with me, waved goodbye, and continued. Before much longer, son #2 was ill too. Luckily, not in the car, but still at least partially on him-self. Our crowded car now smelled particularly funky. I don't think we got to the end of the road — I do not remember the volcano at all, but we got to the Keane lookout spot, took a couple pictures, and turned right around for the six to eight-hour trip back down the mountain.

Around 4 pm we came across a lone female hiker. I drove slowly passed her thinking she would not get off the mountain before dark. She had equipment, and possibly was not concerned about the dark, but I was. I came to my senses quickly, and asked my four passengers, if we could make room for her. We agreed we could, and should. I backed up, and we picked up the young lady, perhaps twenty years of age. We put her backpack in the trunk and she squeezed in with Barbara, and next to "name-less" Jakarta. Wideman #2 moved to the front with me.

Luckily the descent was much easier on our nerves, and our stomachs, than the climb up had been. Barbara asked the bare minimum polite questions of our visitor, who revealed she was American, and had been traveling for over six months. She had recently been in Indonesia, and could speak a little of the language. I am not sure how it came up, but she openly discussed how to piss standing up with Barbara, in case she had to go before we reached civilization at the bottom. Probably from prudish horror, Barbara stopped talking with her. She then turned to "name-less", and conversing in his native tongue didn't stop talking to him for several hours, n'er a word of English escaping from either of their mouths. As we approached the bottom, and nightfall, she gave me directions where she would like to be let off. By this time, I was more than eager to jettison her anywhere.

What none of us expected, however, was that "nameless" got out with her! He said his goodbyes, conveyed he was going to spend the night with her, and may or may not see us tomorrow. He was grateful for the adventure, and shook my hand vigorously, thanking me for having stopped for the hiker. I took her pack out of the trunk, and never saw either of them again.

I know we did see some fabulous exotic flowers, and some spectacular waterfalls, but I would need to go to Hana again to tell you much else. Upon my return to Florida, when I was telling my neighbor of the trip, he laughed and told me he too had been to Hana, but he had flown. Apparently, there was a helicopter that flew to the top about every fifteen minutes. He was there and back in less than one hour. My trip had taken fourteen hours. He wondered out loud what kind of fool was I to have driven it.

Combining my thirty-four Ripley Manager's Meetings, with seventeen Pattison Group meetings, and roughly 100 Pattison Quarterly meetings, it is safe to say I spent a lot of time on the road with Ripley people in different places. I love to travel in general, and Ian was a favorite passenger, but for many places one visit is enough. Baja and Hawaii are two of the places I don't have any real desire to give a second chance too. As the kids of today say: Been there, done that, got the t-shirt.

New Orleans, Post-Hurricane Katrina

I love New Orleans, the people, the food, and the music, are deep within my soul. For a short holiday— an instant pick-me up renewal, there is nowhere I would rather go for a few days. When Ripley's closed the first odditorium on Bourbon Street, I was sad, but it was the right decision. From the beginning we had mistaken people just passing by, having a drink — or six — and having a good time on the street, for customers. We didn't serve alcohol, so they didn't come in. It was a great museum, but short lived, just a mere seven years. Ripley's second location in New Orleans, in Jackson Square, inside the JAX Brewery building, died an even quicker death — less than three years. Its death, however, was from "natural causes", rather than misguided human judgment.

No one could have been happier than I was when Bill Sims, an Orlando businessman, approached Ripley's to build a franchise odditorium in New Orleans. We had been out of the city for ten years, and though some things hadn't changed, some things had. Bourbon Street was still the main avenue of nightlife, but new more family friendly, businesses had sprung up along the river on Decatur Street, and around Jackson Square. In 2003, the time certainly seemed right for a second attempt. That a franchise was willing to take the financial risks, made it an easier decision for corporate office. That Bill had owned other Ripley franchised odditoriums in Ocean City, Maryland, and Key West, Florida, bode well for a good partnership. He knew we had failed in New Orleans once before, but he was willing to gamble.

This second location seemed perfect, a major corner, in a major shopping complex building, with three big draws for neighbors: the St. Louis Cathedral, the Mississippi River, and the world-famous **Café Du Monde** beignets & coffee shop. **Tujagues** restaurant, established in 1856, **The House of Blues** (new since our first odditorium), the **French Market**, and **the Central Grocery Store** (home of the world's best muffuletta sandwich), were also all within walking distance. It was also, coincidentally, right next store to a very good record store, where I spent more than a few hours and a few dollars.

The museum had a small first floor lobby presence, and was primarily on the second floor of the JAX Brewery complex. Signage was small because of Vieux Carré Historic District restrictions, but having a corner, with exposure on two sides, should have been adequate. Visually the show was even better than its predecessor, with the Lee Harvey Oswald assassination vehicle being a primary draw (see Chapter 57). Prior to the odditorium's opening, Bobby Owens, our then director of franchise operations, and myself, had done a major presentation to the city tourist bureau, and we opened with great fanfare and expectations.

Business may not have been as good as we had hoped, but it was decent for the first two years. The worries and fears seemed to have been quelled. On August 29, 2005, however, life in New Orleans changed forever. Hurricane Katrina devastated the city, and though Ripley's physically survived, big nails were driven into our coffin.

Seventeen days after Katrina hit, Bill, his son, Will, and myself, piled into a supply laden SUV and headed west to New Orleans from Orlando. On a good day this is a ten-hour drive. We were prepared for much longer. We knew some bridges were out, and some roads were closed, but until we reached about Mobile, Alabama, we really didn't understand what we were getting ourselves into. At the Louisiana state border, we were detoured north into Mississippi state, and would have to do a big loop of a few hundred miles to enter New Orleans from the northwest of the city. Along the Biloxi coast we had seen dozens of billboards damaged and down, but the highway was too far off the coast for us to see the real horrific damage. Driving north we followed the direct path the hurricane had followed, and saw thousands of downed trees, and other damage of all sorts. The hurricane's path had been perfectly straight — directly up the highway — the path of least resistance.

We entered New Orleans via Lake Pontchartrain, but the trip had taken us fourteen hours, and we missed the 8 pm curfew by a matter of minutes. Our plan had been to sleep in the museum, or the SUV if necessary, as hotels were all booked-up with local survivors, and first responders. Being told we had to turn back, and come back tomorrow, was not in our plan. Cell phones were still in their infancy, and weren't all that reliable in the disaster zone, so the best we could do was drive and pray. After an hour or so of going west, we decided our best bet was to head north on Highway #55, back into Mississippi. It was very dark by this time and in addition to being tired, we were scared. Visions of 1960s racial strife danced in my head. Nothing is more irrational than fear, but, if we ran out of gas we would truly be up Shit's Creek.

Bill drove, Will searched for hotels on his phone, and I looked at an old-fashioned road map. For miles there was nothing. In McComb, we found two small motels, but both were full. Being a hardcore Mississippi Blues fanatic, I associate every little Mississippi town with a musician who came from there. McComb was the birthplace of Ellas McDaniel, aka, Bo Diddley. Staying there would have appealed to me.

It was nearly 2 am when we pulled into a small six room roadside motel in Hazlehurst, and were told there were two rooms available. We had been on the road twenty hours and hadn't had anything but junk food to eat since lunchtime. We shouted for joy, and hugged each other. We would live to fight another day — assuming we could find a gas station in the morning.

I went into my designated room, while Bill and Will shared the other. I was exhausted but I couldn't sleep. All night long — all four hours of it — I couldn't think of why I knew the name of this very small dot on the map town. In the morning it came to me. Though he hadn't spent a lot of time there, Hazlehurst was the birthplace of blues leg-end Robert Johnson, the man who reportedly sold his soul to the devil at a crossroads in the night back in the late 1920s. Chills ran "upside my head and down my spine". Of all the places to land, why here? I took it to be a very serious omen, but I wasn't sure if it would be a good omen or a bad one.

Highway #55 in the daylight didn't seem quite so forlorn, and it was almost comical how little distance we had actually traveled from New Orleans. With luck we managed to find gas. The blues gods, if not the real God, were with us. We figured we should be able to get back into the city in a couple hours, but traffic was bumper-to-bumper almost the entire way back into town so it was past noon when we got to the barriers. I am not sure what Bill had done to receive permission into the city in the first place, but he had the right papers to get us through the blockade. Technically, our museum was out of the disaster zone, but we would have to drive right through many of the very worst areas to get to it. Bill had somehow secured a "military escort" pass.

Everywhere we were led we saw nightmares: buildings down, broken glass, chunks of crumbled concrete, splintered pieces of wood, and garbage everywhere; a body floating face down in a canal; markings on doorways showing "no survivors" — but no people except for one bent over old man with the saddest face I have seen, tending a six-foot square garden in front of a decrepit building that must have been his home less than three weeks before.

The armed soldiers driving a jeep led us straight to our door, wished us luck, then drove away. They weren't gone a minute before a FBI jeep pulled up and inspected our papers. They brusquely told us we had to wear facemasks in this area. The air seemed fine and I thought they were being too serious.

On the outside, our main signage was down — leaning against the corner of our neighbors' store ten feet away — but otherwise, by a miracle of God, the building looked untouched. It didn't take long, however, to discover why the masks were necessary. Bill opened the door, and water came rushing out. Watermarks revealed the water had been about ten inches deep in the lobby. The further in we went, the air got bad really quick. Mold was already everywhere, and the air was filled with debris floating in the head beams of our flashlights. Any thoughts of sleeping here were immediately thrown out the window. Working inside was also not going to be possible beyond a few minutes at a time. Nothing was "lost" to the storm, or to looters, so we determined the best we could do was to take the money from the safe, replace it with a couple of small exhibits from the lobby, and move a few other things up the stairs to the dry second floor. We removed the shrunken head from its display case and took it home with us.

After barely an hour, we gave up. Seeking "fresh" air, we headed to the roof, only to find a man living up there. His family had died, and his house was gone. He had no way of leaving town, and nowhere else to stay. We gave him a tent, several jugs of water, some junk food, some money, and all the extra clothes we had. We offered him a ride, but he had no place to go.

As I exited the building, as if drawn by a magnet, I turned right to walk past the Cathedral, and to gaze upon the Café du Monde. Trees had been properly cut in front of the Cathedral so that President George W. Bush looked good during his speech and the church grounds looked pristine on the aired broadcast as if nothing had happened, but a few feet away, outside of camera view, there was enough green debris and stacked wood to keep the city's boy scouts in fire wood for a year.

As I walked, I called my wife, and amidst tears flowing down my cheeks, I tried to describe what I had already seen, and what I was now seeing: the outside chairs of the Café du Monde stacked up and chained to a fence, the doors closed and the lights out. I had never seen this before. The Café was normally open 24 hours a day, and the patio was always full, even at 3 am. Katrina had closed this institution for the first time in its 143-year history. Gil couldn't understand a word I babbled. I leaned on the fence and wept.

We had one more mission of mercy to accomplish. A brand-new manager had just started to work at the museum a week before the hurricane hit. Her name was Antoinette. I had never met her, and Bill had only met her once, but we had promised to visit her home to report on its condition. She herself, and her small daughter, had been able to flee to San Antonio, Texas.

We were escorted out of the French Quarter, and then left on our own. With Bill driving, and me talking to Antoinette on a phone, we wove our way through the northwest corner of the town, an area I had never been before. My description of things drew no responses but gasps from Antoinette. Destruction was everywhere, and the closer we got to the main canal, which had burst, the worse things got. At one point we unknowingly made a wrong turn. Suddenly, what we were describing wasn't familiar to Antoinette. When we came to a school, with

198

no roof, and only three exterior walls still standing, she realized where we were, and was relieved to know we were going the wrong direction! A couple turns later, we were in a subdivision with virtually no damage. Antoinette's street had no water — not a drop —and her house was intact. A small tree had fallen onto her porch, but nothing was damaged. Another miracle.

Antoinette told us her neighbor, an elderly woman, had not evacuated. We knocked on her door. She was as white as a ghost, and scared of us. She wouldn't come out, but talked from behind the slightly cracked open door. She was relieved to hear Antoinette's voice on the phone, and we were able to give her some food. She had not ventured out of her house in seventeen days.

As if in a funeral hearse, we drove halfway home that evening in dead silence. There was nothing to talk about. We doubted anyone would believe what we had seen and experienced. The following day we were home, still shaken, but oh so happy to be out of Hell.

The odditorium re-opened for business in the new year five months later, but it was hard to get employees, and impossible to get visitors. The French Quarter would remain no-man's land for more than a couple years. Bill fought with his insurance companies for several years. He got no government subsidies as the building was about a quarter mile out of the so-called designated disaster zone, and could really only claim business interruption, loss of a rug, and damage to a sign. He soon had no choice but to close the odditorium.

Bill was a trooper though, and he opened another franchise odditorium in Panama City, Florida in 2006 less than a year later [1], while still entangled in insurance battles. I on the other hand, had great difficulty ever going back to New Orleans. A certain Louis Armstrong song never left my head, but neither did the vision of a messy cathedral, and a closed coffee shop. A documentary film about the aftermath, starring Elvis Costello and one of New Orleans' most celebrated musicians, Allen Toussaint who lost everything in the storm, is commercially available should I ever need a reminder of what it looked like that September.

I thought about going back to New Orleans at Jazz Fess (at the end of April) almost every year, but not until

2017, when Fats Domino died, did I make up my mind to do it. In 2018 the festival would be held in his honor, and there would be several commemorative concerts and a special parade. It had now been 13 years since I had last seen my favorite American city (2). The venerable old restaurants: Brennan's, Antoine's, Galatoire's, Commander's Palace, and the Café Du Monde are all still there, and still must-dos, but the music scene has shifted to outside the Quarter. The festival too has changed. It no longer is just Louisiana musician based, and relies on young pop stars to draw the biggest crowds. The evening tent concerts are gone, and with Wynton Marsalis living in New York, and the deaths of Toussaint, Fats, Charles Neville and Henry Butler, I am not sure who is left to carry the torch. No city I know of has more character and soul than New Orleans, but

Katrina sure knocked the guts out of her — and me too (3).

30

Ripley & Twain:
Walking in the Paths of Giants in India

It is only a theory, but one I feel very confident in proclaiming: Robert Ripley probably loved the works of Mark Twain. He definitely was familiar with the classics, **Huck Finn**, **Tom Sawyer** and **Life on the Mississippi**, all of which he drew related cartoons about, but I suspect he was very fond of a lesser known travelogue called: "**Following the Equator**", first published in 1897 when Ripley was just a young boy.

Ripley would first visit India, seemingly Twain's favorite foreign country, in 1923. He would return a second time in 1936. His 1923 excursion would be the longest time he ever spent in one country in his nearly forty years of traveling. His path was a virtual retracing of Twain's steps, and many of the places and things Twain had written about became cartoon subjects for Robert: Hindu gods, Buddhist life styles, temples, elephants, fortresses, the Taj Mahal, the Ganges River, the Burning Ghats of Varanasi, and fakirs, the holy men who practice all kinds of asceticism and mortification in the name of holiness. In 2008, eighty-five years after Ripley, and one hundred and eleven after Twain, unconsciously, I retraced both men's giant steps across the sub-continent in what would be my longest sojourn too.

I am sure my subconscious self was aware of their footsteps, and may have been secretly guiding me once the path was decided, but it was pure coincidence that I was going to India in the first place, and a further coincidence that the path I chose matched theirs — in reverse.

I celebrated my thirtieth anniversary with Ripley's at an annual conference in St. Kitts, in the Caribbean. I was only the third employee in post Ripley times to have reached this milestone. I was treated to an all-day roast (party), organized by Steve Glum and his then assistant Marcie Pikel. During the day, at random times, they presented me with a song; a personal congratulatory button; pre-recorded messages from past employees and my mother; a diamond studded service boutonnière; an engraved iPod, with songs from my own music collection already secretly transferred on to it; a John Graziano original Edward Meyer cartoon, disguised as a gold record by "Two-Tone" Meyer, a reference to my beard and my love of blues music; and a Gibson guitar (and case) autographed by Mississippi blues man Big Jack Johnson (whom people thought looked like B.B. King in the accompanying photo showing him signing it). It was the best day of my life. I ungraciously, at a loss for words, reminded them I didn't use an iPod, nor did I play guitar. They said I would learn both, but I never did. It's the thought that counts though, and the efforts and meaning behind each gift were not lost or wasted on me. I repeat, it was the best day of my life. The phone recordings from Alec Rigby, my first bosses, Derek and Rita Copperthwaite, and then my mother, recorded from a hospital bed, absolutely tore me up.

That night it somehow got even better.

In a vaguely Indian style restaurant — as Indian as you can get in St. Kitts — I was further congratulated and spoiled. Several people gave speeches — not always coherent, but always heartfelt. Then president Bob Masterson forced me into a swimming pool, fully dressed, but then rewarded both my willingness to drown as well as my thirty years of service, with the ultimate gift — a two-week, all expenses paid, **Passage to India** for my wife and I. Marcie handed it to me in a beautiful decorated board envelope she had hand-made. I cried, but couldn't call my wife to share my joy as my phone had been destroyed in my impromptu swim (1).

In the day's continuing sub-theme of looking a gift horse in the mouth, I wasn't sure why a trip to India had been chosen. The logical answer was that we would soon be opening a museum in Bangalore, and I could combine business with pleasure, but I soon learned that was not the actual reason. Marcie had apparently asked my wife, rather than me, where I would like to go on a company-paid trip. She wasn't really wrong in choosing India, but in truth it would have been a distant fourth choice for me, behind Egypt, China, Kenya (East Africa).

Her having been born in India, and not having been back in over forty years, it was in fact a somewhat selfish choice by her. It turned out to be a very good one.

Earlier in the day, our soon-to-be Indian franchisees, Mr. Prasad and Ms. Upsana, had invited me to Bangalore for the opening of the new museum, so I was now looking at nearly a whole month in India. There would be some work, but for the most part the trip was to be a long, extended vacation. I had carte blanche freedom to organize when and where to visit. We would have to go to Calcutta where Gil was born, but otherwise Rajasthan, in the northwest, was the biggest attraction to me. I thought we would do a trip on the legendary **Maharaja's Express**, nicknamed the **Palace on Wheels**. Marcie had already looked into where the train went, and had provided its itinerary. It sounded and looked fabulous. Unfortunately, they were booked three seasons in advance! I was not willing to wait. I wanted to go as soon as possible. My compromise was that we would do a road, plane and train trip roughly following the Palace's route: from Bangalore to Delhi and Jodhpur by planes, then by car to Jaipur, and Jaisalmer, (rather than Udaipore), and Agra to see the Taj Mahal. From Agra we would take a train to Varanasi then another train to Calcutta. Within each city very little was planned, everything was more or less a spontaneous adventure.

Gil's Anglo-Indian relatives and friends had over-hyped Bangalore as some sort of English-speaking enclave-paradise. Of all the places we went, as a location it was the least notable. We did, however, have a longtime friend there who made it special in a different way. We thought Queenie (Pauline) Peterson still lived in Calcutta (2) — but found out she had moved to Bangalore just a few days before we arrived.

The Ripley odditorium was not in Bangalore proper, but an hour outside of town on the main highway connecting Bangalore to Mysore on the coast. It was fascinating to see the manual labor style construction of the museum, and the movie-themed amusement park we would be in, but the highlight here was meeting the former Minister of Agriculture, Mr. Lockraj who spontaneously picked up a phone, and with one call got a limousine, shut down a market, and by limousine took Queenie and us mango shopping. To have seen the joy on the face of a near ninety-year old as she tried a dozen different fresh picked and cut different kinds of mangoes, may have been the best moment of the entire month-long trip. We would see Queenie three times on this trip, including once after the mango adventure, but after that we would never see her again. She died just a few months later.

The museum was behind schedule and would not open as planned while we were there. I did help with some displays, and did training sessions with employees — one of which ended me up in a nearby hospital after I fainted from heat stroke — but I never actually saw the museum open, or the staff in operation. Combining the non-opening, a hospital visit, subsequent stomach problems, and a stolen passport wallet with credit cards and my American resident's green card in it, you could safely say Bangalore was not a good memory. It was the work portion of this trip, however, so I feel compelled to emphasize these nightmares. Dear reader, please keep in mind I still had three weeks to be in India after Bangalore.

We stayed in a lovely staffed villa, owned by our museum franchise host, Mr. Prasad, which was surrounded by a mango orchard. We were sharing the facility, about a mile from the construction site, with Lon Casey, the Ripley Director of Franchise Operations, a person we knew and loved, and a second gentlemen, in charge of the construction, whom we knew by association, but had never actually met before. We did not exactly get along with him. We had our own cooks —one to make Western breakfast, and one almost exclusively for Gil to make Indian delicacies — and our own chauffeur/tour guide, a wonderful young man named Bartha, who took to Gil immediately because she was born in his home town which he greatly missed.

We had arrived in India in the middle of the night during a festival. There was no work to be done that day and after settling in and having a cursory tour of the site — called Innovative Film City and featuring a dozen other attractions in addition to the Ripley's museum and a Louis Tussaud's Wax Works (3) — we went back into Bangalore for a big dinner. I had tandoori lobster, a dish I had never confront-ed before. Later, on the street we had ice cream. Two cardinal sins in less than an hour, and on my first day in India. One or the other, made me sick, and I never fully recovered for the entire twenty-eight days in India. I blamed the ice cream, Gil blamed the lobster. Either way, there was clearly a lack of refrigeration rules I had to learn. I spent the next twelve hours in washrooms, both elegant and scary, whatever I could find when nature screamed.

The next day, my first day of actual work, I was giving a lecture tour to about twenty soon-to-be staff, and Ms. Upsana. I distinctly remember her asking me if I felt alright. Apparently, I didn't look good. Be- fore she could finish asking me if I would like some water, I was unconscious flat on the floor. When I woke up, I was about a half mile away in Mr. Prasad's second-story office. Gil was fanning me. I had been carried on a stretcher that was sitting propped up against the door; I didn't remember hitting the ground, or being carried away. Mr. Prasad had ordered a car and was preparing to take me to the hospital in Bangalore, an hour away. He was not going to take any chances that an American Ripley VP would die on his home turf.

The hospital was ultra-modern, and a pleasant surprise. I hadn't wanted to go, thinking it would not be up to my standards. It was packed, and somewhat chaotic, but Mr. Prasad obviously knew someone or something, as we didn't wait a minute. I was rushed straight in, past the huge line, and inspected by a bevy of people before I knew what was happening. The treatment and care were exceptional, and the bill was minimal — the equivalent to eight American dollars. The cardiograph showed no irregularities, and the official diagnosis was dehydration. I was given some pills and told to go to bed for forty-eight hours.

I heeded most of the advice, but got out of bed after about thirty hours. The first thing I discovered after getting out of bed, was that my wallet and papers were gone. I like to think that I lost them in the car on the ride home (I definitely had them in the hospital), but I suspect they were stolen from my room while I slept. I will never know. Foolishly, I did not panic, because by some coincidental unseen force of providence, I had taken photocopies of everything before we left Florida. I could still prove who I was, I could cancel credit cards and traveler's checks, and with Gil's wallet, we

could start over again from the top. It was an incon-
venience, but not a vacation breaker — at least not
yet.

The rest of the week went much smoother, and we started
the actual vacation with great expectations. From this
point on we were following in the invisible footsteps
of Ripley and Twain even if we didn't know it.

Our first night in Delhi we visited the Red Fort, and
the adjacent marketplace. On the fort's ground we saw a
laser light show about the history of India, and were
eaten alive by mosquitoes from the nearby river. In the
market, I loudly asked every vendor if they had any
miniature ivory carvings inside seeds. This was something Ripley had once bought in Delhi, and that Gil's
family had several samples of. The seeds are about ¼"
round, and the animals inside cannot be recognized for
what they are without magnification. Usually, they are
elephants. Some seeds have a few animals inside, but
the expensive $5.00 ones have as many as 100! I eventu-
ally found what I was looking for, well hidden in the
back of a dark stall, accessible only to the shopkeeper. I also found a rice writer who performed his magic
right in front of our eyes, writing whatever we requested on a single grain of rice. These were the only
items I bought for the company on the entire trip.

The next day we visited the Qubt Minar iron pillar, a
3rd-4th century twenty-four-foot tall iron rust re-
sistant pillar erected in honor of the Hindu god Vish-
nu. Ripley had posed with it and had his picture taken
with his arms wrapped around it, once a must-do ceremony, but now it was forbidden to even touch it. I faked
a Ripley photo re-enactment.

In Jaipur we rode elephants up to the Amber Castle, and
watched snake charmers in the market place outside the
Royal Pink Palace. We also saw the **Limca** world's record
amber jewel — as big as my fist — and the Gangajalis
solid silver water vessels. These two huge silver water
jars, capable of holding 4,000 liters of water each,
and the largest single silver objects in the world
(again, according to the **Limca Book of Records**), were
made for Maharaja Madho Singh II to store Ganges River
water in during a trip to England to see the coronation
of King Edward VII in 1902.

Driving to Jaisalmer we got caught in a sand storm and we rode camels just like Ripley. We also met the grandson of a man Ripley had met who in 1933 when Ripley brought him to America, had a 109" long mustache. The grandson's mustache, listed in the India Limca Book of World Records as the longest in the world, was a mere 102" in length. He unfurled the entire thing for me so I could recreate yet another Ripley picture of old.

In Jodhpur we stayed in a Heritage Hotel's, round outer building, a luxury yurt of sorts, and saw the amazingly accurate 18th century Jantar Mantar sundial and astronomy complex of Rajput King Sawai Jai Singh II. I also bought my first Indian kurta.

After Jodhpur we deviated from the Ripley-Twain agenda, and visited Ranthambore, to see tigers in the wild. Gil loves tigers and this was a highly anticipated part of our trip. Of the four jeeps allowed in the park each day, only ours saw tigers on April 9th, 2008 — two female sisters. It was the National Geographic nature moment of a lifetime. In an over-sized jeep with twelve passengers, and a driver, we entered the park at 8 am as the sun started to heat up. (We had gotten up at 5:30 in preparation, and to see the sunrise over the mountain).

Within minutes, our driver-guide stopped the jeep and announced he could smell a tiger. We would park right where we were and wait. He was sure one was nearby. I thought he was nuts. I didn't smell anything out of the ordinary. I soon spotted his tiger, however, the first to do so. Initially she kept her distance, but as the clock ticked, she came closer…and closer…and closer. She came right up to my position — the rear left tire — and marked her territory. I could have bent over and petted her if I hadn't been frozen with fear. There was no roof or side to the jeep, the tiger was right there at my elbow. I quietly encouraged the driver to move the jeep. He politely assured me that if he moved it, I would be dead. Best just to piss myself and be quiet.

The tiger was inquisitive, definitely not scared of us, but not aggressive. She was quite obliging to all photographers, until suddenly she roared and ran off about fifty yards into the long brown grass. Seconds later she was in a full fledge battle with a second tiger —

her sister according to our guide. The ensuing battle was majestic, both cats on their hind legs, pushing, shoving, growling, tussling like giant wrestlers. It was awesome in the true dictionary sense of the word, but it was all over in seconds. The fighting stopped, the first tiger sauntered off with an air of victory. The second tiger ambled away in the opposite direction, beaten physically, but not in spirit. She would definitely live to fight another day. Our entire tiger experience was about twenty minutes in length. On the rest of our eight-hour, two-part safari ride, we saw a mongoose, wild peacocks, and hundreds of deer of several species, but no more tigers. The other three jeeps saw tiger shit and tracks, but no tigers.

In Agra we of course visited the Taj Mahal, the undisputed most beautiful building in the world — built in 1632-53 as the final resting place for Emperor Shah Jahan's **second** wife, Mumtaz Mahal. We also saw the Agra Fort where Jahan's son Aurangzeb imprisoned him for bankrupting the country to make the Taj. His prison rooms were sumptuously decorated — he was not exactly hard done by — but from his sleeping quarters the Taj was only visible through a slim slit-style window where Jahan is said to have wept for hours each day.

As both Ripley and Twain asserted, Varanasi proved to be the most unusual place in all India, and probably the entire world. Twain called it a "big church, a religious hive, whose every cell is a temple, a shrine, or a mosque, and whose every conceivable earthly and heavenly good is procurable under one roof…" and Ripley said: "… the strangest places on earth are the holiest. And the strangest and most remarkable city in the world is the holy city of Benares (Sic-Varanasi) on the muddy arm of the Ganges, India's holy river."

Every Hindu in India wishes to die in Varanasi, and the streets are full of fakirs worshiping their gods, as well as near corpses waiting for the divine to end their earthly existence. The scene has not changed since Ripley's or Twain's times, and probably not since the dawn of civilization.

We experienced both the sunrise and sunset rituals (4) on the River Ganges just like they did, and saw: a funeral pyre on the ghats (5), with the burnt ash remains being scattered in the holy river right next to bathers; naked and painted fakirs on every corner, and even a bull inside a cloth shop that officially owned the store. No purchase could be made without the sacred bull's approval. Customers haggled with the shopkeepers, and when they were satisfied with a negotiated price, the attendants approached the bull and verbalized the "proposed" amount. If the bull did nothing the deal was consummated, but if he moved, or made a noise, the deal was nullified and negotiations would have to start afresh. As Ripley noted: "Strange is man when he seeks after his gods." In this case, Nandhi, the bull incarnation of Shiva, the god of destruction.

We regrettably skipped a side trip to Bodh Gaya to see where Gautama Buddha achieved enlightenment under a pupal tree, and instead boarded an overnight train "direct" to Kolkata. Our earlier train ride had been lovely, first class, this third class, fourteen-hour trip, was a totally different experience. It was advertised as being ten hours long, but unlike in England, trains in India are not always punctual, despite the Raj's best intentions at duplicating the famous English rail system through the subcontinent. Twain's train ride from Varanasi to Kolkata had taken him seventeen and a half hours. I was skeptical if our train would make it in any less time, or without some calamity.

Men and women had separate sleeping areas. Gil got a curtained wooden folding couch seat in the aisle by herself. I got a third-story, top bunk, in a room with eight other men, and a young boy. My head was inches away from a ceiling fan that would terrorize me all night. The only thing scarier was the hole in the floor bathroom I had to visit in the pitch dark of the middle of the night (6). On the way I lost my sheet in the climb down the bunk, and didn't dare try to lift it off the sleeping Sikh beneath me.

I was sleepless the rest of the night, and the first to rise in the morning when I was sure I could get up without breaking any rules of co-ed decorum. Gil had a window, but it was too dirty to see out of. Even after sunrise, we were still in the dark. We strained to see out the window, but Gil did not remember any of the multiple stations we passed through. In her defense, it had been a long time since she had been in India's hinterland, and she may never have been on this particular track. Her memory of train stations — hives of chaos with food vendors hawking wares everywhere, micro-worlds onto themselves, each different, yet each the same — was dead-on accurate. Gil was afraid to eat the station vendor foods, though she looked longingly at the puchkas (7) and sweets. All we ate the entire trip was a handful of grapes that an elderly male fellow passenger had given us. Luckily, we suffered no side effects.

We spent most of our time in Kolkata visiting an Anglo-Indian lady named Philomena, a friend of a friend that we had never met. A wonderful sweet older woman who literally opened all kinds of doors for us, Philomena knew several spots from Gil's childhood: Flurry's bakery and confection shop; Niazam's kathi (roti) shop; the Midan (park) where she once walked daily as a child with her father; the Victoria Memorial where she posed at age two and now again at age fifty-three, seated amongst the bright red Calla lilies (sadly the Memorial itself was closed for the day when we were there); the Calcutta Zoo (where I got to see a rare Indian rhino); Tengra, the China-town neighborhood, home of the world famous Hakka Chow noodles; and the Calcutta Museum, the oldest, and probably dirtiest, museum in all Asia.

On Philomena's advice, we had hired a driver for the duration of our stay — cheaper than by the ride, more convenient, and more depend-able. We found Giliane's family home, but came up short looking for her dear grandmother's home (we found the street, but believed the building must have been torn down — all that looked familiar to Gil was the numerous pedicabs and rick-shaws, scurrying everywhere). We found Gil's favorite cousin Lincoln's home, her church, and her school too. The school grounds were closed, but she pointed out the classroom from memory. We went to a Sunday mass in the church where she was baptized, the same church Mother Teresa was buried from, and we went to Mother Teresa's grave, inside the convent where she served the poor of Kolkata for so many years. Unlike Catholic shrines else-where in the world, there was no sign; we had to ask directions of four different people before we found it, well-hidden behind a big wooden gated wall. There was no admission fee and even giving the nuns a donation was difficult.

For one day we hired a professional tour guide to take us to three things Ripley had seen that Gil was unfamiliar with: the Parshwanath Badridas Jain temple, which is entirely covered in broken mirror shards; Kumortuli, a series of streets where potters craft the thousands of ceramic deity statues one sees all over India; and the infamous Black Hole of Calcutta, the site of the most horrific occurrence of the British Raj period. Here, the Nawab of Bengal imprisoned 164 English and Anglo-English soldiers after the fall of Fort William on June 20, 1756, 143 of who died that night of heat exhaustion and suffocation. I once again posed exactly like Ripley had at the temple, and at the prison site.

Lastly, I need to mention two other miraculous moments of sublime hospitality. We were staying in a five-star luxury hotel, named the **Taj Bengal**. On our last day, the kitchen chef gifted Gil a set of small terracotta yogurt pots, called chatties. These are so cheap they are used as disposable fast food containers throughout Kolkata. People finish their snack, and throw the little pot into the streets where the shards almost instantly become part of the road, ground up by cars and foot traffic. To Gil they were a tangible memory, worth more than gold.

Our driver was barely four and half feet tall and as skinny as a rail. I suspect he weighed less than ninety lbs., wet or dry. He spoke very little English, but was never late and even drove us on a bandh strike day when working was illegal; he literally was risking his life for mere pennies. On our late-night return from Tengra with Philomena, Gil left her camera on the backseat of his cab. The camera was worth about $300 US dollars. The more than 1500 photos of India on it, were priceless. We didn't know it was in the car, and weren't sure when we had last used it. Like my Green card and passport from day one, we were sure it was lost for good, never to be seen again. While at breakfast, we were interrupted by one of the hotel's liveried guards. He said there was a man outside — without a customer in tow he was unable to enter the posh grounds of the hotel — who claimed to have something that belonged to us. We weren't sure who it was, nor what this stranger might have that was ours. When we got outside and walked down the driveway, and saw our driver holding

Gil's camera, we jumped for joy. It was yet another Indian miracle. We tipped him every penny we had, about eighty-five dollars, or six month's salary, and had him wait to drive us to the airport. I later sent him more money and photos of him and I together, but I have no idea whether he ever received the package.

It was the trip of a lifetime for both of us. I saw a thousand wonders I could have only dreamed of, and Gil got to do what very few people ever get to do properly: **Go Home**. The adventure, however, didn't fully end until months later.

At home over the next few days, I reread Ripley's 1923 Rambles **Around the World** travel journal, and glanced at my notes inside Twain's **Following the Equator**. I was floored to learn just how many of the exact same things we three had done, and in virtually the same amount of time (one month). The only real difference was the routes we each took. Twain and Ripley were both coming from the east, I started from the West. Ripley's route was virtually the exact same as mine but in reverse. Twain, started in Sri Lanka (Ceylon), and went to a few places we didn't, but eventually got on the exact same trail and like us, ended in Kolkata (Calcutta).

31

Bizarre Buying Bazaars

Inspired subliminally by a popular television show called **"The Antique Road Show"**, in 2013 I dreamed up a Ripley version that I would call **"Ripley's Bizarre Buying Bazaar" (BBB)**. The ultimate goal was to find exhibits to add to the collection — things we could acquire. The plan was to invite the general public to bring objects to a Ripley location, and meet the Ripley archival staff (Angela Johnson and myself) for a free consultation. We would identify "unknown" objects and suggest potential value, whether we wanted to acquire it ourselves or not. We rewarded anyone who brought an item with a free museum pass whether we bought their object or not, and if we did like it, we would negotiate a deal on the spot, emphasizing potential fame over fortune. The promise to put a person's "treasure" in a world-famous museum, and maybe in a cartoon, or a book too, can be a pretty enticing offer regardless of the attached check.

Over a four-year time-span, Angela and I did twelve **BBBs.** Four were held at Ripley company owned odditoriums, one was at a Ripley franchise location, and the remaining seven were held at third party Science Centers in conjunction with **The Science of Ripley's Believe It or Not!** traveling show. Each show was approximately twenty-four hours long, spread over three days (Friday-Sunday). Initially the plan was just to do the four odditoriums in Florida — locations we could drive to and take exhibits with us with minimal travel costs. The first one was in Orlando (June 2013), the second in St. Augustine (July 2013). In terms of new acquisitions these would be the most successful, but they taught us something right away that we hadn't really thought too much about at first. Whether we acquired anything or not, the **BBB** were great free media grabbers. In all twelve locations we would inevitably, without a lot of effort on our part, (the Science Center marketing people worked harder than we did), get radio, television and print coverage. We proved Ripley was newsworthy.

Measuring the success of anything usually relies on statistics. Some people thought our **Bazaars** were not worth their costs (even though we ran very bare bones), based on how few things we actually acquired. It troubled me, and caused me to not do any in 2016, but at the end of the day, I was very happy with the media coverage we got in all twelve locations, and the enormous public goodwill we generated, especially in the non-Ripley environments where we raised the company's exposure and profile to a brand-new younger audience. I don't think we struck out anywhere, and in some cities, I really believe we hit home runs.

The four Bazaars held in Florida were all carried out outdoors, three in slightly protected areas, but the first one was in the wide-open of the Orlando odditorium parking lot. We did have an open tent for some sun protection (that I bought specifically for BBBs, but never used again), but no protection from the heat, or a torrential downpour. We learned very quickly that working outdoors in Florida was risky business.

I should have recognized an omen when I saw one. The very first object brought to us was a Ku Klux Klan hood and robe. It had belonged to the owner's grandfather. She stored it between her mattress and her box spring. I could barely look at it, never mind buy it. I was electric-shocked into realizing just what I was getting myself into, what level of "weirdness" I was bringing upon myself by openly asking people to bring me their treasures. I have still not recovered from the horror of the thought of sleeping on this artifact. I didn't ask too many details, knowing the atrocities the Central Florida Klan had subjected African Americans to in this area in the 1950s. I couldn't help but to wonder if this very outfit — reportedly a high-ranking official's — was involved in either — or both — the Groveland Four alleged rape nightmare (1949), or the Harry T. Moore house Christmas bombing of 1951. I politely told her it wasn't for me and suggested she try the local history museum as a more likely interested party.

We did buy a lot of items at this first event, including several Ramos family art pieces (see Chapter 70), a taxidermy chicken, electric lamp, and a rare New Guinea widow's finger chopper — not the kind of thing I would have imagined someone having in their home. This special shaped stone knife was used by widows to chop off a part   of their middle finger to signify their husband had died. The cut off portion of the finger was then worn as a necklace. The seller's father had obtained it in New Guinea in World War II. The owner had no clue what it was, I only knew because I had bought one once before.

Two other things happened here that would not be repeated anywhere else. On Day One a gentleman a hundred feet off to the right of our tent booth, put down a chair, a beach umbrella and an easel. He never talked to us, or anyone else as I recall, but sat in the shade for quite a while, seemingly thinking we were not aware of him. In a quiet, unobtrusive way he was driving me crazy, whether he knew it or not. When he finally started to pack up his gear, I left my station, and went to ask him what he had been doing. Turns out he had done a watercolor painting of our tent and booth! It was quite good, and as I was in the middle of it, I offered to buy it. He was not interested in selling it, but did let me take a photo of it — which I still have. The mystery artist was Thomas Thorspecken, a former Disney World artist, and a highly respected artist today, with works in the Orlando Art Museum. I didn't recognize or know him, and suspect I didn't offer quite enough for one of his originals.

The real highlight of the first BBB, however, had nothing to do with art or artifacts, it was all about the weather. The first two days we had almost died of heat, and were only kept alive by Joe Kasinski, the then marketing manager at the museum, who regularly brought us ice cold waters (and fans). On Day Three, the middle of Sunday after-noon, we were hit by hurricane force winds and rain. Joe scavenged tarps which we were able to tie on from inside our tent to prevent water damage to our displays, and then he, Angela and I, from the inside, held down the tent from blowing away for more than an hour. Strangely a few people still brought stuff for us to look at, including the aforementioned chicken lamp, but by the time the storm ended, the show could not go on. We ended hours earlier than planned, looking like cold drowned rats, and knew we could not do another BBB outside under a tent ever again.

A month later we did BBB #2 in St. Augustine. We were again outside, but this time under a portico, with building doors immediately be-hind us, so we could make a quick escape inside from either heat or rain if necessary. The highlights in St. Augustine were three life-size motorcycles made from animal bones (see Chapter 70) and three team-signed baseballs. One of the balls was signed by the last Dodgers team to play in Brooklyn, before moving to Los Angeles (1957), featuring Willie Mays. One other was a 1961 Yankees ball featuring Yogi Berra, Micky Mantle and Roger Maris. The 1961 Yankees were arguably the second-best baseball team in history; it was the year Micky and Maris had a home run battle which culminated with Maris breaking Babe Ruth's thirty-four-year old record with his sixty-first home run on the last day of the season. The owner had a vague idea of their worth, but sold them for considerably less than market value because his late father loved Ripley's, and would have been proud to have the balls displayed at Ripley's in St. Augustine.

The Science of Ripley's Believe It or Not! traveling show was built in conjunction with the staff of Sudbury Ontario's Science North muse-um. The whole concept was outside the box thinking for both partners, but would become a long-term ideal relationship. Doing our first non-Ripley's location BBB in Sudbury (August, 2013), made good sense. The traveling show had just opened, Sudbury was stop number one of a proposed eighteen, and because Sudbury is a little far off the beaten path, dare I say in the woods, we thought we might get some North American Indian artifacts, or mining tools, that we would be unlikely to see anywhere else. We certainly didn't get what we expected. The most remarkable pieces were a 17th century Persian chain mail khud helmet, and an eight-foot long collapsible Tibetan monastery trumpet. A giant rock removed from the bottom of a lake during construction of a boat dock — shaped like the face of the Creature of the Black Lagoon — was a comical bonus. We made front page of the local newspaper, and national television coverage. Sudbury loved us, and treated us like visiting royalty.

The six shows we did in 2014 were not generally as productive as the three 2013 shows had been, and in three of them, at science centers in Phoenix, Arizona, (March) Peoria, Illinois (August) and Seattle, Washing-

216

ton (December), what we didn't buy as opposed to what we did, were the highlights. Phoenix and Peoria also had additional interesting events occur while we were there.

In Phoenix, we had a true OMG moment. A seemingly "homeless" man approached our table, set up in the main foyer, with a brown paper shopping bag. From it he pulled out a balalaika. He did not know its name, origin, or anything about it. I was able to tell him it was a balalaika, a common enough Russian musical instrument (I had once seen a large balalaika orchestra on the Ed Sullivan show, so he was noticeably impressed by my nonchalant showing off). Somewhat discouraged that I had no interest in it, he feebly added he also had an old violin in his shopping bag. "Any chance I would be interested in it?" Note, because he didn't know what the balalaika was, he assumed it was of more interest than an old violin. I politely said, not likely, but I asked did it have any sort of story attached to it? Was there anything that made it special? He claimed he had bought both instruments at a flea market. He knew nothing about either of them.

The violin was not in as good condition as the balalaika, but was clearly older. I perused it carefully trying to give the man some level of dignity, and discovered it had a signature inside. It read: "Ano Stradivari". I am sure I peed myself. I was shaking all over, and stuttering like a dumbfounded idiot. One side of my brain was telling me it couldn't possibly be a 280-year old $5 million-dollar Stradivarius violin, but the other part of my brain of course was saying "what if"?! Who doesn't dream of finding a treasure like this in a dusty cellar, or a shopping bag?!

The owner claimed not to have ever heard of Stradivarius, and was puzzled by my obvious excitement. Angela was much more rational than I was, and had her computer out in seconds. Comparing the signature to on-line samples, it sure looked like the real thing, but the fact that there were pages of "fakes" raised a lot of doubts. We held on to it and did research while he used his earned free pass to visit the museum, but we could not come to any conclusion. In the end, I handed it back to him with addresses for several violin and musical instrument experts, telling him he really needed to show it to an expert. I also suggested he not carry it around in a paper bag. Under no circumstances was I willing to part him from a potential life-changing ticket to easy street for the few hundred dollars I would have been willing to risk.

On the Saturday night in Phoenix they had a "twenty-one and over" costume party. We kept our booth up, gave away some books, and I got to be a judge for their costume contest. Seemingly, I did a good enough job that I was invited back to speak at the museum's next evening event — a fundraiser — a month later. They asked me to do a little speechifying, and give private tours. I agreed with the stipulation that my wife could join me. They agreed, .one of the best meals I have ever eaten. There were speakers, including myself, musicians and even a magician. It was a very high-end gala, but we were eating for free. At the end of the night each person in attendance picked a box of cracker jacks out of sponsors' shopping bags. At each table of ten there was one star-marked box. The person with these boxes got a nice small gift worth maybe fifty dollars. Within the entire room, there were two boxes marked with two stars. My wife miraculously got one of these and won a $1200 gold ruby ring, four-times nicer than the engagement ring I bought her thirty-seven years earlier. It was a good night to be Giliane.

Peoria was a much sadder occasion. The best piece we bought was a giant duct tape mural of famous drag queen "Divine", shown in a full-length red gown, looking a little like a giant lobster. The most interesting item we saw, was a 14th century ivory bubonic plague "prevention device". I had heard of such a thing, but had never seen one except for a photo in a National Geographic magazine. The piece was a family heirloom from Germany. It consisted of a string neck-lace with a six-inch tubular piece of ivory, attesting to either Nordic trade routes for walrus ivory, or possibly African trade routes for elephant ivory. Part of the tube was hollowed out, and ornately carved. The wearer would stuff it with absorbent wool soaked in a perfume called pomander, which was believed to attract, and kill the disease carrying fleas. Evidence that it actually worked is scant, but the necklaces were at least very attractive. The owner of this one was asking $10,000, just a little north of my comfort zone.

On the Saturday night, Angela and I went to a minor
league baseball game featuring the Peoria Chiefs, a
farm team for the St. Louis Cardinals. I love baseball,
and it was a good game, but don't ask me the score. All
I remember is two phone calls, the first from my elder
sister Janet, the second from my younger sister Jean.
Both had the same thing to tell me: my mother had died.
Thankfully, I had seen her just a few days previously,
and knew at the time it would be the last time I would
see her alive. She would have been happy to know I was
watching her favorite sport when her time came. It
seemed like divine providence.

The next day I did a big theater presentation, and I
recorded a piece of oral history on my memories of Peoria. I only had one thing to talk about, and I cried my
whole way through it. I pity the librarian-historian
who had to catalog, and label my mourning eulogy to my
mother. Not sure I will ever want to go back to Peoria,
even though it does have wild flying carp in the river.

That December it was freezing cold in Seattle, but it
was the first time I was in that city that it didn't
rain; the clear cold was an improvement on the typical
gray, dreary, bleak, rain I was accustomed to. In Seattle, our little Bazaar made front-page news with a full
color photo, above the fold. The story, however, was
"one that got away". An elderly lady brought in a mummified baby right in front of both a newspaperman, and
a visiting television station cameraman. Everyone was
speechless. I wasn't sure if I wanted the mummy but I
knew I didn't want to buy it on camera, or discuss it
on mic. I pretended not to be interested, but slipped
the owner a message to call me later. She became an instant celebrity, and I was able to fade in-
conspicuously into the background.

The basic story was that her grandfather had been a
doctor in the late 19th century, and had preserved the
body of a child that he had been unable to save. When
the owner called me later, I said I couldn't buy it.
She then offered it to me for free as a donation. Still
not sure what the right thing to do was, I reluctantly
accepted, but then proceeded to second-guess myself all
night. I was relieved when she called me the next day,
and asked if she could renege on her deal. Turned out,
her son, five states away, had seen her on television,

and called her. He considered the mummy his heirloom and was furious with his mother for her considering parting with it without asking him. She had not told him she had already given it away and begged me to be kind. I had no trouble giving it back to her, complete with a sense of relief at not having to make the final decision.

Media coverage in the two biggest cities we did, Houston (2015) and New York (2014), was confined to radio, and not as effective as television or print was in other cities at driving people to our door, but in both cities, we did manage significant acquisitions that would influence some buying decisions going forward.

Although we did buy some space memorabilia in Houston, and we did have a spectacular behind-the-scenes tour of the Space Center(1) which gave me a whole new appreciation for the 1960s journey to the moon, the most significant purchase in Houston was not space related. Robert Wadlow is a seminal figure in the story of Ripley's Believe It or Not! He died in 1940 at the tender age of twenty-two. He was 8' 11" and still growing. Ripley was the first person to heavily promote him, bringing him from small town Alton, Illinois, to New York City in 1936, for both radio and movie exposure. He is the only "thing" other than Shuar Shrunken heads that are featured in every Ripley odditorium in one form or other (wax, photos, artifacts, cartoons, animatronic robots). I had never been to Alton at the time, and though I had met many people who had once seen Robert as   he toured the Midwest endorsing the company that made his giant shoes, until Houston, I had never met anyone who actually person- ally knew Robert.

One of the Space Center's employees had once been Wadlow's neighbor. There were a few years difference in age between him and Robert, but he had been Robert's younger brother's best friend, and he had been the family's newspaper boy. He sold us a book, a video, several news clippings and printed memorabilia, and an unpublished manuscript that he himself had written. In this archival treasure trove were all of Robert's vital statistics from an early age (he was already big at six months, and huge by age six). A footprint, and a shoe poster, even provided the size details for his feet, allowing the Ripley art department to exactly replicate his size thirty-nine shoes for future wax figures. The seller was a wealth of information, and the driving force behind me finally in 2018, making the pilgrimage to the town of Alton.

In New York City, the only Ripley franchise location we visited — they paid our airfare and hotel bill to get us there — I bought the company's first Donald Trump object, a two-dimensional portrait made from American currency. I thought it was funny, and never dreamed he would be a future president. That it was later stolen from the odditorium was a pity, but I have to say I felt cleansed of having bought it in the first place. More significant that the Trump portrait, or a mixed media portrait of Barack Obama bought the same day, were a group of portraits of characters from the **Star Wars** film franchise made from colored staples. I honestly hadn't ever seen a colored staple before, nor do I believe I even knew such a thing existed, but the effects of color, and shadow, in these portraits was spellbinding. Greedo was made with green staples, Darth Vader was made from black ones, and C3PO was radiant in gold. The popularity of these portraits was phenomenal (we got significant print press after the BBB when we displayed these pieces in the NYC odditorium), and they were the launching pad into a change of overall buying direction regarding Pop culture, specifically **Star Wars** and space memorabilia (see Chapter 79).

Despite never hitting a grand slam with this program, I still firmly believe in it. I feel the future of Ripley's and museums in general, is in outreach programs, bringing the collection into the field. The wonder I saw on children's faces, and the smiles on the faces of their elders as they explained Ripley's, and the artifacts we displayed, were heart-warming magic moments for me, worth all my efforts ten-fold. If I were to do it again, I'd want a bigger budget, and a longer period of time for pre-advertising, and maybe a full-week in residence. Whether anything got bought or not, the real measure of success was the number of people met and talked to. A curator can learn more from a five-minute interaction with a child than they ever will from a book, or a boardroom of "experts". Only by meeting the future patron head on, and discovering what they like, what they are really interested in, can a curator grow their collection in the right direction.

32

"They're Going to Put Me in the Movies….
and All I Gotta Do is Act Naturally"

With a face made for radio, my leaps from newsprint, to television, to documentary movies, seems unbelievable even to me. With bad hair, then no hair, a pimply bad-skin face, a big belly, and a too-loud laugh, it is clear it must have been my boyish charm that got me on the silver screen. That and the so-called gift of the gab. Documentaries after all are not about acting, but about talking. All the directors had to do was turn the microphone on. All I had to do was act naturally, look at the camera, and start talking. Presumably people liked the way I talked, and didn't care so much about the way I looked.

Starting in the late 1980s I had done multiple appearances on television, everything from morning and nighttime news programs, to daytime talk shows, to historical documentaries. It was pretty evident I could talk on camera, as well as I did on mic, and by the 21st century, I was more than willing to sit still in front of a camera and just talk, no scripts, minimal prompts, and only the occasional touch up to my bald shiny head required, so as not to blind the camera person. To date my movie canon consists of four performances:

A film about string balls, a film about a serial killer (**the Düsseldorf Vampire**), a film about an incredible strongman, and a film about Li Ling Ai, a Hawaii-born Chinese woman who played a large role in the life of Robert Ripley, and through him, me.

"Twine" was a labor of love about collecting string (see Chapter 58). When I was interviewed by the two-person production team I had no idea how big a part I would have. It seemed like a low budget affair, but I had a lot of fun doing it, and I love the results. It took about ten years to see the light of day. I never saw it

222

in a theater, but I know it did play in some; I was invited to a festival showing but was unable to attend.

"My" second film, the story of German serial killer, Peter Kurtin was made to air in theaters, but I am not sure it ever did. The version I have suggests it only aired on pay television as part of a series called "**Serial Killer Culture**".It is a horrific true story, about a man nicknamed the "Düsseldorf Vampire" because of his lust for blood. It's a tough watch, highlighted by minutely close-up shots of the mummified remains of Kurtin's head which I just happened to have bought. I also had met one of the men who preserved it in Germany in the 1930s. I initially didn't want to do this project, and tried hard to dissuade John Borowski the director, from making it. I don't know how much he paid Ripley's for the privilege to film the head in our museum, but I know I didn't see a penny for my time and efforts. The result is a decent film that presumably appeals to a certain audience. For my part, I have never recommended it to anyone. It's my under-ground performance for mature audiences only. My mother would not be proud.

There is a 1931 Ripley cartoon about a guy named Joe Green, (sic-Greenstein), nicknamed the Mighty Atom, who could bend a steel bar with his hair. The artwork was very eye-catching, and unforgettable. The described stunt is too incredulous to believe, yet is totally true. Ripley's has a couple other cartoons about the Mighty Atom, including one about breaking metal chains with his teeth, that again, the art is so good, I have to think Ripley actually saw this NY strong man perform live somewhere. Ripley's also has a piece of film showing him driving a nail through a board with his hand and stopping a plane from taking off with ropes tied to his biceps. I always marveled at this piece of film, but it was years before I knew it was the same guy as featured in the cartoons, it not being labeled Green, but Greenstein, and with no mention of the nick name — the Mighty Atom. The odds against there being two wildly curly haired five-foot short strongmen with twenty-inch biceps, dressed in a leopard print Tarzan outfit, should have tipped me off a lot quicker, I am embarrassed to say.

Over the years the Ripley cartoons and photos of the

Mighty Atom in the collection have been used several times, both by Ripley's and by third parties (see "**The Mighty Atom. The Life and Times of Joseph L. Greenstein, Biography of a Superhuman,** by Ed Spielman for the best sample). They are etched in my brain, so when I got a call from a film director asking if I knew anything about this baffling man, Ihad no problem claiming to be an expert. I didn't know at first that I was talking to his grandson, Steven Greenstein.

Steven invited me on his nickel to come to Washington DC to be interviewed for a biopic film he was making, titled simply **The Mighty Atom** (released in 2017). My wife and I made a weekend of it, and saw some museums and friends while we were there. The filming took place in a small rented warehouse. There were a couple other people filmed that Saturday morning, most memorably a young strongman who had been tutored by Greenstein during the late years of his life. (The Atom was still doing amazing feats of strength, including a performance at Madison Square Garden, into his eighty's — born 1893, died 1977). I was a little intimidated, but soon realized I was the best speaker of all the people to be interviewed. No matter how good your story is, if you can't articulate it, — can't "sell it" — you are severely handicapped in an interview situation. My years of television experience really helped me nail this one.

It was a couple more years before I saw the results, but I walked away that day with my head swollen almost as big as the Mighty Atom's chest. In addition to a plane ride, two nights in a hotel, a couple free meals for the wife and I, I got paid some cash. A star was born, or at least so I thought.

The film is not fine art, but is an enjoyable viewing. Certainly worth putting on my resume.

Finding Kukan, the story of Li Ling Ai, like **"Twine"**, was one person's passion, and would take years to be birthed. The film, made by Robin Lung of Hawaii, started as a documentary about a 1941 Oscar winning documentary called **Kukan, the Battle Cry of China**. Over time, it became as much Li Ling Ai's life story as it was about Robin's search for a long-lost film.

During the last nine years of Robert Ripley's life, Li Ling Ai was his constant companion and confidant. Some people would suggest she may have been his lover too, but Robin convinced me this wasn't likely the case. She was an author, a dancer, a lecturer, a linguist, and a compassionate lover of all things Chinese — especially the country's people who in the late 1930s underwent horrific atrocities at the hands of Imperial Japan. The original **Kukan** film, made in conjunction with cinematographer Ray Scott, showed the everyday lives of the people of different rural regions of China, and captured in eyewitness detail the devastating bombing of Chungking (now Chongqing). This sequence is riveting, and probably the first color documentary film ever shot in China.

What I have seen of the original film is a masterpiece. Trouble is, as hinted at by Robin's film title, even after years of searching for a copy, no complete version of the film exists. The Academy of Motion Pictures (the Oscars) doesn't even have a copy. Most of what Robin shows of the original film in her film is from a reel that was found rotting in a barn in rural Georgia. Robin spent thousands of hours and dollars to restore the film, raising money slowly through "Kickstarter" website pleas, art shows, lectures and outright begging, but she was still only partially successful in this endeavor. The reel she found had several large gaps in it that have been lost to time.

Robin came to Ripley's, and me, originally for photographs of Ripley with Li Ling Ai, finding the connection between the two people totally on her own. When I told Robin we had film of the two of them, she became my best friend, and in turn, she became a lasting friend of the Ripley archives as she supplied the company with additional photos, previously unknown information regarding Ripley's China Relief efforts of the early 1940s, and most significantly, digitized new versions of our Li Ling Ai film footage. Along the way, we even discovered that Li had hosted a couple of episodes of the first Ripley television show in 1949 after he tragically died mid-season (1). Evidence uncovered by Robin suggest these were not only the first American TV shows hosted by an Asian, but by a woman too — years before Connie Chung!

Just working with Robin and witnessing her passion on so many levels, for so many years, I knew the picture was destined for greatness long before I saw it, but when I first saw a version on her laptop on the patio of a swanky hotel restaurant in Los Angeles, I was numbed. I knew the story by heart by this time, but I had no idea of Robin's directorial additions. I beamed with joy. It may have been her child, but it was my nephew.

When Robin introduced me to the packed house audience, in New York at the DOC — NYC Film Festival world premiere in November 2016, I cried. It is a film of true cinematic beauty. A documentary masterpiece, a must-see for any student of film, history, China, and female empowerment. Li Ling Ai is a queen, and Robin her princess: Hawaii's royal family of documentary film. I'm not too bad either.

The multiple award-winning version shown in festivals around the country in 2016-2017 shows me for about thirty seconds, and has maybe another thirty seconds with my voice over. The version shown in 2018 nationwide on PBS public television has both my section, and Ripley's, tragically edited out to meet the time restraints of network television. Robin apologized. It's unfortunate this happened, but I still thank her from the bottom of my heart for bringing me into her life, and immortalizing Ling Ai's. l believe she, like Li, was robbed in that she didn't get an Oscar. My whole family is pretty proud of this one.

33

Under African Skies

I have been drawn to Africa since before I can remember. First it was just to Egypt, but then to West Africa via a griot named Bai Konte, with help from author Paul Oliver and some other Malian musicians; then, via a nanny named Martha, and Robert Ripley, to East Africa; then lastly to South Africa by Paul Simon, and his ground-shaking album, **Graceland**.

I bought hundreds of African artifacts over the years, from virtually every country, but I have only actually been to South Africa, and it took a long time for me to get even there. Through the kindness of Tinus Maree, and his sister Kristi, I finally got to Cape Town in November of 2016, then again in April 2017.

My biggest "hobby", my real passion, is listening to, reading about, and collecting Afro-American blues music. The great British blues scholar, Paul Oliver, published several seminal books in the 1960s (and later too) that had an effect on me, and his book **Savannah Syncopators**, published in 1970 when I was only fourteen, convinced me there was more to Africa than just Egypt. At sixteen, I had a short-term job with Toronto's Mariposa Folk Festival, where I met Bai Konte, a Gambian griot who played a strange stringed harp-like instrument called a kora, Konte sung in a haunting language, miles beyond my comprehension. Over time I listened to several other African musicians, and could make the connection to the Mississippi Delta blues men that I revered. The deeper I got into pre-World War II Afro-American blues music of the 1920s and 1930s, the more Africa started calling my name. The similarities to John Lee Hooker's hypnotic rhythms to African rhythms, seem to me blatantly obvious now, to say nothing of the string band music of the Mississippi Sheiks, or the fife and drum music of Othar Turner and Napoleon Strickland, musicians I saw at Mariposa in the early 1970s. Long before I knew anything about, or had any interest in African art, African music had seduced me.

In 1985, the late Texas blues guitarist Johnnie

Copeland released an album called **Bringin' It All Back Home**; it was the first ever recorded collaboration between an American blues man, and African musicians. A year later, Paul Simon released his seminal album **Graceland**, recorded with musicians from South Africa. He toured North America with an energetic African vocal group, **Ladysmith Black Mambazo**, and suddenly everyone was listening to African music. Coincidentally, my children were born in 1984 and 1986, and one of their nannies was a lovely Ugandan young lady named Martha Nabungya. Her native music was different again, but she loved both the Copeland and the Simon albums, and they were played frequently in our home for all the years she was with us.

These records, and Martha's stories of her homeland, which she sadly missed, and had hurriedly fled during the regime of Idie Amin, were the gate-openers to my subsequent interest in African art. Robert Ripley spent some time in Egypt in 1923, then North Africa, Morocco, Algeria, Libya and Egypt — in 1930-31, and in 1933, he took one of the longest adventures of his career, traveling the length of the continent from Egypt to Cape Town. Traveling by camel, donkey, boat, plane, train and car for more than two months, he made copious notes; took hundreds of pictures; shot film footage (including the first sound movie of Victoria Falls); drew dozens of sketches; some published in the cartoon, others left undeveloped on scratch pads, train schedules and menus; and acquired a few choice artifacts. Several of these made their way into the Dallas Odditorium of 1936, the Cleveland Odditorium of 1937, and most significantly the New York Odditoriums of 1939-40, where they were featured not just in the odditoriums, but also prominently in the souvenir guide-books. His 1933 travel journal, as written, has never been published, but I have read it several times, and it was my main inspiration for wanting to go to Africa — at least as part of my job.

H.M. Lissauer, who I have discussed earlier (see Chapter 10), had us covered for South Sea Island ethnographic artifacts, but seldom had anything from Africa to offer me. In the late 1980s, Bob Masterson regularly teased me with "you need to go to Africa", but when in 1993, we moved to Orlando, Africa, came to me in the name of one Muhammed Keita, and later his nephew Adjibou Keita, West African art dealers with connections from

Senegal to Zaire. Together, these men supplied Ripley with hundreds of artifacts, weapons, costumes, statuary, masks, domestic utensils, and bead work (1). Muhammed's greatest contribution was the ebony Balué fertility statues that would prove to be one of the most popular Ripley exhibits of all time (see Chapter 15). Adjibou found me the fantasy coffins of P'aa Joe from Accra, Ghana.

I first learned about "fantasy" coffins in an issue of **Smithsonian Magazine**. They showed a photo of a half-size wood carved, robin-egg blue Mercedes Benz car, with the tantalizing, but vague caption: "Carved in Ghana, Africa, this car is actually a coffin." Not long after, I found a copy of the exact same car-coffin in a curio-shop in Santa Barbara, California. Fast forward about ten years, where sitting in my office, I told Adjibou Keita I was no longer interested in African masks and statues; I needed something unique and unusual, something most Americans hadn't ever seen, like coffins that looked like cars. He had never heard or seen such a thing, but he was willing to go looking and with a little research was able to determine at least where they came from.

The next time he was in Africa, he called me in the middle of the night, and said "I found them. How many do you want?" When I clued into what the hell he was talking about, I said, "as many as you can afford to buy." He came home a month later with seventeen. I was good to my word, and bought them all. I would later buy a handful more.

The tradition seems to have started amongst the Ga people sometime in the 1950s, with one family in Accra, Ghana. P'aa Joe, being the #1 designer, basically had a monopoly. They are called "fantasy" coffins because they are made in the shape of something near and dear to the deceased. Sometimes they represent the job they held, other times, simply things they liked. I have a book that lists about thirty different styles, everything from fruits and vegetables, to animals, to airplanes, and different cars being the most common. I bought at least one of every type. My personal favorite is a frilled lizard (think the spitting dinosaur in **Jurassic Park**). Crabs and lobsters for shell fishermen are perhaps the most colorful (and strange shaped), while the favorite with Ripley guests was indisputably the Coca-Cola bottle shaped ones. Bird shaped ones — chickens, roosters and eagles — are by far the largest, the eagle being reserved for tribal chieftains. Accompanied by photos and film foot-age shot by **National Geographic**, virtually every Ripley odditorium now has at least one of these coffins. Collectively they are my favorite African pieces in the Ripley collection.

Around 2012 Ripley's got serious about the concept of traveling exhibitions. The program was first started by John Corcoran who piloted the successful **Science of Ripley's**, but in the mid-teens it was driven forward by Doug Rutledge, an eager number cruncher turned sales person in the company's Business Development wing. Doug's tenure with the company was sadly quite short, but he deserves full credit for the first foreign Ripley traveling show, a show that started in Johannesburg in 2014, traveled to about twelve destinations in the eastern parts of South Africa, and then settled in Cape Town in 2016-2017. Doug had previous experience working with "malls" in Africa and Dubai, and hooked Ripley's up with a conglomerate of partners to tour large South African malls. The show was small, and conservative; the risk was high, but the exposure was worth it. When the "tour" ended, one of the partners, Kristi Maree, suggested she and her brother, Tinus Maree, would like to build a permanent Ripley location either in Durban, or Cape Town. Ripley's felt more comfortable with Cape Town (Bob Masterson and Norm Deska had both looked at Cape Town before), and somewhat hastily a "B-grade" site was located in the Victoria and Albert Harbor, and a "pop-up" museum opened less than two months later.

In the attractions business, location is everything. I call the Ripley's Cape Town a B-location, others may not have been even this kind. The V&A Harbor Region is without a doubt the best possible location not just in Cape Town, but perhaps in all Africa, based on income standards, tourist numbers, climate, foot traffic, transportation routes, all the key ingredients Buzz Price discusses in his book, the industry bible, **Walt's Revolution**. Significantly there are high end hotels, lots of restaurants, and retail outlets for locals and tourists alike, and there were already other existing attractions in the area, an aquarium, a marine history museum, a Ferris wheel, and the ferry boat to Robben Island, site of the prison where South African leg-end Nelson Mandela was imprisoned for eighteen years. The prison is like a national shrine and a must-see for anyone in Cape Town.

Ripley's was quite close to the ferry dock, but a flight of stairs up. The ideal location within the harbor was about 300 yards away, on the other side of a drawbridge, near the marine museum, next to the Ferris wheel, and in front of the main mall entrance. You wouldn't think 300 yards would make a difference, but when it comes to parking and foot traffic, as little as fifty-feet can make a difference. I wouldn't have believed it if I hadn't seen it with my own eyes, and worked that staircase myself for several days.

Of course, the price of rent, and the franchise fee levied by Ripley's, were also significant reasons why the museum failed.

The Ripley staff in Orlando, referred to the location as a "pop-up", suggesting it was never meant to be permanent. Tinus and Kristi knew it wasn't the best location, but it was the best they could do, at least for the time being. Almost from day one they were looking for another site. They saw it as a long-term investment, and though small by most museum standards, they saw it as a permanent business venture. This fundamental difference of opinion probably doomed the location from the beginning.

I had met Tinus and Kristi twice in America, and we had hit it off quite strongly, so when they specifically asked for me to be the Ripley representative to help them with their opening I was very honored, but not surprised. Typically, I would go to museum openings, but not by myself, someone from operations, or the design department, would also go. I am sure the Maree's expected to see both Doug and I, as Doug had been instrumental in doing the financial deal, but Doug, unbeknownst to them had been pulled off the assignment, and would leave the company shortly after. For their money, they were left with just me.

I went to Cape Town on my own shortly after they opened, and did some radio press. I met several members of the staff: Charin, Lish, Tabele, Ganiefah, Wendy, Leigh, Sia, Solo, and Sibong, and worked with them on learning what their exhibits were, Robert Ripley's personal connections to Africa and South Africa in particular, and some sales techniques. I never met a more enthusiastic staff determined to please both me and the owners. All of them were expected to be "guide-hosts" as well as cashiers. Charin Rumble, the "manager", was the eldest, perhaps thirty-five to forty years of age, and the only one who had ever traveled outside of Cape Town. None of them had a car, and most traveled to work many miles by train every day, typically for a four-hour shift. In general, women did not work past 5 pm for safety reasons. Religious backgrounds varied, as did languages. They all spoke perfect English, but several tribal regional languages too: Wendy told me she was fluent in nine languages, and often acted as a translator between staff members, as well as with guests.

On my first visit, Kristi acted as my guide. On my second trip, six months later, I spent more time with Tinus, his wife, Elsebe, and his daughter, Johani, who was now acting as the day-to day operations director. Together they were all wonderful hosts, proud of their city, and their museum. I saw Robben Island — and was deeply moved (when I went home I immediately read Mandela's autobiography, **Long Walk to Freedom**), the natural wonder of the top of Table Mountain, a winery or two, and I even squeezed in a day safari to see elephants, lions, water buffalo and rhinos — four of the so-called "Big Five" animals of the region (2). I also went shopping.

I identified two types of sculptures that I thought would work for Ripley's, life sized animals made from oil drums (turns out these were not actually produced locally, but came from Kenya), and life size animals made from wire and glass beads. I made a deal, using Adjibou Keita as a middleman, to buy several of each, to include: giraffes, elephants, rhinos, lions, leopards, ostriches and gorillas. It would be the hardest, longest, most fraught with anguish two deals of my career. I retired before all of them were finally delivered eighteen months later. A few of them I never did see, and at least two of the oil drum animals arrived damaged. A few were displayed at the Memphis Zoo in a temporary display in the early summer of 2018, but I did not see them installed, and am unaware if the public loved them as much as I do.

Tinus was always very optimistic, and did everything possible to keep the museum open. His inability to get a bigger, better location, however, eventually killed the project. I had hoped to help with the closure in the spring of 2018, and see his wonderful staff one more time, but a severe national water shortage in South Africa made travel unadvisable. Tinus quietly closed the doors after Easter, and I was left with a bad taste in my mouth. I took the failure of the museum, and the tribulations of the South African purchases, both somewhat personally, and they became final straws in helping me decide to retire the following month, on May 18th, ten days after celebrating my fortieth anniversary with Ripley's.

34

Snake Alley & the Key to Burlington, Iowa

In my mind one of the greatest honors anyone can get is
to be given the key to a city. Sure, it is hokey and
the key doesn't really do anything, but the gesture is
very meaningful. It is a genuine sign of thanks, love,
and appreciation for something, presumably of meaning,
done well. Icons like Sinatra, Monroe and Elvis, had
several in their collections. I felt honored to have
one. Burlington, Iowa is not quite, Memphis, Hollywood,
or Las Vegas, but beggars can't be choosers. I can assure you the effect was the same: the city of Burlington, and its mayor made me feel like a king.

In preparation for the Ripley company's 100th birthday
(actual date December 19, 2018, but to be celebrated for
several months in 2018-2019), Ripley's on-line marketing
team Ross Jenne, and Lauren Hubbard, took an idea that
a TV producer named J. Sanchez, and I, had been playing
around with for a couple years. The basic plan was to
honor places in small town America that had once been
featured in the Believe It or Not! cartoon. Both J. and
I, had been in several towns of this ilk, and thought
that there were hundreds of places that could be honored. J. believed the towns would be excited to be me-
morialized as it could attract tourists. Ross suggested
we pick 100 in order to capitalize and synchronize with
the upcoming Ripley anniversary. It seemed like a perfect fit.

I set to work compiling a list of likely candidates. I
quickly identified over a thousand towns without even
finishing looking at every state. The possibilities
were endless. I thought Alton, Illinois, the home of
legendary giant Robert Wadlow, whose 100th anniversary
would also be in 2018, was the perfect choice. J. didn't
dispute my choice, but because of an **Amazon** show he was
producing, called **The Fire-ball Run**, he suggested nearby Burlington, Iowa instead. He had connections already
with the mayor, and because he was going to be filming
there regardless of Ripley's involvement or not, he of-

fered to film and promote Ripley's being in the town as part of an episode, at no cost to Ripley's if we were willing. It was too good an opportunity to pass on.

With a projected deadline of a few months, Ross and Lauren set out to design a cast iron plaque that could be mounted into the ground. They called the program **"Ripley Oddspots"**. Burlington's "odd spot" was called Snake Alley. It is a one-block, 275'-long, cobblestone street, with a gradient of twenty-one degrees, and five-half turns, and two-quarter turns. It was made in 1894, and has a unique uneven brick pattern constructed deliberately to prevent horses from slipping. It is the crookedest street in the world. The plaque would have an etching of Ripley's cartoon of it, and some verbiage. It wouldmeasure approximately twenty-four inches by thirty-six inches set on a four-foot tall post.

J.'s show, **The Fireball Run**, which aired for eleven seasons, is about an annual charity car race, by a group of mega-rich one-percenters. Like the popular network show, **"The Amazing Race"**, teams travel a given route somewhere in America, locating obscure historic artifacts and unique attractions in each city they stop. The contestants paid all their own expenses, and each car sponsored searches for a "missing person". They tended to drive fancy cars, or at least decorated ones. The year before they had filmed at Ripley's in St. Augustine on a trip down the Eastern Seaboard. This year they were traveling through the Midwest, down the Mississippi River valley. In addition to a Ripley plaque unveiling, the Burlington episode would feature a marching band parade, and high school cheerleaders. My job would be to make a speech at the base of Snake Alley, cut a ribbon and unveil the plaque.

By the time the event took place, a couple more details were added. All of the competing cars would have to drive down the alley, and I would too. I would narrate part of the parade, and not only would J.'s crew be filming, but a crew from Ripley's would as well. Ross and Lauren saw the opportunity to make a promo-sizzle-reel that might help them sell the concept to future interested towns. Ripley's team and I descended on Burlington on September 16, 2017.

J. is a very spontaneous guy, and he may have known

what was going to happen, but I certainly didn't. The parade took at least an hour, and as I know nothing about cars, every word of my narration was made up on the spot. By the time it was over, I was psyched up big time to drive a hot car down the alley, but at the last minute, I was made a passenger rather than a driver. For the cameras, including an aerial drone, I would sit and wave, like the Pope, from a gorgeous silver Porsche. Both sides of the alley were lined with cheerleaders, from two competing schools. One side chanted my name, "Edward, Edward, Edward", the other yelled "Ripley's, Ripley's, Ripley's". The car traveled at tortoise speed and almost burnt out its brakes, but the view, and the spectacle were super. I felt like a king.

At the bottom of the Alley, a large dais was assembled, and a marching band drove the crowd of several hundred into a frenzy. Both schools and several businesses had closed for the day to assure a large crowd. I gave a speech signifying the significance of Burlington being the first —#1-Oddspot in the whole country. The mayor, a wonderfully energetic young man, gave a speech acknowledging the honor, and praising Ripley's. Then we two cut the ribbon, and pulled the veil off the plaque together. After several staged photos, and multiple takes to make sure the video got every angle, the mayor returned to the stage for a Longer speech on the history of the alley. He closed by inviting practically the whole town to a celebratory dinner at the convention center that evening, and by giving me personally - not Ripley's — the key to the city. I don't know if J. knew this was going to happen, but the Ripley team sure didn't. As the cheerleaders screamed, and the band roared, I cried like a baby. For once I was speechless. The newspaper photo the next day showed me pumping my fist like a champion.

That night I was again called on to speak at the dinner, and again the town gifted me — this time with a t-shirt and a metal lunch box — both featuring drawings of Snake Alley. There were lots of greetings, handshakes and photos, and the Ripley team were the last people to leave. From the reception we went to a bowling alley, the only place in the whole town still open on a Tuesday night at 10 pm.

My emotional high lasted five days. Over the weekend I

had the key and part of the ribbon framed, and on Monday I quietly, without pomp and circumstance, but publicly, presented the key to Ross. It wasn't an easy decision, but it was the right one. He had worked much harder than I did. After displaying it in his office for a short while, he in turn gave it to the company. It is now proudly displayed in the company's corporate headquarters reception area in Orlando.

To date there is still no Oddspot #2, and I haven't yet seen the Burlington episode of **The Fireball Run** [1]. The Oddspot campaign switched gears rather radically early in 2018, and though I still hope it succeeds going forward, I can't personally endorse it, and honestly don't think any town will get as excited about it as Burlington was. Snake Alley deserved to be first regardless of whom else may follow.

35

De-Acquisitioning; A Bad Decision?
The Jury is Still Out

1989 was the strangest year in my Ripley career. At very least, it was a year of chaos. It followed the last year of a beloved president who was replaced by a not so admired man, and finished with the ascension of Bob Masterson who would in the 1990s lead Ripley's into a new era, a time of awakening, tremendous growth, and radical change. In hindsight 1989 was Ripley's Dark Age.

I didn't totally grasp this in 1989, because for me it was an okay time. Through no particular effort on my part, the late Bjarne Christensen, who would serve as President for about eighteen months (1988-November 1989), liked me, and valued my opinion on everything as he tested the waters. I can't say I had any more faith in him than anyone else had, and I certainly knew he was not as capable a leader as John Withers had been, but I did try to reward his faith in me, with loyalty.

His first radical program was to de-acquisition 100 Ripley original drawings. I worked diligently on selecting pieces that I thought would have commercial appeal based on content or exceptional craftsmanship. The well-established Margo Feiden Gallery in New York City, the successful handlers of well-known caricaturist Al Hirschfeld sketches, was hired to make reproductions, and to sell the originals, with prices ranging from $1,000 to $5,000. Thankfully the deal was never consummated; I kept the file intact for nearly thirty years just in case the proposal ever came back to life.

Sensing Bjarne was open to de-acquisitioning, I proposed the sale of a Ripley exhibit.

While flying on an airplane, I read in a **Smithsonian Magazine** that the institute had bought, and repaired an

18th century Japanese royal palanquin (a sedan chair used to carry royal women). They considered it a priceless Crown Jewel. It looked exactly like one we had in St. Augustine, that had been acquired by Robert Ripley sometime in the 1930s, and featured prominently in his Manhattan apartment in the 1940s. It had been in St. Augustine since the 1950 opening, but was coming out in the 1989 renovation. It seemed criminal to relegate it to a no-air conditioner, Butler building in stifling hot St. Augustine that was the Ripley warehouse at the time, so I asked Bjarne did he think we should sell it. I was sure it was worth more than we had it insured for, and equally sure "Oriental artifacts" were no longer seen as a priority in the company's "new" vision. At the time, I was sure getting some quick cash was better than watching it get stored and potentially damaged. No surprise, Bjarne agreed, and gave me the okay to get it appraised, and then find a buyer or seller.

I contacted the world's two most prestigious auction houses: Sotheby's and Christie's. Both showed interest, but it was Christie's that jumped at the opportunity and sent an expert to look at it right away. They identified it as an exact duplicate of the Edo era Smithsonian twin, and estimated it would sell for at least $200,000. They had our attention.

There was one caveat. They wanted to sell something else of Ripley's at the same time in order to advertise the sale as "from the collection of Ripley's Believe It or Not! and the estate of Robert Ripley". They particularly liked a collection of samurai swords that had recently been removed from the San Francisco odditorium. They also asked about several large ivory pieces that had been removed from both San Francisco and St. Augustine that were original Ripley pieces dating back at least to his 1939 Broadway odditorium.

Times had changed, and there was some doubt about redisplaying ivory anywhere. I had already been told not to buy any more ivory, in order to be safe and politically correct in a fluid environment. Bob Masterson was very opposed to selling any of it, but I was thinking of the safety of the pieces rather than their provenance, and Bjarne was thinking of making a good financial first impression. It was decided we would sell all the ivory (about fifteen pieces as I recall), the swords and the palanquin, but with guaranteed minimums, and free full color advertising of the palanquin. I can't vouch for others, but I was satisfied that it was a good deal.

I went to the auction in New York, and was ecstatic at the palanquin's selling for $265,000, ninety-five thousand over our minimum. The ivories all sold, but the realized prices were barely above the mini-mums, not a one got what Bob, or I, really thought they were worth. In total, I made a half-million dollars that day, and felt pretty good. It was the first and last time I would ever sell anything that belonged directly to Ripley [1].

I met the late Nick Gear, the number two guy with the Jim Pattison Group at the time, on the plane home to Toronto. I liked him, and always respected his opinion [2]. A half-million dollars didn't impress him, and he questioned why we would sell any Ripley assets. He deflated my swollen head very quickly.

Thirty years later, I am still not sure if I did good or bad. I certainly regret selling the ivories, but still think it was the right choice for the palanquin. I would love to see it once again, and hope it is in a museum somewhere, and not in some rich guy's apartment gathering dust — or worse.

Bob Masterson and I have talked about this day many times, and I know he thinks I f*&%ed up, — but I don't think he blames me — he blames Bjarne who as pointed out above, was fired in November that year for reasons unrelated to this story. Bob took over in January 1990, and the company had a new war cry "Let's not do that again", which had several levels of meaning. Bob was the fourth president of five that I operated under, and the longest reigning (1973-to 2010 with the company, 1990-2009 as president).

36

De-Acquisitioning — A Footnote:
Dr. Gerald Gardner — English Witch

In the last chapter I noted that I never de-acquisitioned anything that belonged directly to Robert Ripley aside from the palanquin and the ivories. After writing the chapter I reflected, and decided I did need to add a footnote, there was one other late addition artifact I played a big part in de-acquisitioning.

The Doctor Gerald Gardner Witchcraft collection had no direct tie to Robert Ripley, having been bought by Alec Rigby, Derek Copperthwaite and Charlie Bristol in 1973, post Ripley, pre-Edward Meyer, and in 1986, I didn't give a second thought to selling a large chunk of it. The company had in fact been selling small jewelry pieces from the collection from day one, mainly via the odditorium gift shop in St. Augustine, Florida. In closing the Museum of Witchcraft and Superstition (aka — "The World of the Unexplained"), in Gatlinburg, Tennessee, I became acquainted not just with the history of the good doctor, one of the founders of the Wiccan religion, and a friend of Aleister Crowley, but of a massive library of witchcraft books and hand—written manuscript material that had been used merely as props in two sets regarding ancient and modern witchcraft. Some of the books were very old, a couple dating to the 1500s, and I figured they had value just because of their age. Since Gardner, and his friend Crowley to whom there were several hand-written letters both to and from, both had cult followings, I suspected some money could be made by selling the library, while keeping the artifacts that had been displayed in Gardner's own Isle of Man museum from the 1950s through to 1973.

I made some phone calls, and wrote some letters, and soon confirmed there was considerable interest in Gardner's library, mainly for his manuscript material, and specifically for one large handwritten volume titled **Ye Olde Arts Magical.** Using my best library skills, I made a lengthy handwritten descriptive bibliography, circulated it amongst the underground witch community, and then invited several notable Wiccans and self-proclaimed witches, to inspect the collection. I eventually sold roughly half the books, including the **Arts Magical** manuscript for $40,000 (CDN) to a Wiccan priest living in Toronto. When we met to hand over the books, he wore a full-length Dracula cape, carried a devil-headed cane, and had a necklace made from a bird of prey claw. His female associate was somewhat scantily under-dressed for the occasion in leather and devilish jewelry, and served as a disturbing visual distraction. They were visually scary, and people joked that I might need to have a Catholic priest come in and exorcise my office of any evil they may have left behind. I heard months later that they had swindled the purchase money out of their coven followers and absconded with the books.

I was glad to have the books gone, and to have made back nearly 50% of the original purchase price of the entire Gardner collection while still having the exhibits and a couple hundred more books that I thought I could sell later for about the same price.

Nearly every year for thirty years, someone would want to see the remaining book collection which I duly inventoried, and stored to the best of my ability. Most were not serious buyers, and those who made an offer could not match my asking price of between $30,000 and $40,000. I was never able to find another Wiccan with enough money to purchase the entire collection, and I stubbornly refused to sell the library off piecemeal. The original buyer made a second appearance in 2003, but just wanted the remaining Crowley letters. He was convinced he had bought the best stuff, and believed he had got it for a bargain. I was still happy with the original deal; it had apparently been a win-win for both parties. I couldn't help but wonder if he had learned any magic from the books, but I was too polite to ask what had happened to his cape, his mistress or his coven.

37

Exhibit Thefts: Vampire Killing Kit Guns, Shrunken Heads, A DiMaggio Bat, and Elvis' Underwear.

Petty theft drives me crazy. I am convinced people steal just to prove to someone else they can. Why else would someone want Ripley odditorium show cards, the small descriptive story placards I wrote for every exhibit displayed in Ripley odditoriums? If I was supposed to feel flattered that someone liked my writing so much they stole it, I was not. Rather, I was angered that they made me work to re-write the missing piece. You would be surprised how often these text cards were literally ripped off the walls. Depending on the size of the card, the value of the stolen goods ranged from five to fifteen dollars. Hardly the crime of the century.

We never had more than one theft a year, and over time security systems, everything from motion detectors to video recording surveillance, to basic showcase padlocks, improved to a level where crime was virtually wiped-out. In forty years, there were ten thefts of note, and each one left me shaking my head in disbelief. I hazard to mention them here, in the naïve hope that someone might read this and return the artifacts — or turn in the culprits!

Shrunken Heads

Shrunken heads don't exactly come with a serial number, so tracking a stolen one is nearly impossible. It is hard to imagine what the thief plans to do with the hot property. There isn't a big resale market, and anyone who does buy shrunken heads typically knows everyone else's collection. The stolen property would be questioned pretty quickly. Under my watch there were four separate shrunken head thefts: one in Niagara Falls, one in Key West, one in Australia, and one in New York City.

The head from Key West was found two days later in a

back-alley garbage can. The head in Australia was re-turned in a bag. The two heads stolen from the New York Odditorium took more than two years to surface, but when shown to collectors for sale, they were instantly recognized as coming from Ripley's, and through some careful intrigue, made their way back to Ripley's. The actual thief was not apprehended, but others involved in the illicit trade of stolen property were prosecut-ed.

The Niagara Falls head has been missing for over thirty years. It is unlikely that it will ever be found, but rumors of it being in someone's bedroom just outside of Niagara Falls have circulated, and I remain hopeful that one day I will see it again. This particular head was the company poster-boy shrunken head for most of the 1950s-through the early 1980s. It went missing dur-ing a major renovation of the Niagara odditorium in 1987. It has very long hair, probably the longest of any head in the Ripley collection, and is adorned with a single large red bead on each of its three mouth strings. It was acquired by Ripley himself, and could easily be identified because of the number of existing photos, both black and white, and color, that exist of it, dating all the way back to 1939 when he was displayed in the first New York City World's Fair odditorium. This is the theft that eats away at me. A long-standing re-ward is still offered for its return.

Vampire Killing Kits

It is scary to think what someone might do with a sto-len 180-year-old pistol, but four different 1840s era flintlock pistols have been stolen from Ripley museums. All four belonged to vampire killing kits. Two of the thefts occurred in San Francisco, and in both cases, just the pistol was stolen. In the third case, in Or-lando, and the fourth in Australia, the entire case was stolen. Like a shrunken head, a vampire pistol is also not easily traced, but unless advertised as coming from a vampire kit, the value of just the gun is not signif-icant, and if advertised as coming from a vampire kill-ing kit, any potential buyer is going to have a lot of questions, starting with where is the rest of the kit?

I can surmise that the pistols, being small enough,

244

could be hidden away from eyesight in a cabinet of curiosities to gather dust, but the fear that someone
might commit a dastardly crime with one, is enough to
cause me nightmares. If the thieves genuinely believe
in vampires, they should have taken the entire kits,
the gun will only wound the monster, they will still
need to put the stake in his heart. Kidding aside, the
kit is of course rendered un-displayable without the
gun.

Where Have You Gone Joe DiMaggio?

I suspect it was an inside job, and possibly by the
same crook that removed two shrunken heads from the New
York Odditorium, but I feel the disappearance of a rare
Joe DiMaggio baseball bat (and a DiMaggio autographed
baseball) probably happened on a different evening. One
theft having being successfully executed, a second
bolder one was perpetrated. The crook was even bold
enough to brag.

The value was somewhat less than the two shrunken
heads, but the bat in fact was rarer. It was the number
seventeen of fifty-six signed limited-edition bats,
made in 1991 to commemorate the 50th anniversary of one
of the greatest sports records ever, DiMaggio's 1941
fifty-six straight game hitting streak, a record now
seventy-seven years old that no one has even come close
to breaking. I am way too young to know how Di Maggio
dominated the game during his career, but I am smart
enough to know this was an Olympian feat by a baseball
god. I cherished this bat as if it was Thor's hammer.
It was my favorite Ripley baseball artifact.

The thieves were so cocky they not only stole the bat
and ball, they replaced them with another bat and ball.
The trick worked. No one knows how long the replace-
ments were displayed before the switch-out was noticed.
It was only after the two shrunken heads were stolen
that the entire museum was inspected, and DiMaggio was
found missing.

There are thousands of DiMaggio signed baseballs, I
swear he must have done nothing but autograph sessions
for the last years of his life, but there is only one
#17 bat. To me it is priceless. I keep thinking it will

show up in a sports auction someday, and pray that it will someday find its way back to where it belongs on Broadway.

Elvis Has Left the Building

It is impossible not to laugh. Believe it or not, someone stole Elvis' black underwear from the Ripley's odditorium in Hollywood. I kid you not. What is even weirder, is that a pair of gold lame autographed panties worn by of Madonna, were in the same display case, but they weren't taken. Elvis fans are obviously hardcore.

Whoever wanted these really wanted them. They broke through a cube shaped display case, set the alarm off and escaped undetected through a fire escape exit. The next day papers all across the country reported the theft, all with smart ass attempts at humor. My favorite was a writer surmising the Madonna panties hadn't been taken because everyone had already seen them. The Elvis underpants were custom made black briefs, super stretchy so that Elvis could do his karate moves on stage without fear of a wardrobe malfunction, but they weren't marked in any identifying way. The thief didn't even take the letter of authenticity that was displayed with them. There is a huge market in Elvis memorabilia, but without the letter, they are just old, used black briefs. I am sure the thief's lover wasn't impressed.

There may have been one more theft in my history, but personally, I suspected carelessness over crime. In all my years of shipping exhibits I always used Federal Express. I often joked I would be happy to do endorsement commercials for the company, because I had 110% faith in them as the best in their business. One time, and one time only, did one of my FedEx packages go missing. They could "prove" it was delivered, but the signature was illegible and possibly suspect. I had wrapped the artifact myself, and the box contained more bubble wrap than exhibit. I suspect the actual exhibit was thrown away still inside the box by mistake, rather than stolen… unless perhaps, the kinky Elvis thief had a friend with a similar fetish. The lost piece was a 19th century whale bone corset, only big enough to fit a woman with about a twenty-inch waist.

38

Museums You Should See Before You Die

I have been to literally a few hundred museums all around the world, and love them all — except for the occasional really bad wax muse um. In this chapter I will just touch on a few of my favorites, both Ripley museums and everyone else's too.

The first museum I recall ever seeing was the Royal Ontario Museum in Toronto, affectionately called the ROM. I loved the humongous Haida Indian totem pole in the main stairwell, the mummies, the dinosaurs, and the Chinese fresco "wall". Seeing a skeleton of a dodo bird left a permanent mark on my brain — years later I would buy a casting made from it. It is reportedly the most complete dodo skeleton ever found. I especially loved the giant stone lions at the Queen's Park entrance where I had my picture taken on my 8th birthday. The ROM in the years of my youth was a true window unto the world. It is still exactly where it always was, though greatly expanded into what used to be an adjacent garden, but I am sorry to say, I have not been inside it for more than twenty-five years. I hope it is still a grand dame.

In the same vein, I love Mr. Roosevelt's New York City gem of an even earlier vintage, the American Museum of Natural History, and Oxford's Pitt Rivers Collection in England. It goes without saying that I wish every American could have the opportunity to visit Washing-ton D.C. during their lifetime to see at least one of the Smithsonian Institute museums. My all-time favorite is the Natural History museum, but the Museum of American History, the American Indian, and the new African American History and Culture Museum buildings are all worth at least a half day of anyone's time. My current favorite Smithsonian exhibit, located in the Museum of African American History and Culture, is the Emmett Till display, but the Jefferson display, and Chuck Berry's cherry red Cadillac are all worth the wait.

For science museums, which I am not a typical fan of (excuse me but I still like to read about exhibits, more than play with exhibits), I like Sudbury, Ontario's Science North. Two things make it the cream of the crop in my opinion. First, the fact that it is built around a giant cliff of Pre-Cambrian shield, a wall of which was scarred by a meteorite millions of years ago, and second, the people who work there. It is the only science museum I know where everyone is a scientist. They are all passionate about their areas, and it is definitely not just a summer job for the brilliant youngsters that man the exhibits. I am proud to call the Science Director, Julie Moskalyk, a personal friend. She is the perfect example of what makes the Sudbury team so unique. She has a degree in Lepidopterology (butterflies and moths), and started as a fourteen-year-old volunteer, but now runs the place.

She worked herself up from the bottom rung of the ladder to the very top, and I have a feeling isn't finished yet. The whole of Ontario, and maybe even all of Canada, should be proud of her. Her imprint is now on every inch of the building, and its sister Big Nickel mining museum too. Directors and CEOs from all over the science museum world study her every move. With their revolutionary "object theaters", pioneering IMAX presentations and the best team in the business, Julie has put little-old Sudbury on the world visitor's map.

I am also not the typical "military" or "aviation" museum patron, but the San Diego Museum of Air & Space under the direction of James Kidrick, is another museum that has great displays, and even better people. Kidrick himself has been named the top CEO in San Diego, and I don't know anyone who loves his job as much as this man. All of his top people are hands-on, and it shows both in their craftsmanship – they can repair anything or even build replica planes, like Charles Lindbergh's the Spirit of St. Louis, from scratch, and in their exceptional treatment of theirguests. If you want to see airplanes displayed better than anywhere else in the world does it, this is a must-see museum.

I love all the American Presidential Libraries & Museums, I have seen, and at this minute, I would say the Abraham Lincoln Museum in Springfield, Illinois is the number one museum in the entire country. I love everything about this museum, but its two media presentations, developed and built by Bob Rogers, and his Californian company, BRC Imagination Arts, are story telling at its zenith. I first met Bob while working on Harrison "Buzz" Price's book **Walt's Revolution**. Buzz greatly admired him, and any-one visiting the Lincoln museum in Springfield will instantly admire him too. Trust me on this one, a trip to this museum is worth going hundreds of miles out of your way. The wax figures are top notch too!

There are two other specialty museums that for me, because of their ties to Ripley's, are very special. The Alton Museum of History &Art in Alton, Illinois features a collection of giant Robert Wadlow's personal artifacts. Ripley drew cartoons of him when he was eight, and again at age twelve. When he was eighteen, Ripley brought him to New York for a radio interview. He was also, at Ripley's insistence, filmed with the mayor of New York City atop the Empire State Building. In truth this little museum's collection is not much bigger than Ripley's Wadlow collection (1), but the fact that it is in his home town, and that every person in that town knows his story, and are supremely proud that he came from Alton, makes this my personal favorite small town local history museum.

The Mütter Museum of the College of Physicians of Philadelphia is the only museum my children ever ran screaming from — and they didn't even get to the Venereal Disease section! This museum is not for everybody, it might not even be for anybody — other than doctors but it has the best "pure Ripley" display I have ever seen. The subject is Pica — the affliction whereby people will eat anything, especially metal pins, needles, buttons, coins, jewelry, nails, screws, small door knobs — you name it. The text describes a few individuals with enormous appetites, but the actual display is a large, antique wooden library card cabinet. Each of its couple dozen drawers contains dozens of samples of recovered "food stuffs", a drawer for coins, a drawer for hat pins, a drawer for screws, etc. — literally hundreds of items, removed from dozens of different patients, some dating back to the 19th century. It makes some people ill to think about it, but it makes me smile. I can only imagine the archivist separating them all, and cataloging them for future generations to ponder.

It may be hard to believe, but I did not see every Ripley odditorium during my forty-year stay. I did, however, work on every one, and feel qualified to rate them, at least on my own personal preference scale. Having acquired the majority of exhibits in every one of them I could argue that they all are fantastic. Based on their content, I am proud of them all, they all are my babies. I will encourage you, beloved reader to visit as many as possible, but here I will limit my comments to just three. I hope I make it clear why these are the special ones.

Ripley's St. Augustine, Florida -1950 to present

The odditorium in St. Augustine, Florida is the oldest continually operated Ripley attraction. This alone makes it unique and visit-worthy, but its real charm is that it is in a building called **Castle Warden** that was built in the 1880s as a private residence. Its architecture is special, and its layout is very different from other Ripley locations in that it is filled with small rooms, and every room (more than twenty), has a fireplace in it. These are beautiful unto themselves, but make a designer's job rather difficult — no matter what is on display, the fireplace inevitably is the first thing people notice. It also has wonderful wood floors, a magnificent thirty-foot high rotunda, and a couple large Tiffany-studios 19th century stain glass windows. It's an architectural gem, and on more the one occasion in the 1940s, when it was a hotel run and owned by one of Florida's greatest literary figures, Marjorie Kinnans Rawlins. Robert Ripley actually slept here. It is the only Ripley odditorium that can boast that. It is also haunted, but that is another story.

In 1950 Doug Storer (Robert Ripley's right hand man), Doug Ripley (Robert's younger brother) and a New York City impresario named John Arthur, filled the museum with the hundreds of items that they had obtained from the estate auction of Robert Ripley. Every other Ripley museum that opened prior to 1985 would get the majority of its exhibits from this "central showroom". I can't imagine what it looked and felt like in the 1950s, when it had thousands of displays; it still felt stuffed (and a little stuffy too) when I first visited in 1982 when it "only" had "500 items".

Until its first total renovation in 1989 — thirty-nine years after its opening, this museum was the single best place to get a grasp on the size and diversity of the Ripley collection in its original purist form. It has been renovated several times since 1989, and may have lost a great deal of its exhibits, but it hasn't lost its soul. In addition to Robert Ripley, it is the only odditorium Jack Palance and Jack Haley (the producer of the Palance - Ripley tv show) visited. For me there are more than just the two female ghosts of the women who lost their lives in a 1940s fire roaming this stately museum.

San Antonio, Texas -1988 to present

The odditorium in San Antonio has never moved — at least not yet— but is unique in that it has significantly changed three times. When it was built and opened in 1988, it was a franchise, it had a non-Ripley owner, Bill Phillips, and a non-Ripley designer, Drew Hunter. From the very beginning it was unique, unlike any other existing Ripley's museum. Drew approached it from a larger theme park, theatrical background, and actually sketched his sales pitch renderings on bar napkins! I kid you not (2).

It was the first Ripley odditorium that was more an "attraction", than a museum. You could almost ignore the actual exhibits and simply enjoy the "sets". It had elements of fairground fun houses and haunted houses, and each gallery had its own elaborately themed concept. My favorites were a lost civilization ruins room, and a very glittery undersea gallery that channeled both Disney's "20,000 Leagues Under the Sea", and "Atlantis".

Several years later, the museum was the first franchise bought back by the parent Ripley company. The exhibit collection was dramatically changed, but the basic sets stayed the same. It was a rather interesting combination of second and third generation Ripley attractions where two very different designers clashed in styles. The new people never quite grasped Drew's bigger picture imagination, and tried to force "square pegs into round holes". It wasn't terrible, but it wasn't good either.

When they finally gutted the entire place in 2007, and started again from scratch, San Antonio became my favorite Ripley odditorium. The new second-story height made all kinds of new things possible, including the display of a twenty-four-foot tall toothpick Eiffel Tower, and videos near the ceiling that could be enjoyed without blocking other people's view. The real beauty of this museum is its exhibits, both the quality and the quantity. Its large open warehouse concept rooms allowed the team to stuff it like I imagine St. Augustine once looked. This is a museum you can spend hours in, and still miss stuff. I believe it has the very best of Ripley's in terms of exhibits, something for everyone, big and small, historical and scientific, classy and kitschy, sublime and silly. It must be seen to be believed.

Wisconsin Dells, Wisconsin -1990 to present

Like the original San Antonio, Wisconsin was built as, and in this case still is, a franchise, again meaning it had outside designers, people with new thoughts and fewer pre-conceived notions of what a Ripley odditorium had to look like. The chief designer was Norm Rollingson, a past-wax museum specialist, with aid from his entire family. It doesn't have my very favorite façade — that would be Atlantic City (3)

but it does have a themed exterior. It looks like a Central American pyramid-ruin, and has a parked car hanging precariously thirty-feet up its side — so the building itself, is very cool. Inside, the ancient ruins theme was perpetuated, and in the middle, there is a crashed airplane and a rope bridge. The most outlandish display features the mummified head of serial killer Peter Kurtin on a meat hook, originally inside a refrigerator (see Chapter 32) inside a M.A.S.H. television show inspired medical army tent. Pure Hollywood drama around every corner.

Around 2010, Norm's daughter, Corena, and her husband Kevin Ricks, did a significant renovation to the show adding a computer game element and even more Hollywood thematic elements. Expanding on the lost civilization look of the museum's exterior, they decided to **hide** some of their best exhibits. Going forward, a trip through the museum was a treasure hunt — a real inter-active ad-venture. One-third of the museum's exhibits are hidden. If you want to see them, you have to solve puzzles, and actually "work" to enjoy the experience. Think **"Raiders of the Lost Ark"** meets Robert Ripley. The Ricks' have since expanded this style "game" to another attraction in the Dells that they call **Wizard Quest**. On a recent trip to **Wizard Quest**, I saw more kids having fun with their parents in an attraction than I have in many years. The innovative thinking of Kevin and Corena paved the way for all future Ripley odditoriums.

The common thread to the above three museums, is that they are very different from all the rest. Each has an element that no other Ripley odditorium has. There are newer, and arguably flashier ones, like Amsterdam, but there are none as original as these three. St. Augustine established the bar, San Antonio and Wisconsin raised it [4].

All Good Things Must Come to Pass

Over the years Ripley's closed almost as many odditoriums as they opened. For odditoriums overseas, like Manila, Jakarta, Kuwait, Korea and India, I merely helped out from a computer at a desk in Orlando, verifying the names and values of the pieces in the collection. For many of the closings, however, I was on site to literally pack the artifacts, to take stock of the collection, and to judiciously decide what could be thrown away, or sold, versus what was to come back to the warehouse. Knowing that when I left after a few days of hard work people would be unemployed was always sad, but for the most part, I enjoyed being on site, and learning from the people who had dedicated hours and years to the location. Some of my most memorable times with staff were at closings, when teamwork and camaraderie were essential to getting the job done, quickly, safely, and with minimal damage. This chapter is dedicated to them. Five specific odditorium closings are particularly memorable for me for widely varying reasons (1).

Estes Park, Colorado -October 1984

Alec Rigby had built the Ripley's Estes Park, Colorado, odditorium in 1972, flush with the success of Gatlinburg, Tennessee. To his mind the locations were very similar: both were at the gateway to a much visited National Park with mountains. They may have — on the surface — looked the same, but they were in fact very different places, at least in 1984. In my mind this was the only mistake Alec ever made when it came to choosing a location.

The odditorium was located on the main street in a two-story, turn of the century, combination hotel/ music hall. It was beautiful in a Far West cowboy style. Like Gatlinburg, a lot of people, including families, did pass right by our door, but unlike in Gatlinburg, they didn't stop, virtually everyone was heading straight for the park. There really were no "attractions" to keep them in town. "Tourists" here were hardcore nature lovers, many of whom would rather hike the Continental

Divide, loaded down with fifty pounds of gear, or drive America's highest elevation highway inside a camper with all the amenities, than go into a museum. There was also a lack of watering holes in town, one nice one for "couples on a date", one country western dance hall for twenty-somethings, and one not so nice place for everyone else. Before the week was out the Ripley team had tested all three.

There were three of us, Bob Masterson, Norm Deska, and myself on the mission, working in conjunction with the local manager, Carol Tucker. Bob had recently been on site, and had reported it was very run-down, and it would probably be wise to get rid of it prior to the company being sold (2). Neither Norm, nor I, had ever been to the odditorium. She met us at the airport, casually said "Thank you" to Bob (I had no idea what for) and smiled cautiously at me. Later that evening, I would learn that Bob had told her I was a cross dresser. She expected me to be in a gown and high heels; she had thanked Bob for convincing me to leave my dress, wig, bra, and heels at home. Mountain folk were simply not ready for whatever version of me Bob had painted. This would not be the last practical joke Bob would play that week.

Closing a Ripley odditorium is not an easy job. More often than not, walls are built around certain exhibits making their extraction difficult, some might even say impossible. Estes Park was my first closing, so I had no idea what to expect, and in 1984 there was no computer list of what was supposed to be in the show. I had a binder of Polaroid photos for an inventory, which was maybe 50% accurate at best; it had all the wax figures which were post-Robert Ripley acquisitions, and the most expensive pieces according to an insurance list, but it did not have literally dozens of pieces of "funny money", unusual currencies from around the world which were in abundance here (displayed in a replica bank vault setting), or any "props" — items bought as window dressings for dioramas. In this latter category, were several hand-painted circus sideshow giant banners, worth hundreds of dollars then, but multithousands now, and a family of three taxidermy mounted buffalo (sic — more properly called American Bison, per a cartoon in Ripley's first book, 1929). I suspect these buffalo really were the most valuable items in the building, not just because I now have a deep appreciation for what taxidermy cost, but also because they were originally killed by President Theodore Roosevelt in 1901-03. I repeat, these were not on the inventory, for all intent and purposes, they did not "officially exist".

Once the exhibits were labeled, and packaged, they would be placed in a giant truck parked outside on the main street (bet you can't do that today!). This was estimated to take a week of eight-hour work days. Whatever wasn't an exhibit, was placed into two piles as close to the front entrance as we could get it. One pile was items we would try to sell, but be willing to throw away if necessary, the other was a pile of objects we would take if we couldn't sell them, but only if we had room on the truck for them.

It is amazing what people will buy. We literally could have sold anything. For example, we sold an antique safe, circa 1860 that no one could open; presumably the buyer ended up spending a lot of money to have a locksmith change the antique burnished silver-plated door. As a thing of beauty, it was no surprise that someone would want it, but given it weighed in excess of a 1,000 pounds, and was on the second floor of a building with no elevators (3), we didn't expect to be able to sell it.

There was one thing we were sure we would not be able to sell, no matter how cheap the price. Bob is one of the biggest practical jokers I have ever met. Very early in our "Closing Sale", he had me wrap this particular item in non-see through brown Kraft paper. It was quite large, and the only thing for sale that was wrapped; it was virtually impossible to miss it on the sale pile. Needless to say, every would-be bargain hunter asked what it was. Our answer was, "Sorry I can't tell you, but I guarantee you it is worth more than $100, but today, for you, I will sell it for twenty dollars". It sat on the table all week, and finally on the last morning, a well-known local businessman man who had looked at it repeatedly every time he walked in, broke down and bought it. We begged him to open it on the spot, but he wouldn't. He probably knew he had been had, but he'd be damned if he was going to let anyone know.

Within ten minutes of leaving the building he phoned, asked for Bob, laughed, and said" Well done, You got me." For the princely sum of twenty dollars he now was the proud owner of the Ripley's Believe It or Not! Odditorium's women's washroom, sanity napkin dispenser.

Even this however, was not Bob's coup d'grace in the town of Estes Park. As I mentioned above, we frequented all three bars in the town during our stay. The one we liked best was the cowboy dance hall. The owner's name was Eddie, and like myself, his nickname was "Fast Eddie". For several nights in a row we had tried to convince Eddie that he should buy our three buffalo. We even told him what he could do with them: nail them to the ceiling and call the bar "Fast Eddie's Upside Down Buffalo Bar". We assured him people would come from all over the country to drink and dance in a place with upside down buffalo on the ceiling. He didn't believe us……but……he knew more about those buffalo than we did. In fact, a relative (his grandfather I believe), had been Roosevelt's guide, and there was reason to believe that he had been the man who skinned them for Teddy and a taxidermist more than eighty-years earlier.

Bob was willing to sell the buffalo if we could, but they were in the pile to be put on the truck if we had room. Fast Eddie wanted the buffalo, but he wasn't willing to pay for them; our asking price was a measly $800 for the three, and we would not break up the set. Eddie had made numerous small offers for them during the week, but was convinced we would end up giving them to him. As the truck filled up, it was apparent the buffalo weren't going to fit. We gave Eddie one last chance to buy them. He said "nope", then Bob walked back into the odditorium, and came out with a chain saw. He told Eddie he would cut the heads off, take them, and leave the bodies. He started the piercing, squalling, chain saw for affect. Eddie started screaming, then crying. The buffalo were inches away from losing their lives a second time before Eddie yelled "stop". He wrote the check, and the entire town cheered.

In total we made over $8,000 from that closing sale. Six months later, five Ripley managers went fishing, but more on that later.

I could end this section here, but we did do more than just sell stuff in Estes Park. So for a moment let me digress from the topic of "closings" to some points of personal biography.

Estes Park, or more specifically nearby Rocky Mountain National Park, is one of the most beautiful places in all of America. We didn't have much daylight leisure time, but we did spend one day in the Park. We hiked two trails. The first was a short one, but none of us noted the contour lines, and discovered though short, it was the steepest path in the whole Park. All three of us nearly died climbing to the Continental Divide — only to be met by an elderly couple (at least seventy-five years old), in traditional leather Lederhosen shorts, who did the hike daily! We contemplated throwing them off the side of the mountain.

In the afternoon we did a much longer, but "flatter" trail, and regained some degree of our dignity.

We did have considerable evening leisure time, but it was far too cold outside (first week of October, and lots of snow around), so nature was usurped by drinking, watching "Colorado Slim "(our name for the six-foot, five-inch, 160lbs. cowboy who two-stepped danced at Fast Eddie's every night with or without partners), and watching baseball on Fast Eddie's one television. I mention these details for a reason. First, I am not much of a country western music fan, but it was here I learned the beauty of precision choreographed dancing, which I have loved to watch ever since, and second it was in **"Fast Eddie's Upside-Down Buffalo Bar"** (I am sure those three buffalo must have been nailed to the ceiling by that Thanksgiving) that I first watched baseball.

In October 1984, the Chicago Cubs were playing the San Diego Padres for the pennant. Estes Park is at least a thousand miles away from Chicago, but Colorado didn't have their own team in those days, and everyone in that town cheered for Chicago as their "home team". Go figure? "Fast Eddie" having the only communal television in town, knew if he could get baseball fans to come to the bar, he could make a killing on whiskey, especially when it was cold enough to freeze the balls of a brass monkey outside. Eddie being the marketing genius we by this time knew him to be, was holding a raffle for tickets to the World Series, in Chicago — assuming Chicago, the heavy favorite could beat San Diego. To enter, all you had to do was drink. Each bar order got you one more ticket in the jar. Pure genius. I had never watched a professional baseball game on TV in my life before, but with "World Series Tickets" on the line, I was fixated.

I grew up in a hardcore hockey family, in a hardcore hockey city. "Softball" had been a summer diversion as a kid, but no one I knew growing up watched American professional baseball. The Blue Jays had come to Toronto in 1977, but it wasn't until 1985 that they played above 500, so in October 1984, forced by snow and cold to watch two teams I knew or cared nothing about, I fell in love with America's pastime. Being a contrarian though, I of course cheered for San Diego, led then by the amazing Tony Gwynn — one of the greatest batters to ever play the game. For those who care, San Diego beat the Cubs, so no one from Esters Park went to the World Series that year. The Padres would lose to Sparky Anderson's Detroit Tigers, and not get back to the playoffs again for another fourteen years. To date, they have still never won a World Series, nor have they had a pitcher on their team throw a no-hitter. I imagine the people of Estes Park now vote for the Rockies instead of the Cubs, but I guarantee they don't vote for the hapless perennial losing Padres.

Ocean City, Maryland -January 1987

The last of Alec Rigby's creations, Ocean City had only been built in 1978, the year I had started with Ripley's. Closing it in 1987 after only eight seasons was admitting defeat. I suspect Alec and John wouldn't have closed it if they had still been in charge, but it was definitely an under-performer by Jimmy Pattison's standards, so when it was time to renew the lease, at an escalated rent, rather than re-new, we walked away. It is worth noting that Ocean City is a beach town, and our odditorium was fronted by a boardwalk, and backed by the ocean. It was our smallest location at the time, and was only open a quarter of the year at best (May-September). It was deserted in January, and freezing cold with bitter winds blowing straight off the ocean. The plan was for myself and my assistant Kathy Vader to fly from Toronto to Salisbury, MD., via Baltimore, aboard an old military plane, then drive to Ocean City where we would be met by Peter MacIntyre, our then odditorium manager in Myrtle Beach, South Carolina, another odditorium that at that time closed in the winter. We saw the trip as torture, Peter saw it as a vacation from winter boredom. Peter knew me well, but had never met Kathy. Kathy had been on a plane before, but never a small one, and this was to be her first Ripley out-of-office adventure.

From Toronto, Ocean City is not an easy place to get to. It takes at least two planes, plus an hour car ride. The second plane would be a small "puddle-jumper". We luckily had winter clothing, but only enough for three days, the time we expected we would need to pack the odditorium.

Almost immediately, this turned into the trip from Hell. I swear we could still see Toronto in the distance when the pilot came on, and said a fierce freak storm was hitting Baltimore, we were going to have to fly to Boston. I knew where Boston was in relationship to Toronto, but not necessarily where it was in relationship to Baltimore. A quick peak at the in flight magazine, however, confirmed my first thoughts: "Why in the hell would we go to Boston rather than simply turning back to Toronto?" Apparently, decision making based on geographic locations and climate conditions, was not how airlines worked. Kathy was scared, white knuckled, squeezing the armrest. I was angry.

To make matters worse, there was not a single snowflake to be seen anywhere in Boston when we landed. "Snow storm? What snow storm?" We were told the storm would probably not last too long. We were re-booked on a later flight, but warned to contact the airport frequently as flights would be canceled for a few hours. We didn't have to stay in the airport, and they were willing to keep our bags, so we thought we would venture out and see Boston.

Neither of us had been to Boston before. We knew about Paul Revere, and even the wonderful Harold Edgerton exhibit on slow-motion photography at the Boston Museum of Technology, but we didn't know how much time we had to waste. We considered where we thought we should go to get out of the cold and decided on the **"Cheers"** Bar. To be honest, I didn't watch "Cheers" – one of the most popular sitcom television shows of all time — but I certainly knew about it, and figured we could at least have lunch, and probably a beer. With the help of a cab driver, we found it despite not knowing its real name (4). Fact was, anyone I could have asked would have directed us there; it was by this time a tourist mecca. It didn't really look like the television version, but it was a nice bar, in the Boston-Irish style, and the food was decent.

I don't think we were there more than an hour, but when we came out, it was a whole different world. Snow was blowing and accumulating faster than I could say "where everyone knows your name". The storm was full frontal now in Boston, never mind Baltimore. The streets were a mess, clogged with skidding cars, and it was very clear no planes would be leaving Logan Airport that afternoon, but we still had to go back to the airport and at least get our bags.

We managed with great difficulty to get back to the airport, but were instantly met with long lines, angry people and "no flights today signs". The ticket agent suggested we find a hotel for the night. The line for the phone booth — this was at least ten years before any-one had a cell phone — was very long. Two hours later, it was my turn. I started with the cheapest one-star hotels, and worked my way up the dollar scale through eight hotels (not knowing where any of them were located). Every desk clerk said the same thing: "Sorry No Vacancies" Finally, on the last possible page, I called the prestigious Lennox Hotel. I certainly couldn't afford to stay there, but if the boss balked at the cost, at least I had a witness to confirm that we had to stay there. The desk clerk said "Sir, yes we do still have one room, but it is the honeymoon suite. Do you want it?" I turned to Kathy, and asked the question. I will never forget the look on her face. She knew I wasn't kidding, but she still didn't believe, or want to believe, what she had just heard. I repeated the question, and add-ed, it was either that, or sleeping the night on a bench in the airport. "Is there at least two beds", she cried. Good question, I hadn't asked. Well, being the "honeymoon suite", no there weren't two beds…but as luck would have it, there were two rooms, a suite, with a door between them. I would be paying somewhere in the neighborhood of $200 to sleep on a couch. Kathy would be very comfortable, and we might even be able to still get room service dinner if we wanted.

Someone assured us the only way we could get to the Lennox was by subway, cabs were no longer working, and walking with our luggage was out of the question. The only thing I knew about the Boston subway – the infamous MTA of folk song legend — was that even in the best of weather one was destined to get lost on it. Coincidentally, it turned out that the Lennox Hotel was exactly where we had gotten the cab to the airport a couple hours earlier.

I can still see Kathy's face, it is etched in my brain, but the subway ride I don't remember at all. The final walk from the subway stop was not long, but very difficult. We were cold, tired, soaked right through, hungry and lugging our excessive baggage (bulky winter clothing combined with exhibit packing supplies). The hotel was an oasis. The room was sumptuous, the doors in between could be locked, and the day's special was poached salmon. Our spouses might kill us when they next saw us, but at least we would eat well. We ate in the hotel's restaurant rather than ordering room service because I had no idea how much one would have to tip a room service bell hop in the Lennox Hotel, and I wasn't prepared to find out.

Boston was not the end of the nightmare, as unbelievable as it might seem, rather, it was just the beginning.

It wasn't snowing when we woke up, but there was deep lush snow everywhere. Traffic was barely moving, and no one was out for a morning stroll. The airline telephone operator said that flights would start as soon as possible. It was, however, recommended we get to the airport as soon as we could. By the time we got there, there were no more spaces for Baltimore.

"We can get you to Philadelphia, though", said the perky agent with a toothpaste commercial smile, "and you should be able to get a connector from there."

"Is it snowing there?" I said.

"No sir", she chirped back in a voice that made you want to throttle her.

"Well then, by all means, please put us on a plane to Philly." "With a connection to Baltimore?" she asked.

At that point, I finally remembered, that I really didn't need to go to Baltimore, it was Salisbury, Maryland we really wanted to get to. "Was there anything going there?" To my amazement, she said:

"No problem, the storm hasn't hit there. You can be there in a couple hours".

"No problem", famous last words never to be believed when uttered by an airline employee.

The flight to Philly was pushed back several times between the supposed take off at 9:15 am, and the actual take off at 3:15 pm. As I recall we both spent the day on the phone talking to the office, to our spouses and Peter MacIntyre (aka: Mac) who was now in Ocean City wondering where we were. It apparently wasn't snowing there and as he hadn't seen snow in several years, he thought our tale of woe was very funny. We finally arrived in Philly round about 6 pm thirty-six hours delayed on a supposed seventy-two hour trip. We of course had missed our connection to Salisbury by several hours, but we were put on stand-by for the next flight — arriving at 8 pm in Salisbury. Kathy hated the Salisbury small plane, a Shorts 330 military surplus vehicle, and was extremely happy to finally land in Salisbury. Unfortunately, it was now dark, and snowing hard. The drive to Ocean City was treacherous and did not bode well. Our friend the "snow storm of the century" (5) had punctually arrived in Maryland with us. It was like a ravenous wolf tracking us down.

We were probably the only car on the road going to Ocean City, everyone else was evacuating the beach town, before the only bridge connecting the beach and the boardwalk to the main land, would be closed. Our Quality Inn motel was on the island side — thank God, of the bridge. For forty dollars a night, it was actually ten times better than I expected. It was a very far cry from the Lennox, but we would have no trouble extending our stay if needed – which was a given by this point. It had a restaurant — specializing in flounder (seemingly the only thing they had in the freezer since they served it three times a day), a room with a big television for watching the Super Bowl which we would be in town for (Mac watched the game, Kathy and I opted that Sunday for staring from our respective rooms out at the gigantic powerful waves hitting the shore. They even had a hot tub that Mac used every evening. Kathy and I could see no enjoyment in taking off six layers of warm clothes to have a public bath with Mac.

With Mac in tow, the drive the next morning from the motel to the odditorium though only a mile or two, was still scary in the continuing blizzard. On our first trip to the odditorium we were stopped by the police who thought us absolutely stark raving mad to be out in the storm. He would stop us several more times before our week was over.

The cold, and the several cups of coffee we had drank to fend it off, made the first order of the day an urgent need for a bathroom. This need was greeted with the news – from Lionel Massey, the odditorium's manager – that the pipes were frozen, we would have to use the public beach bathroom on the boardwalk about a hundred yards away. If there had of been a way for Kathy to escape, I am sure she would never have gone to the bathroom, or come back to the odditorium, once out. The next obvious bit of news was that there was no heat in the entire odditorium, we would be wearing our coats, hats and mitts all week to pack – provided we didn't freeze to death venturing out to the bathroom. Kathy whimpered, I scowled, and to our amazement Mac smiled and sang. The song may have been "Always Look on the Bright Side of Life" from the 1979 Monty Python movie "The Life of Brian." Whatever it was, it was annoying, and I was soon thinking of killing him.

I have no recollection of the specific exhibits that were in this odditorium, but we did have a carpenter to help make crates, and some intermittent help at our disposal as long as the violence of the storm allowed them to get from the island to the mainland. The gallery I remember best, was a recreation of an underground church, carved into the walls of a salt mine, the original being somewhere in Poland. Based on a Ripley cartoon from the late 1930s, this was one of the

264

two finest wax figure galleries Ripley's ever did. In the unheated cold building, we felt like we were working in just such a salt mine. Our extremities were cracking and in fear of falling off faster than the fingers, toes, noses and ears of the wax figures that adorned the sparkling white crystal cave. We prayed to be somewhere warmer.

Our original estimate of three days to pack was accurate, but we couldn't make up the two days we had lost, nor could we "will" our truck to arrive on schedule, so we ended up booking one extra day in Ocean City. The adventure was now twice as long as it had been planned for, and we still had no truck to load the exhibits into. The snow had ceased falling, but there wasn't a plow to be had for hundreds of miles, and the police officer still stopped us, or at least stared us down like we were idiots, every time we went by. Snow or no snow, closures or no closures, we were determined that we would "party" on our last night, believing we could finish packing in plenty of time the next morning. Big mistake.

Expensive places had re-opened over the weekend — small mom and pop places hadn't — so we decided to splurge and reward our-selves. The odditorium was at North First Street, but we had to drive all the way to 75th street before we found BJ's, the perfect place for a celebratory last fling in Ocean City.

Just like in Boston, it was fine when we went into the restaurant, but it snowed hard – again — when we were inside (5). We all got good and drunk. Kathy had never had a "Manhattan" before, and didn't realize that Mac was having hers refilled every time she turned her head or went to the — indoor — washroom (utter luxury!). She also ate a little more than she should have, seeing something other than flounder on the menu for the first time in five days. She ordered — and reordered — jumbo bright pink shrimps. She ate voraciously in an endless cycle of shrimp-drink, shrimp-drink proclaiming they were the best shrimp she had ever eaten, and that Mac's "special" drink was so smooth it tasted like it had no whiskey in it at all.

We were just about the only people in the place, but we did party. Hours later, at 1am closing time, Mac and I fought over who should drive home. I knew I was drunker than he was, but I also knew I had way more snow driving experience than he did. Kathy voted for Mac. In retrospect she was too drunk to have been expected to vote with any sort of intelligence. As the "boss", I should have thrown my weight around, but it was exactly because I was the boss that Mac was so persistent. It would not look good on him should any harm come to me, a vice president — or Kathy for that matter.

Mac was in the car less than ten seconds before he backed into a five-foot high snow drift. We had no sand, no shovels, no boots, nothing but our hands to dig us out — and Kathy was too drunk to hold the steering wheel. Mac and I would take turns "behind the wheel", and pushing. The process was unbearable. We were frozen and no longer talking. By the time the car was free from the drift we were at least sober. The keys were mine, no argument. I have never been in a car with Mac as the driver since.

The next morning Mac and I decided to let Kathy sleep it off, we could finish without her. An hour or so later, we phoned her. No answer. Another hour later, another call. Still no answer. We were not actually panicking though. We had finished without her, and had plenty of time to get to the airport. We drove back to the motel, discussing the finer points of alcohol poisoning. When we got back to the motel and she didn't answer the door, it was time to panic. The owner had not seen her, so we were sure she was still inside, but she had now been asleep more than ten hours. He opened her door and we found her still in her coat from the night before; we could tell that she had spent at least part of the night "sleeping" in the bathroom.

We no longer had time to sober her up, so we poured her into the car. I drove Mac back to the odditorium where he would have to wait another full day for the truck to finally arrive before he and Lionel could load it, and drive a thousand miles to our warehouse in St. Augustine, Florida. Kathy and I drove the opposite direction forty miles to the Salisbury airport. She was sick when she saw the miser-able looking plane — World War II vintage, seemingly held together by thousands of rivets. By this time, however, I no longer had any sympathy, or patience. I blamed Mac, and not her, but was adamant that we had to get on the plane. I was not waiting another minute, let alone another day, to get out of town. Both of us having very young children at home — my daughter Celeste was only a month old at this point, and Kathy's two children were both less than five years old — we had begrudgingly been given presidential permission to leave Mac to load the truck without us. I had no pity for either Mac or Kathy. It was snowing again.

We made the flight, though I suspect it was pure hell for Kathy. The snow got worse, and the ride was not smooth — nor on time. We arrived in Washington in another full-fledge blizzard, with our connecting plane already on the runway. I begged the attendant to get us on the plane. I am sure I must have seemed like a crazed lunatic, but a luggage guy heard my pleading and said he could get us to the plane. I paid him twenty dollars, and he drove a golf cart-like vehicle under plane wings, dodging people and vehicles, through the squall. I have no idea whether he thought we were important political dignitaries, or movie stars, but clearly, he was up to the challenge. The plane miraculously waited for us. In fact, it sat on the runway for another full hour after we boarded. A lot of people glared angrily at us for having caused them to miss the window of opportunity for takeoff. Eventually we left, and got home late that night.

Kathy did not come to work the next day, and until now the story of our week in a frozen hell has never been told in full. It is told here not just with her permission, but also with a few details from her recollection and point of view. She worked for me for seven years (1982-89), the second longest term of any of my wonderful assistants, and we are still friends to this day. She holds a very special place in my heart. It may not sound like much, but Kathy's real claim to fame is that she was the first one in the 1980s to go through every last cartoon research archive folder looking for original photos to enter into our computer database. It was she who discovered two of the most iconic photos in the entire Ripley collection, both from the late 1920s: Wang the human unicorn (a Chinese gentleman with a thirteen-inch horn growing from the back of his head), and Alexandre Patty, a French acrobat that could bounce down and up (!) stairs on his head — the king of cranial hop-ping. These two photos have appeared in Ripley books, on billboards, and t-shirts, and in large formats (the original photos in both cases are less than two-inches square) in virtually every Ripley odditorium around the world. To this day the wax figure of Wang, based on that one small photo, is one of the company's most astonishing and beloved wax figures.

Mac is also still a beloved friend, but neither Kathy nor I have ever drank a Manhattan with or without him, ever again. To be totally fair, Mac, being born in Saranac Lake, New York — snow country — could, and still can, drive in the snow, just not on that night.

All in all, not the best Ripley trip, nor the worst — but definitely the single most memorable.

Postscript: In 2001, fourteen years after the closing of Ocean City, Ripley's opened Ocean City Version Two in the exact same building! Believe It or Not!

Chicago, Illinois -August 1987

As the closing of Estes Park is forever linked in my mind with baseball, so the closing of Chicago is linked with blues music and Thai food. By 1987 I had been a blues music fanatic for eighteen or nineteen years, but this was my first time in the Windy City. Here I didn't have to hear Country music each night, I could go to blues bars and see some of my faves:, Valerie Wellington, Eddie "the Chief" Clear-water, Big Daddy Kinsey, Son Seals, and a few other less well-known luminaries. Chicago was – and still is to a lesser degree — a music pilgrimage site for me. As for Thai food, it was the first time I ever ate it — hot spicy mussels in a steaming sauce with lemon grass. Still the best Thai food I've eaten — at least outside of Thailand.

Chicago was the third odditorium Alec Rigby had built (1968) after Niagara Falls, and San Francisco, and the city had been the location of the very first Ripley odditorium in 1933. The 1968 version was unique in that Ripley's owned the property. Other odditoriums were typically closed because they were under-performing, and the rent was more than we were earning. Chicago was a little different. By 1987 it had passed its peak — its

North Wells Street location had gone from touristy, to trendy high-end restaurants. The property values were soaring, and our land was suddenly worth about five-times what we were clearing per year. It was not a difficult decision to sell, close and move on.

For almost its entire history the odditorium had been run by a lady named Gale Madaj. I didn't know her very well — I think we had met only twice before — but she was a Ripley character in every sense of the word, and then some. With medical issues, and knowing the odditorium would be sold, she left before the final days. I often wonder what happened to her; gone but not forgotten. In her place for the last couple months was the company's youngest rising star, John Corcoran, one of the company's longest serving loyal members, and the employee who worked in more locations than anyone else. By 1987 he had worked at three or four locations already, each time being promoted. Prior to Chicago, he was the #2 in St. Augustine. Though there wasn't much "running" to do, Chicago was his first chance to be #1, the manager. He did an exemplary job keeping the staff intact, and an even better job in advertising, dare I say, promoting, the closure of the odditorium. Several stories appeared in the papers, all lamenting the loss to the city, and mentioning the historical connection to the start of Ripley's, and that we would be having a "going out of business sale". When the time came, people were lined up around the block — more people than had been in the odditorium in months. The biggest sales draw were the wax figures.

The wax figures in this odditorium were more papier maché than wax, built by legendary doll maker Lewis Sorenson in the 1950s and 60s. Being very old, and even older in sculpting technique, we had determined we would sell these. Who wouldn't want a wax figure of Charles Charlesworth, the boy who died of old age at age eight, or a four-eyed man, or a human unicorn, or a man with a candle inserted in his head, or a fat man, or Robert Wadlow, or my personal favorite, Genghis Khan. We (6) sold every one, at a considerable profit (more money to be used for a future fishing trip), and all the newspapers showed photos on their first pages of people walking down the street with them over their shoulders. Corcoran was an overnight media sensation, in the papers, and on the television, the interviews were endless. We couldn't help but wonder where all these people had been when we were open!?

We made over $5,600 from the sale of these wax figures on day one. On Day Two we made nearly as much from selling the wood paneling throughout the odditorium. Our biggest helper was a tall muscular man named "AV" Hunter. AV had been with the odditorium since opening day, nineteen years in total, and was terrified at the prospect of being unemployed, but he worked so hard dismantling our lights, walls, and even wood floors, that he had a half-dozen job offers by week's end. In addition to making people pay for "fixtures", which we had no intention of taking with us, we charged people to have AV carry their purchases to their vehicles. He was as strong as the proverbial ox, and this extra fee was given straight to him. He made over a $1,000 for his troubles, and along with a $5,000 bonus we gave him for his nineteen years' service, he was able to pay off his mortgage, and still have enough money to take his wife dancing. AV was one of the best, and most loyal employees the company ever had. He started another job the following Monday. I continued to send him a company Christmas card for years, and I believe John Corcoran still keeps in touch with him.

A great number of the shoppers came hoping to buy "witchcraft" items from the collection of the late Dr. Gerald Gardner, the most famous witch of the 20th century. Ripley's had bought up his entire collection of artifacts and books in 1973. Initially the artifacts were divided into two collections, called Dr. Gardner's Museum(s) of Witchcraft & Superstition, one being displayed very successfully in San Francisco, the other not so well received, in Gatlinburg, Tennessee. Both of these were gone by 1987 and the best of the Gardner collection was now in Chicago. I have no statistics on how many Wiccans lived in Chicago in the 1980s, but it was definitely more than in the whole state of Tennessee where we had been practically run out of town as Satanist for displaying this collection. We didn't sell any of the actual artifacts, but we did sell an Old-traditional Wizard of Oz-like witch wax figure, and a nude "young", modern witch figure. We probably sold more odditorium guide books, featuring a photo of Gardner on the cover, than had been sold in nineteen years of operation.

In addition to what we sold, I recall four favorite items from the Chicago odditorium that we didn't sell. I couldn't advertise any of these with any effect, and certainly they weren't "show-stoppers", in the

P.T. Barnum attractions lingo, but all four were "pure Ripley":

1) A small piece of wood with thousands of layers of paint on it. Owned by a professional painter, he used it every day for several years to test his brushes. It had grown from a half inch thick board, to a six-inch high rainbow riot of color.

Many years later (2010), a small piece of this block was given to Bob Masterson when he retired from Ripley's. He had long said it was his favorite Believe It or Not! exhibit.

2) A petrified orange that was nearly 100 years old. It was almost totally black, shriveled up to about the size of a golf ball, and as hard as a meteorite — which it resembled much more than an orange.

3) A coin that had been lodged in a man's nose for years, until a coughing fit shot it out several feet across a room….and

4) A razor blade that had been continuously used daily by one man for 67 years.

I doubt anyone paid specifically to see these small items, but it was items like this that had been the heart of Ripley's cartoon during his life time (1890-1949), and I suspect I am not the only person who remembers them with a smile on their face.

There were at least two other items much sought after by shoppers. One was a Chinese sword that I could have sold a dozen times (but didn't) that had a painted wood carved sheath shaped like a dragon, with the handle inside the dragons' mouth, and the blade in its tail. This is my favorite weapon from the original Robert Ripley collection, and it was acquired by Rip himself in China in 1923. The second item, was one of two original shrunken heads Ripley had acquired in Ecuador in 1925. It had the longest hair of any shrunken head I've ever seen and was the model for a famous Chess records blues album cover. It was years later fondly remembered

271

by President Barack Obama as his favorite Chicago exhibit from when he was a youth.

This sale wasn't without mishap. Two turquoise Tibetan Dr.Gardner necklaces, my $300 dicta machine (with all my inventory odditorium "closing notes"), a prop suit jacket from the wax figure of Abraham Lincoln, a multibladed Swiss Army knife, and a camera, were stolen. It was no myth that Chicago was a crime-riddled tough town. I can only imagine what might have happened if AV hadn't been there acting as our muscle.

In 2008, as part of my 30th anniversary gift from the company, I returned to Chicago to attend the annual Chicago Blues Festival. I took a stroll down N. Wells Street for old time's sake. I couldn't find the odditorium — the building had presumably been torn down, and the giant crater size hole in the sidewalk a few feet from the old entrance, must have finally been fixed. I did, however, find the good Thai restaurant nearby, and the mussels were just as good as I had re- membered.

Hong Kong - March 2005

The 1990s were a period of great growth for Ripley's. It was the decade that Ripley expanded into Asia and that I traveled the most. The Hong Kong Ripley's Odditorium — a franchise operation — was located atop Victoria Peak, a site available only by a steep funicular that holds only about thirty people at a time. A lot of people went up that ride, but the location went against everything we preached concerning "location, location, location", and the need for steady walk-by traffic. No one randomly found us there. To scale the mountain, was a predetermined destination activity. The odditorium was first class and beautiful, but virtually inaccessible. Needless to say, the odditorium didn't do as well as hoped, and closed after just eight years. I had been in Hong Kong briefly before, but Hong Kong in 2005 was no longer an English colony, and the winds of change were evident. I suspect the new economy and the mass migration of English-speaking Chinese out of Hong Kong since 1997, had much to do with our premature closing.

I had some health issues in 2005 that would get worse post this shut-down, and I feared there would be language issues that would make this the hardest closing yet. With a break for Easter falling in the middle, we allowed ten days for this closing, twice as long as normal. At great personal sacrifice I forfeited a business class ticket for an assistant — Paul Pikel, my warehouse manager and a very resourceful individual (much more so than myself). Despite the agony of a fifteen-hour flight the day after a colonoscopy, taking Paul with me was one of the best decisions I ever made. He was a God-send in every way.

Our on-site assistant was a very petite young lady named Eva. We couldn't have gotten anything done without her. She was the only one who spoke English, and she had family connections for everything we needed: plumbers, electricians, drivers, muscle men, even a chain saw.

The age of garage sales was long past, everything, including a series of granite statues (at this location several of what used to be our standard collection of wax personalities were carved in stone), a giant sixteen-foot long fiberglass Great White shark — a replica of the real-life "Jaws" shark, the largest fish ever caught on rod and reel, and a ten-foot by ten-foot, twenty-five hundred pound piece of the Berlin Wall, had to come home. Paul and I almost killed ourselves moving the statues. The other two things required more than just brawn.

No matter what we needed, given an hour, Eva somehow miraculously could accommodate us. When it came time to move the Berlin Wall, we needed a crane to hoist it up and out of the building, then a virtual army to move it by hand halfway down the hill to the nearest service road. We figured the crane would be relatively easy, after all Hong Kong is filled with hundreds of tall buildings, and cranes are essential to any construction. Where Eva was going to find us enough man power was an entirely different kind of logistics problem. With a smile that would melt snow, she said "No problem, I'll call my relatives and friends." The next morning, very early — we had to work pre-dawn so as not to disrupt the funicular — I swear there must have been two hundred able-bodied men waiting for us to give orders. I was stunned, but had to tell Eva we couldn't possibly pay all these people even if it only took an hour to move the Wall. She was embarrassed, maybe even horrified...I thought because she would have to send them all home, but no, her problem was with me. "Mr. Edward, sir, these people are here to help me [her], they are not expecting any payment". The feeling of family love extended to Paul and I was overwhelming. This little woman taught me more about family ties, respect for elders, and gratitude, than any other individual other than my own mother.

It took considerably longer than an hour to dismantle the front part of the odditorium to get the Wall out, and the downhill movement proved to be a breeze in comparison. I soon learned how the pyramids were really built! With ropes, a couple logs, and lots of man power, it is possible to move anything, even on the side of a mountain. One of Eva's "uncles" was a civil engineer. His plan was to roll the wall flat on logs held by men with ropes, all the way down the mountain. It sounded ludicrous to me, but I certainly didn't have a better idea. At first, I couldn't watch, but working like a fine-tuned machine, a group of men held back the wall with ropes, while another group placed a log in front of it, slid it the length of the Wall, then ran around the other side, and put another log under, repeating this procedure every few seconds all the way down to the truck. It was a choreographed thing of beauty.

At the truck, about fifty of the crew picked up the wall by hand and put it in the back, lifting it with one Herculean heave-ho. I was speechless. Stunned, I didn't know what to say, or do. Eva called her "uncle" the engineer over, but before I could say or do anything, he actually thanked me on behalf of his family for giving them the great honor of helping Eva's friend! The best we could do in return was buy them all a small bowl of noodles from a nearby stand. They were beaming with joy. They were duly impressed that I could use chopsticks, and I never enjoyed a lunch with fellow workers more.

The next day, neither brawn, grace, luck or man-power were what we needed. We needed a chainsaw.

For several days our helpers had smirked, and guffawed, when I told them we would be taking the Great White "Jaws" shark with us. Being in the middle of the odditorium, surrounded by numerous walls and hallways that

were obviously built after the shark had been installed, this on the surface seemed impossible, and
laughable (7). "Boss man" was obviously crazy. Well,
since no one was willing to tear down any walls — what I
really was expecting them to do — the only solution
would be to carve up the shark into smaller pieces
head, fins, tail — which could be carried through the
labyrinth with-out too much difficulty. Eva was not only
up to the task of finding a chainsaw, she wanted first
crack at the shark, and scared the workers shitless
when she, like a horror-film monster, sliced its head
off in a relentless attack of sheer aggression. It was
evident she was having fun, so needless to say there
were suddenly several volunteers to finish the butch-
ery. Paul and I laughed hysterically. We had no idea if
our art department would be able to put the shark back
together, but the spectacle we had just witnessed was
well worth the experiment.

I mentioned earlier, my health was not the best at the
start of this trip. The time frame of the trip encom-
passed both Good Friday and Easter Sunday. I had hoped
to get to church both days. Good Friday service didn't
happen, but Easter did. In the middle of the night on
Good Friday I got a phone call from my wife Giliane. In
tears and incoherent, she pronounced my recent doctor's
visit had confirmed I had prostate cancer. How she managed to have the courage 10,000 miles away, to call and
tell me, I have no idea. I was shaken to the core, but
I was determined not to panic, nor to tell Paul and Eva
if possible. We still had a lot of work to do, and five
days to do it. We knew in advance that no one would
work Good Friday or Easter Sunday, so these days had
been pre-planned as vacation. Unable to find an English
speaking "Catholic" service, Paul and I decided to
spend Good Friday in Macau. Rather than mope, I did
everything to the extreme. Paul, ten years my junior,
couldn't keep up with me. I was sure I would never see
Macau again, in fact, I was thinking I might not see anywhere again. I knew prostate cancer was a potential
killer, so live life to the fullest was my war cry. In
Macau I ate street food — the best Chinese doughnuts
I've ever eaten (Paul wouldn't try them), and we followed the patterned sidewalk of the main square to a
Catholic church which Giliane believes was where her
great grandparents were married. A nun gave me directions to where I could find an Easter service in Hong

275

Kong.

We worked a "soft" day the next day, given that many of
our workers simply didn't show up. Paul and I ended the
day at a famous floating dragon shaped restaurant that
I had seen on an old television episode of "My Three
Sons", a popular show in the 1960s. We ate outside on
the deck, at a railing edge table for two. We joked that
perhaps the host thought we were "a couple", and had
given us the restaurant's most "romantic" table. We
proceed to have a multi-course Peking duck dinner, and
under the stars it did seem strangely romantic. At some
point in the evening I told him it was absolutely im-
perative, come hell or high water, as my father use to
say, that I get to Mass in the morning. I didn't say why
— I didn't want to wreck one of the best meals I have
ever eaten (8) with the Big C news.

With Eva's help we found the designated church the next
morning, but the service was not in English. It was actually in a combination of Chinese and Filipino Taga-
log. Apparently, the church was built and sustained by a
congregation of Filipino prostitutes. Paul was totally
lost, but I at least could follow the service, and actually sang along to the hymns I knew.

After Mass we visited every religious (Buddhist) temple
we could find, and at some point I told Paul why. It
was months later, in an email, before I told Eva.

Most people either don't know, or forget, that Hong
Kong is a small island. A lot of people do live on it,
but the majority work there, and live across the harbor
in Kowloon. The Lucky Star Ferry terminal harbor dock,
and the ferry boat ride across the channel, offer the
most beautiful views of the two cities. On our last
night, Eva took us to Kowloon to shop for souvenirs —
she modeled "kimonos" for Paul to choose his wife,
and she took us to a seafood restaurant to eat live
crab — not just alive when you ordered it, but alive
when it came to your table! We ate crab, but not one of
the live giants they specialized in ($100 American dol-
lars). Eva's chainsaw shark performance assured us she
could kill a crab, but when we saw one crawling on the
table next to us, to her merriment we opted out.

Every restaurant in Kowloon was packed to the gills
that night, and the mad rush from Hong Kong to the Kow-

loon restaurants every night is the wildest shove-fest maddest dash of humanity I have ever witnessed. Eva explained to us that virtually no one owned a kitchen, real estate was far too expensive for anyone to afford a room you couldn't sleep three of four people in, so people ate immediately after work before going home. If you wanted to get into a restaurant before midnight, it paid to race down the streets of the harbor like an Olympic sprinter. She told us not only did her family not own a kitchen, but also she personally knew no one who did. I could not tell her how large the kitchen was in my modest sized home in Orlando. Once again, she had taught me just how much I took for granted. She was wise beyond her years.

It's been thirteen years since I was in Hong Kong, but I still remember Eva clearly, as well as the sights and smells of Buddhist temple incense, Peking duck, and Godzilla sized crabs. I survived my cancer, but I never once, from that trip on, took time, travel, or anything else for granted. I count my blessings daily.

Jackson Hole, Wyoming - September 2015

Jackson Hole was a small franchise odditorium, in a marginal location. It opened the same year as Hong Kong (1997), but surprisingly outlasted it by a full ten years. Dedicated, hardworking, creative, and humanistic owners were the difference. The odditorium was built, co-owned and run by Norm and Heather Rollingson, their daughter Corena, and their son-in- law Kevin Ricks. Kevin and Corena's children would all work summer jobs in the odditorium too as they grew up. I doubt a more beautiful and loving God serving family exists in all of America.

Norm Rollingson had over thirty year's experience in the attraction's industry before becoming a Ripley franchisee. He had worked as an independent designer on wax museums across the continent, and had built Ripley's Newport, Oregon odditorium as well as having done renovation work in several others. He and Kevin, using designs by Kevin and Corena, built Jackson Hole from the ground up, despite advice from Ripley's HQ that Jackson Hole was not an "A" location. Many people thought he was nuts — and he might have been, but he was quite clear

277

that he was wanting to settle down, and would be happy being "comfortable"; he was not concerned with being "rich". I can only compare him to the first apostles: he gave up everything he knew (except family) to live a simpler life based on Christian ethics and morality. I have always admired him, and Kevin and Corena, who physically operated the odditorium, are cut from the same cloth [8].

By 2015 the writing was on the wall, both for the odditorium, and for me too [9]. I volunteered to do the closing wanting one more chance to spend time with Norm and Kevin, and to perhaps end my travels out west where my first closing had been thirty years earlier. I also loved Jackson Hole, and wanted to share its physical beauty with Angela Johnson, my assistant, while at the same time giving her first-hand "closing" experience that she would benefit from at some point later in her career [10].

The Jackson Hole odditorium was unlike any other Ripley odditorium. In square footage it was small (around 8,500 sq. feet), and it had only two galleries (rooms), one on the first floor, and one on the second, an overhanging balcony. Most of the exhibitory was "nature", or Wild West themed. It also featured a small crashed airplane right in the middle, that Norm — a pilot — had trucked all the way from a flea market in Florida. In dismantling the show, we left the plane to Norm, but took everything else, including: a white buffalo; two bears; a horse; a flying dinosaur skeleton (the odditorium had huge ceiling height); an 1890s Gold Rush era Alaskan snow sleigh funeral hearse; a 3,000 lb. Haida Indian totem pole (bought by Robert Ripley in 1937 in Seattle, Washington's Ye Olde Curiosity Shoppe, and displayed in his garden in Mamaroneck, New York for the last decade of his life); a monstrous collection of Western style belt buckles (collected by one individual); and an enormous twenty-foot in circumference ball of solid barbed wire — very heavy and very sharp.

The acrobatics required to dismantle the pterosaur from the ceiling were left to Kevin's sons, Angela and Corena dealt with the belt buckles — they were mounted with a staple gun in rows to boards attached to every inch of the walls of the second floor — there were over 10,000 of them — Norm played with the airplane, and

Kevin and I, with various employees and personal family friends, dealt with the three biggies.

Removing the totem pole, the hearse-sleigh, and the barbed wire ball, all required serious building demolition. Kevin looks like a cross between a lumberjack and Thor, so he got to wield the sledge hammer. The totem pole was on the ground floor, but was on a supporting wall holding up the second floor; it would have to be removed last just in case the second floor of the hundred-plus year old saloon might collapse. The ball was also on the first floor, and would require two walls to be removed, and an enlargement of the back door in order to get it outside into the back alley. The hearse-sleigh was on the second floor. There was a back "door" (more like a sliding grain silo wall), but it was a good twenty to thirty-feet down to the ground. We couldn't lower it down, and we certainly couldn't just drop it. Made of wood and glass, it measured about twenty-foot long by eight-foot wide, and weighed close to a thousand pounds. Having lived in the small town for years, Kevin knew everyone. It was time to call in a few favors, and first up was a call to Bob Choma, a guy who owned a construction company with a forklift. The lift was raised as high as possible, and extension forks were added for length. Next, Kevin and a couple other mountain climbers scaled the forks, and the side of the building, to lower the hearse-sleigh. While they risked life, limb and exhibit, I closed my eyes and prayed.

Once out of the building, the forklift had to be driven in reverse — there was no room to turn around – down a ten-foot wide, fifty-yard long alley. The team accomplished it like it was something they did every day. Pizza was there sole reward. Seeing how "easy" this had been accomplished, someone suggested perhaps this was the way to deal with the barbed wire ball too. Measurements were taken, and though tight, the conclusion was it could be done — except, a crane would also be needed once the ball was at the front of the building, in order to avoid the building's front awning. Another friend could be counted on for the crane, but we would have to wait until the following night, late after dark, in order to close the street to traffic. Kevin also knew the may-or, and got the street closure permit with a simple phone call. It pays to have friends — especially in a small town.

Before I describe how the extraction of the ball was accomplished, I need to mention one of the greatest marketing/advertising gimmicks Ripley's (in this case, Norm) ever did. Norm always knew how to save a shekel or two, and had driven all the odditorium's exhibits from St. Augustine, Florida, to Jackson Hole himself. The barbed wire ball had required a flatbed truck all of its own. The truck was adorned with signage advertising that the ball was headed across country "to Ripley's Believe It or Not! Jackson Hole, or bust". He had made newspaper and television headlines in every state he drove through. It was brilliance in the style of the greatest showmen. What this meant, however, was that the ball had never been inside a closed truck. Assuming we could get it in, how the hell were we going to push it to the back? Then even more problematical, how would it be removed at the other end back in Florida?

The next day over a scrumptious meal of game — deer, elk and bison — in a restaurant that must have had a 1,000 taxidermy head mounts watching us eat, the team unanimously decided the Florida extraction was a problem for another day and someone else!

That night, at 10 pm, wearing two pairs of work gloves, with straps around the ball tied to the forklift outside, we pushed, shoved, huffed and puffed the ball across the floor, mangling everything — including ourselves (everyone was cut at least once), that got in the way. Kevin being more than worthy, with "Mjolnir" in hand, widened the door a little more. We all closed our eyes, and held our breath, while the five-ton ball dropped out the door, and unto the forklift. The lift did a momentary, spontaneous, reverse wheelie, the back-end leaving the ground like a bucking bronco, until it was wrangled back on to the ground by Kevin's manager Steve Deyholos, and the dozens of witnesses who had gathered to see the most exciting thing to happen in Jackson Hole in a long time. Once balanced, and settled, it still had to be driven out the narrow alley, in reverse, and turned 90 degrees into the street. I have never seen more precision driving (11), but this was still so-called child's play compared to attaching it to a smallish crane, and lifting it thirty feet in the air over the corner of the building and then over the street of parked cars.

Kevin's buddies were in full control. Helpers were on the roof of the odditorium, and the truck, to protect structures, and to push the arm of the crane as necessary. Angela and I, armed with flashlights, directed the odd passing car around our assembled traffic pylons. The only thing we took for granted, to quote Bob Dylan, "was that God was on our side".

Movement was inch by inch, and very slow, but eventually to loud cheers, the ball was lowered back onto the waiting forklift, and placed on the lip of the truck. There was virtually no room to move, so no one could be inside the truck behind the ball. Standing on ladders, we held the ball in place for a few quick seconds (Thank God it didn't fall out, crush us and roll down the street), while the forklift, now in elephant mode, rammed the ball with the forks and drove it as far back as possible. With machine driven momentum, we man-aged to roll it almost to the very back. A little more delicately we used the forklift to load the hearse sleigh in right behind the ball. The two items took up a considerable amount of the truck space, but Kevin was confident everything else would fit, noting that a lot of smaller items could be put inside the hearse.

It was nearly 2 am when we went home. It was only in the cold bright autumn daylight the next morning that we could truly appreciate what we had accomplished with borrowed tools, determination, a group of good Samaritans, and a family of angelic souls.

That morning, Sherpa-style, we formed a long line, and passed boxes from one person to another, out the front door, down the street, and onto the truck, and with Kevin's skilled packing, finished loading the truck in record time. Driven by a hired driver, the truck was gone by 10 am.

Earlier in the week Kevin and Corena had taken Angela and I for a sunrise scenic drive around the Grand Teton's National Park. It had been freezing cold — literally twenty-seven degrees Fahrenheit — but worth it. The autumn colors had started, we saw a herd of antelope and a moose, and the sunrise reflected on the granite snow topped mountains reminded us we were truly in God's country. Inspired by that experience, we asked if it was possible to get to Yellowstone National Park for

281

a few hours, and were told it was certainly worth trying. Given the time it would take to drive there and back, we would only have a couple hours in the park, with little time for getting out of the car, but Angela, always game for one of my spur-of-the moment adventures, would have said "let's do it", even if we had only five minutes. It turned out to be time very well spent.

Wesaw Old Faithful erupt — yet another reminder of God's unexplainable power and mystery — and around 4 pm as the sun was starting to set, we had a true epiphany. Rounding a corner at the side of a river, a bull elk bolted out of the woods, over a small hill, and crossed inches in front of our car, while I squealed the brakes to avoid hitting it. Barely slowing to see us, it descended a gully, and waded into a river. Angela, with phone-camera in hand, flew out of the car at my command — imagine a movie style tuck and roll — to get the majestic creature on camera. I drove a few feet further down the road in order to park safely, then ran back at top speed. The elk was now in the middle of the river gingerly testing the bottom, as if knowing there was a sharp drop off somewhere ahead. Climbing a sandbar, with the golden sun reflecting on the water all around him, he stopped, stared straight at us, and bellowed. Turning to the north, he bellowed again. Turning once more to the east, he bellowed a third time. Then slowly he stepped off the sandbar up to his neck, swam a few yards, then rose to his legs again, and slowly waded out onto the opposite side of the river, bellowed once more, and then was gone. For anyone who has not heard the mating call of the elk, a sound used for years by monster movie makers, including the roar of a certain T-rex in a well-known dinosaur movie or two, it is the most resounding, unforgettable sound in all of nature.

The ground quakes, and the hairs on your body stand straight up. Joshua's trumpet couldn't have been louder or more resounding. Angela and I were dumbstruck. We could not believe what we had witnessed, especially since Kevin had assured us elk were still in the highlands as the rut had not yet begun, and the chances of seeing one, never mind a huge-racked bull, was next to nil. Angela, the great photographer she is, not only got stills, but video too. Anytime I need any reassurance of God's splendor, watching this video can send my heart soaring once again We drove back almost the whole way in silence. That night we bar-hopped, listened to some live country music, drank a couple too many Jack Daniel's whiskeys, and smugly pretended we were locals. After all we had seen God in "them thar hills".

The next morning, we all met up for one more giant breakfast at the little cafe next to the odditorium where we had eaten every morning all week: eggs, waffles, muffins, fresh berries, bacon — enough to sustain us for the long flight home. The goodbyes were very hard, drawn out, and tearful. Like ten years before in Hong Kong, but for different reasons, I was thinking these were people, and a place I might never see again (12).

Part Four

Heads I Bought,
Tales I Tell

40

Fish Tales: My Biggest Catch — a Moose

I have bought numerous albino creatures over the years: birds, a squirrel, a beaver, a lioness, an alligator (a leurcistic specimen rather than a true albino (1)), two buffaloes, a giraffe, and a bull moose. All of them are noteworthy acquisitions, but the moose is by far my favorite, at least in part because I was fishing, not hunting, when he was first brought to my attention.

Ripley fishing trips pre-date me by at least a couple years. I know Alec Rigby and Chuck Theilen did some trout fishing in the 1960s, and there had been at least one Northern pike and pickerel expedition on Ontario's French River circa 1982-83 that I wasn't involved in, but I will take **almost** full credit for making them a Ripley tradition at Ripley's annual conferences. I attended thirty-four of these conferences and fished on everyone that was on water. On conference free days — no seminars to attend — I organized, rented boats, and led excursions off several Caribbean Islands, and a of couple lake trips too. On a couple of these trips the gang was shut out. Sometimes we were too cold, sometimes we were too hot, and sometimes somebody would be deathly ill (I speak from experience), but we always had fun, and on more than one occasion we celebrated by eating the fish we caught. For a bargain price, many restaurants in the islands will cook your fish knowing that the bar bill will more than compensate for the deeply discounted food bill. We did this at least five times, and they were amongst the best meals I have ever eaten. Not much can beat fresh wahoo, mahi, tuna, grouper or snapper, cooked on a beach, accompanied by ice cold beer.

In the 1980s John Withers (Ripley's then president), and Bob Masterson (then VP Operations), instigated three French River voyages. John and Bob liked salt water fishing, and did do some fishing in the Islands at Ripley conferences, but they were much fonder of freshwater fishing. To those French River voyages, Bob and I added a speckled trout trip in Quebec, and two fly-in trips to Lake Kesagami in Northern Ontario. Bob also led two memorable ice fishing trips, one being our first co-ed excursion held during a severe blizzard; no one should have been out that day, and only Bob caught a fish. It was a large beautiful lake trout, so big that he had to submerge his upper body in the freezing water to wrestle it by hand out the fishing hole!

It was the big one that didn't get away.

Consider the above a long pre-amble. This chapter is really about a moose, not about fish or fishing, (kind of like Norman Maclean's **"A River Runs Through It"**, eh?), but I thought you the reader might need to understand the fishing culture that existed at Ripley's before you could really appreciate this fish tale.

Fishing for Arctic char, or lake trout, was out of our price range. If we were going to do a "fly-in", we would have to stay in Ontario, and fish for pickerel and/or pike. Every angler dreams of doing a fly-in trip, to fish where no other fisherman has fished before (or at least not too many others). John, Bob and I were no exception to this rule. Bob and I would spend hours considering how it could be done, and where we should go. Bob was (and still is) a better fisherman than I will ever be, but he grew up in the States, so he didn't know Ontario as well as I did. It was my job to do the research, and pick a place. It was Bob's job to talk John into at least considering it a possibility.

There is a huge Sportsman's Show every Fall in Toronto. It used to be held on the grounds of the Canadian National Exhibition (I assume it is now held in the city's expansive downtown convention center). I thought this was the best place to start our search. The three ofus, plus Norm Deska (then Ripley controller) and Mark Grunwald (VP Finance) planned to spend a day at the show.

After several laps of the show floor, and countless hours of "what-if arguing" we settled on Lake Kesagami Lodge several hundred miles due north of the last road stop — Cochrane, Ontario, near the tip of James Bay. Just about as far north in Ontario as one can go. We would be fishing for pickerel, and trophy sized Northern pike.

The following June 12, 1985, the five of us flew from

Toronto to Timmins on two separate small planes, (we had way too much luggage for us to all fit on one plane), from Timmins to Cochrane. We would spend the night in this mining town and catch a float plane the next morning.

Cochrane is a small, typical Northern Ontario town best known for being the moose capital of Ontario. It's a hunter's paradise in the Fall, but too far north to have any real summer tourism. In June it gets about eighteen hours of sunlight. We arrived at 10:20 pm, but it looked like 6 pm. Our lodging, the Northern Lights Motel, was "basic" at best, and the selection of places to eat and drink boiled down to two places. One nice enough to take your wife or date. The other, a men's drinking hole that quite possibly had never had a female customer. Paying a whopping six dollars for a cab, we chose to go to the latter.

The first thing we saw was the stuffed head of a full grown bull moose on the wall in the far corner. In the moose capital of Ontario this would normally not be worth mentioning, but holy shit, this moose head was pure white with pink eyes! It was astonishing. Upon close inspection, the adjacent wall showed three photos of local hunters with the full moose prior to butchering and subsequent taxidermy. My God, it was like a vision in the wilderness. We were all excited, but especially John.

As President, and until just a few months earlier, part-owner of the company, John's pocket book was a little thicker than that of the rest of ours combined. He wanted the moose, and was willing to buy it, right then and there, no questions asked. He approached the bartender with bank roll in hand. He assumed the bar keep must also be the owner of the bar. He was wrong, the bartender certainly knew the owner, but was not in a position to speak on his behalf, or to phone him at 11:30 at night. John at first wouldn't take no for an answer. He proceeded to make a pile of cash on the bar, and repeatedly said "How much"? The bartender pleaded he couldn't sell the moose. John eventually raised the stakes so high, he said he would buy the whole bar, just to get the albino moose.

I am pretty sure the bartender keep didn't believe him.

We assured him the money wasn't stolen, and that John was the President of the world famous museum company, Ripley's Believe It or Not!, and really could afford to buy the bar if necessary. He had heard of our television show, but not of our odditoriums. Our sales pitch was going nowhere.

John was beside himself by this point — he couldn't fathom that someone in this remote little dive could turn down the thousands of dollars that were laying on the cracked and faded Formica bar. It was all Bob could do to keep John from starting a fist fight. Bob ushered him away from the bar to watch the late-night news recap of the Blue Jays baseball game (John was a huge Jays fan in the 1980s before anyone else caught on to the team), and I stepped up to the bar, to try a much softer approach.

I told him I understood the moose, nor the bar, was his to sell, but I assured him we were serious; we were really from Ripley's Believe It or Not!, and we really were willing to pay top dollar for an albino moose head. I told him we were leaving town early the next morning to go fishing, but I gave him my business card and begged him to have the owner phone me in a week.

Eight years went by.

One day in early 1993, in the Toronto office, I was asked to take a collect call from Cochrane, Ontario. I didn't know anyone in Cochrane, and I had only ever been there one night in my whole life. I joked, "Maybe it's the guy from the bar with the albino moose"?

It was.

For most of my Ripley career my business card was also a free pass to Ripley attractions. The bartender had kept it for nearly eight years in the hopes that someday he would visit Niagara Falls. He now owned the bar, and the moose. "Did I still want it"? I may have shit my pants — of course I did!

I bought the moose head, and the accompanying photos for considerably less than John had laid out back in '85 in the Cochranebar. It wasn't cheap, but it was a bargain. I have bought several other albino specimens over time, at least six bigger than my moose, and I have bought at least three other moose heads, but none of them make me smile like the Cochrane albino. Who else can say they went fishing and caught a white moose, eh?

Postscript: I told you this wasn't a fishing story, but just in case you doubt my veracity, we did go fishing the next day, for four days. As a group we spent twenty-nine and a half hours on Lake Kesagami and caught 135 fish, fifty-four pike, eighty pickerel, and one perch. Norm led the way with thirty-five fish caught. I was second with thirty-one. It was the best fishing I have ever done.

41

One that Got Away #1 — the PEI Sperm Whale

Herman Melville's **Moby Dick** is one of my all-time favorite books. I am pretty sure it is the only book I have read three times, going back to it years later, and seeing it differently each time. I love the majesty and mystery of whales, and of all the whales, the sperm whale seems to me the most mysterious. It can dive the deepest, stay under water the longest, produces ambergris, and has big teeth. It may have been the leviathan that swallowed Jonah, and it definitely was the one that swallowed James Bartley, "The Modern Jonah" in 1891. It is typically associated with warm waters around the equator, and in the Indian Ocean, but in 1989, one beached and died on the north shore of Canada's smallest province, Prince Edward Island (PEI). The timing seemed fortuitous, as we were on schedule to open a Ripley odditorium that summer in Cavendish, PEI.

In Florida you hear about small whales, Pilots, and Minkes, beaching a few times every year. Until 1989 I don't recall ever hearing of a big whale beaching, and certainly not in Canada. That year there were actually a few, including an enormous blue whale, but the beaching of a sperm whale so far from its known habitat, was front page news. I reacted as quick as lightning. I wanted to buy a whale. I had seen the skeletons of whales displayed in a few museums, most significantly in the Niagara Falls Historical Museum, in Niagara Falls Canada (1), and I knew a sperm whale skeleton would not just be a unique display to our collection, but a real coup for the company, something that would raise our image to new heights of credibility.

With a man on the ground in PEI, the new franchisee, Tom MacMilian, we contacted the CBC national news team that had first reported the beaching, the National Parks and Recreation team (the whale apparently was on-government owned park land), the local university, and a construction team. Everyone wanted the whale re-moved immediately before it started to stink to high heavens, and no one but Ripley's seemed to want it, so by default it became ours with the proviso we moved it PDQ.

With Melville as my only reference point, I thought we could hire a team of fishermen (there are lots of those on PEI), flay it, dump the flesh in the ocean, and walk away with the skeleton. Unfortunately, it is not quite that easy. It smelled horrific within a matter of hours, so there was no time to flay it, it had to be moved immediately. Tom miraculously found a team willing and able to do it, and he found a farmer a few miles down the coast from the beaching site that was willing to let us bury it on his beach front property. We would haul it by boat to the new location, and then put it in the ground for what we thought would be just a few days, a temporary solution to an over-sized — thirty-eight-foot long, sixty-ton problem.

Throughout my career I was always happy to say "I got a guy for that"; no matter what might be needed, I knew someone to call on for help. In this case, I called Henry Galiano of **Maxilla & Mandible**, a bone store in New York City. Henry had been my go-to bone guy for about five years at that point. Henry had experience with just about any kind of animal skeleton you could name, including dinosaurs, and was as excited as a kid in a candy store at the prospect of cleaning, and articulating, a sperm whale skeleton for a museum display. He couldn't wait to get started. The fact that it still had its flesh didn't initially worry him, nor did the fact that it needed to be buried. He too thought it would be simple to hire a team to flay it, and in truth, I believe he would have done it himself if necessary. We flew him to PEI, and he oversaw the whale burial. Only a couple of photos were taken as the whale was already decomposing. Henry described the smell as putrid, and noticeable for miles along the wind-swept coast, and reported that the farmer was in a real hurry to get it underground. Fortunately, Henry had the foresight to hand draw a small "treasure" map of where the whale was buried. This map would be very important a year later, and even more important twenty years later.

PEI has a long cold winter, and conversely, a very short summer. Henry broke the news that he didn't think the cleaning work could be completed before the end of summer. He recommended we wait until next spring. From the start, I had imagined the whale being displayed in the new odditorium, and being a big selling point in their first year of operation, so I was disappointed. I had a lot to learn about whales, and PEI.

The following Spring, we sent Henry back to PEI. Using his sketch map, the whale was uncovered, but not excavated. Despite almost a full year in the ground, the whale had not decomposed at all. In fact, it was in better condition than when we had buried it! There were no insects underground to eat the corpse, and the cold North Atlantic Ocean clay was in fact preserving the whale as if it had been buried in ice. We nearly cried. Soil experts and fishery experts both agreed, it would be twenty years before the whale would be decomposed under these conditions. We did cry.

On the upside, the whale had been free, and we hadn't spent a great deal of money. On the down side, the skeleton would definitely not be displayed in PEI, or for that matter anywhere in Canada.

Fast forward ten years to 1999 when Bob Masterson was building Ripley's second aquarium in Gatlinburg, Tennessee. Bob, wanted to hang a whale skeleton from the rotunda ceiling. "Whatever happened to the PEI sperm whale", he asked. I may have been the only person who hadn't forgotten it, but I was all for letting sleeping dogs lie, sort to speak. Rather than revisit it, why not buy a cheaper, bigger alter-native, I proposed. In the interim, the entire Niagara Falls His-tory Museum had been sold, including the P.T. Barnum humpback whale skeleton, and as it turned out, I was good friends with the buyer, William, "Billy" Jamieson of Toronto. I knew he had a buyer in Dubai for the skeleton even before he owned it, but I also knew he had made a casting of it before he sold the original. I could buy a casting for about one-third the estimated cost of digging up and preparing the sperm whale, and it would be ready a lot quicker, in three months compared to eighteen!

I bought the humpback, and officially gave up on the sperm whale. The file was buried as deep in the archives as the skeleton was in the cold unforgiving PEI ground.

Fast forward another ten years to 2009. The predicted necessary twenty years in the ground for decomposition was now up. The company would now like to hang a whale

292

skeleton in the lobby of the future Ripley's Aquarium of Canada. As the removal out of the country of the now endangered Sperm whale would likely be nigh impossible, having a place to display it in Canada would be ideal. I had no desire to visit this old wound — twenty years later — but had no choice but to look into the possibility of excavating it. Henry Galiano was still around, but semi-retired, and no longer interested at all. Luckily, Tom MacMillian was still around, and could find the farmland. The land (and house), however, no longer belonged to the man who had let us bury the whale twenty years before. The new owner (who had been there more than ten years) was unaware that she had a whale skeleton under her beach. Tom reported that the land looked very different than he remembered it; he was not sure we would be able to find the whale, even if we got the owner's okay to proceed.

In a conversation with Henry, I learned of his "treasure map" drawing. Thank God there was at least a hint of where the whale was buried. Henry was willing to relinquish the map, but he was not willing to get involved. Therefore, with map in hand, I flew to PEI in May 2010. Word was out that Ripley's was coming to the island looking for a long "lost" whale skeleton. I thought the term "lost" was a gross exaggeration, because I did have a map, regardless of how simple it was, but I played along with the media thinking the reluctant owner would love the media attention. I was wrong. My appearance was indeed big news on the island, and was covered by all media, including CBC National news, which unearthed, and aired, footage of the beaching and burial twenty years earlier. I was being touted as a modern treasure hunter, and was photographed with a shovel in hand.

On our visit to the site Tom and I were met politely, but with reserve. The owner did not like the thought of news people, construction workers, and tourists, traipsing over her property all summer, and told us in no uncertain terms. We were able to inspect the land, but soon found the map no longer reflected reality. We were able to calculate land erosion, to estimate the skeleton's distance from the ocean not very much by this time — and we now were concerned that the skeleton may have already washed out to sea, or at least be very close to surfacing. The location in respect to the house, was no longer determinable — a barn building on Henry's map was gone, a fence line was gone, another fence line had been built in a different place, and there was now a forest blocking part of the view from the main house. Realistically other than aerial to ground radar surveillance, it would be impossible to mark an exact location without digging up half her farm. She laughed us off the property.

A month or so later, I received a detailed letter from a lawyer. There was a long list of non-negotiable points that if we would comply to, the owner would let us dig up the land in the Fall of the following year after she had spent another summer on the property. On its own this made the proposal absurd. Summer in PEI typically ends mid-September. Winter starts by October. If we didn't dig in the spring it was impossible to get the job done in one season.

The other restrictions on where we could dig, how many hours a day, etc., etc., and my favorite, that we would have to build her a new retaining wall when we were finished, were all non-starters. Her cash payout request may have been the only thing we were on the same page with. The letter ended very threateningly, warning us not to bother the owner in person again, but to deal exclusively with her legal representative firm.

When the Ripley's Aquarium of Canada opened in October 2013, Toronto would have Barnum Humpback whale casting #2 hanging from the ceiling.

In 2015 I would try — timidly — one last time. Tom MacMillan was now retired and Ripley's Cavendish PEI had a new owner, Matthew Kelly. Matthew was a lawyer by trade, and knew the law firm that had read me the riot act. He made some headway, and maybe Ripley's will try again in the future, but I suspect before that happens, some farm machine will either unknowingly plow up a few bones, or someone will dig in the ground and find a big black lump that is still perfectly preserved like a Siberian mammoth in a glacier. Either way, I don't foresee it ever hanging in a Ripley attraction. For me it is a really big, "one that got away".

Postscript: When the whale first beached in 1989, the Canadian Government took part of the lower jaw bone, and three teeth to do a necropsy. At some point, unbe-

294

knownst to me, these were returned to Tom MacMillan. I
first saw them in 2009, and recommended he put them on
display in the Cavendish odditorium. I am not sure if
this in fact ever happened, but somewhere in PEI there
is physical evidence that this great "white elephant"
of a whale really did once exist. The teeth represent
Melville's, Queequeg's, and Ishmael's, legacy to me and
Ripley's (2).

42

Mummies

Many countries in antiquity mummified human remains for religious and ceremonial reasons. I have seen mummies from Europe, China, Peru, and from Egypt. I will mention a couple Peruvian specimens in the paragraphs that follow, but my emphasis here in this chapter is on Egyptian mummies: cats, falcons, ibises, human hands, feet and heads. I will also discuss so-called "dime museum American mummies".

I don't know when I first became fascinated with mummies, but it was probably around age eight, when I had a birthday party at the Royal Ontario Museum, in Toronto (The ROM). The museum had a couple Egyptian mummies, in basic glass and metal cases, stacked on two shelves — the sarcophagus lid on the top shelf, and the mummy, still in the bottom of the case, on the lower shelf. I don't believe the mummies were of any significant pharaohs, or persons, and my recollection is that they were probably all New Kingdom vintage, but I loved the ROM's Egyptian gallery, and having nothing to compare it with, considered it a very good collection.

The second mummies I remember seeing, were displayed at the Niagara Falls History Museum. Compared to the ROM, they looked a little worse for wear — dirty, dusty, poorly lit, and dare I say it, "old". It looked like no one had done anything with them for millennium. The fact that it took an outside researcher to discover, and prove one of the mummies in this collection was perhaps the most important mummy in antiquity, Ramses I, is proof of their sad neglect. (1). There is no disputing that any mummy, in any collection, anywhere, has a sordid past — somewhere and sometime along the way grave robbers were involved. I saw my first complete Peruvian mummy in the home of Torontonian Bill Jamieson sometime in the early 1990s. Folded up in a fetal position, the skull had no wrappings and stared straight at you with a grimace of agony. It was the most terrifying mummy I had ever seen. I loved this mummy, but there was too much recent news of current grave robbery going on in

Peru for me to feel comfortable even thinking about acquiring it. I did in fact already own a couple Peruvian heads, one skull, and one with skin still attached, but these had some documented provenance attached, and had already been in private hands for quite a while before I bought them. I am not suggesting there is an official "statute of limitations" on grave robbing, but I am suggesting my moral values changed somewhat over time. When I bought those two heads, I saw nothing wrong with it, and probably never even thought about grave robbers. When I stared at Bill's full mummy I envisioned grave robbers with their shovels still in hand, staring back at me. From that moment forward, I only ever gave consideration to Egyptian mummies, South Americans mummies were taboo.

I must say, however, that the two Peruvian, Moche culture heads I purchased in Europe, in the 1980s, are amongst the best heads of any sort I ever acquired. One had three-foot long braided hair, some colored cloths bound in the hair, and heavily patinaed bronze discs in its eye sockets. It was in mint condition, and is shockingly beautiful. The second, is a bit of a different story. It still has a full face of skin attached to the skull, sharp wooden pegs in its mouth, and a small pouch of skin attached with sinew to the forehead. The skin pouch is the remains of a scrotal sac. It is not "beautiful" by anybody's definition. I dare say there are probably no two identical heads to these in the world. Both heads date from c. 800-900 AD, and were removed from Peru in the early 20th century.

I have never bought an intact Egyptian mummy. My whole mummies were all early 20th-century dime museum mummies, some with no real human parts, others very human, but preserved with arsenic by morticians, not by natron the salt commonly used in Ancient Egypt for mummification, by temple priests. Two of these were x-rayed, and thoroughly studied by two experts, Ron Beckett and Jerry Conlogue, and shown on a television program called The National Geographic Mummy Road Show (1997-2003). I got to be the dumb as dirt sidekick as they did all this really cool science stuff. It was the most fun you could ever have with corpses. These two very legitimate scientists and historians, shared a lot in common with Anthony Bourdain. They didn't look like they knew what they were talking about, were often quite irreverent, traveled all over the world in a recycled food truck, were passionate about what they did, and were willing to share their knowledge with everyone. Like Tony, they were downright lovable.

For Ripley's they came to the company's warehouse and x-rayed several mummified cats and birds (with mixed results — most were perfect, but some had no bones in them at all), and looked in great detail over every inch of the two dime museum mummies we had. As part of their investigation, and to be used in the show, we took the two mummies to a local hospital for CAT scans. The hospital excitedly agreed to the plan, but only if we did it early on a Saturday morning, and the doctor could add children of his staff to the cast. It was a great idea, giving kids a first-hand look at history and medical science working hand in hand. This, however, did mean the mummies would have to come home with me on a Friday night, and spend the night in my guest room. Little did I know that my daughter had invited a college friend home for the weekend — to stay in the guest room. His scream at finding two mummies on his bed could behead a block away. Luckily, my wife was not home at the time, and I did not tell her about our guests until much, much later. The mummies slept in archival boxes, on the floor, not in the bed. My daughter's guest slept on a couch in another room.

The stitching on both bodies — called "baseball stitching" — suggested the date of both mummies to be 1905-1920, consistent with the first wave of Egyptmania in America, when every museum wanted a mummy, and many morticians were willing to give them one. Elaborate legends declared them as natural weather and desert created American mummies. One was supposed to be a 17th century Indian, the other a 19th century gambler-cowboy, both from Arizona or New Mexico (2).

Both, more likely, were from Chicago. One died from tuberculosis, the other had a very unique pathology. CAT scans showed he had a spike in his head, but it was revealed that this was accomplished post-mortem. The real cause of death were severe abdominal injuries: a heavy blow to the thorax had broken a rib, which punctured both his heart and a lung. It was the first time ever on the show that Ron and Jerry could unequivocally determine a cause of death by looking at a mummy. They described his death as being instantaneous and extremely painful.

Outwardly, both these mummies were in excellent condition, both having been prepped like early taxidermy specimens with arsenic. Arsenic is a deadly poison that can kill you, but also preserve you too.

I became good friends with Ron and Jerry over our three days together, and got a lot of kudos when our two episodes aired. A little later Ron and Jerry took one of our wax sculptors, Barry Anderson, with them to Peru to make castings of some famous mummies for a subsequent episode. Ripley's later donated the tuberculosis mummy to their institution of study in Maryland.

A few years later I had cause to have a cat scan at the same Winter Park medical institution we had used for the mummies, and by the same doctor we had worked with for the show. He had a picture of a mummy, me, Ron and Jerry in his office. He asked me to autograph it, and told me his son still talked about the day the Ripley guy and his dad had let him touch a "real" mummy. I imagine it was a teaching lesson that no kid there that Saturday morning would ever forget. I know I haven't.

When it comes to real Egyptian mummies it has to be stated I have never been to Egypt. Most of the mummies I bought were acquired in America, a couple from Maryland, a couple from New Jersey, a couple from California and a whole flock of birds from Florida. The two best pieces in the collection, an 18th Dynasty human head, and a large cat, were from England.

The Great Stromboli, and his fire eating wife Sylvia, were old school traveling circus people, part gypsies, part Barnum, part Wizard of Oz. I dealt with Stromboli (aka: Danny Lynch) for over thirty years, but never met him. A mutual friend and associate, John Turner (former Ripley manager in Blackpool, England and St. Augustine Florida), who was from England, but whom I had met in Florida, had introduced us and was my liaison. Stromboli traveled around England with a small show that was part circus, part lecture. Along the way he collected artifacts, and animal oddities. Some of these pieces he used in his presentations, but the majority were simply things he found interesting. Whenever he needed money, for what-ever reason, he would contact John. John would visit him, and send me a list of Ripleyesque things, everything from tribal weapons, to chastity belts, to two-headed cows, to an Egyptian mummified cat (3). Stromboli's mummified cat was the largest one I had ever seen, and was in perfect condition. He didn't really want to sell it, however, and it took months of coercing to get him to consider parting with it. To my surprise, against all expectations, he said he wanted to trade for it, rather than sell it for cash. I had never done this, and never did it again, but his proposed deal was too good to say no to. In addition to the cat, he would also give me a Fiji Island mermaid — one of the great hoaxes of all time, in exchange for a shrunken head. At the time of this deal, I had no mummified cats, and only one mermaid one that had been acquired by Ripley in the 1930s. Monetarily, the deal was pretty even, but I had at least a couple dozen shrunken heads; I could afford to part with one, and he wasn't really fussy, any head would do. I liked him way too much to give him a bad one (new, or in poor condition), and gave him one worth several thousand dollars. He was happy, and so was I. We both felt like we had "won" the negotiation — and that is one thing I learned early in my career, if you want to do repeat business with someone, both sides have to feel like winners. You can't beat someone up and expect them to come back for a Round Two. I always prided myself on offering fair prices. The cat came with x-rays, but Ron and Jerry updated them for us. As it turned out, the inside was as good as the outside.

The cat was first displayed in 1989, in a large malachite stone and glass pyramid shaped display case, with the x-rays on the side, in a small room in the St. Augustine odditorium. I have not studied "pyramid power", and remain very skeptical about ghosts, but the room where the cat was displayed was right underneath the room where two ladies had burned to death in the building in the 1940s. People had for years claimed to occasionally see the ghosts of these women looking out the window of these two rooms, but after the cat was installed, the sightings increased to the point where the company eventually started giving after hours ghost tours of the building. Believers made the connection to the cat and the pyramid as "portals" to "the other side". I am ambivalent about ghosts, I don't believe or disbelieve, but I have never seen one. In this room, however, I believe you can at least feel one.

300

I did eventually buy a full mummified human head from Stromboli, and a human hand as well, but St. Augustine is where I discovered the largest part of the Ripley mummy collection: an entire flock of birds, falcons that represent Ra the sun god of Egypt, and ibises that represent Thoth, the Egyptian god of writing, magic, wisdom, and the moon. I consider this purchase important because it shows that "stuff" can be found just about anywhere if you are looking. I bought this large group of bird mummies, within a mile of the Ripley location. The odditorium manager had never been in the shop, and the shopkeeper had never been in the odditorium. I simply walked in one day because I liked the antique shop's window display. I am sure I made the shopkeeper's day (maybe, week, maybe month, maybe even year), and afterwards it became a regular haunt for me every time I was in St. Augustine. I even ended up giving them several restoration projects. It was a great find right in the museum's proverbial "front yard". They were the only mummies I ever found that weren't in a private collection.

I have met people who collect just about anything you can name, and for the most part they love to talk about their collections, but people who collect mummies, and other kinds of body artifacts, are typically, and understandably, very private people. I have purposely withheld the names of people still alive in this chapter to respect their privacy. I know them by name, and in some cases would call them close friends, but in general, I don't think they would want the world to know them, and collectively as a group, I know they are not too willing to discuss provenance. I'm positive that no one I ever bought from personally was a grave robber, but knowing they may not be able to vouch for whom they bought something from, when dealing with mummies, "Mum's the word".

43

One that Got Away #2 — Atta Boy

Ripley's acquired up to 1,200 new exhibits a year during my stay averaging nearly two a day, every day of the year, year after of year… yet there were many exhibits we simply said no to. Some we couldn't agree on the price, some the seller changed his or her mind not to sell, and of course there are ones we walked away from, either because we were uncomfortable with their provenance, or their authenticity… or sometimes, believe it or not, they simply were too weird even for Ripley's!

I like to call these the "ones that got away".

Collectors and archivists are always looking for the one that got away, whether it was them that "lost it", or someone else. One of my "Holy Grail' desires, was to find "Atta Boy" — an item Ripley had in his possession in 1933, but seemingly let get away.

"Atta Boy" is known to me in five formats, an original Ripley cartoon drawing from March 8, 1931, a dust cover from Ripley's second book in 1931, and three photos believed to have been taken at the first Ripley Odditorium in Chicago in 1933. The cartoon calls him a mummified five and a half-inch baby from Bolivia. The photos are labeled in Ripley's hand writing, "a shrunken human body from the Jivaro [sic-"Shuar"] Indians of Peru".

Either way, this is an exhibit I sure wish I could have found.

There are two mysteries: according to the cartoon it was on loan to Ripley. Why did he not buy it? Historically, the company virtually never borrowed exhibits, they acquired them outright. Assuming Ripley gave it back to the owner, where did it disappear to, never to cross paths again in the company's 100-year history.

Over the years there were a few false leads: we were actually offered a real Shuar shrunken body — but it was female, and more like eighteen inches than five and a half. There was an Explorer's Club in Chicago that had a shrunken body that was pretty damn interesting, but not our guy (despite the Chicago connection), and a couple years ago, a mummified "creature", considered to be an alien, was found in Bolivia that looked similar, but not exactly like "Atta Boy". **"The Huffington Post"** out of New York had a field day with this story and even called it, "Atta Boy" until I provided them with Ripley's photos which showed the size being close, but proved their little guy looked very different from our long-lost character. In the end, their guy was studied by some experts who determined it was not an alien but a child's skeleton with a hereditary malformed skull.

So what is "Atta Boy", and is he still out there waiting to be rediscovered? My guess is that it is a fetus mummified by natural high altitude, desert-like climate conditions. I hope it is still out there some-where. I would pay just to know he still exists, more to actually see him, and a lot to bring him back into the Ripley collection, where he so belongs. (1

44

Heads I've Bought, Tales I Tell

It's a bad joke, maybe even tasteless, but more than one interviewer called me Ripley's "head guy". I confess, I even said it myself on occasion. I never counted the number of human heads I acquired, but a safe estimate would be around 250. The largest number would be shrunken heads from Ecuador, South America, but there were also skull bowls and skull drums from Tibet, carved skulls from Borneo, cannibal skulls from New Guinea, clay-over-modeled skulls from several South Sea Islands, skull trophies from the Philippines, skulls decorated with water buffalo horns and feathers from Myanmar, voodoo skulls from Haiti, Zaire and Cameroon, even a few skulls and heads from Europe, all in addition to the mummified heads discussed in an earlier chapter (see Chapter 42).

I tend to use the words skull and head as the same thing when I am speaking. Skulls may have all kinds of ornamentation, but they have no skin. Heads have skin. Asian and South Sea Island skulls can be subdivided into two main broad types, those of the deceased that were kept in reverence as part of "ancestor worship", and those brutally taken in combat as "war" trophies. European skulls and heads roughly fit into two similar categories: reverence and criminal.

Collectively the estimated 250 heads and skulls came from all over the world, some from auctions, most from collectors. I bought my first skulls from H.M. Lissauer; I also bought a couple notable heads from him (see Chapter 10). Others were acquired from collectors in Maryland, Florida, Louisiana, and California, and from auctions in New Hampshire, New York, England, and Germany. I also bought some on-line from Belgium, and I even had heads hand delivered, a couple by post and couriers, a couple brought to my office in a brown paper bag, and a couple hand delivered in an ice cooler.

Ancestor Skulls:

Tibet was one of the only countries Ripley never traveled to, but he did go to Nepal. In Katmandu, Nepal, in 1936 he bought dozens of Tibetan artifacts, many made from human bones, including skulls. Monks in Tibet used both skull bowls and skull drums, made from the skulls of special persons, in religious ceremonies. They also used the skull caps of family members as alms begging bowls. All three objects were believed to be endowed with spiritual powers, and were revered as sacred objects. Often, they were decorated with semi-precious jewels, like turquoise and carnelian, and small silver skulls. Ripley had a couple of examples of each, and displayed them in his odditoriums as early as 1937. Over the years I bought numerous examples of all three of these objects of ancestor worship, most from H.M Lissauer who went to Nepal at least once every two years. Sometime in the 1990s, the traditional kapali skull bowl was replaced by a heavily ornamented skull complete with a haunting face made of silver. I suspect these were more for the tourist trade than for monasteries, but for museum display purposes they are considerably more dramatic than the traditional style.

Tribes in the Pacific South Sea Islands (1) also worship the skulls of their ancestors, and decorated them as part of their reverential observance. These skulls are generally referred to as "clay-over-modeled", because the skull is completely hidden by natural substances, starting with clay, but also including human hair, shells, feathers, nose bones, and paint. Perhaps because the skull is "hidden", but probably more because of the elaborate ornamentation, these are the most sought after ethnographic skulls by typical collectors and museums. The first, and best, came from Lissauer, who acquired them directly from Islanders on his travels. He considered them more valuable even than Jivaro shrunken heads. Several in the Ripley collection came from **Hermann-Historica**, a German auction house — the Germans having been amongst the first explorers and colonial powers to exploit New Guinea. A collection of over twenty different heads — the core of the Ripley collection, came from a private deal with **Christies Auctions** of London in 1988-89, before they started doing ethnographic auctions and loosening their restrictions on selling human body parts — more on that

305

later.

These kinds of heads were openly displayed in communal houses, and historically could have been identified by tribesmen. The most unusual "one" in the Ripley collection is a cylindrical drum-like stand, made of brightly painted tree bark with four pointed posts. Each post bears a different decorated skull, presumably all members of one family. One might call it the New Guinea version of Vlad the Impaler's castle fence. Beauty is in the eye of the beholder, but all of these types of skulls are works of art; I consider them beautiful. Voodoo skulls on the other hand are not as easy to look at. They tend to be smoke charred black, and lack any other form of decoration. They are considered to have spiritual powers, but not necessarily for good. They may come with other ceremonial paraphernalia, including animal bones, and though held in reference by the loa, or priest that uses them, they are feared by the congregation, and hidden away when not in ceremonial use. Ripley's has samples from Haiti, the country most often associated with voodoo, but also from Africa, where voodoo, known there as hoodun, originated.

Cannibal (trophy) Skulls

The most elaborately decorated cannibal skulls are associated with the Asmat tribe of New Guinea — Ripley acquired one in Port Moseby in 1932 — but cannibalism was also practiced by the Dyaks of Borneo, the Igorot (Bontoc and Ifugao) (2) of the Philippines, the Naga of North-Eastern India and North-Western Myanmar, and tribes in Fiji and Taiwan. Ripley's has skulls from all of these areas excluding Fiji and Taiwan (3).

Like ancestor skulls, these too can be considered beautiful pieces of ethnographic art. Skulls from New Guinea typically have bone nose ornaments, beans and shells, and grey cassowary bird feathers. Dyak skulls from Borneo, are magnificently etched and carved, then darkened brown, almost like a copper patina. Naga skulls occasionally have feathers, but colorful ones, and more often than not, large water buffalo horns protruding from the sides; visually these look demonic and devil-like. The Bontoc of the Philippines, also liked to decorate their skulls with water buffalo horns,

306

whereas the Ifugao merely blackened them, but then either mounted them to wood boards to display, or wove several together to display on shelves as a way of boasting of their prowess as hunters.

Medieval Vehmic (Oath) Skulls

Most people have either heard of, or seen on television, the use of swearing to tell the truth by placing one's hand on a Bible. In Medieval Europe, before the printing press and when Bibles would not have readily been found outside a church, a monastery, or a castle, and still later, because the average person couldn't read, legally binding oaths were often made by placing your hand on a human skull. This was practiced in many parts of Europe, most notably Germany, where traveling judges who held "Vehmic" courts would bring their own personal oath skull to the trials. The skull might be that of a holy person, or a relative. Sometimes they bore etchings, but sometimes they were painted in monastic scribe style with flowers and quotations. These too can actually be quite "pretty". Satanist and Wiccans in more modern times also "swore" allegiance on etched skulls, some featuring a pentagram.

Every oath skull in the Ripley collection was acquired via an auction. I never found one of these in the collection of an individual. I suspect there is some inherent taboo, or at least a suspicion of bad mojo.

Skulls and Heads I Didn't, Couldn't, Wouldn't, Buy

The most prized skulls no doubt, are those of paleolithic pre-history the skulls of cavemen. I did buy a perfect replica of a skull, now named after Henry Galiano of New York who found it in a box in a widow's estate, that is believed to be from Southeast Asia. It visually resembles the so-called "Java Man", one of the first hominid cavemen ever found. I was never lucky enough to be offered a real cave man skull, but as these are obviously super rare, and expensive, most likely I would have passed on it if I had of seen one for sale.

307

The other kind of head I never bought are called moko makai — the fabled tattooed heads of the Maori of New Zealand, made famous by Melville's Queequeg character in the novel **Moby Dick**. These are heads — not skulls — the skin and hair are still intact, and the skin is heavily tattooed. The tattoos tell tribal stories and lineage. These heads can be directly traced back to their original owners.

Twice I did have the chance to buy one of these. The first time I simply couldn't afford it — but I definitely wanted it. By the second time, the Maori had successfully claimed repatriate rights to any that existed anywhere in the world. If you were not Maori, owning one would land you in jail for a long time. In lieu of the impossibility of ever buying a real moko makai, Barry Anderson, a friend and former Ripley wax artist made me my own personal resin sample. It sat behind my desk for years, mildly disturbing all visitors. It gives my wife the creeps, so it is now hidden away in the most unused portion of my house. I can't lie, these are the most unique heads in the world, and they fascinate me. Anyone ever traveling to New Zealand needs to visit a Maori historical site to see them in their ceremonial places of honor. If on the other hand you see one anywhere outside of New Zealand, do the right thing, and report it to the authorities.

Ripley's Most Iconic Exhibit:
Genuine Jivaro shrunken Heads

Call me out on a double standard. I never had any qualms about buying shrunken heads. The distinction between them and moko makai is a fine line, but for me it all came down to legality. I would hate for Ripley's to ever have to send back their collection, but if the Shuar tribes of Ecuador, and Peru, ever became as strongly organized as New Zealand's Maori, and owning a shrunken head became illegal, then I would grudgingly suggest doing the right thing — but boy would it hurt. At the time of his death, Ripley owned two shrunken heads, a short-haired one, and a very long haired one. Sometime after his death in the 50s, two more were added; photographs of these were widely circulated for more than thirty years. One, lost to the collection in the 1980s, had long hair and red beads on its mouth strings. The other is Asian and bald, and is probably the most valuable head in the Ripley collection because of its rarity. It is certainly the oldest, having been carbon dated to the 16th century (Try to imagine what an Asian was doing in South America at the time of the Spanish conquistadors!? In the 1950s Ripley's advertised him as being a Chinese missionary. His DNA confirms his origins, but not his occupation).

Two more heads were added in the early 1970s, making for a total of six when I joined in 1978. I bought my first head in 1985 for $500. When I retired, there was over 110 in the collection, the most expensive having been bought at an auction for $17,000. Clearly, I bought a lot of shrunken heads. I never formerly "studied" them, or their creators, and I have never been in Ecuador or Peru, but I am somewhat of an expert on the subject based on exposure and experience.

Shrunken heads only come from one place in the world — the border area separating Ecuador and Peru. Historically, the tribes that made them were called the Jivaro (pronounced "he-var-o"), but this is their Spanish name. Amongst themselves, they are collectively called the Shuar. I often told people that one of the sure methods of distinguishing a fake shrunken head from a real one, was the place of origin. A person claiming they had a genuine shrunken head from Mexico, Africa, or Australia, right away made their head suspect. There are of course several ways to tell fakes from real ones, most requiring nothing more than experience, and a trained eye. The novice can easily be fooled, and there are way more fake ones on the market than real ones. For anyone wanting to buy a real shrunken head, or simply wanting to learn everything that can be learned about shrunken heads, I recommend a heavily illustrated book by James Castner, titled: **Shrunken Heads Tsantsa Trophies and Human Exotica** (2002). Many of the heads shown in this book be- longed to Ripley's when it was published, and many more, including the very exotic specimen on the cover, were added to the Ripley collection post-publication.

There are obvious fakes, ones made of rubber with nylon hair, and sold from the back of comic books and in touristy gift shops. Slightly higher on the scale of fakes are ones with real skin, but not human, monkey or goat being the common leather of choice. These tend to have very perfect features, because they have been cut-out, rather than shaped by fingers, and hot rocks. These typically have fake hair, but sometimes do have real hair.

Actual genuine human heads come in two types, based on age and use, and several subcategories based on hair style. The most prized heads are called **tsantsa**. They were taken as war trophies as an act of revenge for a crime against a member of the avenging warrior's family. The most valuable ones predate 1911 when the explorer Hiram Bingham infiltrated the Peruvian jungles. The 19th century is considered the Golden Age of shrunken heads. There are a few older ones, such as Ripley's "Chinese missionary", but the jungle is not the best place to preserve anything, and the natives that created the heads typically only valued them for a year, then discarded them. We can probably thank the early German explorers for the preservation of the majority of real **tsantsas**, and later Hispanic tradesmen who recognized there was a European museum market for them, then later a tourist market too.

Genuine **tsantsas** are very dark in color, they have been well preserved by open fire smoke. They have thick natural vines strung in their mouths — the vines are inserted through the lips and are used to hold the captured "soul" of the victim inside the head cavity. The head cavity is hollow (the skull is removed from the head before the shrinking process starts), hard and about 3/8" thick, and generally with long hair. There are no barbers in the jungle, nor any reason for natives to cut their hair short. They may have feather, or insect carapace earrings. More elaborate ornamentation, such as coffee beans, shells, jaguar skin headbands, or feather hats, typically adorn only more modern tourist quality heads. Today, due largely because of the late Canadian collector Bill Jamieson, authentic **tsantsas** can fetch between $30,000 and $100,000 (US$). The ones in the Ripley collection were all bought at much lower prices.

The second type, heads created for the tourist market, post-1911, and for the most part pre-1930, are a little more commonly seen on the collector's market. They are easy to recognize by a number of details. First, they tend not to be well smoked — darkened. Their creators were in a hurry, and didn't take the time to preserve them well. As a result, they often have bug damage and skin cracks, and are even missing features. They may have mouth strings, but typically not long ones, and typically they are made of string, not natural vines. There is a preponderance of misshaped heads, some being seriously "conical" rather than round. These can look quite disturbing. These also tend to have short hair, rather than long flowing locks.

There are exceptions to every rule, such as the Ripley Chinese missionary head, but as tribal warriors were typically male Shuars, Negroid heads with Afros, Caucasian heads with mustaches, extra small heads of children, female heads, and heads with parts of a body still attached, are heads created for the tourist trade. They may fetch high sale prices because they are "rare" (especially heads with torsos or whole bodies), but they are the results of deliberate murders and grave robbing. Some of these heads may date from as late as the 1950s.

Ripley's does have female heads, children's heads, Negroid heads, Caucasian heads (typically Spanish in origin) and two female torsos. They do not have a complete shrunken body, of which I know of four. I did once have the opportunity to buy one of these (4).

The two female torsos are very special. They both have small shrunken breasts, clearly identifying them as female, and shoulder stubs. They were both bought from Christie's Auctions in London, the property of a German collector. One was in "mint" condition, but with a tar-filled body. The other, hollow, and not as well preserved, looks vaguely Tahitian or Samoan with a wild mop of curly black hair. It had once belonged to novelist Ernest Hemingway. It is the crown jewel of the Ripley Shrunken head collection in my opinion.

Until 1992 auction houses would not publicly sell shrunken heads. This all changed when a small auction firm in New Hampshire sold two heads — to Ripley's — formerly the property of one Eugenie Shorrock. A collector of ethnographic objects and snake skins, and a contemporary of Ripley's, she owned and ran a serpentarium for much of her life. Bob Masterson and I went to the auction determined to buy both heads being offered. We paid the most we ever paid for the first one, $16,000 plus commission and taxes; the audience was astounded. We got the second for under $6,000 because no one was willing to bid against us. We were mavericks. We set the auction world on its ears that day, and changed the future of Ripley's forever. For the record, the second head featuring a jaguar headband, was the better of the two heads.

The entire world now believed all shrunken heads were worth $16,000. They heard so on the radio, saw so on television, and read it in their local newspaper — articles were syndicated as far away as Australia. Up until that day you could have counted the Ripley shrunken head collection on two hands, and Ripley's had never paid more than $5,000 for one. In the next few months I bought twenty, from twenty different people who had them for a couple generations stored away in shoe boxes in their attics. They had no idea there was a market for them. They of course now all wanted $16,000 for theirs, and it took me three years to bring the price back down to under $7,000 where it belonged, but because of that auction, and that publicity, shrunken heads were no longer taboo to talk about or sell. Pretty soon other auction houses got into the act, clearly seeing there was a market to be tapped. For the next twenty-five consecutive years (1992-2017), I was able to buy at least one shrunken head a year — and in some years, a lot more than just one.

My favorite purchase was of a pair of heads, sold as a man and wife, mounted inside a small custom display case. These were literally brought into the Ripley office in person, inside a brown kraft paper grocery bag. The owner had inherited them, and didn't really know what they were, but knew she didn't want them in her home. They were in good condition and a real bargain.

I also got one — unsolicited— in the mail. Again, the owner didn't want it in her home, and gave it to me no strings attached. I suspected it was going to be a fake since she was willing to give it away, but it arrived in a small box wrapped in Peruvian newspapers dated from 1908. She probably had never even opened it to look at it.

In the early days of the internet you could buy and sell shrunken heads on-line. I was too leery, and cautious, to buy individual ones, but I bought an entire collection housed in Belgium. I never met the owner, and don't know anything about him/her, but the heads were all in excellent condition, and included two genuine tsantsas worth at least five times what I paid for the entire collection. It was too good a deal to walk away from. I lost count of how many 19th century, or older, **tsantsas** are in the Ripley collection, but safe to say they rep-resent only about 10% of the collection, maybe 15% tops. To get two at once was a coup.

In 1994 I bought two virtually identical heads from H.M. Lissauer who brokered them for a collector in Hamburg, Germany. For overall appearance, both condition and decoration, the "Hamburg heads" are the two best heads in the Ripley collection. They both still have intact long natural fiber mouth strings, yellow and red macaw feather earrings, more than twenty-inches in length hair, and even the original fiber necklace string — yes, the Shuar wore these heads as necklaces! Lissauer himself had never sold a shrunken head, being a specialist in South Sea Island and Asian ethnographic items, and never considered them as valuable as cannibal skulls, or clay-over-modeled skulls. Needless to say, I got these for much less than they were worth then, and considerably less than they are worth today. Lissauer sold me a couple others as time went on, but not as good as these ones, and not as nicely priced.

My biggest shrunken head coup came in 2004, at least in part thanks to Professor James Castner of the University of Florida. As mentioned previously, he published the definitive book on shrunken heads in 2002. In that book there are several beautiful heads that were owned by a collector named Robert White. I knew of Mr. White, but had never met him, or even seen photos of his collection. He was well known in collector circles for having the largest collection outside of Ripley's. Almost simultaneously to the book's publication, via a long-time third-party associate, Warren Raymond — someone I knew who had a couple heads of his own and had sold Ripley's a couple over the years — I learned that White's collection was up for sale. Warren knew Robert and the collection well, but could not possibly afford the whole collection. Acting on my behalf — earning a com-mission — he brokered over thirty heads to me, in-cluding the most decorated, composite, head known to exist. The head itself is a 19th century **tsantsa**, but the beetle wing earrings, the macaw feather headdress, and the bead and shell mouth strings were all added to it at a later date. In this case, it is "too good to be true", but visually, for museum display, it is the most magnificent head there is — nicer even than ones that have sold publicly for $80,000+.

In 2006 Castner wrote a second book, titled **"The Tsantsa Homicides"**. It is a work of fiction — a murder mystery book. It takes place around the University of Florida where Castner teaches a course on entomology — the study of insects. Castner first got interested in shrunken heads by studying the beetles that Shuar bee-tle wing earrings are made of. He first visited me, and the Ripley warehouse, to see a shrunken head decorated with these iridescent green bugs. His real interest in the heads started with that visit to Ripley's. As a thank you gift for my hospitality, he made me a charac-ter in his novel. My name has been changed, and my sex too, but anyone reading about Ms. Ibanez, and the real-istically described Ripley warehouse, will have no trouble identifying me. I have no idea how many copies of the book have been sold, but this is one of my proudest achievements, right up there with having my own TV show cartoon character, and receiving the key to Burlington, Iowa.

There is one last shrunken head tale, however, that sits even higher in my pantheon, and that is a book tour I did in 2007 to promote **Ripley's Search for the Shrunken Heads**. It is my favorite Ripley book, and it took me to several places across America, England and Ireland that I otherwise would have never gotten to. It got me a private viewing in Trinity College, Dublin, with the **Book of Kells**, one of the most important books in the world, and on the cover of **Fortean Times** (with a feature interview), the world's premier magazine on the unbelievable and the unexplainable. The tour also put me on a big stage in Palm Beach, Florida, where I got to speak for ninety minutes in front of about 200 people including Arlette and Alec Rigby, the man who first hired me thirty years before. After the lecture he hugged me, and knighted me with a mock rolled up honor-ary doctorate of shrunken heads, and pronounced it the best lecture he ever attended. My heart, and my head, both grew ten sizes that day.

The Ripley shrunken head book is wonderful, and truly is my favorite of all the Ripley books I worked on, but ironically, it doesn't have much to do with shrunken heads, nor is it the book I believed the company should have done. I envisioned it as a serious tome, featuring the unedited words from Ripley's 1920s personal travel diaries. The final version does have excerpts from those diaries, but is an elaborate children's pop-up book. I doubt anyone has ever read it, they simply look at the fabulous design and special effects. For the record, it sold well in Europe, but not in America. The print run was small, so it is now a hard to get collector's item. I myself don't even own one, and no, I don't have a shrunken head in my house either, not even a fake one.

Postscript:

There are two other heads in the Ripley collection that don't fit nicely into any of the categories discussed above in this chapter. I can't take full credit, or fault, for either of them. Both are heads, not skulls. Both were bought with my approval, but discovered by my long-time associate John Turner. Both raised moral issues, and one broke my written in stone law that thou shall not buy anything "**pickled**" (pre-served in liquid).

The first, was a third century AD head of a Christian martyr that I suspect was stolen from a catacomb. It is tastefully, and artistically, presented in a reliquary of Italian origin and design. I assume it came from the collection of a noble. Reportedly, it found its way to England during the Crusades. I cannot vouch for its dark history.

The second, is the dissected head of a French criminal, circa 1800. In appearance it looks similar to the Peter Kurtin, Dusseldorf Vampire head discussed in Chapter 33. Most likely it was dissected and preserved to study in relation to "normal" heads, like Kurtin's head was, but it isn't mummified, it is "pickled" inside a glass block, floating like a goldfish. It is the only "pickled" artifact in the entire Ripley collection. It is hard to look at, but mesmerizing at the same time. No

one has ever formally complained about it being displayed. Perhaps they don't think it is real? (5).

45

Freak Animals

Despite having bought an awful lot of "freak animals", animals with unusual birth defects, I don't have much to say on the subject. I can only think of one that had any sort of adventure attached to it, and in that case, it wasn't me who had the adventure. With only one or two exceptions, freak animals all came to me, typically by phone, occasionally by letter. The process was always the same:

"Hello, my name is Gus. I am a farmer, and last night one of my cows gave birth to a two-headed calf."

ME: "Well thank you for calling Ripley's sir. Is the calf dead or alive? Did it die at childbirth?"

"It's dead."

Me: "Do you wish to sell it"? "Yes, I sure do!"

Me: "Well, we can do one of two things. We can buy the carcass as is. If you haven't already, please wrap it in a big garbage bag and put it in a freezer right away. Do not let it sit too long or it will be useless to anyone. Or, if you wish to get it locally preserved by a taxidermist, we can buy the finished mount from you. How much are you hoping to get for it?"

Well I've been cattle farming all my life, and I have never seen anything like this. It's got to be worth a million dollars!

Me — calmly, with authority, "Well I have sixty-seven of them, so I am afraid it isn't worth anywhere near a million dollars to me". "Shit, no fooling, sixty-seven of them?"

Me: Yes sir, and that's just the ones I've bought. I see three or four every year.

"Well then, how much will you give me?"

Me: "For the skin, $500, but if you get it mounted, and we like the workmanship, maybe $5,000." (1).

Angrily: "Damn, I not selling it that cheap".

Me: "Well sir that's what it's worth to me. You have my number. Call me if you change your mind…Goodbye."

A couple weeks later, Gus, who has not had any luck finding anyone that will buy just the carcass, or anyone that has ever mounted a two-headed animal either, calls again:

"Will you give me $1,000 for it,"

Me: "Sorry Gus, $500 is the best I can do." "Okay, sold. What do we do now?"

Me: "Give me your address, and your phone number. I will send you

$250 as a down payment. When you get my check, call me, and I will arrange to have the carcass picked up. Do not take it out of the freezer until the truck comes."

A few weeks later, the carcass arrives packed in dry ice on the front porch of Carl Pepi's **Jonas Brothers Studios**, in Brewster, New York the very best taxidermists in the business, and for over 30 years, the only company I trusted to do Ripley's taxidermy.

Calves, and the occasional full-grown cow, were the most common freak animals I acquired, but what follows is as complete a list as I can recollect. Some of these had no abnormalities, but were acquired for general interest. The majority, have extra limbs, followed by two-faces, followed by two completely separated heads.

Domestic Animals:

-calves: multi-limbed, two-faced and two-headed

-full grown cows: multi-limbed and two-faced

-colts: two and three-legged, and miniatures

-pigs: two-headed, two-faced, cyclops, hydrocephalic, and multi-limbed

-sheep: unicorns, two-headed, multi-limbed, and cyclops

-chickens, roosters & ducks: multi-legged, and multi-winged

-kittens: two-faced, and two-headed

Wild Animals:

-parrots: two-headed

-peacock: two-headed (2)

-crows: two-headed, and multi-winged

-squirrels: two-headed, and two-tailed

-monkey: three-armed

-rabbits: two-headed, and upside down-headed

-snakes: two-headed, and giant

-frogs: multi-limbed

-turtles: two-headed, and with distorted shells caused by plastic pollution

-tortoise: with a tusk embedded in its shell

-foxes: two-tailed

-deer: two-headed, and multi-limbed

-buffaloes (bison): multi-limbed

-moose: just heads, but with giant antlers

-big horned mountain sheep: horns locked in battle

-cougars: hit by lightning, and large

-mongoose with cobras (in battle)

-alligators: multi-limbed, with unusual objects found inside, and giant ones

-Komodo dragon: largest in captivity

-lions: largest shot by bow and arrow

-hyena: shown attacking a lion

-bears: killed by a frying pan; killed by a porcupine, wearing a car tire

-elephant head: with two-trunks

Albinos

-white black bird

-squirrel

-porcupine

-beaver

-buffaloes (bison)

-alligator

-lioness

-giraffe

-cobra snake

-moose

Nearly 40 different kinds of animals: quite the menagerie!

The four-year old, full-size African elephant, with two working, fully developed trunks, one over top of the other (not side-by-side), is easily the most impressive animal in the collection, but it still came to me simply by a phone call. I actually had a big game hunter working in Africa to find a reported albino giraffe. He found the giraffe, but called in the middle of the night to say he had found something in Botswana even better. I couldn't fathom what could be better than a full-grown albino giraffe and assumed he was drunk, or that I was dreaming. He was right, the elephant is even better. I bought carcasses of both, shipped them to America and had them DNA tested before spending the money to have them mounted. The elephant has been displayed in a number of locations; the giraffe just in NYC., and Gatlinburg (3).

I have mentioned the albino moose previously (see Chapter 41), but I like my giant moose head with eight-foot wide antlers almost as much. The actual moose broke a pane of glass in a trapper's cabin in Alaska, and froze and starved to death when it couldn't get its head back out of the window. We displayed the head mounted to a wall with a prop window built around it, complete with cutesy cottage faded curtains.

Paul Springer of Mineral Springs, Wisconsin, is Ripley's King of Cows. I lost count of how many two-headed calves, or six-legged cows Paul found me over the years, but it probably was nearly twenty. Paul is a farmer with a heart of gold. All around Wisconsin it is well known that if someone has a freak animal, born alive, and they don't want it, Paul will buy it, then raise and nurture it for as long as it lives. When it died, he would then call me.

It started with a giant sixteen-year old steer that Paul called Beauregard. I know of no other freak animal that lived as long as Beauregard, and I have to imagine Paul spoiled the animal terribly to get it so big and old. Inspired by Roy Rodgers and his horse Trigger, Paul wanted to get his friend preserved, but couldn't afford it. Someone told him he should call Ripley's, and he did. After I bought Beauregard, Paul must have put my number on speed dial. Hardly a year went by where he didn't call me at least once. I used to tease him that there must be something bad in the water in Wisconsin. I sporadically did get cows from all over the country, but Paul knew who to call when one was born on his farm or nearby, and was by far the number one supplier.

One time he called and got my son Curtis on the phone. I was "busy" and not wanting to get up off my butt to answer a late-night call. Curtis yelled from the other room, "It's a guy from Wisconsin". I said, "take a message". Next thing I heard was Curtis saying "Is it dead, or alive?" followed by, "Dad, I think you really need to talk to this guy!" What's his name", I asked as I approached. "Paul Springer", Curtis said. "He says he knows you." Even as a ten-year old, Curtis knew you don't get phone calls about two-headed cows every day.

Multi-limbed creatures as proven by Paul, can live a normal life for years, provided the farmer gives them extra attention in the early stages. Most freak animals are stillborn, but if born alive they are still in danger of starving because their mother more often than not will abandon them. If the farmer won't hand feed them, they will die. This is particularly true of two-faced, and two-headed sheep, pigs and cows. Even under loving care, these seldom survive more than a few days.

When I heard of the birth of **Star**, a two-headed calf born in Virginia, just after New Year's, 2010, I thought we should get film footage of her while she was still alive. There was a great sense of urgency as she was already nearly a week old, and wasn't moving much. I couldn't go, so I sent Todd Day, our intrepid movie cinematographer, radio show tech, and all-round gadgets guy, north to farm country on a freezing cold January day. The calf didn't move at all; it may have been breathing, but it certainly appeared lifeless.

There was nothing for Todd to film, or even get decent still photos of, since the calf wouldn't (or possibly couldn't), stand up. Ill dressed for the weather twenty below zero — and ill equipped, Todd made the best of the situation: he decided to interview the family members on what they thought of Star. That day we discovered the one thing Todd couldn't do — an interview. To be fair, his subjects said the same things over and over again, and Star just laid there motionless. Todd brought back several hours of film, but in the final used production, there is less than thirty seconds from the "Great Farm Misadventure", the rest of the film is Paul Springer, or myself, talking about freak animals in general.

Star lived for forty days, the longest I had ever heard of until January 2017, when "Lucky, from Kentucky" died after managing to live for 108 days.

Freak animals, cows in particular, are an iconic part of Ripley's history, and I can't imagine there being a time when a child is not fascinated with a mutant animal, especially if it looks "cute". I seldom passed on any one I was offered, and truly felt there was always room for one more in the Ripley zoo. I regularly said: "I would not stop buying two-headed animals until I found something with three-heads. Find me something with three-heads and I could retire happy". I still haven't seen this Holy Grail. Cerberus, where are you?

46

One that Got Away #3: The Chupacabra

The most notorious of all the items that "got away" was a sample of the most common type of offerings we turned down — so-called aliens and mythical creatures.

In a nutshell, I said "no thank you" to items of this nature because to date no one has been able to give the 100% assurance of authenticity that I needed before Ripley's could put the company name on whatever it might really be. Rest assured I have been shown unexplainable things that I found "unbelievable", and was amazed by, but if "we" couldn't prove it, I couldn't buy it.

A little more than fifteen years ago I first heard the word "chupacabra", a so-called creature somewhat like a monkey, but with wings, that sucks the blood out of the throats of goats – the word literally translates from Spanish as "goat sucker". The first chupacabras were supposed to have lived in Puerto Rico, but as the myth has grown over the years, sightings have also come in from Florida and Texas. In 2005, I actually traveled up into the mountain rain forests of Puerto Rico looking for evidence of chupacabras. I met many people who said they had seen one, or that their goats had been killed by one, but no one could produce any hard evidence for us to use.

Fast forward a couple years, and imagine my excitement when I got a phone call from a local Orlando farmer who claimed to have caught one and had it in a jar — preserved in alcohol and formaldehyde. I couldn't wait to see it, and excitedly told dozens of people that my long search was over, I was about to come face to face with the legendary chupacabra.

Well, talk about disappointment…..

The man had something in a jar alright, but it was definitely not a chupacabra. It looked exactly like a TV show X-Files style "grey" alien…not as exciting as a chupacabra would have been to me — but still pretty OMG exciting….

Unfortunately, it wasn't an alien either. Against my visitor's strong objections, I put my hand in the jar, and felt stone. I pulled the alien out of the jar, knocked it with my fist, and then hit it on the kitchen counter to prove it was a carved stone, and nothing from space, or the swamps of Florida, and definitely not worth the king's ransom he was asking for it.

Language was a barrier and I never got a believable story from him, but needless to say, I didn't buy the alien-chupacabra, and to this day, I still haven't seen one of either that I would purchase. Tag this as "One that got away".

47

The "Or Nots"!

There are three types of exhibits displayed in various Ripley odditoriums that are fakes — items not meant to be believed. Accompanying signage is always forthright: these are fakes — some people may believe they are real, but shouldn't. The most popular of these are Fiji mermaids (spelled Feejee by P. T. Barnum), followed by fur covered fish, followed by wolpertingers. Ripley had ambiguously featured the mermaids (sic-mermen), and the fur fish in the cartoon in the 1930s, so adding them physically to the collection did not seem a stretch. Wolpertingers, however, I take full responsibility for; they were a 1990s addition to the collection, and if Ripley had ever heard of them, he had ignored them as obvious mythological fakes.

At age fifteen, with no full-time summer job, I was happy to go with my parents, and sisters, on what would be are last full-family vacation. My father had five weeks of holidays (based on thirty-years' service with the same company) that he typically took in July as the pharmaceutical plant he worked at always closed for at least two weeks every July. Most summers we would do a week-long road trip, camping and fishing, and then spend the rest of the time at the family cottage in Huntsville, Ontario. In 1971, my father finally bent to my mother's wishes — and threats — and bought a canvas top tent trailer. It wasn't exactly luxurious, but it was a big step up from sleeping in a tent on the ground; and it was certainly easier to assemble. That year we would reverse the normal plan, and go on a long camping road trip, and only spend a week at the cottage. In exactly twenty-eight days we drove across Canada, from Toronto, Ontario, to Victoria, British Columbia and back. I loved every minute of it, and still can recall all the best bits (seeing my first topless woman, in a river outside of Vancouver), and worst bits, stranded for hours with a flat tire outside of Moose Jaw, Saskatchewan), of this epic adventure. Here, however, I am only interested in a store on the main street of Banff, Alberta, a small town in Banff National Park — one of the most beautiful places in the world.

At fifteen I was heavy into my "Indian phase". I had long hair, wore a buckskin jacket — no matter what the temperature — Grey Owl (Archie Belaney) was my hero, and Dee Brown's **Bury My Heart at Wounded Knee** was my gospel. Much of this trip was dedicated to seeing Indian petroglyphs, pictographs, and ancient hunting grounds. Alberta had been the last stand of Sitting Bull, one of my heroes.

In what I would like to believe was more an authentic Trading Post than a simple tourist shop on Banff's main street, I was enamored by a window display of beaded moccasins. Two pairs in particular caught my full attention. Most likely both pairs were meant for show, maybe to be worn at a traditional powwow dance, but certainly not to be worn daily by a sixteen-year old kid from the suburbs. Both pairs were beautiful, and ornately decorated with colored beads. The big difference was that the basic cloth attached to the deerskin was black on one pair, and white on the other. The black pair cost sixty dollars, the white pair forty-five dollars. I liked the black pair best, but couldn't afford them. I bought the white pair, and though they haven't been "wearable" for years, I still have them, and proudly display them with other Indian artifacts on my fireplace.

But I digress….

The moccasins in the window got me into the store, but it was the Fiji Island mermaid in a glass case near the pay counter that may have changed my life. I couldn't stop staring at it. There was no signage with the piece saying what it was, but a nearby nickel postcard identified it as a "real, authentic mermaid". I was spellbound. Six years later, my first Summer with Ripley's, I would learn this "monstrosity" was affectionately called a Fiji Island mermaid and one somewhat like the Banff store creature, had made P.T. Barnum filthy rich in the 1840s when he promoted it as a real mermaid from the Islands of Fiji. Fiji being the legendary Cannibal Islands as reported by Herman Melville, and other writers and sailors of that time, no one was likely to rush off to Fiji to either find another one, or prove Barnum a humbug. It was the greatest hoax of his career, and perhaps of all time.

The original Barnum mermaid according to etchings of the time, is really quite frightening looking, and impossible to identify. By the 20th century, every dime museum had to have one, and a company in Boston was making replicas that were cleverly taxidermy half-fish, half-monkey specimens. In 1933, Ripley published a photo and story, claiming he had found a real merman in Japan. His picture looked exactly like the Banff creation, and for the most part like all other subsequent mermaids whether they were found in Africa, Europe, Asia, or the United States. Even one I bought in New Guinea was fundamentally the same, but a little bigger, and with some clay covering to preserve the fragile fish skin.

A couple years later, Ripley again repeated his claim, this time saying he had found one in Aden. Clearly sailors were spreading the mythical beauties around the world.

In 1939, when he opened his Broadway odditorium, he was ready to display his merman to the general public. He made some fantastical association to it and Sir Walter Raleigh, but now openly stated it was a fake — part monkey, part fish, and proceeded to debunk Barnum.

I learned all this in my first few days at Ripley's. In 1985, now in charge of exhibit acquisitions I tried to buy the Banff mermaid. It was still there, but not for sale. With a little bit of research, however, I discovered there were a few of these around in similar stores around the world, including a famous one in Arkansas and a giant one in Seattle, at the Ye Olde Curiosity Shoppe — a favorite shopping ground of Ripley in the late 1930s. It became my passionate mission to buy one.

I don't think I ever found one as nice as the original Ripley merman, but I eventually bought about 20 mermaids/mermen from around the world. I even found two different people who for a price would make me one. Imagine, making a living by faking fakes!

Virtually all of the Ripley mermaids/mermen are posed the same — as if swimming, with one clawed hand extended forward, while the body rests on the other hand. The mouths are always open to display the frightening, small, but sharp, teeth. The tails are very fragile, and most have broken off; it is possible some were even made that way. They come in two basic sizes, the most popular are thirteen to fifteen inches long and are made from rhesus monkeys. A second size, including the original Ripley mermaid/merman, is about twenty-five inches in length, and considerably more substantial in weight and girth. I am guessing, but the monkey might be a chimpanzee. The exception to all rules, however, is the Seattle mermaid. I surmise it is made from an orangutan as it is nearly five feet long. It also has what appear to be real nipples. If Columbus had seen this maiden, he may have convinced a lot of people back home that mermaids really did exist. Fiji mermaids are one of my all-time favorite acquisitions. I wish I owned one of my own.

Fur covered fish — specifically trout — are another great hoax that Ripley was ambiguous about. In the late twenties he reported seeing one in a museum in Edinburgh, Scotland that was labeled as if it was an authentic fish, from the frigid cold waters of Canada's Lake Superior. A few years later he wrote about this fish again, but this time he made it clear that he personally didn't believe it, but he did not openly call it a fake. Anyone that has ever swam in Lake Superior understandably might have their doubts. The lake is cold enough that a fur skin would seem like good Darwinian evolutionary solution to the lake's frigid temperature. Anyone who has ever inspected a fur fish up close, however, can immediately tell the basic fish is an Eastern Speckled (brook) trout, covered in domestic bunny fur.

In 1985 while researching Fiji mermaids, I discovered Ross Jobe, a taxidermist in Sault Saint Marie, Ontario, on the shores of Lake Superior. Ross's claim to fame was that he sold fur covered fish in two sizes — farmed twelve-inch speckled trout for $25 each, and various sized wild lake trout that he caught himself, for seventy-five dollars. I bought about thirty of them, one for every museum at the time, with a few left over to give away as promotional thank you gifts. I don't like them as much as the mermaids, but they bring a smile to everyone's face, and it is amazing just how many people think they are real!

I wish I owned one of these also.

Wolpertingers are a little different than the mermaids or the fur fish. I have never met anyone "fooled" by them. The taxidermy combination of creatures is just too hard to imagine. Wolpertingers — animals that are half-bird, half-mammal, do however, play a role in Germanic myths, and perhaps in days gone by were seen as real possibilities. The animals according to their mix are said to have certain characteristics (2), and as a "species" are collectively "evil" forest dwellers that like to torment, and sometimes, eat, small children. Scary stories were told of them to prevent children from idly running away into dark foreboding forests. That the animals all have wings gives credence to their ability to hide in trees and sweep down to scoop up their unsuspecting kiddy prey.

Specimens I purchased include: raven-rabbits, owl-rats, hawk-gophers, and winged monkeys that I am sure were the inspiration for the flying monkeys in the Wizard of Oz. My personal favorite, however, is a beaver, complete with giant protruding teeth, attached to large bird of prey wings. I know if I ever saw one of these things flying towards me, I would die of fright long before it ever picked me up, or attempted to eat my face.

The common circus-sideshow term for all these make-believe creatures is "gaffs". It is safe to say most were originally made to fool the unsuspecting naïve public in the name of profit. In a simpler time and place, they probably did fool a lot of people, but they also made them laugh and smile at the same time. Today's special effects creators are light years beyond these simple fakes in quality and realism, but they seem to have lost any concept of "maybe" or "what if", and are designed purely to scare the shit out of their audience. I love dragons, and dinosaurs and even aliens, but I wish I could still find an old-fashioned mermaid, fur fish, or maybe even a taxidermy "catfish", for my mantle.

48

One That Got Away (#4);
Despite Being Landed

Cow and pig hairballs have always been part of the Ripley collection,- dating back to the 1930s. Pig hairballs tend to be oblong and spikey. Cow hairballs are
usually perfectly shaped solid globes of hair and very
smooth. Pig hairballs seldom are bigger than a softball. Cow hairballs can be bigger than basketballs (1).

One of the first promotions we did after the company
moved to Florida in 1993, was to have a cow hairball
contest, a search to find the biggest cow hairball in
America, maybe even the world. We still had a few in
the warehouse, but we were down to tennis ball sized
ones, and we really did wonder how big they could get.

We offered some prizes, and put out the call in the media that we were looking for the biggest hairball we
could find. Over a period of about three months, we received over 300 hairballs from all parts of the country
— unfortunately none from overseas. Most were softball
size, about twelve inches in circumference. There were
a few ugly, nasty pig ones, and there were some obvious
giants, ones measuring over thirty-inches in circumference. All of the entries were photo-graphed, measured,
placed in brown shopping bags and stored in an empty
office. The cow hairballs don't smell, but the pig ones
do; they had to be separated from the herd pretty quickly before Lisa Pascella and I, the official King and
Queen of Hairballs, died of asphyxiation. The whole
contest was a hoot, definitely one of the strangest
promotions we ever did, and certainly the silliest contest. The winning ball was forty-two-inches in circumference.

Fast forward about twenty years.

My master bedroom at home has an adjoining bathroom. My
wife was in the bed watching the morning news. I had
just come out of the shower, and had the door cracked
open a few inches to hear the news. A story came on
about a guy trying to raise money for an operation for
his "pet" tiger. He believed the animal, named "TY",

had a giant hairball caught in its throat that was preventing it from eating, and was affecting its breathing. The tiger was living on a game farm near Tampa, Florida, about a hundred miles away.

Within minutes of my getting to the office, less than an hour later, I had contacted the owner. I said Ripley's would pay for the surgery in return for getting the hairball. There was serious potential PR good will in this benevolent act: "RIPLEY'S SAVES TIGER" — would make a catchy news headline, and though I had no idea what a tiger hairball would look like (domestic cat hairballs, are not round, and not solid), I assumed the company would get a cool exhibit out of the deal.

A couple days later a wet, stinky blob of no distinguishable shape, was hand delivered to my office door. The smell was strong enough to kill an elephant. People ten feet away were instantly coughing and gagging. No one could get close enough to even look at it. It definitely couldn't stay indoors.

Genius that I am — duh — I placed the slime in a beer cooler, the kind you take on picnics and camping trips, and placed the cooler underneath the back-step entrance of the warehouse — to let it air in the Florida sun. Dumb idea, especially knowing people regularly stole stuff from our nearby dumpster.

Less than an hour after I put it out there, the cooler was gone — stolen — seemingly with the hairball still inside. Go figure. I imagine the conversation between the thieves:

"This is Ripley's Believe It or Not! They have the best garbage. Hey, look at that mint condition brand new cooler. Let's steal it and get out of here quick."

I would have paid anything to see their faces when moments later, after running to safety, they opened the cooler. I am surprised the next day's news headline wasn't: "Boys Found Dead. No Sign of Physical Injury or Foul Play, but Unidentified Mysterious Object (with an accompanying photo) Suspected".

We did have the foresight to take a couple pictures of the ball — and we definitely got a hell of a story — but thankfully, this is another exhibit "that got

331

away".

Postscript: A month or so later, the grateful tiger
owner came to our office — with Ty, a full-grown Bengal
tiger. Ty was in a cage in a truck in our parking lot;
several employees flocked to see him. The owner put him
on a leash, and walked him up and down the driveway
like a dog. I enthusiastically — read unthinkingly —
went right up to it, and petted it on his nose and
forehead, just like I do with my house cat. I guess I
figured if it was walked on a leash it was fully tame.
It was more than an hour later before I realized just
how dangerous   a stunt this had been. Several people
couldn't believe my bravery. I couldn't believe my stupidity. The next time I petted a tiger it was on the
rump, and the tiger was heavily chained.

49

California's Cathedrals

My family camped a fair bit when I was growing up, so from an early age I liked the woods, and the Indigenous People who I associated with living in the woods. The first time I remember anyone declaring trees, and spots in the woods to be God's natural churches, was in the book **"Pilgrims of the Wild"** (1935) by Archie Belaney, aka, Grey Owl. My copy of the book had the most beautiful sun-drenched forest photo on the cover. It was a black and white photo, but you could clearly envision the stream of gold penetrating the dark green and black forest. Grey Owl, one of my first favorite writers (1), was describing the virgin pine forests of Temagami, Ontario. Wonderful as those trees are — and they are very special, being one of the only remaining virgin forests in Ontario — they pale in comparison with the redwoods and sequoias of Northern California. The very first trip I took on behalf of Ripley's was to California in the fall of 1978. I fell in love instantly with San Francisco, and seeing my first redwoods in nearby Muir Woods, gave me "goosebumps". A few years later, on a longer extended trip in Sequoia and Kings' Canyon National Parks, I knew exactly what Grey Owl had been talking about. It was like seeing, and touching, the face of God.

I am a possessive bastard. I love — and have to — own things. Seeing things you love is one thing, borrowing them (when possible) is another, but I knew instantly I had to buy a redwood tree. I eventually acquired three two coastal redwoods, and one sequoia, and a fourth got away (2).

The Ripley cartoons are filled with dozens of fascinating redwood stories and facts, including the differences between the three sub-species of these majestic giants, but for my purposes, all you need to know is that redwoods are redder in color, and taller than sequoias, but sequoias are larger in circumference. Both grow incredibly old (over 2,500 years), and tall, upward to 370'.

333

My favorite redwood tree cartoon involved a man living in a still standing tree. My first redwood purchase was a "log house" -three rooms carved into the inside of a fallen redwood log. The man who had carved it, had lived in it for over thirty years! It had a kitchen, a bedroom and a sitting room. After living in it during the 1920s-1940s he sold it and it became a US state fair attraction in the 1950s-70s. Over time, I met many people who had seen it in places as far afield as Oregon, Massachusetts, Missouri and Florida. I knew it simply from an oversized postcard. I bought it sight unseen. It measures about fifty-feet long, six-feet high by six-feet wide and you can walk right through it from end to end.

In 1995 it cost Ripley's $40,000, a fair bit of my annual budget at the time. I considered it "a steal", one of the best deals ever. When I got a phone call saying it had been delivered to St. Augustine, they asked:

"What do you want us to do with the truck cab?"

I didn't at first know what they were saying, and then once I understood, I was convinced it was a mistake. I knew the purchase of the tree included the trailer it was mounted to, but I was not expecting the front end of the truck to be part of the deal — but apparently it was. With no difficulty I was able to sell the cab for $65,000, more than a 50% profit on the price of the tree. No one could argue that this wasn't the deal of the century.

The climate in Florida has not been kind to the tree, or the trailer, but I still love this tree and would love one day to sleep in it. It is parked in the garden adjacent to the driveway at the St. Augustine, Ripley's Odditorium. I cannot visit that odditorium without first going through the log. It is definitely one of my all-time top ten purchases.

Sometime early in 1986 I visited the Historic Niagara Falls Museum (HNFM), reportedly the oldest museum in Canada, once visited by Abraham Lincoln, and home to several artifacts concerning Niagara Falls daredevils — the people who went over the Falls in barrels and other contraptions in the early 1900s. I was with brilliant museum designer Anton Gosley, one of the three or four most creative people I know. He was working on renovating our Niagara Falls museum. We were at the HNFM specifically to look at Niagara Falls related exhibits, but it was hard to miss the graffiti carved humpback whale skeleton, the flat-face squished nose taxidermy lion (the most ridiculous stuffed animal on display anywhere), or the hollowed out giant sequoia tree stump in the center of the floor in the first gallery.

A few years later Ripley's considered buying the entire museum, the collection and the five-story building. Based on notes I had made back in 1986, we decided to pass. There were certainly things we could use, but more that we couldn't, and we had no interest in the real estate at the time. Torontonian legend, William ("Billy") Jamieson, eventually bought the whole collection. (Bill and I were good friends). He made a fortune off this collection. He kept lots of it for his own "museum" gallery on Toronto's Adelaide Street, but he sold the big pieces, including the mummy of Ramses I, a royal Hawaiian bird-feather robe, the whale skeleton (once owned by P.T. Barnum), and the giant sequoia tree stump.

I bought the tree stump in 2008.

It came in sections, and was hollowed out so you could walk into it. When I first saw it, it was shamefully covered in business cards; it made you laugh, but it also made you cry. It was approximately twenty-five feet tall by about sixty-feet in circumference and at least ten people could stand inside. The tree had been cut early in the century and was definitely a one-of-a-kind perfect thing for Ripley's. I was glad it came in pieces, each supported by heavy duty iron braces. Transportation was not a critical issue, but like with the "log", we really had no place to display it, and we would end up displaying it outside in Jeju Island, Korea. I have not seen it in years and have no idea how well it has fared. I suspect it may not look like I remember.

Back in 1978 in the California National Parks I had seen cross-section slabs of redwoods displayed with time lines pointing out significant dates in history in relationship with the growth rings of the tree. I had always imagined doing a display like this, but getting a slab of a redwood which were heavily protected as early

as the 1950s, seemed an impossibility. Then in 2012, at
the annual IAAPA (International Association of Amusement Parks and Attractions), held that year in Orlando,
I saw a fantastic display of a thirteen-foot in diameter slab. The owners, two brothers from Paso Robles,
California (the town Marilyn Monroe and Joe DiMaggio
honeymooned in before going to Korea in 1954), said they
had five more slices, three identical in size, and two
from the top of the tree that were smaller, measuring
eight-foot in diameter. Always a firm believer in
"cheaper by the dozen", on the spot, I bought the one
in front of me — saving a considerably amount of money
on shipping and handling, and then went to California
four months later, to inspect and purchase the other
five. While there, I also bought a fantastic human skull
with an Indian spearhead embedded in it; the brothers
had found it in a creek near their home. Once you have
seen the thirteen-foot slabs, the eight-foot ones don't
look so impressive, but when you learn that the small
pieces came from the very top of the tree — more than
260' high — they can carry their weight on the wow
scale. For the record, this tree had fallen in the
woods one year before Monroe and DiMaggio passed through
Paso Robles. Actually, it had lived a few hundred miles
away, and had been trucked nearly sixty years later, to
Paso Robles where the "Woods Brothers" had their lumber
yard and furniture making factory.

The tree that got away, was a second sequoia, and it
was another "log house". It was more "elegant" than our
redwood log house, and measured nearly twelve feet in
diameter. There were five rooms — including two bed-
rooms, and a very comfortable shower room! The kitchen
had glass cabinets. The present owners had lived in it
from the 1950s through the 1990s, pulling it on a
trailer across the USA, and for a while, residing in it
in New Zealand!

Negotiations had gone on for months by the time I got
to the Pocono Mountains of Pennsylvania to seal the
deal. From the start, there had been great concern for
the size. The owner had measured "the tree" down to the
quarter-inch, and we had determined we would be able to
get it into our Orlando warehouse facility. Unfortunately, he hadn't measured the trailer the tree was on,
and had neglected to tell us the tree couldn't be taken
off the trailer. The tree was bolted to the trailer,

and the bottom was not safe if we were to attempt to unbolt it.

I was heart-broken. This piece was truly unbelievable, and I had visions of our construction team actually living in it, but the two extra feet in length, and about an extra foot in width, were deal breakers. I walked away empty handed, and never heard from them again. For the record, the sequoia tree was carved to look like a wine barrel, and had been inspired by a giant cask in Heidelberg Castle, Germany, built in 1751, that holds 58,124 gallons of wine. The German cask was once featured in the Ripley's cartoon.

I am very content with the three trees I got, and I won't cry over the one that got away, after all I bought enough wood to make a real cathedral in the wilds if the need ever arises (3).

A Forestry Footnote-One that Got Away #5

No trees can compare to the redwoods and sequoias, but a couple others I came across are worthy of at least a mention.

Long before I got my first redwood, I managed with the help of Chuck Thielen, the manager of Ripley's San Francisco when I first started, to acquire two slabs of bristle cone pine trees. These really don't look impressive at all, but the bristle cone grows only in very small areas of California and Nevada, and is believed to be the longest living tree in the world. Ripley's pieces are over 4,000 years old. The trees live in poor soil at sub-alpine elevations of 11,000' just below the tree line, where little rain falls, and where virtually no other vegetation can grow. They don't grow tall, and typically are stunted, and gnarly looking. The Ripley pieces though extremely old, are only about twenty-four inches in diameter, and dull grey in color. The growth rings, however, are well defined and quite easy to count for a very patient person (1). It would be virtually impossible to get a slab of a bristle cone tree today.

Before working for Ripley's Chuck had been a forest ranger, and he knew and loved trees more than anyone I have ever known. He found a government contact for the bristle cone pieces while hunting down redwoods, and personally culled the two pieces in the Ripley collection. He was convinced they would make as good an exhibit as their larger redwood brethren. We displayed them in a similar manner, matching historical dates to growth lines. The average person is underwhelmed; but the occasional botanist that visits, shakes with ecstasy.

It was Chuck who introduced Ripley's to some other very interesting trees too, a grove of seventy "man-made", oddly shaped trees near Santa Cruz, California (2). The trees were planted, grafted and nurtured by a Swedish horticulturist named Axel Erlandson (1884-1964). More than a dozen of the trees at different times, starting in the late 1940s, had been featured in the Ripley cartoon. At the time I saw the grove in 1980, which had originally been the man's back garden, the attraction was called **"The Tree Circus"**.

Over the years the "Circus" changed hands a few times, and at least twice, under Chuck's lead, we tried to buy the whole forest. The location made it a hard sell. It not only wasn't on the "beaten path", it was far off the path, and deep in the woods. You certainly couldn't see a thing from the closest secondary roadway. It was so sad to see the trees die from neglect that I had suggested — to the horror of every-one, especially Chuck — that we simply cut the sections of the most visual ones, and display partial trees in our museums. There was one that had a heart in the middle, another that was latticed, one that had a square in the middle and even one that was shaped like a chair. Eventually, before it was too late, Michael Bonfante invested millions of dollars, and dug up all the trees that were still healthy (approximately forty), and moved them south to Gilroy, California where twenty-five are still on display at **Gilroy Gardens**, a roadside attraction that gets thousands of visitors every year. Chuck would be very proud (3).

51

Chasing History

I have always been a history buff, and many of my favorite Ripley exhibits, items that I personally acquired, are historical in nature. I may not have been
conscious of it before 2007, but at least in the back of
my brain I always thought history was a big part of Ripley's that is to say, the telling and showing of little
known, or fantastical aspects of it. In 2007 at the
opening of the Ripley's odditorium in New York's Times
Square, an arrogant newspaper reporter who admitted he
had never been to any other Ripley's attraction, flat
out told me our ten-foot by ten-foot segment of the
Berlin Wall didn't belong in a Ripley's odditorium. The
implication was that we weren't good enough to own such
an important piece of history. My feathers were very
ruffled that day, and going forward from that moment
on, I made a much more concerted effort to add historical, and educational exhibitory, to the collection. My
firm belief has always been Ripley's is not just an entertainment attraction, but an educational one too. I
saw myself as at least part teacher, with a mission not
just to save history, but to display it to the "common
man". If an item, say a wall, or a gun, or a dinosaur
bone, wasn't unusual unto itself, but there was an unbelievable back story to it, and we could afford it, why
wouldn't I try to buy it and display it? It still makes
me steamy today to think of that day and that conversation.

The Ripley history collection is full of small quirky
bits of history: wood from Lincoln's log cabin, a photograph from and of Hitler's yacht, a canteen found at
Gettysburg, or Ripley's favorite, a small bottle of
mange, found in the bombed-out ruins of Chapei, China,
circa 1932, but there are some much more significant,
pieces too. I will leave the most significant — the
Ripley space artifacts — for another chapter of their
own (see Chapter 79), and concentrate here on just a
few random personal favorites.

Elephant Armor

Robert Ripley owned three or four suits of medieval soldier's armor. I can appreciate them, but I don't know
why he acquired them. For me, they aren't "unusual"
enough to warrant a place in the collection. The first
piece of armor I bought was for a cat. It's unlikely
the cat was comfortable, or of much use in battle, but
he must have looked good, and he was safe from arrows.
I also bought modern samurai style cat armor, but I am
sure it was totally for show. I bought a suit of dog
armor specifically to illustrate a Ripley cartoon about
a heroic medieval dog, and I bought a suit of horse armor just because it was the only one that was ever offered to me. It wasn't until I went to India in 2008,
and saw a suit of elephant armor, that I got excited
about "armor".

All school kids learn about Hannibal invading Rome rid-
ing on elephants, and it doesn't take much imagination
to visualize the fear and havoc an elephant coming towards an army at twenty-plus miles an hour would cause,
but shamefully, I had no idea elephants in Mogul period
India were not only used in warfare, but were heavily
armored in European style protective metal gear to
boot. I was led to believe by museum authorities there
were maybe only three of these suits of elephant armor
still intact in the entire world. I was, however, assured there was a second kind of elephant armor — made
up of chain mail blankets — that could be found for the
right price in many parts of northwest India [1].

Less than a year later, I had the good fortune to meet
a gentleman who worked for the Stratford-on-Avon Armory
in Shakespeare's home town in England. He initially
contacted me because he was interested in vampire killing kits; it was only by chance that he mentioned the
armory was de-acquisitioning a large part of their collection — including a full set of "composite" Indian
elephant armor. All of the pieces were authentic, but
not all from the same suit, or even same time period.
The pieces were an amalgamation of 16-18th century
plates, and mail. It was a must buy.

The deal took several months, and ended up including
various other pieces, including two more sets of horse
armor used in the 2004 Hollywood blockbuster movie Van

341

Helsing. The armor came attached to a paper mâché and foam full-sized elephant, complete with a howdah on the back, with three wax figure warriors inside. It stood an incredible twenty-seven feet high, and weighed more than a ton. The ears are covered in chain mail, the eyes have hooded metal covers, and the front knees have huge four-pronged spikes. The whole ensemble is the most frightening looking war machine imaginable, and clearly what inspired World War I army tanks. I confess I sat on her back before the cabin was repaired and re-installed. With the beast between my legs, and from the towering viewpoint, I felt invincible.

Dinosaurs

Like many little boys, I knew my dinosaurs almost as soon as I knew my ABC's. It amazes me that youngsters can tell you the names of a dozen prehistoric crea-tures, but can't pronounce the word "spaghetti", or spell the name of the state they live in. I grew up wanting to be an archaeologist, and after visiting the Badlands of Alberta and seeing Triceratops bones in situ, I felt it was my destiny to someday buy dinosaur bones. It took Stephen Spielberg to help fulfill this calling.

My moving to Florida was the single most significant thing to happen to me in 1993, but a close second was the release of the film **Jurassic Park**. It was the last movie my family saw in Toronto, just days before we moved. My then six-year old daughter hid between my legs for the entire film. My eight-year old son was glued to the screen, and repeatedly listed off all the species we were seeing. I was mesmerized that the dino-saurs of my youth looked so real.

The very next day I told the boss we had to buy some dinosaur bones this film was going to be the biggest hit of all time — even bigger than **"Jaws"** (2) — and we had to catch the trend. He agreed, the purse strings were loosened, and I went shopping. The first stop was China where hundreds of nests of dinosaur eggs had recently been found. I bought about a dozen nests, ranging in size from three eggs to sixteen. Today, single eggs may cost as much as a thousand dollars, large nests are worth a king's ransom.

342

Next, I went looking for signature pieces, T-rex teeth, Stegosaurus plates, and ceratopsian horns. I knew I could not afford whole skeletons, so pieces would have to do. I bought claws, feet, giant leg bones, and eventually casts of full heads: T-rex, Allosaurus, Triceratops, Chasmosaurus. Before I was finished, I got two actual Chinese Stegosaurus variants, a small Apatosaurus, two fifteen-foot wingspan pterosaurs, two mosasaurs, two prehistoric crocodiles, an Archelon (giant turtle) casting, two Diatryma terror birds, two Utah raptor castings and a replica Archaeopteryx plate — perhaps the most famous and important fossil of all — the first to prove that birds descended from dinosaurs.

In less than two years I acquired more than 100 fossil pieces. Prior to that, the only fossils in the collection were trilobites and ammonites, small creature fossils that can be bought at any fossil fair or rock shop for a few bucks.

For twenty-five years I never officially stopped buying fossils, but as market prices soared once China stopped the trade of their supplies, purchases became less frequent and more specialized. I eventually branched out into prehistoric mammals, and added ancient woolly mammoth hairs, giant sloth claws, giant beaver, rhino and saber tooth tiger skulls, and complete mastodon skeletons.

In 2016 I took a major road trip through Montana, Wyoming and South Dakota. I visited hallowed Indian grounds at Wounded Knee and the Little Bighorn, and with friends of the Black Hills Institute got to work on some fossils in their research facility. With a small broom, and a tooth brush, I got to help uncover a Pachycephalosaur, the head-butting dinosaur featured in the 2018 version of **Jurassic Park**, and a T-rex skull — a long time dream fulfilled.

The last official company interview I did for Ripley's was about the "ethics" of private collectors buying fossils. I understood the question, but was more pissed off by it than philosophical about my answer. I do own a couple very small fossils, and a couple other "replicas", but I could never afford to be a collector of fossils for myself. I struggled to make it clear to the reporter that I bought for a museum company, not for my living room. At the core, I have always felt myself more a librarian than an archivist. I have always wanted to share everything I bought. I don't like collectors who hide their treasures from the public, but I certainly don't begrudge anyone who can afford to buy treasures that institutions can't (or won't). I love the Ripley fossil collection that I built up from nothing to a "substantial" private holding, and am very proud of it. I still read every article about new fossil findings with great interest, and I can think of nothing that pleases me more than seeing a five-year old in a Ripley odditorium lecturing his stunned parents, or grandparents, on the monsters of pre-history.

Abraham Lincoln

Ripley's has a large number of American presidential pieces, mainly connected to Kennedy, Washington, or Lincoln. I am a Canadian, so maybe my vote doesn't count, but for my money, Honest Abe was America's greatest president. Though I did buy several unusual portraits of Lincoln (made from human hair, butterflies, computer keys, etcetera), and a custom made, extra-long Lincoln bed, the best Lincoln artifacts I acquired all relate to his assassination by John Wilkes Booth.

One of the first big auctions I attended was with Bob Masterson at **Butterfield& Butterfield Auction House** in San Francisco. We bought a number of "western" pieces, including a cannon made out of a log, and a peg leg with a concealed pistol and wire trigger attachment — used by an itinerant street thief — but the prize piece was a derringer pistol made by Henry Derringer in Philadelphia in the 1860s for actor assassin John Wilkes Booth. It is beautifully engraved, and as far as guns go, a work of art. It is one of a matched pair.

The Lincoln assassination story is one of the most written about moments in American history, and I thought I knew the story pretty well, but in 1994 it was news to me that Booth had two derringers that fateful April night in the Ford Theater. This pistol was one of them, the other belongs to the Smithsonian Institute and resides in the Ford Theater museum in Washington, D.C. Until the 1970s, more than 100 years after the trigger was pulled, no one was sure which of the

344

two pistols was the actual murder weapon.

As the story goes, after the fatal shot, Booth jumped from the balcony to the stage, breaking his ankle before making his dramatic escape. During the leap a derringer fell from his vest pocket onto the stage. It was recovered immediately, and considered the "smoking gun". Twelve days later, however, when Booth was finally cornered and gunned down in Virginia, an exact duplicate derringer was found on his person. At the time no one thought twice about it, and our gun toured as the murder weapon for the next fifty years, unchallenged. Sometime in the 1920s Lincoln experts started to ask questions, but it was another fifty years before criminology and ballistics were advanced enough to prove once and for all which gun was the murder weapon.

Though the gun being auctioned was not the murder weapon, the back story was fascinating, and the provenance impeccable. The gun would be a showpiece amongst various other pieces related to the assassination already in the collection, existing cartoons, and a wax figure of the President. Bob seemed to want it even more than I did, and we came away with the treasure.

Derringers are very small guns. They can be concealed in your hand, and will fit in any pants pocket. Bob paid for the gun on the spot, and carried it out of the building in his pocket. Not trusting our hotel, he carried it all evening, down along the wharf to the Ripley Odditorium, and even to dinner (3). The next morning, Bob went to the airport very early expecting to fill out required paperwork for us to be able to carry the derringer home on a plane. I thought Bob may have had special permission as a military vet, or former security guard, for somehow to my amazement he was able to keep the gun on his person. He not only ever relinquished it, I don't believe he ever even showed it to anyone (4). Our purchasing of the gun made television and newspaper headlines around the country, and it was a real feather in our caps. Within a week I had an offer for 33% more than we had paid for it, and over the next ten years I could have resold it a dozen times. I don't think the company has ever displayed it well, and at times though fundamentally opposed to selling our artifacts (see Chapter 35), I wondered if we shouldn't have flipped it.

Ordinarily, I didn't buy very much jewelry, but I made exceptions regarding Washington and Lincoln, and acquired several lovely pieces, most of which contained locks of the presidents' hair. Lockets containing hair locks have been exchanged by lovers for centuries, but in the 18th and 19th hair jewelry was associated primarily with mourning.

As Lincoln lay dying, after he was shot in the head, his head was shaved in order to look for the bullet. Someone present had the foresight to collect and keep the shaved hairs. For this reason, there is more Lincoln hair available on the market than any other president, and after his death virtually every woman with any connection to the president had a sample — typically kept in a brooch or locket, and worn in respect for the late president. The best sample – actually two pieces — in the Ripley collection both came with provenance directly tied to Mary Todd Lincoln, the president's widow. One is a small brooch with a border of rubies, about a half inch square, the other is a silver locket, ornately engraved. Both contain under glass a depiction of Lincoln's Kentucky log cabin home — woven from locks of his hair, collected the night of his death. The smaller of the two is not very detailed, and its value rest more in the rubies than the hair, but the larger one, about two inches by two inches is a wonder to behold. The response by causal viewers is disbelief. The response from anyone who has ever done any kind of "needle work" is dumbstruck awe, followed by the word "IMPOSSIBLE"!

One of the last things I bought before my retirement might be the most controversial piece I ever acquired. Like the Booth derringer, it has impeccable, indisputable, provenance, direct from the original owner, but somewhere along the line something happened to cast doubt on its back story. The piece is a bugle, reported to have been played by Lincoln's personal military guard's bugler as a call to arms the night he was assassinated, then again, days later as his coffin boarded a train for his long ride home, and then at each stop along the train's journey from Washington to Springfield, Illinois. That such a bugler existed is not in question, every detail of his life and military career is known to experts, but what song was played is disputed. "Taps" was listed in all later literature, but in 1865, it was not yet in wide circulation, and whether this is the actual bugle that was played is also disputed. The bugle as it exists today appears to be a composite with some parts dating from the 1870s.

The bugle was offered, and later sold by a reputable auction house. Information brought to light literally the day before the sale, caused them to take it out of the sale, but a few months later with a modified description, and a devalued price, it was offered a second time. I would have bid the first time, but doubt I would have got it because of the price, but at the reduced price, I couldn't resist. If it is ever totally debunked, then I made a mistake, and paid too much for an antique bugle. In the meantime, however, it is a haunting memorial of the loss of America's greatest president. The display verbiage as I wrote it, states what is known for sure, and leaves the question of authenticity to the reader, to believe or not.

The Berlin Wall

I consider the building and the tearing down of the Berlin Wall, the two most significant historical events of the second half of the twentieth century. Knowing that, it should be no surprise that I rank the acquisition of sixteen, ten-foot by ten-foot pieces of it, as one of my greatest achievements. To the best of my knowledge Ripley's has more Wall at least extant pieces — than anyone else in the world. We chased history, and through perseverance caught it, and preserved it for future generations that hopefully will never in their lifetimes experience the reality of anything so dastardly as the Berlin Wall.

For days before the Wall fell in November 1989, people watched the news in anticipation that something major was about to happen in Berlin. President Reagan had exhorted President Gorbachev to tear down the Wall, and people sensed that if Gorbachev wouldn't, German citizens would. Norm Deska greeted Bob Masterson and I every morning that month with: "If and when the Wall falls, Ripley's should get some pieces". I don't think we ignored him, but we weren't as convinced as he was that it would Fall, and we at least at first, weren't sure it was something that people in America would pay to see.

On the brink of the breakthrough on November 12, he at last convinced us.

Within three days of the Fall, I had made contact with the son of an American ambassador stationed in Berlin, who would ultimately broker the deal for me. I was introduced to him by my friend Drew Hunter who at the time was living in Dallas, Texas. He was sure he could get as much of the Wall as I might want. At the time my vision was fairly small, I was thinking handfuls, not complete sections.

Eleven months later, Bob, Norm, myself, and Sylvia Matiko, the company's VP of Franchise Operations, and our would-be German translator, flew to Hamburg, Germany to look at a collection of tribal artifacts in a harbor side curiosity shop Bob had previously discovered (we bought roughly eighty pieces, including colorful Ceylonese snake masks, New Guinea hook statues used to hold cooking ware, and a large, one-piece, solid teak elephant. From Hamburg we all drove to Berlin to look at what remained of the Wall. Sylvia and I would try to get a feel of the land, while Norm and Bob would continue on the next morning to Munich to investigate properties for a potential new odditorium.

Only a small portion of the Wall was down at that point, mainly close to the Brandenburg Gate, the dramatic symbol of 19th and 20th century Imperial Germany. There were crowds of people everywhere, some selling jewelry made from small bits of the Wall, and others actively chipping away small pieces for souvenirs. Watching people interact with the Wall, either by touching it, or walking through the holes — something I intentionally did several times with tears rolling down my face — was one of the most moving experiences of my life. My distant, several generations back, relatives were from Germany, but I didn't consider myself to have any real ties to the Wall, yet it tore apart my heart. With a rock smith's small hammer, and a Swiss army knife, I went to work immediately. My goal was to fill an empty suitcase with as much rock as I could lift. I collected nearly sixty pounds worth.

Pretty soon I came to realize that there was not going to be anything unique about small pieces, for display we would need big pieces — whole slabs if possible.

Sylvia did her best asking anyone and everyone who we needed to talk to in order to "buy" big pieces, but armed soldiers merely shrugged their shoulders, and said the Wall was "free", and would be completely torn down "soon". Nervous that we might already be too late, I left Berlin with my suitcase full of fist size pieces. The custom agent weighed the bag and joked "what did I have inside, a bunch of rocks?". I laughed and said, "Yes, exactly". He thought I was crazy, and let me through without even charging me for the excess weight.

Once back in America, using my Texas connection, I went into over-drive, and from about twenty-five pre-identified slabs, hand-picked sixteen that I thought were the most visual, the ones with the most colorful slogans or images.

The soldiers had been right, the Wall came down shortly after. Pieces were cheap. It costs nearly ten times as much to ship our purchases, first by truck to Hamburg, then by cargo boat to Miami, then by truck to St. Augustine, than it did to buy them. It is impossible to say who "owned" the Wall, I have no idea who we actually bought it from, but money was distributed to politicians, soldiers, and construction workers, with no questions asked. Nearly two years after the initial breakthrough, I had 160 linear feet of the Wall. Drew Hunter, and the Dallas Ripley odditorium, got the first choice as a reward for their role in the acquisition, and chose a wonderful image of an orange butterfly rising above rows of barbed wire (in Berlin the actual Wall was topped by barbed wire).

It would be nearly thirty years before all sixteen segments were duly installed in Ripley locations around the world. In the interim, I saw individual slabs, some only five-foot' wide by ten-foot high, in various museums around the world, including a piece in the Reagan Presidential Library, and another in the Gerald Ford Presidential library, but I have never met anyone with more than one slab. Ripley's has enough that if it wanted, it could build a wall around one of its odditoriums.

I don't care what any New York journalist thinks, I believe Ripley's did good in preserving — and displaying — the Wall, and I think this acquisition might just be my proudest moment (5).

As a footnote, in 2017 Angela Johnson and I, met a man who claimed to have been Ronald Reagan's personal body guard back in 1989, and had a public storage facility in Florida filled with hundreds of small pieces of the Wall. He had a handful of brick size pieces, but most were about the size of a quarter.   Bagged with a picture postcard, a military star-shaped Russian badge, and a small piece of barbed wire, he had made a decent living in the 1990s selling them in souvenir shops for eighty-nine dollars apiece. I didn't have the courage to tell him how much I had paid for sixteen ten-foot by ten-foot pieces, but I did buy a hundred pieces from him, that I used as promotional gifts and contest prizes for the next two years.

52

Funny Money-Yap Stones &
Bird Feather Coils

The world's most unusual form of currency comes from the Island of Yap, in Micronesia. Called "rai", this money is also the world's largest, sometimes as much as twelve-feet in diameter, and made of solid stone. Try putting that in your purse, or pocket.

My first exposure to this monetary marvel was an early 1940s Believe it or Not! cartoon. With American soldiers fighting in the South Pacific during World War II, Ripley drew dozens of seemingly incredulous, unbelievable cultural items so that the folks back home would know just what their sons, daughters and husbands were facing so far from home. Some of these items were based on Ripley's travels in the South Pacific back in 1932, but most I suspect came from the pen of the incomparable Norbert Pearlroth, Ripley's head researcher, a man someone, even at this late date, should write a book about. The original "rai" cartoon had also appeared on the cover of a small Rip-ley pamphlet created in the 1960s for the United States mint on the subject of "money". From photo evidence, I also knew Ripley's had quite a large one of these donut-looking stones at some point in the 1960s-1970s outside in the gardens at the St. Augustine odditorium. Apparently, this stone was on loan from Grover Criswell, a respected Floridian numismatist, but it was long gone by the time I first asked anything about it. Bob Masterson, had seen it in St. Augustine in the mid-1970s and had actually built a cabana to display it under (1).

In 1987-1988 I read about rai in a **"National Geographic"** magazine, and decided I just had to buy one of these stones. If their size and uniqueness wasn't enough to get anyone excited, learning the stone from which they were carved from actually came from another island and had to be moved across the open ocean by dug-out canoe, was a certified WOW moment of disbelief. I had to get at least one.

351

By this time, I knew where Yap was, and even knew one person who had been there and seen rai in situ. Mr. Lissauer (see Chapter 10), assured me they indeed still existed and could be seen all over the island, but to the best of his knowledge it was impossible and illegal to remove them from the island (2). Too stubborn, and too dumb to take "no way' for an answer, I contacted the writer of the magazine article, who nonchalantly said I should write to the king of Yap with a formal request. The king had several on his palace grounds, and could probably afford to spare one. It didn't sound as stupid then to a naive young man of thirty-two as it does today, after all there were pictures in the magazine, so the guy had probably met the king in person, but I wisecracked: "Just where will I find his address, and how long does it take to get a letter to the island". To my total shock, and disbelief, he said: "I'll give you his facsimile (fax) number. He'll see the request the same day you write to him". The fax machine, a visual medium phone connection was a pretty new state of the art invention at that time, so I was stunned to imagine the king of Yap had one. Turns out he had the only one on the island, and enjoyed playing with it. I heard a positive response from him almost instantly.

After a few more written interchanges, I was granted two, three-foot in diameter stones from his personal collection. It would take weeks, even months to finally get them, but they came just in time to add one to the newly renovated Myrtle Beach, South Carolina odditorium, two days before their grand re-opening on July 4, 1988. I am not sure where they are today, but they are still in the Ripley collection, and aside from one I've seen in the Smithsonian Institute, they are still the only two I have ever seen, let alone touched.

Over the years I did buy some other forms of "funny money", but most of Ripley's money collection predated me. The only other currency I personally could get excited about, were scarlet honey eater bird feather - coil money, from the Islands of Santa Cruz. Made entirely from thousands of small red feathers, sewn on a leather backing, these coils are often fifteen-feet in length. Four coils could buy a canoe, ten would buy a wife. The bird they are made from, a member of the family Mzomela cardinalis, is extremely endangered today. The rarity of the feathers presumably stopped the production of the currency, called tevau, sometime around the early 1950s. I think I bought four of these. They are worth thousands of dollars today, but like rai, are real hard to export to anywhere without a royal procla- mation, or at least a king's say-so.

53

Man's Inhumanity to Man

The original Ripley collection has a number of very grizzly torture items, some dating back to the 16th century, and others with provenance from a famous Nuremberg, Germany collection that first toured America in the late 19th century. I have every reason to believe Ripley personally saw that collection in his youth. He knew about it, and the Ripley archives has a published catalog pertaining to it. In 1928, whilst in Germany, Ripley acquired an Iron Maiden torture device, quite possibly the one listed in the catalog — the catalog has no pictures and has been a source of "best guess" identification ever since it was printed. By 1933 he also had a medieval chastity belt. By the 1950s, there were enough torture items in the collection to have a museum of torture on Broadway in Times Square, as well as a perfectly diabolical torture gallery in the Tussaud's Wax Museum in Niagara Falls, which I first viewed as an eight-year old on a third-grade school class excursion. (I remember asking why Hitler was in the same gallery). In the 1980s, I had bought a couple more chastity belts, a perennial favorite with me and Ripley patrons, and a few other small pieces, like coal tongs, flesh pinchers and thumb screws. In 1992 I entered the market of the macabre in a big way, and over the next twenty-five years I would frequent this market place regularly.

At the age of thirty-six, long past the age of self-discovery, I finally made my first trip to England. My three best friends had gone to Europe when I was only sixteen. I was too young to join them, and no real opportunity had arisen in the twenty years since. I was starting to doubt I would ever get to the homeland of my mother's family to see any of the things my friends had written about. The early 1990s, however, were the time where I went to most auctions in person, rather than shopping by phone or on-line, so in 1992 the time was finally right for me to go abroad.

We had an odditorium in Blackpool, and a brand new one in Great Yarmouth, both of which needed an exhibit insurance inventory reconciliation, and by chance, Christie's Auctions in London was going to auction the personal torture collection of the royal executioner, Albert Pierrepoint. I flew to London, attended the auction, then took the train east to Yarmouth, then another train northwest to Blackpool. I saw half of the country in one short week. Bob Masterson was with me for the initial London portion of the trip.

The Pierrepoint collection would give the average person the creeps. Several mantraps — large metal traps used by the nobility in the 17th and 18th centuries to capture poachers hunting illegally on their estates, nooses, hangman's masks, lists of people hung by generations of the Pierrepoint family, and literally dozens of kinds of shackles and restraints, including one or two "balls and chains". I didn't have a lot to spend, but the plan was to bid a little on everything, the more I could get the better. Virtually every torture implements we owned was on display, and this auction was seen as one stop shopping to refill the warehouse shelves.

Bob and I were quite successful that day, especially regarding the man traps — we got all but one of the ones that were sold — but we weren't the day's biggest buyer. That honor went to a Frenchman who resembled a cross between a death mask and a cadaver. He was scarier than anything that was up for sale. In addition to frequently glaring us down anytime we bid, he repeatedly stopped the proceedings demanding a translator. I don't know if he really needed one, or whether it was merely a tactic to throw us off our game, but he succeeded in frustrating us at every turn. Reportedly, he was shopping to open a torture museum in the south of France. Money seemed to be "no object". Like us, he bid on everything. He spent thousands that day, but we still got the press. The next day on the train to Yarmouth I was recognized by a group of footballers looking at my picture in the morning papers. They bought me my first ever Newcastle Brown Ale, and kept me talking for the whole train ride.

The Brits know a thing or two about medieval torture, but the "best" stuff, the stuff that will really make people squirm comes from Germany. **Hermann Historica Auctions** out of Munich hold two gigantic auctions, in May and October, every year. Inevitably they have witch catchers, metal pronged forks on long handles used to put around a suspected witch's neck without having to touch and defile oneself by touching a witch; pears of agony, a spring-loaded device forced into orifices of the guilty (1); thumb screws; shackles; and branks, iron masks worn as objects of shame and ridicule by criminals for "petty" offenses such as bragging, gossiping, and small thefts, but also adultery. In 2006, much to my amazement they had a 16th century Iron Maiden in their catalog, the only one I ever saw besides the one Ripley bought in 1928.

The Iron Maiden is associated with the Spanish Inquisition, and witchcraft. Though it is called a torture device, the word "torture" is a misnomer. Anyone subjected to her embrace would instantly be killed. She consists of a heavy wooden body that opens in the middle, like a set of doors. Inside she is lined with multiple metal dagger-sharp spikes, each aligned to pierce a vital organ when the doors are closed. The resulting body would be so terribly mangled that it would be dumped directly into water rather than be handled, the Maiden usually being set up on a bridge.

I am not sure if no one saw the catalog, or if people didn't bid on this one of a kind tour de force thinking it would go for an astronomical amount, but whatever the reason, it had only two serious bidders, myself, and a man whom I believe was my old friend the Frenchman from 1992. This time I wouldn't let him beat me. I may have never been more determined. I not only wanted the Maiden, I wanted to make sure he didn't get it. As luck would have it, he went down without much of a fight. I later learned his torture museum had failed; money that day mattered.

This Iron Maiden, much better constructed than the Ripley-bought one of 1928, is the Crown Jewel of the Ripley torture collection. It has a terrifying metal devil-faced head piece, much like a brank mask, very sharp intact metal prongs, and it is in near mint condition. It has an engraved date of 1565 on one of its metal bands, and anyone doubting its authenticity need only do DNA tests: it has several visible blood stains. As previously stated elsewhere (see Chapter 15), there is an excellent video of me being taunted by her.

The torture of criminals didn't stop in the Middle Ages, though, or even in the so-called Age of Enlightenment, and it didn't just happen in Europe either. Two of the nastiest pieces of "torture weaponry" ever devised, the garrote and the guillotine, both reached their peaks of infamy in the late 18th century, and were still being used in some countries as late as the 1970s and 1980s. Ripley's Spanish garrote, used to strangle pirates, comes from St. Augustine, Florida, and was in use at least as late as the 1820s. Public executions using it occurred in the town square across from the Catholic Cathedral, and the City Hall. I bought it, and several other pieces of Spanish, pirate torture items, at a public auction, just outside of town. The locals wanted to dispose of it, to remove the blemish from their town. I put it on display in the Ripley's St. Augustine odditorium for all to see. I don't believe you can hide history, it is cyclical, it will come back to haunt you if you don't learn from it.

One of the very last things I acquired in my career at Ripley's was a French-style, portable guillotine. It wasn't from France though, it was from the Louisiana-Texas border, circa 1800, and I bought it in New Orleans from the finest antique store in America. Apparently when the justice of the peace journeyed into the hinterland of sugar cane country, justice could be very swift. Chop the head off of the accused right now, on the spot, ask questions later. The blade weighs over 40lbs.

In the theatrical musical and the movie, **"Chicago"**, in the song called the "Cell Block Tango", the audience learns about the first woman in America to be hung. Ripley's has the actual gallows this historical event was committed on. I bought it at an auction in Chicago. Between 1977 and 2005, was used as an unlabeled "prop" in a children's Western themed cowboy park. No one looking at it would have known it was real. The park had bought it directly from the Cook County Jail where it had been in storage for more than fifty years. It is unique in appearance, and in history, in that it is big enough to hang four people at the same time.

In 1923 a murderer named "Terrible" Tommy O'Connor was sentenced to be hung in the Cook County Prison for killing a police officer. Just four days before the execution was to take place, Tommy escaped. A huge man-hunt followed, but Tommy couldn't be found. Four years later, in 1927, death by hanging was outlawed in Illinois, replaced by the electric chair. The Cook County prison officials, ever optimistic, didn't want to give up on Tommy, and decided to keep their gallows in case he was someday recaptured. As he had already been convicted and sentenced to die by the gallows, Tommy would not be able to be executed any other way, without a retrial. Tommy was never seen again. The authorities waited fifty years, before they decommissioned the gallows. In all likelihood, Tommy died twenty-six years earlier in 1951. If he was still alive in 1977, he would have been eighty-seven years old. If by some miracle he was still alive in 2006 when I bought the gallows, he would have been 116-117 — potentially the oldest man in the world.

The sale of the gallows was contested by the Chicago Historical Society who thought it should be given to them. They couldn't afford an auction, but thought it was criminal for the gallows to be sold — especially to someone outside of Illinois. The auction took place on December 11, 2006. It was after 1 am before I won the fight on the phone. The next day the papers lambasted the auction house, and were even harsher on

the state government. How had this piece of local Illinois history been sold to a Canadian owned company stationed in Florida? They called it a travesty. I called it preserving history when no one else was willing to.

With the gallows we got an archive of things related to Tommy and the gallows — Tommy's pocket watch which he had turned over when he was arrested, his mug shots, and a list of everyone that had been executed on the gallows. The list shows the name and date of one, Sabella Nitli, executed 1923 for murdering her husband, the real life "Ekaterina Chtchelkanova" of Bob Fosse's musical masterpiece **Chicago** "Pop, six, squish, Cicero, uh uh Lipschitz".

Tommy may have had it coming, but unlike Nitli he got away.

Electric chairs started to replace gallows in American prisons in the 1890s, and by the 1920s-1930s, states that allowed capital punishment had also introduced the

358

gas chamber as an option. I had no qualms about acquiring an electric chair from Kentucky, or even clothing worn and autographed by Charles Manson, but purchasing an authentic gas chamber chair was one of the hardest purchases I ever made.

California, long considered the most "liberal" state, never used the electric chair, but installed their first two-seater gas chamber in 1938, and used it more frequently than any other state but one, before the death penalty was abolished. It is still strange to me how, of all the implements of man's inhumanity to man I have acquired, and there have been lots, only the Ripley San Quentin Prison gas chamber chair from the early 1940s, is difficult for me to touch and talk about. I often couldn't even look at it.

Perhaps it is visions of the Holocaust [2] that prevent me from seeing anything in it but horror, or maybe it is the fact that we know the exact number and names of the people that died in the San Quentin gas chamber, but something about this chair shoves me outside my comfort zone. I certainly don't see justice or mercy when I look at it, but like with the Cook County gallows, I do believe objects like these implements of destruction have a place in museums. I firmly believe you can't sweep history under the carpet. You simply can't ignore the darker moments in history, as if they never happened. In fact, to learn from them, we not only can't ignore them, but we have to openly talk about them. Dialogue and education are the only means we have to prevent another Spanish Inquisition, or Reign of Terror, or Holocaust. Acquiring and displaying a gas chamber chair is my personal reminder that we have to confront our demons in order to conquer them

54

Accidents Do Happen

Call me a sick-o, but I have to admit, some of my favorite Believe It or Not! stories are miraculous near-death survival stories. The Ripley files are filled with guys with drills going into their stomachs, a swordfish sword into their heads, pitchforks through their feet. The list is endless, and it is impossible not to say "OMG how did that happen, and how did they survive?" when you read this kind of story, or see photos and x-rays illustrating them. For the purpose of this chapter I will discuss just three of many such stories. These are not necessarily the most horrific I could relate, but ones in which I met the survivor personally. I caution that this material is graphic.

Back in the 1940s Ripley's ran a story about Ivory Hill, an African American man living in Louisiana that had crashed a car into a wooden fence. He had been impaled on a large two and a half -inch diameter post — it went straight through his stomach. Miraculously, he walked to a nearby hospital with the post through his abdomen, and out his back. Someone took four photos of him, one from each direction, showing not just the pole, but the blood too. Ivory looks sedated, but perfectly calm. In 1984, as Ripley's designed the first New Orleans odditorium, I suggested we do a wax figure of Mr. Hill (for local flavor), and later, posed for it for the wax sculptors who made it.

In the first week of the museum being open, a guest named Jack Thompson, a local truck driver from New Orleans, moments after he had entered the show, returned to the front desk, and asked to see the manager. I happened to be in the office with Jack Webster the manager when Mr. Thompson was let into the office. Introductions and pleasantries were barely finished when Mr. Thompson pulled up his shirt to reveal a large circular scar on his chest, with a matching one on his back. He informed Jack and I that he had a similar accident to Ivory Hill, except that the fence post that he was impaled on was a metal pipe, not wood, and his accident had happened only a few months previous. If we were interested, he had a medical re-port, photos of himself impaled on the pipe, and even a thirty-inch segment of the pipe that had been through him and cut so that he could fit into an ambulance. Like with Hill, the pole was not removed from his body until he got to the hospital.

In exchange for making a wax figure of him to match Ivory Hill's he would give us the above items, including the actual pipe. It was a quick handshake deal. Within a year Mr. Thompson's figure, posed on a hospital gurney with a metal pipe through its stomach and back (as seen in one of the photos he had given us), was on display in not just the Bourbon Street odditorium, but several other odditoriums as well. The real piece of pipe for some reason I can't remember, was sent to Myrtle Beach.

My next victim, was also named Thompson, and he too literally walked into my life in much the same manner. Tom Thompson entered himself in a contest we ran to find the most amazing Believe It or Not! story in San Antonio. The occasion of the contest was the opening of the franchised Ripley museum across the street from the Alamo. The success of the contest was largely the result of advertising by the **San Antonio Express**, the newspaper that happened to be the longest continuous newspaper in the country to still be running the Believe it or Not! cartoon — at that point just shy of sixty years. The winner of the contest was guaranteed an article in the paper, a place in the new museum, and an original drawing by Drew Hunter, the museum's artistic director. We had dozens of entries, but Tom was the hands down winner.

I was sitting at the judge's table where each entry had to present their story, or thing, to me and the other judges. Mr. Thompson didn't have anything in his hand, and looked totally "normal". One could not have guessed his "entry". He started slowly, telling us he was a school teacher now, but as a teenager, he had been hit by a car. He was hesitant to tell his story in such a public forum, but asked if he could show us something that would explain it. Given permission, he then had someone hand him a large x-ray. The x-ray showed a skull with a five-inch metal plate bolted to it. After a very audible gasp from the judges, he calmly, quietly told us that the picture was of his skull. For about ten years, he had been living with a third of his skull missing, replaced by a metal disc that looked surprisingly like the bottom of a kitchen colander.

He won the contest, and his x-ray was displayed in the museum for twenty years. When it was removed during a renovation, Tom wrote to me and complained. I told him it was beyond my control, but seemingly appeased him by letting him know that copies of it were still on display in at least two other Ripley odditoriums. When the San Antonio museum celebrated its thirtieth year of operation in 2018, I talked to Tom again. He was happy to hear from me, and excited to learn our web team was doing a blog about him. He verified that the plate was still in place, and that he was still proud of the fifteen-plus minutes of fame Ripley's had given him.

Sometime in 2000 during the first season of the Dean Cain-TBS-Ripley television show a man walked into my Orlando office wearing a small cap, and carrying a large brown shopping bag. His voice was a little slurred, but otherwise, he seemed "normal". I welcomed him in, and asked if I could help him. He wanted to be on our television show. I politely told him I couldn't assure him a spot at least for now, as the show had finished filming for the season. I had no way of knowing at that point whether the show would be renewed for a second season, but seeing the disappointment on his face, suggested that he tell me his story, and I would keep him in mind.

He took a seat, and took off his hat. I could clearly see an indent in his bald head. Before I could say a word, he pulled a fifteen-inch serrated dagger out of his shopping bag and plunked it on my desk. The knife had blood stains all over it. I quite possibly fainted.

Michael Hill of Jacksonville, Florida had been stabbed in the head with this gruesome knife and was now sitting just a few feet across my desk begging to be on television as he needed to pay for recent hospital bills (1). He was willing to sell me the x-rays of the knife in his head, and the knife, and he alluded to the possibility of get-ting film footage of himself in the hospital the night the stabbing occurred. Apparently, totally by coincidence, a college journalism class was touring the hospital ER when he was brought in, and a student had filmed him on a gurney, with the knife handle protruding from his head, the blade deeply embedded inside.

In record Ripley time a deal was consummated, and a check was turned over to Mr. Hill for the knife. If he could procure the film there would be more money, and if the film was good, I felt safe to say we would get him on TV. His story, with the amateur film, became the opening story of show number one, season two. His x-ray has been displayed in several odditoriums, and the knife after having been shown of television, was made a permanent odditorium display too, complete with blood stains.

As author, radio personality Paul Harvey used to say, "and now for the rest of the story".

Not only did Michael Hill survive a ghastly stabbing to the head, he wasn't the intended victim! Michael had been at his sister's house when the doorbell rang. She was in the kitchen cooking him dinner, so Michael went to the door, opened it, and a huge muscular arm plunged the dagger into his head. The assailant then fled as Hill crumbled to the floor. The would-be assassin was Michael's sister's former boyfriend. He had meant to kill her.

55

Matchstick Models,
A Case Where "Bigger is Better"

Matchstick models maybe the most quintessential Ripley museum exhibit of all-time. Every Ripley museum has at least one, and depending on how you count, the company has well over 200 models in its collection (1). A couple in the collection date from Ripley's time, but most were bought from 1970 onward, and the best from after 1985.

A few of the pre-1985 models were made in prisons, model making seeming to have been a popular prison recreational activity both in England and the United Stated at least as early as the 1930s. Ripley's also had a few random pieces that lacked any known provenance. The majority of the collection, however, came from four remarkable builders, Reginald Pollard of England, Len Hughes or Australia, Ken Applegate of California and Florida, and Patrick Acton of Gladbrook, Iowa. I never met Reg Pollard, but I had personal experiences with the other three gentlemen.

The company seems to have met Reg sometime in the early 1970s, probably when they first opened in Blackpool, England in 1972. Reg and his wife Madge lived in a countryside cottage near Manchester. It had a wonderful name something like, (but not): Rose Garden, Bexhill-on-the-Sea, and if you closed your eyes, you could imagine the whole menagerie of Beatrix' Potter's characters frolicking in their garden amongst the June strawberries. Reg had no use of his legs and was confined to a wheel chair bound during the period I knew him (1978-87). He wore a neck brace and only his hands were functional. He suffered from arthritis and had taken up model making as a form of therapy. His wife Madge wrote all his correspondence.

Reg was the first, and one of only a handful of artists, that Ripley's ever commissioned to make exhibitory. He initially was making models of cars, ships, and trains in the thirty-inch size range. We asked for bigger models than typical: a five-foot long space shuttle, a six-foot tall Eiffel Tower, a seven-foot tall Leaning Tower of Pisa, a seven-foot long Mississippi steam boat, an eight-foot long San Francisco cable car, a ten-foot long London Tower Bridge, and his crowning achievement, a thirteen-foot long, three-quarter scale, one million matchstick, 1907 Silver Cloud Rolls Royce (a replica model of the first Rolls made).

Reg kept detailed notes of how many hours he spent, how many days of the month he worked, how much glue he used, and of course the important statistic, how many matchsticks were used. Madge would write me lovely progress report letters, and assure me that the projects, though physically taking over their house, were what kept Reg alive. Each of Madge's letter would have a careful account of monies owed from Ripley's. Most of our commissioned models took him about six months to complete, the Rolls was nearly three years from start to finish. The Rolls was started before I became the exhibits guy, but it is one of the first exhibits I can claim any ownership to. I made sure Reg was paid in a timely way, and I encouraged him as much as necessary to not get discouraged by his failing health, and pushed him not to give up. The finished car, with over one million matchsticks, was for quite some time the longest model we had, and until thirty years later, was the only one with more than a million sticks. In 1987, when completed, it was displayed in Niagara Falls, without its canopy roof (due to low ceiling heights). In 1992, it was moved to Orlando, where it was displayed much better in a 360degree walk around viewing area, with the roof, and a mirrored floor which revealed the intricate undercarriage. In 2013, it became a key part of a six-year traveling exhibition called **The Science of Ripley's Believe It or Not!** Some museums where it went used the roof, but most didn't. It has had to have a few repairs (in one city a child tried to climb into, it, luckily the running board broke before they made it inside to the seats), but considering its age, and the number of times it has been moved, it still looks super, and arguably is one of the greatest matchstick models ever made [2].

The Rolls was the last model Reg made for Ripley's. He continued to make some smaller models for his friends and relatives, but he was not willing to take on another giant.

As if it was God's way of passing a baton, I first met Len Hughes in Surfer's Paradise, Australia in December 1988. At the time, he had a museum of **Matchstick Marvels** in the remote northern Aussie town of Darwin. He wanted to sell the whole collection, including the building, but we weren't interested. Four years later, we didn't take the building, but we did take virtually every display from inside it — the only piece we didn't take, because he wouldn't sell it, was a giant perfectly round globe. He wanted it for his living room in Maroochydore, Australia, down near Brisbane.

Len's work was almost as good as Reg's, but typically a bit smaller. He was definitely much more prolific, however, and having started at a young age, had hundreds of models (3) by the time we purchased his collection in 1992. My very favorite was a five-foot in circumference Roman Colosseum, but his Leaning Tower of Pisa, complete with the adjacent Baptistery domed building, though not as tall as Reg's, was even more detailed. The real oddity in his collection was a forty-four-foot long model of the Great Wall of China. It came in eleven, four-foot segments, and was only eight-inches high and three-inches wide, but when on display in Darwin, it took up an entire gallery by itself. Ripley's has never displayed it in over twenty-five years. The packing of the roughly seventy different displays and hundreds of pieces was accomplished in record time by myself, and our Australian odditorium manager, Russell Murphy. Russell was my hero. He not only organized the supplies, the truck, and the secondary team, he even managed to find us a great dinner when the day was done. I had requested good Australian lamb, but we were too late in the evening, and everywhere we tried was closed. We ended up settling on seafood, a delightful plate of "Morton Bay bugs". Though they do look like some prehistoric giant bug, they are in fact a kind of slipper lobster native to Australia's Morton Bay. For those who like to argue about the merits of Maine Lobster versus Caribbean lobster, I say you are both wrong, Aussie "bugs" win the argument hands down, no pun intended — they have no claws.

This was the biggest, and most expensive purchase to that point in my history. I celebrated by returning home with an upgrade to first class, the only time I ever flew international first class. Like Dustin Hoffman in **"Rain Man"**, I can highly recommend Quantas not just for its safety record, but also for its service and comfort.

Ken Applegate learned how to make matchstick models in a California prison. The company only bought three pieces from him, and of these, I only bought the last one, a twelve-foot long model of the Challenger Space Shuttle, complete with an extending "Canad arm", and a separate pay load working satellite.

Chuck Thielen, our long time San Francisco museum manager bought Ken's first model, an eight-foot long delicate replica ¼ mile dragster; it was displayed in San Francisco's front window for over thirty years. Bob Masterson, who first worked in the San Francis-co Ripley's in the early 1970s, fell in love with it, and bought Ken's second model, a ten-foot long Peterbilt truck, when we opened in Myrtle Beach in 1976. At one time or another both of these have been displayed in Prince Edward Island, Canada, but I believe neither have been in more than three locations in their forty-plus year history. Matchstick models can be moved, but with great care, and Ken's have some delicate small pieces that make them poor choices for traveling exhibitions, or frequent location changes of any type. Despite their beauty and magnificence, these two pieces have never been on television.

The space shuttle I bought, like Ken's other two models was made directly from professional blueprints. Ken wrote to NASA from prison requesting blueprints and got them. How's that for a Believe It or Not!? The model was installed in San Francisco in the mid-2000's in a full gallery on space designed around it as the center piece. Todd Day made a terrific special effects presentation simulating the sound, and smell, of a shuttle lift-off.

I had known of Ken for years, and had talked to him on occasion even when he was incarcerated, but when he called one day from Florida, I was taken way back. He wanted me to visit him in his trailer in the woods to see the shuttle; it had taken him nearly twenty years to complete. I saw plenty of pictures of it before I decided to pay an in-person visit. It wasn't that he lived far away, the problem was, I was intimidated by him. He was very unsettling on the phone. I couldn't imagine what he would be like in person. Being the coward that I am, I took my wife, two children and my son's best friend Jarrod with me on the short road trip, for moral support.

Ken lived well off the grid, no street number, no town, just a trailer, and a woodworking shop in the woods. Everything about the trip was like an episode of **The X-Files**. After an obligatory tour of the model and the wood shop, the kids played in the woods. Gil and I went inside the trailer. She watched television in the far corner, while Ken and I negotiated at the dinner table. We sat directly across from each other. He stared me in the eyes. I stared at a rifle mounted on the wall above him and tried to remember just what he had been in prison for. I could barely think straight. I paid less than his asking price, but more than I ever paid for a matchstick model before or since. He brow beat me for every last nickel.

Patrick Acton of Gladbrook, Iowa, is in a class all by himself. He physically makes his models differently that the other three gentlemen, but he combines the best skills of the three. He is detail oriented, he is prolific, and he understands Ripley's mantra of "bigger is better."

I have known Patrick for more than thirty years. I think the first piece I bought from him was a very detailed aircraft carrier, complete with about a dozen miniature planes on its deck. For the first couple of years, everything we bought from Patrick was a ship, and everything was bought after it was completed; he was not commissioned, nor did we encourage him to make more models. He was pretty good, even without Ripley's help, in getting press coverage of his newest pieces as they were completed, and one way or another we usually heard about them after the fact. When we learned he had made a human figure (two to be exact, a cowboy, and a mounted Paul Revere), it was time to pay him a personal visit.

Gladbrook is a very small town, with literally only one street of significance. On that street, next to the town's only movie theater, there is a one room museum,

Patrick's **"Museum of Matchstick Marvels"** It is a fairly large room — the building was probably originally a department store, perhaps a Woolworth's and contains about seventy models. Patrick, who has been decorating it since 1977, never imagined himself having his artworks in any museum beyond his home town. I walked into the room and my jaw hit the ground. There were several ships, most in the two to three-foot size range. They were detailed and perfectly made, but for the most part smaller than I was interested in. There were however, the two human figures, some larger sailing ships (Columbus' Santa Maria), and the largest matchstick model I had ever seen, the United States Capitol Building. It was smack dab in the middle of the room, and clearly his Crown Jewel. He had never really considered selling anything, and the Capitol Building definitely was not for sale. The cowboy and Paul Revere were, and along with about ten other pieces, they became Ripley property that day. The cowboy went to Branson, and Paul Revere (4) went to Atlantic City.

In addition to visiting the museum, I spent time at Patrick's house that day, and saw where and how he builds his models. His house was quite modest in size, and his workshop probably measured no more than twelve-foot by fourteen-foot. With a big work table in the middle, there was hardly enough room to walk around the edges. I couldn't fathom how he made several of his bigger pieces in such cramped quarters. The answer was he builds them in pieces, and never assembles the complete model until the pieces are moved to his museum. He literally can't "see" the end result, until it is finished. If he has built one piece wrong, the whole model is at risk of not coming together, something akin to doing a jigsaw puzzle for days and finding out it's missing a piece.

After buying Len Hughes' complete collection I thought I would never buy another matchstick model, the company had enough for eternity, but it was impossible to pass on Patrick's because his varnished models were just so much better looking. A few years did go by, however, where we did not buy from Patrick. He was not upset by our lack of interest, and in fact used the time to build up his own inventory, but when he sold two very large magnificent pieces to one of Ripley's European competitors, Ripley's stepped back in to prevent the competitor from getting anymore pieces. Ripley's had to consider commissioning specific pieces in order to monopolize Patrick's time. At this point Patrick still had a "real job" as a career counselor at a local college, and there were only so many hours he could commit to his "hobby".

The first plan of attack was to pay Patrick another personal visit. This time I flew into Gladbrook on the new Ripley private jet. It was my first time on the plane, and maybe the first non-crop duster to ever land in Gladbrook's corn field airport. It was a powerful first impression. I met Patrick at his museum, then took him to lunch at the town's only diner. In turn Patrick introduced me to everyone in town, assuring them that I was not there to buy his museum, just a couple things in it. As it turned out, I only bought one item — a large "crooked" doll house inspired by a children's story. (He still wouldn't sell the Capitol building, nor his now largest piece, a space shuttle with launch pad).

What did happen, was Ripley's committed to pay Patrick an annual salary for the next three years in return for three new pieces, and the existing crooked house. To have the time to work on them, Patrick was ready, and willing, to retire from his school job going forward. We would suggest "subjects", but Patrick would have a fair bit of leeway, the only strict rule was the models had to be bigger than the two he had sold in Spain — Hogwarts Castle and Minas Tirith, two movie inspired fantasy castles each with over a ½ million matchsticks. We had to be able to advertise whatever he made as "the world's biggest matchstick model" (based on physical size, if not literally the number of matchsticks).

Over the next three years Patrick worked religiously in his little basement workshop and produced a seventeen-foot tall replica of New York's twin towers World Trade Center, a floating replica of the International Space Station that measures more than fifteen-feet in each direction, and a twenty-two-foot long, ten-foot tall, steampunk style train locomotive with wings, and moving parts. Each one in turn was the best matchstick model ever built. Ripley's eventually managed to buy out the Spanish competitor and take ownership of Patrick's two fantasy castles too. All of these five models have a

370

secure place in my pantheon of all-time best purchases, and yet none of them are the very best of Patrick's creations.

At the end of Patrick's three-year term, he asked if I would sign on for a year-long extension. I did, and I did again two more times after that. His next model was a two-headed dragon. It was a bit smaller than his three previous pieces (about 300,000 matchsticks), but it has a motion sensor that makes its mouth light up and roar, while flapping its wings. Prior to this piece Patrick had no electronics experience. My only direction to him had been that whatever he built had to be able to be suspended from the ceiling. He chose the dragon motif, and most importantly, making it a two-headed dragon, a perfect complement to the company's large two-headed animal collection.

A year later, I again asked for something that could be hung from a high ceiling (the hardest area to display adequately in a museum). I already had two space shuttles, and he still wouldn't sell the one he had on display in Gladbrook, so the possibility of a "fantasy" space ship was suggested. He ran with the idea, and wound up creating his opus — a fifteen-foot long, twelve-foot wide **Star Wars** Millennium Falcon. Like the dragon, it has motion sensors that activate lights, movement (the radar dish swivels, the guns go back and forth, and landing gear drops from below), and sound. I like to call it a giant 960,000 matchstick music box, as John Williams iconic theme song blasts out from within the model.

By the time anyone reads this, Patrick will have finished his last matchstick model for Ripley's. It was started under my auspices, but with an increased demand for inter-activity (more electronics, less art), and more and more direction being given to Patrick rather than letting him do his own thing, I happily gave up the reins as his Ripley contact. I followed his progress for several months, and will regret it if I never see the piece in person. Based on progress photos I've seen, his full size "working" **Dukes of Hazard** Dodge Charger should be the biggest and best matchstick model ever assembled. Past, present and future model makers will have no choice but to bow down to the master.

Post script: I probably should have said it up front, but just in case you are wondering, matchstick model makers buy their matches straight from the factory — sans the sulfur ends. With ignitable sulfur in place, a work of matchstick art could be lost in a puff of smoke at any time. Perhaps Nero was playing a matchstick violin while Rome burned?

Cinderella and the Wood Cars of Venice

When the Ripley office was in Toronto there was a very good high-end men's tailor shop on the southwest corner of Yonge and Bloor Streets, the city's two largest cross streets for subway transfers, the Bloor line running east-west, the Yonge line running north-south. For my years at college, and the next fifteen years at Ripley's, I passed this men's clothing store, called Stollery's, twice a day (1). I could never afford to shop there, but I looked in their right-angled corner windows very often. Seems to me they changed them every weekend.

One Monday morning they looked very different than they had ever looked before. It was still elegant and orderly, but the clothes were hung on a clothes line, from one end around the corner to the other rather than being on shelves or mannequins, and the clothes were more or less all the same color — pale brown. It was impossible to just walk by no matter how much of a hurry I was in. Upon closer inspection I discovered all the clothes were made of wood! Socks, shirts, a hat, jackets, even a woman's bra, all carved from wood and stained to highlight knots and grains. They were not wearable, but they were beautiful, and true works of art, ingenious in concept and craftsmanship.

The store was closed, but I returned via the subway at lunch time, went in and inquired. They were hand carved, in Venice, Italy, and all by one man, Livio di Marchi, a passionate and talented artist with a giant handlebar mustache in the style of Salvador Dali. The pieces were for sale. The clerk, however, looked at me with disdain, inherently knowing I couldn't afford such masterpieces. He said very little, but he did give me a glossy six-inch by nine-inch booklet with the information I would need to contact the artist.

I'm not sure if I was just too excited to think logically, or whether I just assumed a guy in Venice could speak English, but rather than rely on the post, I decided to call him that same day. It was the start of a

373

strange but beautiful relationship that would go on for more than twenty years. Livio did not speak a single word of English and I never met him in person. All correspondence, verbal and written, was carried out with a lovely woman who I fantasized much have been a raven-haired gypsy. She had the most exotic voice I have ever heard. Her English was not great, but much better than my Italian. When I told her, I worked for a museum and wished to acquire pieces of Livio's work she was ecstatic. I am sure she didn't know what a Ripley's odditorium was, or maybe even where Toronto was, but neither detail mattered, Livio was very anxious for exposure in "America". Nothing was consummated on that first call, but she sent me an even fancier sales catalog. On the cover, and again in a centerfold, was a wood carved Jaguar car — floating in the Grand Canal of Venice. I couldn't believe my eyes, and I couldn't read Italian. It looked like a wood carved boat, shaped like a car, that actually worked in water! I don't think I even looked at the clothes in the rest of the catalog. I had to call Venice again.

Exact in every detail, it may have looked like a vintage 1930s Jaguar car, but it in fact was a working motorboat, made to be used in Venice's annual Fat Tuesday, Mardi Gras pre-Lenten Grand Canal parade. It measured over twenty-one-foot long, and weighed nearly two tons, and yes, it was for sale. I forgot about the clothes entirely and started to save my pennies for a car instead. To make it affordable both in weight and cost, I bought it without its engine. Livio threw in a carved women's stiletto high heel. It was one of the last significant pieces I acquired in 1993 before Ripley's moved to Orlando. Both items have been displayed in Ripley's odditorium in Pattaya, Thailand since that museum first opened in 1995. The museum walls were built around the car, and in all likelihood the car will have to stay there until the museum closes and the walls are torn down.

About a year later, now in Orlando, I received an updated catalog. In place of the Jaguar there was now a pumpkin shaped, full-size carriage pulled by four carved carousel style horses. If possible, it was even more magnificent than the Jag. It was a must have acquisition. Pictures in the catalog showed it in the water, with St. Mark's Basilica and the Doge's Palace in the background (2), but also on land, pulled by real white stallions. This carving could be used on land or in the water! Livio had used it in the most recent Lenten parade, but he had actually built it to be used on land for his daughter's wedding.

This was a close the sale selling point. Not only would Ripley's be able to display it, but we could actually use it on land for promotions if we chose. Call it a moving billboard if you will. Visions of Cinderella were dancing in my head. It took four years for the dream to become reality.

In May 1998 I would use the carriage in the greatest PR stunt of my career. Ripley's former receptionist and my then current assistant, Aida Quinones, was to be married on May 2nd. I asked her if she wanted to be a real-life Cinderella? Not only did she yes to using the carriage to arrive at the church on her wedding day, but also to use it in her after the ceremony photos too. As my good luck would have it, she was to be married in Orlando's main downtown cathedral, and she was planning to have some photos taken in the nearby Lake Eola Gardens, the city's premier lake and park, a perfect backdrop for a bride and a pumpkin carriage.

Getting Aida to agree to use the carriage was the easy part. Getting a parking permit, and a parade permit (the main street of the town would have to be closed for at least a couple blocks), would be infinitely more difficult, and more difficult again, would be finding stallions and a liveried carriage driver qualified to drive a giant pumpkin.

I found the horses, two large chestnut Belgian draft horses and driver, via the telephone directory yellow pages located about 100 miles away in Ocala, the center of Florida's race horse country (3). The woman I spoke with could rent me horses, and she had an experienced coachman — though our pumpkin was not like anything he had driven before, there being no driver's seat, and he would have to stand at the back and not the front, praying the horses did what they were told. The driver had his own livery costume, complete with top hat, and he had all the necessary reins and horse paraphernalia. He even supplied the trailer to transport the horses.

When Orlando's female mayor saw the rig she acquiesced to my unusual requests for a police escort and closed streets, with only two stipulations. First, that we paid for three closed parking spots and four different streets. She wanted us to make a square loop rather than a linear path between the church and the park, and back, to maximize the number of people that would get to see the spectacle. Second, because she would not be able to attend herself, she wanted a photo of the carriage, the wedding couple, and the cathedral for her office. No problem.

Everyone I had talked to in order to make this event happen was a hopeless romantic. People were willing to do just about anything I asked, and even the police officers directing bewildered traffic were delighted to see a real Cinderella, in a real pumpkin carriage, make an appearance in downtown Orlando.

The procession to the cathedral went off like a charm. The post-service trip to the park was also near flawless, with people lining the streets to watch, and media people everywhere snapping photos and shooting video from every direction, but the ventilation in the carriage was not adequate for the hot Florida climate. We had provided the newlyweds, Mr. & Mrs. Duncan and Aida Dortants, with an ice chest, sodas, and champagne, but the heat still almost got the best of them. It was well over 100 degrees Fahrenheit in the carriage, and they were just a little frazzled when they disembarked in the gardens a short twenty minutes later. The story was carried on every local television station, and photos later appeared in celebrated wedding magazines around the country. It was the most beautiful wedding I've ever been to. Cinderella, or at least Disney, were pea green with envy.

Livio made three more cars that I am aware of, which is to say, I acquired. A small round roofed Fiat, a replica 1953 Mercedes Gull Wing with doors that opened bottom to top, rather than left to right, and in 2000, his crowning glory, an F-50 Ferrari. Di Marchi had always joked that every Italian man wants to own a Ferrari. Like the Jaguar and the pumpkin carriage, all of these were boats, made to be used. Di Marchi, in addition to using them in the Lenten canal parade,- frequently used the Benz and the Ferrari to drive to work, or do his shopping. He sold Ripley's the Fiat almost as soon as he had finished it, but the Benz he kept for a couple years, and he toured the Ferrari in car and boat shows around the world before finally parting with it in 2009. It was actually on display in Las Vegas when I bought it.

The Fiat and Benz had their engines removed before they were shipped from Italy, but with the Ferrari already being in America, our deal was struck to include the engine. We had visions of sailing this ship.

The first time we put it in a lake it didn't do so well. As a result, we changed the engine (to help it go faster), added sealant around the entire bottom, and even added pontoons to it to raise it higher in the water. To date it has successfully sailed three times in America, once in a Florida lake, and twice in salt water — once in the Atlantic Ocean for an episode of a Jay Leno car show, and once during Fleet Week in the Pacific Ocean off San Diego. After that event it was displayed as part of a temporary Ripley traveling exhibit in San Diego, ironically, at the Air & Space Museum. The only other places it has been displayed to date by Ripley's were at an IAAPA (International Association of Amusement Parks and Attractions) convention where it helped the company win "best booth at the show" honors, and at Bob Masterson's retirement party. At that party every guest had his or her picture taken with it at the entrance as if they had arrived at the function in it. In terms of a "photo op" it doesn't get any better. I don't know anyone who doesn't want their picture taken with a sexy Ferrari!

Between the Fiat and the Benz, I also bought a Di Marchi Vespa motor scooter, and the last things I bought from him, were the clothes I had first seen at Stollery's nearly twenty-five years earlier: two pairs of cowboy boots, a jacket, a "leather" bag, a pair of pants that was a chair, and a replica of the artist's signature hat.

Regrettably, I have never been to Di Marchi's studio in the Tyrol Mountains, north of Venice. The alpine styled house has exterior "bricks" that are wood carved books, placed with spines out as if on library shelves, and the roof is one giant book, opened in the middle and set upside down on the walls. The gate and the fence, and all the furniture inside, are also made of wood. It looks a little like a fairy tale building, or a ginger bread house — but a lot bigger! It is a wood carver's paradise.

Lee Harvey Oswald on the Auction Block

An attraction named The Tragedy in U.S. History Museum sounds like it is **supposed** to be "**sad**" right? A museum in St. Augustine, Florida, operating for years under this name, however, was "sad" for a whole different reason, and it could be argued, was actually comical in a perverse way. It was definitely the worst maintained museum I have ever been in, and though it will sound like an exaggeration, the entire town of St. Augustine hated it. It took them years, but eventually the good city fathers ran the owner out of town. It was a terrible Catch-22. The owner had a poor location that the city made access to difficult. He had no customers, and locals bad mouthed him, and scared away tourists. With no customers, there was no money. With no money, he had no way of keeping up appearances, which in turn scared more customers away. I visited the museum three times, but was the only one in the place all three times. The wood showed visible dry rot and mold, and you didn't have to look to far to see bugs of several kinds.

The displays in the place were a personal collection of artifacts, big and small, old and new, of significant tragic moments in American history. Most of the exhibits were directly related to death or murder. The museum did have some excellent exhibits, but having so many morbid stories all in one place, and displayed under less than ideal conditions, made the museum a pretty grim experience. The average fairground haunted house would seem like a fun house in comparison to this museum.

When the museum finally ceased to operate in 1998, the bulk of the collection was auctioned off by a small local firm, with no pre-advertising or mailing list, just flyers posted to local telephone poles for notices. It attracted everyone in town, but my guest, Drew Hunter (who was living in nearby Jacksonville, Florida), and I were the only people from out of town, and likely the only people with more than a few hundred dollars budget. If there had of been a barn, I could compare it to

an old fashion country barn auction, but it wasn't even
that organized. It was held in an open field. The auctioneer was under a canvas tent, but the potential buyers were exposed to the brutal Florida sun, and many
had to stand. Drew and I were fortunate to be amongst
the small elite down front who had least had a folding
chair.

That day I bought some small pieces related to James
Dean, World War II and Hitler, and Lincoln and slavery,
but I had come to buy three cars: Jayne Mansfield's
death car, a mid-1960's Buick, Lee Harvey Oswald's 1954
Hudson "Kennedy assassination" car (owned by Oswald's
neighbor, Buell Wesley Frazier), and the 1963 ambulance
that took Oswald away after he was shot by Jack Ruby.

Upon viewing, the Mansfield car was scratched off my
list immediately. I didn't expect it to look pretty,
knowing that it had been mangled in her death accident,
but I didn't know it had been outside in a field for
quite a while, displayed inside an 18th century slave
cage, safe from people, but not from the elements, or
vermin. Animals had definitely been living in it, and
might still have been for all I could tell. I was
afraid to go anywhere near it, never mind buy it. It
did not sell that day as it had no bidders. I believe
it was sold a year later, and has since been restored
and displayed in a car museum in Ohio.

The car I really wanted had once belonged to Lee Harvey
Oswald's neighbor Buell Wesley Frazier. It was a 1954
black sedan with a lot of chrome. On the day of John F.
Kennedy's assassination, Frazier had driven Oswald to
the Texas School Book Depository, and Oswald's rifle —
the murder weapon — was wrapped up in the back seat.
Oswald had told Frazier it was a package of curtain
rods.

The car was in decent shape, presentable, but still
needing some work, mainly on the tires. I had come to
the auction thinking it would sell for around $100,000.
When I saw the auction facilities and the crowd, I
thought it might only get half that. The auctioneer
started at $500,000, thinking the bidding would go
north of that figure, but there was dead silence. He
did his best telling its provenance and its importance,
but you could hear nothing but crickets chirping, and

frogs croaking. He reluctantly brought the call for an opening bid down to $400k, $250k, $100K, $50k. At that point he threatened to take it off the stand and not sell it. The audience at first just laughed at his bid suggestions, but now grew hostile in a way I have never seen again at an auction. It was more like a scene from a 1960s political protest rally. The crowd was screaming that the auction had been advertised with "no reserves — everything must sell", there were many people who wanted to bid on the car, but not for thousands of dollars. He eventually asked the audience what anyone was willing to bid. A farmer dressed in denim overalls, said $1,000. I sat back and watched as about ten people bid $100 a time, up to $5,000. It was painful. I bid $6,000 figuring no one was going to counter. Someone bid $7,000; I suspected he was a "plant" since no one had been willing to go more than a $100 a bid just seconds before, so to scare him off, I bid $8,000, and once again you could hear crickets. The auctioneer was near tears, and did his damned best to raise even another $100, but after a prolonged hammer count: "Going once, are you sure? Going twice: people this is absurd, this is a million-dollar car. Going three times, all done…sold". The car was mine. I was immediately everyone's best friend, except for the auctioneer (and presumably the owner). I don't think they had ever seen anyone spend $8,000 on a fifty-year old car, or maybe on anything. There was an audible buzz in the crowd as rumor went around that I was from Ripley's and the car was going to a real museum.

The next auction lot, was the very ratty furniture from Oswald's apartment, reportedly where the assassination had been planned. No one showed any interest in any one single piece, so the auctioneer bundled it all together: a bed, a bed spring and mattress, a dresser drawer, a mirror, a chair, a desk and a wire garbage basket. Again, the auctioneer pleaded for an opening bid, but couldn't get one. He worked his way down to where I was comfortable. I opened the bid and got the entire room's worth of furnishings — complete with photos of the room's interior showing the placement of each piece for a price of $6,600. I was having a very good day.

Next up was the 1963 Oswald ambulance. It was in near perfect shape having been taken out of service very soon after Oswald's murder. It needed a car wash, but otherwise looked as good as new, the only item in the whole museum that I could say that about. The auctioneer gave the audience a fair warning that he would not sell this item for a paltry amount. If no one seriously wanted this piece of history, then he was willing to face any law suit for false advertising that anyone might want to set against the auction house. The crowd booed him vehemently. Looking straight at me, the auctioneer asked me if I would open the bidding at $10,000. Emphatically, I said no, the car was not worth as much to me as the murder vehicle. Sensing no one else was going to bid, I offered $5,000. The auctioneer, unable to raise another bid, suggested I pay at least $8,000, the same as the previous car. I refused. I called his bluff, and he called mine. I wouldn't budge, and the car was not sold. (1). The audience literally was yelling:" Sell it to the Ripley guy", and about half of them left in disgust when the auctioneer wouldn't budge. I stayed a little longer, but refused to bid anymore. The sale had become a farcical circus.

Drew and I were both interviewed by the local St. Augustine and Jacksonville newspapers. I boasted that the car would go straight to our odditorium in Grand Prairie, Texas (a suburb of Dallas), and Drew, as that museum's designer, elaborated on how it might be displayed. The story with a photo of the car was widely circulated, and seen by the odditorium's owners in Dallas, who rather than being excited, to my surprise, thought it was too controversial an artifact and wanted no part of it. I was dumbfounded. I wasn't too worried about the newspaper proclamation because these things tend to be forgotten after a couple months, but I now had no idea where I would put the car.

The car was transported to storage in Orlando where it would end up sitting for over four years. It eventually was first displayed in New Orleans (the second Ripley New Orleans location in the JAX's Brewery complex at Jackson Square), but after that museum prematurely closed due to Hurricane Katrina, it was moved to San Antonio where it has been ever since.

Over the years I would acquire several artifacts related to John F. Kennedy, and a few more things related to Lee Harvey Oswald (1). Both these personalities are of immense interest to museum goers, but the mystic behind Oswald, at least in terms of audience response, suggest Kennedy's assassin is the most interesting thing about Kennedy. The Oswald-Frazier car is a physically big item; it takes up a lot of floor space to display. In contrast, Oswald's mortician's toe tag certifying his death, with a small lock of Oswald's hair attached, takes only a space less than four inches square to display. Guess which gets more attention?!

I bought the Oswald toe tag from a radio station disc jockey in Wisconsin in 1997 as part of a fund raiser for a charity. He had bought it from an auction house in New Jersey. It cost him the same price as I had paid for the car; it cost me a little more. This little object has long been one of the most talked about artifacts in the Ripley collection. Late night talk show radio deejays in particular always had a field day with it, as did their listeners, and because it was listed on my official company bio, dozens of interviewers, no matter what the subject of the interview was supposed to be, would ask about it, often as their ice-breaker initial question. The biggest surprise to people was that anybody could have this — why wasn't it in an FBI file locked away, or at least in the **Smithsonian**? The simple answer was it belonged to Oswald's mother, and at one point needing the money, she had put it up for auction.

More than twenty years after I bought my toe tag, a second, almost identical, Oswald toe tag came up for auction. It sold for considerably more than I paid for mine, despite dubious provenance, the story being an ambulance worker had stolen the real one and replaced it with one he wrote himself. Both have about the same amount of hair attached, both say the exact same words, and both are the exact same kind of card. The difference is one is hand-written, while the other is typed. I am inclined to believe, mainly based on provenance, but also on the length of time it took for the second one to surface, that Ripley's has the real one. Much like everything else concerning Oswald, and the Kennedy assassination, however, I suspect the truth will never be known for sure.

58

Really Big Balls

"Call Ripley's. This man has really big balls! Five of them!" In ascending order: one four-and-a-half foot tall string ball, one plastic bag ball, approximated six-foot high, one barbed wire ball, about seven-and-a-half foot high, one rubber band ball about ten-foot high, and one nylon cord ball more than thirteen-foot high and forty-feet in circumference [1]. Three of these are the biggest balls of their type on the planet, and the barbed wire ball was the world's biggest when it was built. Saying I have big balls is an understatement. I have HUGE balls.

Making giant string balls seems to have got its origins in the Great Depression of the 1930s when frugal people of little means collected all kinds of string to be re-used rather than discarded. Postal workers in particular were drawn to this unusual "hobby". The Ripley cartoon featured several balls in the 1930s through the 1950s, and one of these was even featured on a Ripley Christmas card, but it wasn't until the mid 1970s did Ripley's shine the light on three string balls of epic proportions.

Giant balls made out of other items: aluminum foil, rubber bands, wool, plastic bags and barbed wire to name the most common, seem to have sprung from a different source at a much later date, based on competition, for the sake of claiming to own "a record". No doubt The Guinness Book of Records, first published in 1955, had something to do with the compulsion. A Ripley television show in 2004 definitely accelerated the trend.

In the very last planned Dean Cain Ripley show [2], in a segment hosted by Kelly Packard, people who had made large balls from various items were featured. One of these was a giant plastic bag ball, another was a very large rubber band ball. Both would inspire collectors to make the future balls of these types that are now in the Ripley collection.

In a stunt of pure idiocy, the then world's largest rubber band ball, weighing 4,600 lbs., was dropped from an airplane one mile high over the Mojave Desert in Arizona to see if it would bounce. It didn't.

A helicopter was wrecked during the filming, and the ball, traveling nearly 400 miles per hour, exploded creating a huge crater. Law suits and damages included, the episode is rumored to have cost four million dollars to produce.

Joel Waul of Lauderhill, Florida watched the episode in astonishment. That very night he started a project that would take him six years to complete — the making of a 9,032 lb. rubber band ball that dwarfed the size of the previous record holder. Joel frequently contacted me to report on his progress and when the ball became too big for his bedroom, and had to be moved outside, it became a regular news story, crews filming it as it grew mushroom like in his driveway. I don't know what the deciding factor was, but one day he called and asked if I wanted to buy it. The price was reasonable, but the additional cost to move it was the real issue. In addition to a flatbed truck to load it on, we also needed a large crane to lift it. Naturally, we made a media event of the moving, decorating both vehicles with Ripley Road Show magnetic signage so anyone who saw it on the road would know exactly where it was going. Joel gave a speech while standing on top of the ball, and dozens of neighbors breathed a sigh of relief that the eyesore was leaving their neighborhood. Hundreds of photos were taken and later used in books and on-line for years after. The ball itself — made from multiple types of rubber, including car tire inner tubes (the bigger the ball got, the bigger and heavier the rubber bands had to be in order to stretch around it), proved to be problematic. We had to reshape it somewhat to get it in our warehouse door, and it was too big – and heavy — to display in most of the company's locations. After a couple years in the company warehouse (3) it finally found a home in one of our sister attractions in California. Some people called it my albatross.

Lyle Lynch's giant barbed wire ball (see Chapter 39), though much smaller than our big rubber band ball, or the giant string ball, I think it may be my favorite of the three. It seems to have more personality to it; it was born of love and idleness — not competitiveness. It also is the most impractical, being dangerous to even touch, never mind roll it to increase its size. Pictures of Lyle with it — he looks like a real cowboy and the fact that he named it — Clonia — suggest he loved it, and didn't make it for the money. It was a perfect piece for our Western-themed Jackson Hole, Wyoming, odditorium, where it was displayed for nearly twenty years. I helped move it twice and it has my blood in and on it. It is a real testimony to man's ingenuity, frugality and sense of humor. You can't look at it without laughing and wondering — "but why"? (4).

My grandmother collected string. As a poor farm girl growing up in the 1930s I have no doubt she started out of need. Her balls were never real big, however, softball size seemed to be the extent of her building, because she reused the string, subtracting from her balls faster than she added to them. Other old ladies I met were more compulsive in their collecting.

Generally speaking, big string balls tend to originate West of the Mississippi, but the biggest true string ball (no twine, no cord, no nylon) that I ever put my hands on, came from about two miles from my home in Winter Park, Florida. It was four-and-a-half feet in height and diameter, and weighed about 1,000 lbs. — just the right size to be hauled in my 1993 Dodge Caravan, the first vehicle I owned after moving to Florida.

My near neighbor had cold-called me in the office, and asked me if I wanted it — for free, just come and get it. She had warned that it might be difficult to get out of her house, as it was in a back room, the same room it had been built in over a lengthy number of years by her recently deceased mother. Getting it out of the house proved easy enough, my son and I rolled it out a pair of sliding glass doors into the backyard. Getting it into my van, however, was a whole different problem. We couldn't lift it; it would have to be rolled in. At first, we tried the back door, but it didn't open high enough. It would fit through the side door, but we would need a ramp to roll it onto. We had brought a large piece of plywood for just this use, but it broke in two the second the ball was on it. The owner was able to supply a two by four. By placing the two broken pieces of plywood on top of the two by four, and giving one quick mighty heave, we got the ball inside the van as onlookers laughed, and cheered. The next step was to drive it slowly about two miles over Winter Park's infamous cobble stone roads.

My son Curtis was pretty young at the time — about nine years old — and not the strongest kid. I had hoped he could "hold" the ball in place while we moved, but I was wrong. It moved once, and he screamed. For his safety, I put him in the front seat beside me, leaving the ball to do its will. We had barely restarted when the ball went crashing through the door — we had forgotten to lock it — and was now rolling wildly down the quiet suburban street. Luckily, there were no parked cars, and no witnesses other than ourselves.

Getting it back in the van was even more difficult the second time. We still had all the wood, but we no longer had the sloped driveway to build up speed for the big push. It took us almost an hour. We were able to laugh out loud about it later, but that Saturday afternoon it was a stressful "oh shit, what are we going to do" moment, hopefully never to be repeated.

Francis Johnson of Darwin, Minnesota, single-handedly built the most impressive string ball in the world. It had been moved once in the late 1950s to New York City where it was shown on Gary Moore's **To Tell the Truth** television game show – how they got it there I have no idea — but for the most part from 1950 until he finished building it in 1979, it sat on his front lawn tied to a giant tree. He used a rigging system, and a tractor to lift it in order to add twine to it once a week. This ball is entirely made from farmer's binder twine, and is perfectly round — a thing of true beauty. I greedily wanted it from the first moment I learned of its existence. When I heard of Francis' death I wondered what would become of it. When I got a call from his nephew, Harlan, sometime in 1991, I was ecstatic. Francis' farm and the ball had "been left" to Harlan; he was hoping to get rid of the ball from his new front yard. Was I interested? You bet I was.

Darwin, Minnesota is a very small town, probably the smallest town I have ever stayed the night in. If memory serves me correctly the population was 164 people. Harlan wanted me to make a presentation to the townsfolk regarding Ripley's, and what we would do with the ball. The meeting would be in the basement of a combination church-town hall, the only building in town big enough to hold "the whole town". I was excited by the prospect, and encouraged that he thought the whole town would be interested enough to spend an evening with me. I would stay the night in Harlan's home.

Harlan was not quite honest with me, or at least he wasn't exactly forthright. He may have legally owned the ball, but he didn't understand the town.

This was pre-laptop-power point era. My presentation would include a short film bio on Robert Ripley, but comprise mainly of me giving a formal podium speech accompanied by 35mm slides of various existing Ripley exhibits and museums. I was good at this sort of thing, and though this wouldn't be my typical school group audience, I was ultra-confident that I could wow them.

I had a rental car, but Harlan suggested I drive to the church with him — in his pick-up truck. I didn't think anything of the offer, and was happy for the conversation and quick tour of the town, including a viewing of the ball, now inside a glass walled silo in the town common, across the street from the **String Ball Café**, on Main Street. I suspected nothing, and if Harlan did, he certainly didn't let on. I think he may have had a hint of what was about to happen, but I believe he was caught pretty much off guard too, and may not have invited me into his home had he foreseen the evening's dramatic conclusion.

When we arrived, the church hall was full. I was pleased, and feeling good; I thought I was a celebrity. The people seemed friendly. They shook my hand, and looked me in the eyes.

In the words of Bob Fosse, I gave them the old "Razzle Dazzle". I told them my life story, the places I'd been, and the people I'd seen. For ninety minutes, I was the ultimate slick salesman trying to sell Ripley's to the uninitiated. No one said a word. They stared blankly at me. You could have heard a pin drop in the room. I thought they were mesmerized. I was wrong. They were angry.

At the end of my presentation, after a second of proverbial frog croaks and cricket chirps, from the back of the room, a large scary woman growled:

"Why the fuck would we give away Francis' ball. It's the only damn thing this town has got going for it."

Amidst cheers for her, I was resoundingly booed off the podium with cat calls and other expletives. I looked for help from Harlan, but got nothing but a shrug and rolled eyes. It was obvious he was not in charge, and not in line with the mood and thinking of the rest of the town. I felt sorry for him more than I felt for myself. I could leave town — quickly — but he would have to live amongst these people, presumably well after that night, and the next day.

One by one the angriest of the people took the podium. They all vowed to do whatever it would take to keep the ball in town — it was their lifeline. One person suggested if Ripley's wanted the ball so much, they should build a museum in Darwin! Another showed a guest book signed by over 1,000 people who had visited the ball since it was moved "downtown". Another showed me a sweatshirt they planned to sell to tourists. I tried to argue that if we moved the ball to Orlando the proposed site of the next new Ripley museum — it was likely a couple thousand people would see the ball every day for years. I could put Darwin on the map. Francis, the ball, and the town would be famous, known to millions all over the world. This was answered with:

"Who gives a damn about those Florida tourists. No one in Darwin can afford to go to Orlando. We would never see the ball that "we" grew up with again."

I was the devil incarnate for even thinking the ball could leave town, and Harlan must clearly have been out of his mind to have suggested it to me. The people believed the ball belonged to the town, not Harlan. It was their collective soul, and given the chance I would see that it would be their savior.

After nearly a full hour of vitriolic ranting, I was told in no uncertain terms that I should leave town and never come back. The issue was not open for further discussion. Harlan and I were escorted out the building, into his pick-up truck, then followed all the way to his home. By this time, I was scared — they knew where I was going to sleep!

Both Harlan and I were shaking. I felt I had just escaped the mob scene of the 1932 Universal Studios **Frankenstein** movie. He apologized profusely, and offered me a couple other things from Francis' barn — some wood whittling, (pliers and chain whimsies carved by Francis himself when he wasn't tying knots in twine), and a giant collection of hardware store advertising aprons — poor substitutes for the ball, but at least I was getting something for my trouble. I didn't sleep a wink that night, and watched deer in the backyard; they seemed so peaceful after such a violent encounter.

In the morning, in my own car, I took a last look at the big ball. I considered having breakfast at the String Ball Café across the street, but decided to just buy a commemorative sweatshirt, a lasting souvenir that I never wore, not even to try it on.

Thus, ends my relationship with the Francis Johnson's string ball…… but it is not the end of the story.

Literally on the plane back to Toronto, I read a magazine article about a guy named J.C. Payne of Denton, Texas, who in just a couple of years had built a bigger ball than Francis'. I was skeptical to say the least, but I of course would have to look into it — and maybe buy it instead.

I had Mr. Payne on the phone the next day. His ball was inspired by Francis', but also by another ball in Cawker City, Kansas. He, and for the most part me too, dismissed the Cawker City ball because it was being built by the whole town as a long-term community event. It wasn't yet as big as Francis', but with string being added by hundreds of people on a regular basis (they actually created an annual "String Ball Day Parade and Celebration), it was clear it would eventually be "the world's biggest ball of string". J.C. in Francis's honor, and for his own wish for string ball immortality, was determined this would never happen.

Like Francis, J.C. was not averse to taking donations of "string", but he insisted that only he could add it to the ball — the ball had to be just one man's endeavor to be fit to compare to Francis' big ball. Unlike Francis, however, Payne used easily acquired nylon twine, cheaper and more accessible than real binder twine. Some people would call this cheating. I didn't think Payne's ball was as nice as Francis' ball, but I wanted a big ball badly, and there was no disputing it would be bigger than Francis' in a matter of weeks. I acquired it for a third of what I had offered Harlan for the Darwin ball.

By this time, it was too late to buy the ball for Orlando, but the company was already well on its way to developing a franchise in Branson, Missouri — about as close as I could hope to Texas when considering a future home for Payne's ball and the task of moving it from Denton.

Payne had built his not exactly round ball in a barn, in a vacant muddy field. The plan was to pull it out as far as necessary by a tractor, then lift it with a crane. The tractor got stuck, the ball flattened on the bottom under its own weight, and when finally lifted, stretched in a dozen different directions. By nobody's definition can it really be called "a ball".

It was driven through northern Texas, Oklahoma, and Missouri on a flat-bed truck. It was then ceremonially dropped with a resounding thud on a vacant lot in Branson. Over the next several months a Ripley odditorium was built around it — the most pre-planned Ripley design of all-time. The roof of the building was lowered on last. The "ball" is still there; the building would have to be destroyed to even dream of moving it.

Another chapter in the saga ended — but still not the end of the story!

A number of years later in Orlando I was approached by JC and Bryan Duggan, a father-daughter documentary film making team. They were planning to make a film about string balls, and wanted me to do an interview, and narrate a portion of the film. This was to be my "motion picture debut". I didn't expect my part to be more than the traditional couple of minutes interview, and though I love documentaries, I certainly had no expectations that anyone would watch a film about string collectors. I gave an impassioned interview, retelling the Darwin/Denton story. The interview went longer than I had expected, but the Duggan's were great listeners and I was really having fun. Safe to say, I got carried away by the limelight.

It was several years before I heard from Bryan again, and truthfully I had totally forgotten him and his daughter's little film. Imagine how surprised I was to learn the film was finally finished, and I was in the whole damn thing, not just a cameo, but the main character! The film also was much more about Ripley's string ball adventures than the people who made the balls in the first place. I was shocked, but honored. I loved the film. It was quirky, I looked and sounded good, and I could actually envision people at film festivals watching it and maybe even voting for it for some obscure award. There was one change I had to demand. The Duggan's had brought my Frankenstein film analogy to life — there I was on the silver screen edited into the mob scene from the classic horror film! I assumed I hadn't yet been forgotten in Darwin, and that Harlan probably still lived there. It was a funny, and brilliant scene, but it had to go. I certainly didn't want to make any more enemies in Darwin, and I definitely couldn't afford a lawsuit. The Duggan's acquiesced. The scene was removed, though I suspect a few original versions still exist somewhere.

A finished film still does not mean a published, released film, and it was 2013, nearly a full ten years from the time of my interview to when the film debuted. It played several film festivals in 2013, and received some decent reviews. It was packaged with a poster and a cover with an endorsement quote from me:

"In the world of weird, this is about as good as it gets".

The film still exists and you can buy it on Amazon. My legacy as the man with the world's biggest balls — is captured on celluloid for all the world to see.

59

Serendipity

I always liked to say that Believe It or Not! exhibits could be found anywhere, all you had to do was keep your eyes and ears open, and when the time came, react quickly. I may have had big balls on my mind those two fateful dates, but I could still seize the moment when destiny called.

On the same day I picked up the world's largest rubber band ball, I also bought a full-size stage coach made from toothpicks, and the day before **I didn't buy** the Darwin string ball, I bought about fifty unique medical quackery devices, including two very rare working **psychographs** — phrenology machines that reveal your inner character by interpreting, and charting, the bumps on your head. Lauderhill, Florida where the big rubber band ball was a three-hour drive from Orlando. The day I was to pick up the ball I drove the distance with the car radio on. I don't remember the station, but it probably was NPR. A man who had built a life-size replica of a 19th century Wells Fargo stage coach out of thousands of toothpicks was being interviewed. His story was wild. He had to build two extensions onto his house during the several years it had taken him to build the carriage. He was not a model maker per se, but a hardcore amateur historian of stagecoaches and the pony express. His wife wanted him to get rid of the coach. It was over twelve-feet long and ten-feet tall. He was literally asking the host if there was a museum somewhere in America that would take it.

I could barely believe my ears. I pulled off the road at the first gas station and phoned the office. Within minutes I found the guy, and was making an offer on the coach — sight unseen. The following week I was in Waynesville, Indiana looking at the largest, most elaborate, toothpick model I had ever seen.

It is infinitely more interesting to look at than a big rubber band ball.

It is a shame that it is painted red and yellow so as

to look exactly like a real Wells Fargo carriage, because this hides the fact that it is completely made of toothpicks. It is so realistic, no one believes it is toothpicks. The wheels alone defy logic — how do you make a round object out or straight-line objects? It probably was the best exhibit I bought that year. Somewhat ironically it ended up in Branson right next to the Payne string ball. God does indeed work in mysterious ways.

The discovery in 1991 of Robert McCoy's collection of medical quackery in St Paul, Minnesota wasn't quite as serendipitous, but it still was far beyond my expectations, and helped heal the pain of the following day.

I had been told about this collection, housed in a small museum, and the collector who looked like a carbon copy of W.C. Fields, including a big red bulbous nose, but I had not been told that the museum was failing. "Dr." McCoy was willing to sell almost everything in the building. A look at my trusty **National Geographic** atlas (one of the best presents my mother ever bought me) confirmed that I could fly to St. Paul, then easily drive to Darwin the next day. It happened to be the end of November, just a few days away from Thanksgiving. St. Paul was frozen over and one of the coldest places I have ever been; I doubt I could last there more than a few hours. What the hell was this place like in January was all I could think of.

I bought dozens of items, shock machines, vibrators, radium belts (to increase male potency) as well as a pair of – **Dinshah Attuned**

Color Wave Semaphores (aka: Spectro-Chrome Therapy machines), that displayed various color lights that were reported to heal just about any ailment simply by baring your chest (particularly good for women) to the reflected color light. Quackery indeed. All of these objects were sold legally on the common market between about 1850 and 1920, and several of their inventors — true charlatans — even made millions of dollars from them. Phrenology at least on the surface, can be argued to be a pseudo-science; everyone has bumps on their heads, and the followers are in no imminent danger from the products sold to them by the established experts.

Popularized in the mid-19th century by L.N. Fowler, the

followers of phrenology believe that the bumps on heads can be read, some-what like tea leaves, to reveal one's personality traits. There are posters and even a well-known marble bust, that outlines the different regions of the head (somewhat like a butcher's cow chart). Phrenologists, and the practice, had never disappeared, but the pseudo-science regained strength in the early 20th century becoming a fairgrounds fad, based largely on the invention of the psychograph, a machine that not only could read your bumps, but provided a printed read-out of what they mean. People actually lined up and paid real money for the experience. I believe it was Barnum, but maybe it was Fields, who said: "a sucker is born every minute".

The machine is well made, with a solid wood seat and cabinet housing a metal "reader" attached to a stand with a large metal "cap" that resembles a futuristic hair dryer, or maybe a machine to teleport you to another dimension. Comical looking, the "patient" sits on the chair, the cap is lowered onto his/her head. Its metal hammers are set in place around the wearer's head, to read one's bumps and the ticker-tape spits out its findings. Each bump is interpreted on a scale of one to five, one being bad, five representing good physical well-being.

The following are excerpts from my initial reading that cold November day back in 1991:

Know Yourself — Psychograph Inventory of Your Potential Powers, Capacities, Characteristics and Tendencies.

Suavity — 4 — Superior — Your capacity for courtesy, tact, diplomacy and consideration for others is marked.

Hope — 2 — Low Average — "Look up, not down; forward, not backward." Cultivate a trust in the law of compensation. High expectations and creative imagination.

Execution — 5 — Very Superior — Capacity for endurance of pain and hardship should not blind you to others. Achievement should be of mutual benefit.

Sexamity — 5 — Very Superior — An amorous nature of

this degree, unless inhibited, seeks association with opposite sex but may not demand physical contact.

Friendship — 5 — Very Superior — You may become staunch and devoted to your friends and may draw a host to you by exercising this capacity consistently.

Faith — 2 — Low Average — lack of trust may prevent you from being swept off your feet but it may also block you from accepting authoritative short cuts.

In total I scored twelve 5's and twelve 4's, one 3, and two 2's — not a single 1.

"Dr". McCoy told me there were only eight of these machines — made between 1903-1908 — still in existence, and only three of the eight were still in working condition. It was impossible for me to not buy both the ones he was offering. They are maybe the craziest looking gadgets I ever bought, or for that matter, ever saw, but they were a must have. I imagine some people really thought I needed my head read when this invoice had to be paid.

PS: The "Dr." also assured me the readings were accurate, and told my full inner story, but then again, he also presented me with my own diploma granting me the degrees from the Kansas City College of Medicine and Surgery of "Doctor in Medicine and Master in Surgery".

He may have looked like W.C. Fields, but in reality, he was more like The Great and Powerful OZ.

One that Got Away #6 –
The Emperor's Gemstone

The best jade in the world is very dark green in color. The commonly used jade for jewelry is called mutton fat jade. It is quite pale in color, sometimes even translucent, and is quite soft and easily broken with bare hands. The cheapest jade is called nephrite by jewelers, and is the grade of choice for most large jade sculptures. Jade comes in dozens of different shades of green between the two extremes of clear and dark, and isn't necessarily even always green. I have a jade bear that is mottled pink and brown that the average person would never guess was made of jade. My large Chinese guardian Foo dogs (lions) on the other hand, are so dark they look more black than green.

Before I went to China in 1996 all I knew about jade was that it was a semi-precious stone, but I did my research before I embarked on the most exotic shopping trip of my career. The first thing I learned was that it was historically the preferred stone of the Emperors. Next, I discovered that though the best jade carvers were Chinese, historically located in the Guangdong region in the south-east of China, the very best black jade comes from British Columbia, Canada. None of the twenty-one large jade sculptures in the Ripley collection are made of Canadian jade. They cost a lot of money, based on size and weight, but not millions of dollars like people generally think when they hear the word jade, and see something that weighs more than a ton.

In a formal meeting I had mentioned to Jimmy Pattison, that I had seen a large multi-headed dragon boat made of jade that I was considering buying. He asked if this was something I was really keen on. He had seen large jade sculptures in British Colombia made by native craftsman, and he was sure he had seen something like what I was describing in a hotel in Guangzhou, China. I told him of Robert Ripley's love for all things Chinese, and that it would be exactly the kind of thing he would have had in his homes. I also told him jade in its raw form was in fact a "real" believe it or not, because it stays a constant temperature. The Emperors of ancient China loved to use it to make furniture because it was cool to the touch in the summer and warm in the winter. I must have impressed him with the bit of knowledge I had, for in the next breath he was offering to send me to Guangzhou, to find out more about "dragon boats". As one of Canada's premier businessmen, Jimmy recently had been a part of a government picked group to go to China and discuss foreign trade at the highest levels. China was not open to individual travelers at this point, but he could pull some strings and get Norm Deska and I an invitation to the next annual Guangzhou Arts & Crafts Fair — the biggest convention of its type in the world. I was speechless. In the next few days he kicked open all the doors, and Norm and I were China bound in less than two months.

Guangzhou was formerly known as Canton. It is not far from Hong Kong, and by Chinese standards has a moderate degree of European-Western influence. It is a huge city, with a population of more than fifteen million today — every one of them, seemingly, getting around by bicycle. I had never been anywhere with so many people, and so few cars. Aside from the crowds and the bicycles, the thing I remember most was bamboo scaffolding everywhere. To say there was a construction boom would be a great understatement; I spent time every day watching people fearlessly climb hundreds of feet in the air on flimsy looking bamboo scaffolding with no harnesses, or safety equipment of any kind, wearing traditional Chinese woven hats rather than hard hats, and often barefoot. My eyes were open wide, and I was astonished. I understood Ripley's fascination both with the country and with this city – where in 1923 he had been held prisoner where my hotel now stood during an uprising between Sun Yat Sen and Chiang Kai-Shek.

Norm only stayed with me a couple of days, and then he departed for Hong Kong where we had a newly opened odditorium. For the duration of my trip I had a translator named Julie Smith who was a Godsend.

The fair was in three giant interconnected buildings, and was a maze of every imaginable product made in China, from children's toys to tractors, and ots of jade and camel bone carvings in between. I was totally unprepared for the size, quality and quantity of the carvings. I didn't know yet that all jade wasn't priceless, nor that ivory had been replaced by camel bone, and that the centuries old carving techniques of historic Canton were still flourishing, just with a different medium. There were things in every direction I wished to buy. With a bottomless pocketbook I could have bought literally hundreds of pieces. In the end, I bought twenty-five, seventeen jade sculptures and eight camel bone pieces.

Almost every vendor we met tried to get us to go off site to their "factory", where they could show us much more than was displayed in their small booths. We were somewhat frightened to do so, but on the third day we acquiesced. Our trip up country into the hinterland proved to be memorable. Julie sat in the front with the driver, and the salesman. Norm and I sat in the back. The car was a Mercedes, but at least twenty years old. It was in bad shape, and had no door handles. We were prisoners. The drive was over two hours long, in some parts picturesque, but in others, bleak and foreboding. Our only stop was in a planned housing community where the jade workers lived. Each house was identical. There were no street names, nor house numbers; we couldn't fathom how anyone could find their home in the dark, or if they were drunk.

The factory was immense. There were hundreds of carvers, each working with primitive tools on a specific part of a sculpture. Each sculpture was designed by one artist, but carved by dozens. Everyone had a specialty: hands, heads, birds, dragons, chains. How it would all fit together was an enigma. Within seconds, I broke the first thing I touched, a delicate jade chain. The commotion was volcanic. Norm was convinced we were in big trouble — our fear of Communists was almost as great as our ignorance. Julie was able to calm the storm — she probably admitted I was a clumsy ox — but it was clear we now had better buy something. We no longer were just looking.

Dragon boats — replicas of a style of actual sailing ships used by the Emperors for centuries, and so called because they appear to have a tail in the rear, and have multiple dragon heads in the front — were my main interest. They came in all variants of color, and ranged in sizes from four-feet, to sixteen-feet, in length. I bought five that day, and five more before leaving the country, but even more spectacular than the boats, were two jade royal carriages (chariot-like covered rick-shaws). They were more or less identical, but one had brass trim on the wheels, the other was all jade, and that was the one I purchased. The cost wasn't quite a king's ransom, but almost.

That night we celebrated our very successful day with a meal of "gooey duck".

Guangzhou is actually famous for snake dishes, and I had my heart set on trying snake, but after being shown eels about five times they assumed we didn't know the difference — we learned that It wasn't snake season (who knew!). Apparently, there were no snakes to be had anywhere. Gooey duck was a distant second choice. Gooey duck is not "duck", nor is it gooey — it is a rubbery giant "Geo duck" clam. In Toronto it was common to see Geoduck clams in fish tanks at the entrance to any decent Chinese restaurant. They are often as big as plates, and are very ugly. They do not appear to have any redeeming qualities, but I like clams — a lot. I regularly tried to convince my wife to let me buy one, but she had no interest, and as they were an expensive delicacy, I was not worthy of the cost just for myself. I told Julie this is what I wanted to eat. She had no idea what I was talking about.

We traipsed through the kitchens of several restaurants. We saw every kind of seafood, some bats, and a fox, but no gooey duck. I was beginning to think it was a communist plot, or at least revenge for the broken jade chain. We at last found the elusive gooey duck. Julie was beside herself, giggling and guffawing. She said she was fond of it, but apparently in China it was called "elephant's trunk", or "elephant tongue", and indeed as soon as she said it, we could see why. With the clam shell fully opened the giant clam oozes out in a long tube shape. Held upright the shell looked like big ears, and the clam a gnarled wrinkled trunk. It looks disgusting. Norm was not enthused, but he was willing to try despite it being sold by the pound, and the smallest one they had was going to cost us Ninety American Dollars. Nothing ventured, nothing gained. Luckily, we did order a couple of other dishes.

The elephant tongue was presented sushi style, prepared three different ways, all sliced paper thin and laid out on the decks of a decorative serving boat. It looked absolutely beautiful, worthy of a gourmet food magazine cover. Julie took one piece from each deck and declared it delicious. Norm and I loaded down our plates expecting Nirvana. One bite of each style and we both had enough. I have never tasted anything so vile in my life. Four beers later I could still taste the mere forkful I had eaten. Once bitten, twice shy. I have never gone near gooey duck again.

Irony: Gooey duck until World War II was unknown in China. It comes from only one place in the world: Puget Sound, Seattle, Washington, USA., and it is harvested almost exclusively by Native Americans. I assume they traditionally ate it, but today nearly 100% of the harvest goes straight to China. The average American, or Canadian, has no taste for it.

Norm departed the next morning leaving me to buy as much jade as I could, and to visit a camel bone factory in the hopes of getting some of those too. The camel bone was not as prevalent at the fair as the jade, and cost considerably more. Like the jade, for each sculpture there was one designer, and dozens of carvers. Each colossal piece was made from thousands of small pieces. Over time these would prove very difficult to move without damaging them, so once installed they tended to stay put. Most of them came in faux wood cabinets with lights. They are exquisite, and for me, more beautiful than the jade.

In addition to five more dragon boats, I found a firm that made "thousand" armed Buddhas (1), and another that made giant eight-foot in diameter, six-inch thick jade good luck coins adorned with carved bats and flowers. I bought three of each, and the Buddha carver gifted me with a pair of twelve-inch high Foo dogs which now guard my reading room.

It needs to be mentioned that I carried no checks, and only as much cash as I needed to buy street food. At the start of each day I had to visit the American Express office and borrow against my gold card. By the end of the week they got to know me very well, and must have thought I was a millionaire. They had no idea what

401

I was buying every day, but they knew I was spending a lot of money, the daily maximum $10,000 they would give me. I was their best customer.

There were three other things I had hoped to find at the fair, smaller in size than the jade or camel bone sculptures, but no less amazing:

  1) An ancient earthquake detector, or at least a replica of one[2].

  2) Two-sided embroidery — each side depicting a different image, but the reverse being invisible to the eye from the opposite side.

  3) Paintings done inside clear acrylic balls.

I did not find #1, nor #3, at the fair. I bought both the company and myself samples of #2, my personal one showing a gold dog on one side and a silver cat on the other, both embroidered to a paper-thin screen, mounted in a wood frame.

I must have walked miles up and down the aisles convinced the left the buildings on the last day empty handed, only to turn the corner to find a street artist painting some on the sidewalk. She had traveled a great long way to attend the fair, but had not been able to afford a booth inside. She spoke a dialect seemingly unknown to anyone, and could not find anyone to help her, so she had set up shop outside on the corner as close to the hall as the authorities would let her. Miraculously, Julie understood her; Julie's mother it turned out had been born in the same region more than a thousand miles from where we were standing.

The woman had two sizes of the balls. The acrylic was apparently more valuable than her talent as the big balls cost considerably more than the little ones, despite the increased difficulty of doing the golf ball sized ones. Each ball had a small hole in it at the bottom, and the brush was inserted through that passageway. The smaller the ball, the smaller the hole, and the smaller the brush. I bought samples of both sizes, both for myself — a large tiger one for my wife, a small panda bear for myself — and the company. The cost for ten was less than a decent Chinese meal in Orlando. For the artisan, it was an annual income.

On my last day, virtually broke, I decided it was best I go to Hong Kong by bus rather than the planned train ride. Julie got me to the station, and on the bus, but then waved goodbye. I was now entirely on my own in China for the first and only time. The bus ride was more of an adventure than anything to date had been.

The distance didn't look like much on the map, and I had all day, so I was not concerned with time. I was prepared to sit back, watch the scenery go by, and reflect on the wondrous week I had. Going to China had been a magical dream come true. I had "no expectations to pass this way again".

The bus was old, decrepit, and smelled like an Asian grocery store a mixture of a thousand unknown smells. It was going to be full, and everyone had 'baggage". I may have been the only person with actual luggage, but the hodgepodge of sacks, cardboard boxes, and grocery bags, made it look like the biggest flea market imaginable. I found a window seat halfway back. I was joined by a toothless old woman whom I could barely see behind her packages. She made eye contact, and I spoke in English, but she closed her eyes and went to sleep before we even pulled out of the station.

The scenery was predominantly green, and rural, flecked with small farms. I saw an ox or two plowing fields, but no cows, a few pigs, but no sheep. Every farm had a pond, and every pond had ducks, hundreds, even thousands of them. Ducks were everywhere, sometimes in baskets in yokes across people's shoulders, sometimes in rickety, open air lorries, and sometimes on leashes being walked to market. I had eaten duck as part of almost every meal for the last week, and now saw why. I had to assume their wings were clipped in some fashion as I saw none flying.

The scenes on the bus were as wild as those along the roadside. It was soon very apparent why the bus smelled like a grocery store. Virtually every passenger but me had food to eat, and I am not talking American bagged snacks, but real food. One man even had a coal burning hand-sized "hibachi" on which he preceded to barbecue bird parts in the center aisle. Clearly there were no rules, for health, or safety. Passengers freely shared both hot and cold food across aisles, and left the remains under their seats. I assumed the bus had to have mice or rats that dined on the leftovers. I stared so hard my eyes popped out.

Without notice we came to a military juncture; the international border between Mainland China and Hong through, no questions, no delays, my passport was stamped without the guard (agent) even looking up at my face.

It was dark before I pulled into Hong Kong, via the Kowloon Ferry, but the trip though slow and long, had been memorable. I was grateful for having been ignored, persona non grata. That night I dreamed of ducks taking over the world. In the morning I ate duck congee, and left homeward bound via Los Angeles.

It would take months for my four different containers to arrive in Orlando, and I was nervous the whole time. Despite shoddy crates, not a single item sustained any damage. With minimal packing material, and nothing "state of the art", twenty-five delicate giant pieces made it half way around the world in perfect condition. This feat was never repeated; virtually every one of the pieces has since suffered some damage. Warehouse people lack the personal love the artist has for their own work and seldom are as careful in their handling and packing.

I would get back to Hong Kong, and nearby Macau, nine years later, but to date I have not returned to Mainland China. Beijing, Xian and Shanghai are still on my bucket list. I would eventually buy more jade and camel bone sculptures, but without going overseas. Within a year of my first visit, a camel bone company set up a branch office in Seattle, and soon anyone could buy pieces on-line. The prices were higher, but the convenience made up for the price hike.

I have never seen a store selling the type of jade pieces I got, but I assume there is one somewhere that at least sells the ships, for I have come across a few of them in private collections, and high-end Chinese restaurants all over the world. The only other one I acquired was the biggest one I ever saw, eighteen-feet in length, and almost ten-feet tall. I found it in a collection in Majorca, Spain.

404

I did, however, later acquire three jade pieces that I never saw anything like them for sale in China, all three were of human form. Two were mutton fat jade life size replicas of the famous terracotta tomb soldiers of Xian. I suspect these were produced in Xian specifically for the tourist market, but I found both in America. They stand about five-foot, four inches, tall, and weigh about 800 lbs. each. Like the real terracotta soldiers, they come in two pieces, the body is all one piece, but the head is another, and is removable for shipping.

The single most interesting jade piece in the Ripley collection, however, was found in Prince Edward Island, Canada — a two-thousand-year old Han Dynasty jade imperial burial suit. There are only a handful of these known to exist. Like mummies, it likely was robbed from a grave at some point, but whether recently or centuries ago, it is impossible to know. This was an item I had first learned about in a college Chinese history class, and having recently seen one in Hong Kong's national museum, I knew exactly what I was looking at.

The "suit" is humanoid in form, including a head, presumably made after the wearer was dead as they would have to be sewn into it for it to fit exactly around the body. The purpose of the jade "armor" was to assure immortality in the next world. Both Hong Kong's and the Ripley's one, were originally made up of hundreds of squares of pieces of jade intricately connected by 24-karat gold wire. Virtually everyone ever found was in pieces, the gold "thread" having been pilfered. My burial suit has been lovingly reassembled, but with home stereo quality copper wire, instead of gold. Hong Kong's suit still has all its original gold. Even with modern copper and not a hint of the original gold, there is about 100 lbs. of good quality jade, and the rarity of the artifact makes it one of the most important historical pieces in the Ripley collection.

Part Two: The Jack Mamiye Jade, and Other Oriental Treasures, Collection — Jade that Got Away

I have seen many marvelous, and priceless collections. Somewhere there is a person that collects anything you can name. Collecting is definitely an obsession, and usually even a collector's own family can't comprehend why they collect what they do. I collect music records and CDs, and books, and I am passionate, and fanatical about my collections. I know I spend more than I should, and I ran out of room to properly care for them years ago, but I can't stop. I'm possessed, but not crazy.

The most impressive single person's collection I ever had the pleasure to peruse — with the thought of acquiring — belonged to Jack Mamiye, a resident of New Jersey and Florida. Jack grew up in China and San Francisco, and has collected Oriental objets d' art, his entire life, everything from small opium bottles to a solid jade bed big large enough to sleep ten. His collection fills two houses, and a warehouse, and I suspect by now has overflowed into the houses of his son and his grandson. He owns a king's ransom in jade alone, and I'm talking several giant pieces of good Canadian black jade, not just nephrites and mutton fat jades.

Jack's collection despite my best efforts is one that got away. I visited his home in New Jersey once, his warehouse twice, and his Florida home twice. Five visits over as many years, each meeting held over a glorious home cooked lunch, all for naught, except for the development of a life-long loving personal relationship I value the trust and friendship shown to me by his entire family, more than the jade would ever have been worth to me…but I do still have to tell you a bit about the collection.

Jack has a chariot just like Ripley's one. He has at least five dragon boats, all as good or better than Ripley's. He has a jade throne, as big as some people's apartments — easily a full wall in even the biggest home; the aforementioned canopied bed — you would need at least three king size mattresses to cover the very hard jade flooring — a couple jade jars big enough to hide people in (picture Ali Baba's 40 thieves!); a twelve-foot tall jade peach tree with thousands of jade leaves; and a pair of life-sized black jade herons. Add to these, approximately 1,000 small pieces — yes, I did a full inventory of every single piece in the collection — and you have the jade collection, but then there is the rest of the stuff: carpets, ceramics, glass wares, weapons, dolls, jewelry, and ivories.

Jack first came to my attention because he has a 1949 era ivory sculpture that consists of over two dozen elephant tusks; it depicts a young Mao Zedong in a rural village scene. The central piece of the sculpture is a fisherman with a net. The fishermen's net is the single most incredible ivory — or camel bone — sculpture I have ever seen, hundreds of times finer than an actual fishing net, more like the weaving of a cottage screen door. Jack values this one piece as being worth more than all the rest of the collection combined.

This piece of ivory, not to mention several other more manageable in size priceless pieces of ivory, were the reason we never came to terms. Almost everything Jack had was for sale(3), but only if the Mao Ivory was part of the deal. Ripley's had only once ever de-acquisitioned any part of the original possessions of Robert Ripley — we sold his personal ivory collection in a Christie's auction (see Chapter 37). It was impossible now to reconsider the moral issue. Ivory was taboo — at any price — for Ripley's after 1989.

My vision was to use the collection to recreate Ripley's Manhattan studio, a thirteen room, three-story high apartment that at one time had nearly 1,000 Oriental artifacts in it.

Photos of his dining room are amongst my favorite in the Ripley archive photo collection. The artifacts obviously wouldn't be the same, but with Jack's collection we could have captured the feeling, the opulence and the elegance of the Ripley mansion. We discussed loans, donations, installment payments, but nothing was destined to work. The Ripley team did not share my vision. I eventually reluctantly gave up this dream.

Jack has already gifted me a delicate, beautiful pair of jade wedding cups that I hope my children will one

day use, but until then I dream of him leaving me something bigger in his will.

Jack, China, and jade have a special place in my heart.

61

David & the Generals

For almost as long as I knew him, Alec Rigby encouraged me to buy big pieces that could be displayed outside. He had a vision of a Ripley European-style sculpture garden, but the trouble was we only had one real place to put the experiment to trial — St. Augustine, Florida — and that city has restrictions on what can be displayed in their so-called historic district. We used to joke — seriously — that you couldn't even paint a white fence white without consulting the historic board to make sure your "white" was an "approved white" and quite often it wasn't. Over time Ripley's would acquire land in Branson, Missouri, and Grand Prairie, Texas, adjacent to parking lots, and display some exhibits outside, but for the majority of my history, the only outdoor location was at Ripley's St. Augustine.

When I joined Ripley's, the grounds of St. Augustine had a whitewashed stone sculpture of a Spanish style ox cart, a wishing well, a dredged up giant ship anchor, three North American Indian totem plaques, and two large Oriental bronze guardian statues. At an earlier date they had a large Oriental dance figure, and a large donut shaped Yap money stone. During my time, I added a metal crocodile, a redwood log house, a car bumper stallion and a seventeen-foot tall marble replica of Michelangelo's **David**. I removed the North American Indian pieces to other Ripley odditoriums.

The Guards and David are worth discussing in some detail. Both are valuable, both have interesting pre St. Augustine histories, and both break city codes. They have been deemed signage, rather than sculpture, and as such are considered potentially dangerous distractions to drivers. The Warriors luckily have been grandfathered in, as they have been at the entrance way since 1950. David had a much harder time getting dispensation.

The Guardians, two very large bronze statues depicting two ancient Chinese generals (warlords), known as Li Chi and King Kang, real personages from the 9th century AD, have two other names: collectively, "The Guardians of Heaven" and individually, "Halt all Evil" and "Chase all Evil." Similar replicas and representations of these warlords, appear in Japanese and Korean history and art, and the Rijksmuseum in Amsterdam has a Japanese wooden pair almost as impressive in size and age as the Ripley ones. The Ripley statues are at youngest, 18th century, and could be much older.

When and where Ripley acquired them is unknown, but there is movie footage taken in 1940 showing workmen installing them at the bridge entrance to his Believe It or Not (BION) Island home in Mamaroneck, New York. There, they were mounted on gravestone -like granite plinths, with their names etched in Chinese. They are mentioned in several articles at the time, with a different age stated in almost every case. In the Fall of 1949, when the estate was sold, they were moved to St. Augustine, and have now rested on either side of the main entrance to the Ripley odditorium there since (nearly seventy years).

The weather, and people, have not been particularly kind to them. The patina of the bronze darkens and the statues gather mold regularly. To combat the fungal growth, the statues have repeatedly been painted black. When I first saw them, I had no idea they were actually bronze.

In 1989, proving the city father's right at least to a point, Li was badly damaged in a car accident. An underage teenage drunk with no insurance, driving a stolen pick-up truck, plowed through about fifty-feet of picket fence, and only stopped when she rammed head first into Li. Kang was not untouched, but was still standing. Li was in pieces in the street and on the sidewalk.

There was no one in little St. Augustine who could repair them, and it was quite a chore to find someone anywhere who could. The work was eventually done in Chicago, by a firm of metal art restorers our chief designer Bill Myhill found after weeks of searching. Li, with the help of a crane, was picked up and shipped off to Chicago, leaving Florida for the first time in thirty-nine years. After removing multiple layers of black paint, and seeing the real Li underneath, it was quickly decided Kang needed to go to Chicago too; the statues had to look alike. It took over a year to repair them both, but they looked a thousand times better when they made their triumphant return. They now get annual maintenance and have only needed one more real good work-over since their car accident. From that day on I could say: "Oh, I have a guy for that", anytime anyone made a query about repairing a monumental statue.

As it turned out we needed them a couple more times, both times again in St. Augustine (1).

Michelangelo's Renaissance masterpiece **David** is made from one solid piece of Carrara marble. It is over seventeen-feet tall, and weighs in excess of 12,000 lbs. (six tons). It is the pride of Florence, Italy, and perhaps the best-known piece of statuary in the world. Believe it or not, there are two near perfect replicas of it, both made from marble from the same quarry that Michelangelo used. Ripley's owns one, and it is outside in the odditorium's garden at St. Augustine. The other, the last I heard, was in a shopping mall in Australia.

The Ripley statue was made for the 1963-64 World's Fair in Flushing, New York. After the fair it was moved to the site of the Movieland Wax Museum in Buena Park, California, just a few miles from Disneyland. It stood there unmolested for roughly forty years until bought it, and moved it to Florida. For the record, it cost me more to move than to buy.

Ripley's needed permission from the city to put him up in the garden, and were approved, but with the stipulation that the statue not face the main street; he had to face the small unused side street. Though David's penis has historically been ridiculed by art critics and ladies alike, as tiny and out of proportion, sitting at about average eye level to passersby, it was still too big for St. Augustine's city officials. We were forced in the name of modesty, to plant a hedge around him, not to be less than seven-feet tall. It is almost too comical, but we of course complied.

No sooner was David hidden from the view of the street, and staff, then graffiti began to appear, usually written on his ass, but in other places too: David's parts are now subject to regular bathing. David, the poor fellow, I dare say has been indecently fondled by thousands of people, women and men both, no doubt. As anyone who has seen him, or the original in Florence, will

411

attest, it is safe to say he is truly a fine specimen. His ass apparently begs to be groped, and behind the veil of a ten-foot high hedge, who knows what other indecencies have been enacted on the splendid youth.

Vandalism to art happens in museums everywhere, not just at Ripley's. Both Michelangelo's actual **David**, and his magnificent **Pieta**, have been attacked, and damaged by evil deranged people, and no longer can be seen up close for fear of further hostilities. It greatly saddens me, and I don't know what the answer is. The most common question I was always asked by designers was if an exhibit could be touched. The answer almost always should be "no" — but when it is "yes", someone needs to be prepared to do regular maintenance.

I don't know if Alec ever saw David in St. Augustine, but he would definitely find his hedge-cloth hilarious. I don't think he would approve, and if alive and still in charge, I could see him fighting the city board with every ounce of his strength. I certainly can see him in the dead of the night with a hedge clipper.

One that Got Away #7 —
An Ear Wax Figure of Galileo

For my entire career I bragged that I got the best mail. It was like Christmas almost every day. I used to circulate the best letter of the week. Many letters were requesting materials from the cartoon archives:

"Dear Mr. Ripley: My grandfather was in Ripley's, can you send me a copy?"

To be fair, sometimes they had a clue why their relative was in the cartoon:

"Dear Mr. Ripley, my mother was in the Ripley cartoon. Her name was "Merry Christmas". Was her item ever in one of your books? Can you send me a copy?"

Occasionally, they might even know the date of publication, or at least have a close idea:

"Dear Mr. Ripley I was in the cartoon on July 24th. I think it was in 1956. Is it possible to get a copy of that cartoon?

All of these types of letters were always answered, and with technological improvements to our database, more than 95% were answered positively with the cartoon being found. The other 5% either were published in the mid-1920s where our collection had some big gaps, or more often than not, were never in our cartoon, the writer mistaking our cartoon for one of Ripley's "knock-off competitors", like John Hix's **Strange As It Seems**" or Gordon Johnston's **"It Happened in Canada"**. In the early years when a lot of the searching was done by hand, I charged for my time. As the machinery lessened the search time, sometimes to mere seconds, I waivered the fee. The satisfaction I got from helping people was one of my greatest joys. The thank you letters I received often burst my heart. For example, an elderly Jewish man who lost a signature ring, recalled that Ripley's had once done a cartoon on the Jewish symbol used on his lost ring. He knew the symbol name in question depicted "Matthew" but no other details. I found it very easily, much to even my surprise, with just the two key words, Matthew and ring. I emailed the man a copy of the cartoon. He phoned me crying, thanking me profusely (his lost ring had been a gift received as a child from his parents). His having the Ripley cartoon drawing would allow a jeweler to replicate it. He promised to send me a gift for my "trouble". I assured him there was no need, it was simple, no trouble, and most importantly, **my job**. A week later I got a $100 American Express gift card in the mail, with a lovely letter.

The second largest "kind" of mail received, were offers to sell something to Ripley's. Some were of no interest, many of them led to exhibit purchases, and still others, were absolutely unbelievable.

One was a piece I had framed and put on my wall for me to stare at every day, while shaking my head in wonder. A man in Hong Kong sent me a note on a small scrap of paper, with a small portrait of himself, and a plastic baggie with a dozen small pieces of white balls of fluff from his belly button. Yes, belly button lint! The sender did not think it weird that he had collected it, nor that he had mailed them to Ripley's half way around the world. What he asked in his letter was "Why is my belly button lint always white?" I am pretty sure I didn't answer this one, but I could never help wondering if he ever wore a colored undershirt?

Another example is without a doubt the all-time best letter I ever received. In 1995, a man named Paul Rosa, published a book titled **"Idiot Letters: One Man's Relentless Assault on Corporate America"**. The book includes a letter that eventually found its way onto my desk. The entire letter is hilarious (as is his whole book), but I will only quote a few lines.

From paragraph one:

"As a young boy growing up in Dyer, IN. (population 10,500) in the 1930s and 1940's, my family frequently went to various wax museums across the state…the "Hoosier State" had quite a few of these attractions and we would visit them ten to twenty times each year".

From paragraph two:

414

"Well in 1941 (I was 12) I began wondering why there weren't any **ear** wax museums! My family (Mom, Dad, Tess, Agnes and Rufus) all agreed that it was a terrific idea, and thought I should "create" the first ear wax statue…. Every few days I would carefully swab the insides of my ears and store the precious yield in a small tin (cigar) canister…. In 1947 ….I finally had enough ear wax to complete a pair of feet….my masterpiece would be: Galileo".

From paragraph three:

"…My family consistently offered to contribute their ear wax, but I politely declined, explaining it would diminish my accomplishment."

From paragraph four:

"…The work on Galileo never stopped…. By 1982 (age 53) only the head and face still needed completing…Well, I'm 64 and retired, and the spectacular face of Galileo was finished one week ago!

From paragraph five [the last]:

But now I'm thrilled about the possibility of sharing my achievement with the world. Are you interested in getting involved?"

Rosa wrote his series of unusual witty letters hoping to get answers from "Corporate America". The book is laid out with his letters on the left side, the answers he received on the right. He literally made idiots out of some of the biggest companies in the world as they at-tempted to intelligently answer his off-the-wall requests.

The letter above was not initially addressed to Ripley's. It was sent to a wax museum in Colorado. They responded with a two-line letter: "…we have no place for it in our museum", followed by a closing suggestion:

"However, you may wish to contact Ripley's Museum in Orlando."

Mr. Rosa did just that — he sent it directly to our Orlando odditorium, not to our headquarters. Excitedly the odditorium manager, had the good sense to forward it to me, amazed at the possibility of having discovered the find of the century.

There is no letter response from me in Mr. Rosa's book, I simply couldn't believe what I was reading — despite an accompanying rough sketch of the ear wax Galileo. I thought it sounded too wild and crazy to be true…but I couldn't take the chance of ignoring the letter in case it was real!

Rather than sending him the written response, and a XL t-shirt that he requested, I phoned him. Imagine my disappointment to learn it was all a hoax in an effort to get a silly written response for a future book. I had been duped. Me, the guy paid to determine fakes from real oddities, had almost been taken in, hook, line and sinker despite several obvious clues (1).

In truth, I was more an idiot than all the other people "he got", but unfortunately for him, and fortunately for me, there is no evidence of my gullibility. There is no letter response from the Vice President of Exhibits of Ripley's Believe It or Not! in his book. The ear wax Galileo wax figure, though I still think it would be a truly unbelievable exhibit, that I definitely would buy if such a thing really existed, is, not surprisingly, one that definitely got away.

63

Sworn to Secrecy — An Untold Chapter

For nearly twenty years I had the privilege of working with two very talented artists, Bruce Miller, a thin as a rail guy who in addition to having his own creative genius, could fix anything someone else had made. Before working at Ripley' he had worked for Universal Studios. He had made several of their dinosaurs and their original King Kong in the 1980s. His first boss at Ripley's was Barry Anderson, a stocky, somewhat emotional wax sculptor, with a Hollywood movie background. He had once been a regular on the show Miami Vice. Both these men were passionate about Halloween. Most years at the annual Ripley costume party they tried to outdo each other, with Bruce typically winning, and Barry coming in a close second, but one year they doubled up on their talents and came together as Stan Laurel and Oliver Hardy. The costumes, make-up and acting were spot on perfection, but even this was not their finest Halloween moment.

In early October 2009 I received a very clandestine, mysterious phone call from a theme park design company based in Cincinnati. They knew me by name as they had worked on the design of the Ripley odditorium in London the previous year. I didn't personally know the person on the other end of the phone, but they were calling on behalf of the White House. Would Ripley's be willing to work with them, gratis, to design a Halloween party at the White House. I was shocked and honored. I immediately said yes, knowing however, that my role would be minimal, simply the liaison, for the two people Bruce and Barry — who would make something very special and memorable happen.

Bruce did create a giant spider, but otherwise, because of the time restraint, everything else we sent to the White House was already in our warehouse: a vampire killing kit, a 1920s dime museum replica mummy, a Bela Lugosi Dracula cape, and wax figures of a witch, a wolf man, a mummy, Dracula, and Vlad the Impaler. It was unfortunate that Bruce and Barry didn't get to do the actual install, as they would have "killed it", but we were oh so proud of our contribution. The President every year celebrates, Easter, the Fourth of July, Thanksgiving, and Christmas in some public way, but unknown to me at the time, this was the first ever Presidential Halloween party. The party was for the families of soldiers fighting in the Middle East; children from all over the country were entertained by Ripley's in the White House and out on the lawn.

I recently read Michelle Obama's book, **"Becoming"**. In two paragraphs on page 336, she describes this event as her first significant accomplishment as the "First Lady". Apparently, no one thought it was a good idea to spend thousands of dollars frivolously having fun during the height of a period of economic turmoil. She was told the "optics were bad", but she fought to have the event and won.

Ripley's is not mentioned by name, there is a chance Michele didn't even know that we were involved, but Bruce's giant spider is mentioned, and Michelle who gave out candy dressed as a leopard, says she and the President had a great time. Quote, "As far as she was concerned the optics were just right."

Until I read these two paragraphs, I had totally forgotten this story! Until now, I have kept my promise of total secrecy. I have no notes, names, or phone numbers, just one "secret" email address marked on my day calendar as evidence that I once worked for the White House and the Obama administration.

64

I'll Drink to That —
One that Almost Got Away

My very first on-line auction came about purely by chance. It was late in the afternoon on May 31, 2001. I was about to shut off my computer for the night, and I noticed a new unopened email. It was from Sotheby's Auctions. Since the dawn of the internet, I had regularly received auction house emails, but typically not from Sotheby's. Ripley's has made some big purchases from them, but somewhat sporadically, and not often enough to be on their free catalogue mailing list. I hadn't seen this auction catalog in print. The email caught my attention immediately, the title page picture being of a giant Tiffany ivory and silver elephant-shaped beer stein that I recognized from a photo in the Ripley archives. I noted that the auction was actually starting in less than twenty minutes.

I quickly verified that the elephant stein was indeed one that had once belonged to Robert Ripley. I then in full panic mode sought out Lisa Pascella, the office manager whom I knew would still be in the office, and had much better computer skills than I. I had no idea at that time how to follow and bid in an on-line auction. By the time we were set up and ready to bid, we had already missed some lots, but I immediately recognized more steins that I was familiar with from Ripley bar photos. Nearly every item in the auction had once belonged to Ripley, but the auction house didn't know it. Officially they were selling the Pabst's Brewery of Milwaukee Stein Collection. Ripley's name did not appear anywhere in the catalog on my computer screen.

To this day, I hate on-line bidding, and avoid it as much as possible. When it has been necessary to bid on-line, inevitably I have sought help. This was the only occasion Lisa ever assisted me; in later years, Angela Johnson did all "my" on-line bidding. I'm a technophobe, I hate "forms", and I am a lousy typist; I simply can't keep up with the pace of on-line bidding. For this auction, I sat on the floor surrounded by about forty archival photos of Ripley's Mamaroneck Island home's bar and beer steins, while Lisa sat at my desk, showed me each auction lot on the computer screen as they came up, and bid when I identified the lot as being a Ripley stein, and one I thought we should try to buy.

The auction went on for hours. We purchased sixty-four different lots, with a total of approximately eighty individual steins. We did not get the elephant stein, which sold for an impressive $225,000, pre- commission and taxes, but we did get several massive silver steins, a trophy size copper one, one made from a nautilus shell, several ceramic ones, including a lovely military Mettlach set, a handful of crystal glass steins, and most significantly, a stein that Ripley touted as the world's largest, capable of holding sixty-three bottles of beer.

There were several lots I wasn't sure of, and others that we bid on but didn't get, but we got just about every "unusual" one offered. The origin of these steins, which I knew, but somehow the auction house didn't, was significant, and I dare say if Sotheby's had of known, they would have made a lot more money that day.

Not only had the lion share of the steins once belonged to Robert Ripley, but Ripley had bought them directly from the Anheuser-Busch family in St Louis in 1938, a fact well documented in the Ripley archives in correspondence, print and photos. When Ripley's estate was auctioned off in 1949, the Pabst Brewery had bought the majority of the steins. They definitely knew the Ripley connection, and I am sure someone must have known the Anheuser-Busch connection, but that they "forgot" it or deemed it insignificant 50-years later, is a shocking case of neglect of archival provenance.

The neglect was further illustrated with the sale of the world's largest stein. Its lid was sold as a separate lot about an hour after the stein as no one recognized it as the lid! I paid very little for the stein (a lot less than I was prepared to go), which was listed as "incomplete, missing lid", but then three times the asking price for the lid, which was listed as a 19th ceramic sculpture. To my amusement when the steins were later delivered Ripley's handwritten two-inch by three-inch museum reader card listing its origin, its size, and its capacity, was still inside the giant stein!

I wish I had of had time to peruse a catalog, as I am sure we missed some gems, but I am very grateful that Lisa was willing to stay late that night, and that we made the killing we did. This collection is one of the few items dating directly from Ripley's time that the company knows exactly when they were bought, whom from, and how much was paid. Based on photographic evidence it is clear that they were one of Ripley's most prized possessions. A few are now displayed in a couple different odditoriums, but the majority, including the giant, have been in New York City since that odditorium opened in 2007.

For me the beer steins have another personal significance beyond being my first on-line auction. They also were the subject in 2010 of my first paid public speaking event at the Stein Collector's International Convention in Myrtle Beach, South Carolina. My then assistant, Anthony Scipio, and myself, drove to Myrtle Beach for the weekend, and were paid handsomely for a ninety-minute presentation on the collection. The members were fascinated by the Ripley history, but shocked at how much I had paid for many of the pieces. They didn't value the provenance like I did, and only saw the current market value price as being significant. The silver tankards, which fetched the highest auction prices, were the ones that they found the least interesting, pointing out that most were probably for show only, and may have never actually been used to quaff a cool one — which at the end of the day, is what steins were created for.

65

Toilet Paper Wedding Dresses

I haven't watched daytime television since the summer of 1972 when I didn't get a summer job, and had nothing else to do for two months. My wife on the other hand watches a lot of daytime TV news and talk shows and if she saw something Ripley's worthy on a morning talk show, she would always call me at the office to tell me. I never had a television in my office, but there was always one nearby. One morning she called me and said: "Turn on the Martha Stewart show, they are talking about a wedding dress contest in which all the dresses are made from toilet paper! The dress ladies are in Florida". Definitely Ripley worthy material.

On the show there were a couple of ladies in beautiful wedding gowns that from a distance were unidentifiable as toilet paper; they looked like couture dresses from a bridal salon. Two sisters – Susan Bain and Laura Gawne were being interviewed. The dresses had just won the first ever **Cheap Chic Wedding Co. Toilet Paper Wedding Dress Contest.** The sisters were the founders of Cheap Chic Weddings.com, an on-line company created to help brides plan weddings cheaply, within a budget. My wife and I were extremely fortunate that we got our wedding hall for free, but I think we still spent about $5,000 on our wedding. Today, the national average spent to get married is $34,000. It's insane how much some people spend, and for those who don't have it, Cheap Chic Weddings is a Godsend.

The Cheap Chic web page offers tips on where to buy flowers, rent stemware, make your own veils etc. good advice for every aspect of wedding planning. Toilet paper wedding dresses probably started as a lark, not meant to be taken too seriously, but obviously a real option if anyone really wanted to save money. The concept certainly caught my imagination, whether anyone actually got married in one of the dresses or not. I was talking to Sue, the company's spokesperson, within a couple hours of that first television airing.

For the next twelve years, Ripley's was a financial sponsor of the annual contest, and three times I would be a celebrity judge. The first time I was the MC, and the final runway event occurred in the Ripley odditorium in New York. The media just loved the fashion show. The company had outgrown their South Florida home base, and taking the event to the Big Apple probably increased their exposure a hundred-fold. It definitely helped grow the number of contestants every year going forth.

I gave them my time and our location for free, and we in exchange got to keep the top three dresses for display. It was a marriage made in heaven. Susan and Laura had already whittled the selection down from over 1500 entries to the top ten. With two other judges, we selected three finalists from the group of ten, to win the prize money. The rules stretched over time, but initially no material other than toilet paper could be used, and most importantly, the dress had to be wearable — at least once. The best dresses would typically consist of at least twenty rolls of paper, and would also include toilet paper accessories, like hats, bouquets, shoes and purses.

The Ripley event was a great success, but the venue still wasn't big enough to hold the crowd of photographers and writers that showed up. For my second judging, the contest was held at a New York City rooftop restaurant. For the third one, we were in a rented art gallery.

After each event Susan and Laura would hand deliver the winning dresses to our office in Orlando and take some additional publicity photos. We were always assured three dresses, but typically each year ended up with five or six. The Ripley collection is now well over thirty strong, and as promised, the dresses have been featured on the Ripley web pages, in Ripley books, and in odditoriums all around the world. In Branson, Missouri, five are displayed together with the world's largest roll of toilet paper, a donation from the company that made it.

As a judge, I got to meet the models and the artists to ask questions about their entries, and what they would do with the prize money if they won (prizes included $10,000 in cash, as well as Ripley location trips). Most of the designers were smart enough to hire a model if they made it to the top ten runway event, and in my last judging, I admit my judgment was definitely swayed by a West African model who flirted shamelessly with me.

At least half the dresses were made by young would be Vera Wangs studying fashion, but there were also dresses made by housewives and grandmothers, and of course there were some male designers too. Most designers were excited by the prize money, but others were much more interested in being "discovered". They knew every fashion and bridal magazine in the country would have a presence at the judging, and television time was a given bonus, win or lose. Having their creations displayed in a Ripley odditorium at a future date, was icing on the cake.

Over the years with the help of the company seamstress Olga Irizarry, I dressed several Ripley ladies in our dresses for photo shoots. We even had our own televised fashion show (during "Florida Fashion Week"), that included toilet paper wedding dresses, as well as other garments made from paper, soda tins, gum wrappers, and candies! As escort to the women, I wore a tuxedo worn by Larry Hagman on the television show **"Dallas"**. I was never successful, however, in tempting a woman to actually wear a toilet paper dress to their own wedding.

66

One that got Away #8 - Pass the Cake

People in England, and Canada too, use "fruit cake" as wedding cake. A lot of people don't like fruit cake and I suspect a lot of cake gets wasted — thrown away the second the happy couple isn't looking. Americans use any regular cake, typically something the bride really likes, but in so-doing they miss out on a wonderfully quaint British tradition, the custom of keeping a piece of wedding cake, sometimes for years! Single guests at the wedding are expected to put the piece of cake they have been given as a "favor" under their pillow that night, and dream of a future husband. The newlyweds put any leftover cake in their freezer, and keep it there until they have their first child. The cake is then eaten at that child's baptism.

I'm not making this up. Until relatively recently I had a piece of cake from my mother's second wedding in my freezer, a piece of my elder sister's cake, who has now been married more than forty years, and it was only two years ago when my mother-in law moved into an assisted living facility that she parted with a piece of my then thirty-nine-year old wedding cake. For those who may now be gagging, or at least asking "How in God's name?", I should elucidate: English fruit cake has about a gallon of rum or brandy in it. The cake is "pickled", and technically will last forever. I personally wouldn't eat a forty-year old piece of cake, and I will eat just about anything, but at least in theory, you can. Of course it will help if you like fruit cake in the first place, which I must confess, I don't.

I have never attended a royal wedding, or for that matter even been invited to one, but, I have acquired a fair number of pieces of royal wedding cake, most notably from Queen Elizabeth and Prince Phillip, Lady Diana & Prince Charles, Prince Charles and Camilla Parker Bowles, William and Kate, and most recently Harry and Meghan. Strange as it may seem there is a market for these pieces of cake, and they come up for sale at auctions quite often. Prices typically are in the $1,000 to $5,000 range, but every now and then, they go higher.

The first piece of wedding cake I tried to buy — spoiler alert, it got away — belonged to the Duke and Duchess of Windsor — the former King Edward VIII who abdicated the throne of England in order to marry the love of his life, American divorcee, Mrs. Wallis Simpson. The cake, along with 3,310 other lots — an astounding 40,000+ individual pieces — were auctioned by Sotheby's of New York on September 11, 1997 in session number one of an eighteen session, nine days, sale of the century.

I was only really interested in three lots, a set of children's jacks used by the Duke and Duchess on the Edward R. Murrow **"Person to Person"** television show on September 28, 1956, inside an inscribed silver presentation box, a set of audio tapes of the Duke's live broadcast on a Ripley radio show dating from 1942 (imagine that: Ripley's didn't have a copy, but the Duke of Windsor did!); and a sixty-one-year old piece of the couple's wedding cake.

I was well known to Sotheby's having recently bought numerous items (read, spent a lot of money) in a couple previous auctions, and they alerted the press that I would be amongst the hoi-polloi attending the opening session of this monumental auction. CNN actually had a stage set up in the streets to do interviews, and our publicist made sure I was on their list.

It was a very weird scenario. The elevated stage was literally blocking traffic in the middle of the street. It looked a little like a boxing ring, and there was a "step and repeat" Sotheby's-CNN branded backdrop so that they could snap a still picture of you in case they decided to use a voice over instead of a video clip of the sit-down interview. I greatly amused them by saying my primary interest was in the wedding cake. They had to scramble to even know what I was talking about. Of all the things to want, why would anyone want a sixty-one-year old, two-inch square piece of cake? It was listed for $500-$1,000. I told them I was prepared to go much higher than that, and I did.

I bid the astronomical amount of $25,000 — and it wasn't enough! I was the under-bidder, the cake sold for $26,000, or $29,900 with taxes and commissions all

426

in.

The buyer was a young Japanese man, probably no more than twenty-five years old. He was inundated by the press, but spoke no English. He and his fiancé were featured the next day on **Good Morning America,** but even with an arranged translator, they didn't say enough for anyone to get a story. I got no idea where the money was coming from, or if there was a back story as to why they bought it. All I understood was that they were in love.

Enter the under-bidder to the rescue. I didn't get the cake, but I did get the majority of the press, including a round two with CNN and a mention in **People Magazine.** I politely answered all their questions regarding the cake, but as much as possible steered them to the two other items we did get — the jacks and the audio tapes. It was kind of like not getting my cake, but still getting to eat it.

The nine-day auction, the longest I have ever heard of, netted Sotheby's a reported twenty-three million dollars. Enough to buy a few bakeries, even in New York City.

67

Baby You Can Drive My Car
The Peel P-50 & the Peel Trident

I am not sure how I first learned about Peel cars. Someone may have seen the episode of "**Top Gear**" the BBC's high rated car show (circa 2002), and subsequently told me about seeing them there, but I have a feeling I already knew about them — somehow — long before that. Perhaps, my British friend John Turner knew about them having lived near the Isle of Man where they were originally made? It matters little in the long run, but the point I want to make is that some-how, I discovered them, rather than them discovering me. From the beginning, our relationship was strained because they believed they were bigger than Ripley's, and much bigger than I perceived them. The "**Top Gear**" episode was in fact brilliant, but hardly seen in America, and not something I needed to advertise to promote the cars "our way".

There are less than thirty vintage original Peel cars in existence. They are the smallest ever manufactured car in the world, and were made on England's Isle of Man in 1963. I am sure no one ever foresaw them being driven on "real" roads any-where else. They are flimsy to say the least, and more like big toys than real cars. The originals have no reverse gear, no turn signals, no mirrors, and no windshield wipers. They also had little ventilation and no air conditioning — which the second and third generation versions still don't have.

There are two styles, a one-seater Peel P-50, and a two-seater, Peel Trident. The Trident features a plexiglass dome, and looks like a flying saucer from the 1960s children's cartoon show, **The Jetson's.** Both weigh less than 200 lbs., and measure less than six feet long. They both have only three wheels, two in the front and one in the back, and are not what most people would call stable. They come in three colors white, bright red, and dark blue. All but one of the Ripley's started as red.

Ripley's acquired film footage of 1963 cars being driven around the Isle of Man, but all her cars are replicas made in the 21st century. The big difference being they are battery powered and not gas engines. This was a plus, they couldn't go as fast, but they could be driven indoor, including in building elevators. The first eight Ripley's ordered were made by hand in a London vicinity private garage. After selling a handful of these to Ripley's and other collectors, the newly formed company was eventually able to build a proper small plant, increasing production, and decreasing the wait time for delivery. Ripley's first order was for two, then six more, then six more, then four more — eighteen in total over a five-year period.

We learned the hard way, that though "legal" as delivered in England, they were not deemed road worthy in America, and we wanted to drive them. Our thoughts were they were good exhibits, but would be even better moving advertisements. We initially got around the problem by only driving them in driveways, parking lots, and on beach boardwalks. For our second order of six, we ordered several bare minimum improvements to make them road worthy. For our last order of four we changed them quite dramatically — new suspension, better tires, seat belts, bigger motors, and improved ventilation (but still not sufficient!).

The cars simply are not safe — they shake like a willow tree even at twenty-five mph — and they are just too darn hot inside to stay in them for more than a couple minutes. They are great attention getters though, and on two occasions Erik, "The Lizard Man", Sprague pulled me in Peel Cars using cords attached to his ears in front of large audiences to great applause. We also shot a film with four different cars and drivers inside our offices that was huge media hit. When Todd Day added sound and special effects to it, it could have passed for lost footage straight out of Charlie Chaplin, The Keystone Cops, or Buster Keaton.

One of the first things we did once our cars were legal, was to film me driving one on Orlando's busy streets. I already had experience driving them in parking lots and indoors, and for short distances on New York City's 42nd Street and around London's Piccadilly Circus, but this was to be a real test. It was the scariest thing I ever did.

The distance traveled was less than five-miles, from Ripley's office, to Ripley's Orlando odditorium, but I had to traverse three roads, make two right turns, and one big major intersection left turn. The longest stretch of road was a major artery with a fifty-mph speed limit. I was driving a P-50 with a reported top speed of 30 mph; I only hit twenty-eight mph when the car felt like it was going to blow up.

For the trip, I had a car in front of me, and a car directly behind me, both filming the entire trip. A television station helicopter followed me from above. Every passing car scared me, getting way to close to me to get a look, and more often than not, a photo. They had no way of knowing I couldn't go any faster to get out of their way and that any turbulence they caused pushed my car closer to the curb. A large truck almost blew me right off the highway, and when he realized I was in danger he pulled away at such high speed that he sucked me into his vortex which scared me even more.

By the time I arrived at the odditorium twenty-three minutes, later I was soaked right through. The temperature inside the car was approaching 120 degrees Fahrenheit. At the odditorium I drove right into the building before getting out and letting a large newscaster get in. The cars are advertised to hold 300 lbs. and a person up to six-foot-six-inches in height. He was a supreme test for both restrictions. Getting him in was difficult, but funny -think overstuffed circus clown car. He drove around the parking lot, and luckily managed not to tip over, though most of those present couldn't watch expecting it to flip at any second. Getting him out — now soaked and smelly — proved him to be a real trooper, but the station rightly cut the scene out of the aired segment.

For the next two weeks of my life virtually everyone I met told me they had seen the segment which had been aired three different times. They called me crazy, and they didn't even know how scared I had been! Angela Johnson is the only other person who has driven a Peel car on a major road (see Chapter 20), but no one else has ever driven one on a freeway, and most of the driving from that day forward has been indoors at conventions.

68

Cruisin' With Art Cars

I define an art car as an ornately decorated car that still can be driven. California and Texas are the meccas for art cars and their artist owners, but they turn up just about anywhere if you keep your eyes open. The two most famous art car artists are probably Larry Fuente and Harrod Blank. Both started in the San Francisco Bay area. The most famous art car parade, where art car artists from all over the country congregate once a year, is in Houston, Texas. I bought one car made by Harrod, drove around in one other, and I bought four that were featured in Houston parades.

Larry Fuente of Mendocino, California didn't need me or Ripley's, by the time I found him, but his work was the first significant art I purchased back in the mid-1980s, and I would credit him to awakening me to a definition of "art" that was unbelievable, and more than just a hobby. Maybe not "fine art", but certainly "professional".

Larry was one of the first "art car" artists, people who decorate working cars, that I ever heard of. He had two, one was a Camaro, with headlights that looked like eyes, the other a vintage Cadillac with pink flamingos for fins. Both were covered with beads, glass shards, and toys, in a rainbow of colors. I wanted the Cadillac, but was pretty sure it was not for sale. The Camaro was a distant second choice, and would be replaced on my shopping list by several pieces when Ian Illjas, our then San Francisco odditorium manager, and I went to meet Larry in person.

I asked Ian to book a hotel. I was unaware of the "trendiness" of Mendocino, California — all I really knew about the place was that it was where the San Francisco hippies all went to following Altamonte, and the end of the "summer of love" era. I had no idea it was a wine and food mecca. I couldn't fathom why Ian came back with exorbitant price quotes. He assured me that there was nothing cheap in that town, and the prices he got were as low as possible. I was cheap, and never liked to spend much on hotels (I still don't, give me a nice meal over a nice room anytime), so I said "at that price, then, let's share a room. It will only be for one night".

The car ride from San Francisco north to Mendocino should take about two hours, but we didn't get on the road until late, then got caught in Bay Bridge traffic, and almost immediately once on the other side, lost in fog. The further north we went, and the closer to the coast we were, the thicker the fog. We never saw an inch of the fabled coast-line, and it took us nearly five hours to get to our destination. We checked into what would now be called a "boutique motel" cloaked in fog and late-night darkness. We couldn't see a thing.

Upon opening the room door, we were bedazzled. A fire was roaring, classical music was playing, and decanted wine was on a table ready for drinking. Only one problem. There was only one bed, a beautiful king-sized four-poster with muslin drapery. Clearly the reservation desk had assumed Ian and I were a couple. I slept on the couch. No harm, no foul, just a lot of laughs. It was probably the nicest hotel room I ever stayed in.

The next morning, when we opened the drapes we discovered one more reason the room was so expensive. The motel was cantilevered off the side of a cliff, the ocean was about 200 feet straight below us. The view was incredible.

Larry lived like a hermit in the woods, a couple of miles outside of town. The town was aware of him, and secretly revered him as a local hero, but on the surface were scared of him. In addition to the two cars, he showed us a full-sized horse; a pig; a sailfish done in the same style as the cars; a football field sized depiction of the city of San Francisco made out of silver colored toasters he was currently working on; and a working "Cow-a-saki" motorcycle, an actual Kawasaki motorcycle covered in a cow skin and head, which he regularly rode along the cliffs and the beach. Like the Cadillac, unfortunately, it wasn't for sale. We ended up buying just the horse. The fish, called "Big Game Fish", because it is made entirely of board game pieces, including dominoes, scrabble tiles, dice and chess men, now hangs in the Smithsonian. Pictures of both cars circulated for years, but I have no idea where they are today. The Cadillac is still my all-time favorite art car.

I first met Harrod Blank at a film festival in Toronto where he was debuting his film **"Wild Wheels"** — the story of how, and why, he first decorated his Volkswagen, **OMG Car** (1), and subsequently became infatuated with other people that decorated their vehicles (2). The film went on to do very well on the documentary film festival circuit, and spawned three books and a second film. Any art car worth mentioning is featured in Harrods's films and books, and his word is the gospel on the subject. At the time he may have only had one vehicle, but he soon had three. He drove all over the world in his second one, a van covered in cameras. Many of the cameras, which were donated to him, actually worked, and he filmed remotely from inside the van.

My family had the opportunity to ride with Harrod and his team, all around Winter Park, Florida, inside the vehicle to see how he operated. It was a magnet. No matter where he drove, the van caused traffic jams, and anywhere he parked it he became the focus of attention, all while he secretly documented the reactions of onlookers from inside the vehicle.

By the time I bought Harrod's third car, another Volkswagen, called **"Pico De Gallo"**, covered in playable musical instruments, an instant party on wheels, I had bought several other decorated cars, including a limo covered in glass marbles, and had been introduced to Rebecca Bass, the Queen of the Houston art car scene.

From Rebecca I acquired two different cars, one called **The Ungrateful Dead** in honor of the Grateful Dead rock band, and one called **Strawberry Fields**, in honor of the Beatles. Both cars were designed by Rebecca, a school teacher, but made by her students. Both cars were "best of show" winners in Houston annual art car parades. The cars were both large, long Buicks, and covered with jewels and beads like Mardi Gras floats. One had several depictions of famous musicians (mainly deceased), the other had imagery pertaining to specific Beatles songs. Both were amazing pieces of art. Crawling at about five mph, and getting about 5 miles per gallon of gas, I drove my daughter Celeste, and a group of students, in the Winter Park High school Homecoming parade inside the **Ungrateful Dead** car. It was much more fun than driving the Peel car in heavy traffic.

One of the very last exhibits I acquired before I retired in May of 2018, was an art motorbike that Harrod had made me aware of nearly thirty years earlier. I discovered it in a car museum in Branson, Missouri where I was shopping for a 1960s TV show Batmobile (not bought). It is only about three-feet wide and five-feet long, but ten-feet high. It is bright red, sexy, and very feminine. It can fit two people, but is probably best driven solo. I posed a Marilyn Monroe look-a like in it for the Ripley web page, but never got to drive in it. Believe it or not, it is a motorized three-wheeled stiletto high heel shoe! Ideal for anyone — male or female — with a foot fetish.

69

Sometimes Even Gold Doesn't Glitter

One of the most expensive items and most glamorous, in the Ripley collection, is an English Austin Mini Cooper, covered in one-million Swarovski crystals, called **"The American Dream"**. The crystals that cover every inch of its exterior are arranged to form ten different scenes of Americana: an eagle, a flag, Mt. Rushmore, the Capitol Building, the iconic Hollywood sign, etcetera. Each crystal on average, cost about a dollar-fifty. I first heard about it from the Atlantic City Ripley's odditorium manager Chris Connelly. The car was on display in a neighboring casino that had it on loan for a few months, but would be giving it back to its creators and owners in a few weeks. Chris re-ported that the owners didn't want to move it back to Canada, and were hoping to sell it. Was I interested? Yes I was.

As it turned out, I knew the creators, Ken and Annie Burkitt, a British couple living in Niagara Falls, Canada. In the 1970s-1980s they sold Ripley's three coin covered cars, two Minis and a MG sports car. The coins on these cars were gold plated, and the cars were very popular museum lobby exhibits [1]. The crystal mini was in a whole different league; it made the gold coin cars look downright dull. All that glitters is not just gold.

At the time of our purchase we were building a museum in London and the Burkitts were wanting to make another crystal car, to be covered in iconic English imagery like the Queen, Princess Di, the Tower of London, Westminster Cathedral etc. I wanted to buy both, but Bob Masterson was too nervous the second wouldn't be completed in time, so we bought the "American Dream", and never mentioned the other one to our London franchise partners.

Before we would ship it out of Florida, to London, however, we had a use for it in Orlando. It would be the feature attraction at Bob's 2008 IAAPA inauguration (see Chapter 22). Mounted on a giant rotating stand custom made just for it, we would place it at the entrance to the auditorium where the function was to be held. No one coming in the door could miss it, in fact they might be blinded by it when the spotlights were added.

The auditorium dining hall was a long way from the building's loading docks. Even though it would easily fit in the Convention Center's hallways, we were not allowed to drive it indoors; we had to use a freight elevator, and push it the rest of the way through a narrow back tunnel-like hallway. Touching the car anywhere was difficult, the crystals are sharp, and pop off pretty easily. Getting the car to the entrance took several people more than an hour. Once at the door we were faced with the near impossibility of getting it through the entrance way. I was as nervous as a moose, which is twice as nervous as a goose, I steered while a team pushed. There was less than an inch to spare on each side. We lost a couple crystals, but our conservator, Bruce Miller, had time to replace them before the lights went down, then on again. The car looked like a giant disco ball under the spotlights. The only thing brighter was the smiles on mine and producer Steve Glum's faces.

Several hours later at 1 am, after a very successful event, it was time to pack up all of the exhibits we had displayed, and leave the room empty as if we had never been there. Ideally, we would have loved to have done the breakdown the next morning, but we didn't have that luxury. It was after 2 am when we moved the car, but at this hour the security staff was almost non-existent. There was no one to stop us from driving it the length of the building, once through the narrow doorway. I told everyone to close their eyes and proceeded to drive it clean through the first time, no pushing, no grimacing, no lost stones. I certainly couldn't do it a second time for all the gold in Tot's tomb.

One of our London franchise partners was Alec Rigby the former CEO and owner of Ripley's (1963-1985). He had never completely disappeared from our lives, but in 2007 he had come back into it with a bang, picking both the New York and London locations, and being a minority partner in the franchises. Alec understood what a "lobby exhibit" was — something that was worthy of advertising, and one of the best things in the whole museum,

436

which could be placed in the lobby, and used as a "come-along" or "loss-leader" to attract passersby. He wanted to put the car in the London lobby. When the designers told him it wouldn't fit, he said break down the wall and place half the car in the lobby, and half in the next room. If it could have been done, it would have been a very good display, but no one thought it could be done. The wall was load-bearing. If the car was to be used, it was going to have to be on a different floor of the museum. All of the museum except the lobby was accessed through a standard elevator. Under no circumstances could the car fit in the elevator, not even if stood up on its back bumper (God forbid, but this was actually suggested).

If Alec couldn't have it in the lobby, he wanted to at least use it in an unforgettable promotion. Under the direction of Ripley's senior project manager, David Hill, the car would be airlifted by crane more than five stories high above London's famous Piccadilly Square, and dropped through a newly carved out section of the roof into a fifth-floor gallery. David did the job bright and early one cold winter morning, and got world-wide press, to my knowledge the only on- air appearance of this otherwise "shy" worker-bee. Alec was more than happy. It wasn't as outlandish a stunt as his trying to buy the Battlefield of Hastings back in 1972, when the Blackpool Odditorium opened, but it certainly got London's attention. A new kid was definitely in town.

Truth is, the car was not a big deal on the fifth floor, the ceiling was too high, so the lighting wasn't ideal, and there were too many big colorful items up there already, including a giant animated T-rex, competing with it. The car had to be set back from the railings to avoid vandalism, and looked quite lost in the unglamorous "warehouse" gallery environment. It only stayed there a couple years, and was replaced by a red knitted Ferrari that could be assembled and disassembled after being loaded in the elevator.

The crystal car then went to the lobby of Baltimore. It looked good there, but was seriously abused and lost lots of crystals. After a couple years in the warehouse, and a much-needed restoration, it was moved to Gatlinburg, Tennessee.

Postscript:

One time during a warehouse-sales pitch tour to a group of prospective partners for a museum in Dubai, I proudly showed off the crystal car as the crown jewel in our collection. One of the gentlemen said nonchalantly: "Nice, but my brother has one just like it, but his is covered in real diamonds." It's a good thing I didn't buy the Burkett's second car.

The last big item I purchased from the Burkett's was a London double-decker bus completely covered in gold-plated English big pennies, some dating back to the 1870s, and worth some money on their own, even without the gold. This had been Ken's "goose that laid the golden egg". For years he had used it as a mobile bill-board, driving it around Niagara Falls, Canada, and charging people for a ride, and charging local businesses to advertise on its sides and interior. I first heard about it when a town just outside of Toronto had a charity fund raiser, in which, for a couple bucks, people were to guess the number of coins on the vehicle to win a trip to England. The answer was in excess of 60,000.

About ten years later, by a strange twist of fate, my mother and step-father mentioned it to me. They had seen a strange gold colored bus parked in a farmer's field a few miles outside their small town of Cobourg, Ontario. They had not gotten close to it, and couldn't tell it was gold coins, but said the gold was blinding in the summer sun. They thought I would be interested. The next time I was In Canada I went looking for it. Yes, it was still outside in a field! I recognized it instantly as the handiwork of Ken and Annie Burkitt.

Turns out the farmer rented his barn in the winter to the Burkitts to store it, but in the summer when he needed the space, the bus was pulled outside to pasture for the summer. It could be clearly seen from the highway on a clear summer day, and was a sight to behold. I wasn't bold enough to walk up to the front door of the farmhouse and inquire, but having contact info for the Burkitts in my trusty black book, I called Ken. Yes, he and Annie had made it, and yes, he still owned it, and yes, it was for sale. The bus itself was made in 1961, in England. The coins had been installed in the mid-

1970s. It was now fifty-five years old and not in the best condition. In fact, upon close inspection, undetectable from ground level, there were very few coins on the roof, the bus having hit the bottom of an overpass bridge getting from Niagara Falls to Cobourg (a distance of about 150 miles).

Another year would go by before I could convince Bob Masterson it was worth buying. We were about to open the Great Wolf Lodge in Niagara Falls. What if, we drove passengers back and forth from our Clifton Hill attractions (a Ripley Odditorium, A Tussaud's Wax Museum, a Moving Theater and a Guinness World Records franchise), a few miles up the Niagara River to the lodge where it could stay parked overnight? It was a good idea. I bought the bus, but the idea for its use never panned out, in fact the bus became an albatross around my neck for the rest of my career.

The purchase of the bus was made while sitting on a giant tree stump in the middle of the field. The bus was operable, but I would have to find a capable licensed driver to move it off the property, and it would have to have its lights repaired, and new license plates purchased, before it could be driven anywhere. Not insurmountable problems, but not cheap, and not easy either. We decided to have it towed to Niagara Falls, where Ken could oversee maintenance repairs, as well as work on the main areas devoid of coins. The roof was not a major concern since no one could see it. Ken found a mechanic that could work on it, and a place to store it, but weeks, turned into months, and the summer season was missed. We now had to face a winter where the bus would have to be stored outside. Shining the bus up would now become a new very big job. We ended up missing another full summer season, and now Bob was on the verge of retiring. His predecessor had no interest in the bus, except to decrease the rent we had now been paying on it for nearly three years. One month in Niagara, cost more than one year in the barn in Cobourg.

We considered sending it by boat to Orlando via the St. Lawrence Seaway. We also looked into sending it by train, but ultimately decided that to drive it the entire way was the most economical way. Ken found us the very lovable, congenial, Harvey Gordon who not only had driven the bus around Niagara thirty-five years earli-

439

er, apparently, he had already driven it once to Florida (and back), something I was unaware of. He predicted top speed would be forty mph, and told us that because of this, and the buses' twenty-eight-foot height, he would have to travel by back roads. The bus was too tall for many interstate overpasses — something we already surmised based on our "near-naked roof". We had to buy him a "special" trucker's GPS system that would list the usable roads.

It took Harvey nearly two weeks to get the bus to our museum in St. Augustine. He got several citations along the way, and lost a bunch more coins, no doubt some to vandals when he slept nights in the bus parked in Walmart parking lots. I had not seen it for three years, and barely recognized it. I literally cried. The interior was now disgusting (vermin had been living in at some point), and hundreds if not thousands of coins were missing. I lost any hope of actually using it as a means of transport (St. Augustine was another town where we had three attractions spread out around town that we thought driving the bus back and forth between them would be a good money-maker). I wasn't even sure we wanted to park it where people could see it — at least not until some extensive work had been done on it. We put it in the museum parking lot for a couple weeks, but coins continued to disappear. It was soon decided to move it to one of our lesser visited properties, a pioneer Sugar Mill north of town. A year later we were forced to hire Harvey again to move it to a storage facility in Orlando.

The plan was to get the Burkitt's to spend a winter in Florida reap-plying as many coins as we could procure. I bought several pounds worth in England, and paid a fair bit to have them gold-plated in New Jersey. The most I could find would still not be enough to redo the entire bus; the roof would still most likely have to be unfinished, meaning we could only display the bus where no one could see the top. I thought the Burkitt's were unreasonable with their repair estimates, and delayed the repair another season, during which time Ken died.

Annie was sure she could repair it without Ken, with the assistance of her two sons, but I wasn't so sure. Her price would now be even higher. I would have to lodge three people all winter, and transportation costs would be tripled by bringing both the sons from other locales (neither lived in Niagara Falls). No one else in the office thought it would be money well spent, and eventually I gave up trying to make a deal work. The bus became my biggest ever white elephant.

Ten years have now gone by, and the bus is still not show worthy. Out of sight, out of mind. Harvey is the only one who still cares. For several years he would unexpectedly drop into my office one day in late December/early January; having retired, he vacationed each winter in Florida. We would reminisce about the bus, and the Burkitt's, and he would let me know, he loved driving "the old girl" and would be happy to move it again, anywhere in North America, if we ever decided on a place it could be displayed. I don't regret having bought it, but it was a case of my vision not jarring with anyone else's. It haunts me, and I once in a while see it in dreams, gleaming in a field near Cobourg.

70

The Ripley Art Gallery

A lot of what I bought, especially in the last ten years, I would call "art". This evolved from the growth of foreign odditoriums which demanded less reading of English cartoons, and in turn the need for more exhibits that could be hung on the walls in their place (1). The art wasn't always "beautiful", but I always aimed for "compelling" — something that stirred an instant emotional response. The majority of the items were bought more because of what they were made of than the aesthetics of the finished piece. Many could be described as "folk art", but for some people that conjures images of amateurish quality. Some pieces like a train made from soup tins, were indeed amateurish, but the lion's share of my acquisitions, whether it was an item made from matchsticks, coffee beans, car parts, or gum wrappers, etcetera, were of high quality, and the works of exceptional mind blowing talents.

Over the years, I often told artists, I couldn't make them rich, but I could possibly make them famous. I can honestly say I "discovered" several unknown talents, and raised their profiles from obscure to at least, "I can no longer afford them". In this chapter I will discuss a few random choice pieces bought before 2000, and then in part two, concentrate on the works of a group of Florida artists from whom I bought several pieces, and definitely had a positive effect on their futures.

One of my "early" favorite art pieces was a thirty-foot by twenty-six-foot mural of Vincent Van Gogh made by Cornelius Bierens, constructed of postcards of Van Gogh paintings (2). Other favorites were "paintings" made of burnt toast, and portraits made from laundry lint.

Our first toast art pieces came from Japan, and were depictions created by Tadahiko Ogawa, of old masters like Da Vinci, Rembrandt and Botticelli. Inspired by Ogawa, we later found a toast art artist in Northern England that did works based on famous Spanish paintings, and a huge portrait of Einstein. Still later, we found a third toast art artist, a Mexican artist, who also preferred replicating religious works of Spanish origin. All three of these artists were discovered via newspaper articles, Ogawa, believe it or not, from the infamous scandal rag **The National Enquirer.**

Likewise, the first lint artist, Slater Barron of Newport, California, came to Ripley's via the Enquirer, and years later we bought "lint art" from three other people that were all inspired by works of hers they saw in a Ripley odditorium. From Slater we bought several portraits of English royalty she already had, but also commissioned pieces of the King of Thailand, Chin Shih Huang Ti, the ancient emperor who unified China and built the Great Wall, and even a life-sized John Wayne.

Robert Ripley acquired only a handful of two-dimensional wall art pieces of art in his time, and they tended to be oil paintings. From the beginning, however, he did have an eye for unusual statuary. Two of the very finest exhibits in the original Ripley collection are fine art wood carvings, the Japanese **Hananuma Masakichi** self-portrait, and the French **The Devil and the Damsel** (see Chapter 77). I started buying three dimensional sculptures in the 1980s, but it would be years before I got anything worthy of being mentioned alongside those two masterpieces. In fact, much of the sculpture I bought was, comparatively speaking, "junk" — literally.

I was buying art made from recycled materials, long before anyone called it that. Leo Sewell of Philadelphia, may have been the first "junk artist" in America. He made life-sized animals, including ducks, dogs, donkeys, and elephants from discarded "found" broken toys, collected from the streets and garbage cans of his neighborhood. I estimate I bought more than thirty of his figures. At one time every Ripley's had a couple in its lobby. I also bought life-sized human figures made by Anton Schiavone of Pittsburgh, from A&P used brown grocery bags. He did everything from a self-portrait, to a cow-boy, to Michelangelo's **Pieta**. These were a little "rough", but the fact that his whole neighborhood collected the bags he used, all from one store, made his artwork a great Believe It or Not! story (3).

By the mid-1990s I had started to acquire "big" sculptures, animals and dinosaurs made from car parts. My first dinosaur was a skeletal Allosaurus by Jim Garry. I was so taken by one of his works I saw from my car while driving through the suburbs of Washington, DC, that I went to the front door of the home and asked the owner who made it. To my surprise it was made by Garry, an artist that Ripley's had featured in its cartoon, and on a television show ten years earlier. I only bought two pieces of Garry's, but I wished I had of bought twenty. He made a Diplodocus that was over seventy-feet long! Simply amazing.

My next dinosaurs, plus a horse, and a gorilla, were made of chrome car bumpers. They are very different than Garry's work, full bodied rather than skeletal, but on the same humungous full-size scale. The three dinosaurs, a Triceratops, a Stegosaurus and a Tyrannosaurus rex are called Chromosaurs. Only the gorilla will fit indoors, the other four sculptures are all displayed outside.

By the 2000s, I had started to frequent art festivals as likely sources for Ripley exhibitory. Florida in the "winter" (November through April) has one of these somewhere virtually every weekend, including in my home town of Winter Park. In 2008, I met Bill Secunda of Pennsylvania, at the Winter Park juried annual spring festival. Bill's tent had several small sculptures and one life-sized one made entirely of nails. The workmanship was exquisite, but the bulk were too small to excite me. The one large piece was not for Ripley's — a depiction of the crucified Christ on the cross (4), but it sure caught my attention. We talked and I told him I was most interested in "large" pieces. He told me he had a full-sized moose, but it was not yet for sale; it was on hold for a big art show later in the year in Grand Rapids, Michigan. He encouraged me to come see that festival, which was being touted as the largest, and most moneyed prize art festival in the country. I am not sure why I didn't go the first year, but I went for the next consecutive eight. Secunda won a top ten prize that year with his moose, and I subsequently over the next couple years bought it as well as an elk, a buffalo, and a couple of bears.

Artprize, a three-week long annual festival in Michigan, attracts quality artists from all over the country, because of its prize money initially $1 million, but now down to $400,000 — and its wonderful citywide involvement. It is perfectly run and offers every genre of art in every possible kind of venue, from pizzerias, to churches, to parking lots. I did not attend in its first year, but still bought three of its money winners, and in the next eight years bought an average of ten pieces per year. In 2017, I only bought one sculpture, but should have bought at least a dozen others.

The festival is literally one-stop shopping, even though I hazard to guess that when it began it was not meant to be a sale, but only a show. Over time, and I think Ripley's (Angela Johnson and I), were prime reasons, artists were just as interested in selling to us as they were in the prize money. After the third year, artists, who worked with recycled objects, knew they had more of a chance at getting my money than they did winning the prize money, which typically went to more conventional art. Each year I did radio, television and print interviews, and by the fifth or sixth year, voters were listening to my "choices", and artists were contacting me to make sure I saw their entries.

In addition to Bill Secunda there were several artists who I would end up buying their entries from every year, plus additional pieces of their work not displayed at Artprize. Justin la Doux's whimsical metal animal sculptures were perennial favorites, as were the air-soft BBs portraits of John O'Hearn, both local Michigan artists.

A total list of the pieces acquired at Artprize would take several pages to record, but the following are a few of the most noteworthy:

    -a full size rhinoceros made from wine corks (each representing a bottle drunk by two neighbors)

    -two murals made of sequins: "Glitter Girl" and a clown fish

    -four different car-size birds of prey made from cutlery

    -portraits made from colored push pins

    -four sculptures made from musical instruments

-a half dozen fantasy rocket ships made from 1950s vacuum cleaners

-a pointillism Pieta, and a David portrait created with thousands of minuscule black dots...and

-Paul Baliker's second year entry, a thirteen-feet in circumference driftwood sculpture called "**A Matter of Time**".

A Matter of Time was the third-place winner in 2009, a prize worth$250,000, but the artist was robbed. It deserved first place, and in my humble opinion, was either the first, or second, best piece of the more than fifteen thousand entries I would view at Artprize over eight years (4). In the mind of the artist, it was unfairly penalized because someone stole a piece of the sculpture before the judges had viewed it.

It was a couple years later before I bought Baliker's masterpiece, and in the interim, using driftwood found on his beach property near Cedar Key, Florida, he made a slightly smaller, but very similar piece, called **Ocean's 11ᵗʰ Hour. A Matter of Time** shows "Father Time" holding a globe, and forty-four different animals on the brink of extinction. In structure it resembles the face of a giant clock, with a bald eagle sitting at high noon. **Ocean's 11ᵗʰ Hour** shows the same "old man time" holding an hour glass with twenty-two sea creatures facing the same unsure future. Bought basically two for the price of one, they were the most expensive non-auction purchases of my career.

Elsewhere (see Chapter 24) I mentioned the acquisition of two, twenty-two foot tall car parts robots bought in Thailand. These proved to be immensely popular as photo ops in the "selfie" era and led to the purchase of a couple of dozen other eight-foot and twelve-foot tall, similar robots. When they grew out of fashion, the Thais turned to **Marvel** Super heroes, and **Star Wars** figures. Combined, these three categories of statuary are the largest single medium art form in the Ripley collection. They are also the most popular, regardless whether they are displayed in Africa, Asia, Europe, North America, or the Middle East.

Of the dozens of metal statues I acquired, there is one hands down favorite. I love dinosaurs, in all forms: real skeletons, wood carvings, paintings, car tire, chrome and car parts, whatever, but John Lopez's farm implement and tractor parts T-Rex is in a class by itself. Modeled after the most famous T-rex of all, Sue, that was found near his home town in South Dakota, it is scarily real looking with its huge six-inch teeth, ten-foot high elevated tail, and piercing eyes. Amongst the tractor parts, there are actual tools that were used by paleontologist Pete Larson to excavate Sue.

I bought this T-rex in 2014 on a life changing road trip through Montana, Wyoming and South Dakota. I viewed about a dozen of John's sculptures, located throughout towns in South Dakota, and would have bought any of them if I hadn't seen the T-rex, which wasn't even finished at the time. A welder before he was an artist, John's horses, his bison, and his Texas long horn steer, named "Maverick", are preeminent pieces of Western "cowboy" art, and would be show stoppers in any museum in the world. The man deserves to be ranked amongst the elite of American artists. It is very safe to say I can no longer afford him.

Part Two: The Florida Art Scene

Central Florida has a large, vibrant art scene in proportion to its medium-sized population. At least nine different artists, in addition to Paul Baliker, are very noteworthy in my buying history. Of these nine, all but one was the source of at least two pieces in the Ripley collection, and one family far and away is responsible for more exhibits in the collection than any other single source.

Larry Behnke who lived in the forest north of Gainesville, in a house he built himself, was my only one hit wonder. His house was full of his art, mainly abstract paintings, but though his work was good and interesting, there was only one piece that caught my attention, and cried to be bought. Sitting smack in the middle of the main room, on a table, stood a two-foot high giant brown resin thumb. Upon close inspection you can see thousands of whitish slivers inside the resin, and the occasional pink or red sliver. The giant thumb is a lamp, and when the lamp is turned on, you can see the slivers are finger and toe nails! The majority, collected over thirty-five years, belonged to the artist, the colored ones with spots of nail polish, were from his daughter. Many people were totally repulsed by this thumb, but it had a magnetic power; it was impossible not to stare at it and con-template the artist's obvious obsession. I had once been given a paperweight with a few dozen nail clippings, but this thumb has over 10,000 clippings, literally a lifetime's worth.

Eric Shupe is another artist living near Gainesville. He too is located a little off the beaten path. He does have neighbors, but I suspect most probably don't know what he does for a living. Eric collects cutlery, for the most part, nice silverware, not typical restaurant quality tableware. Like Bill Secunda, I discovered Eric at the Winter Park Art Festival, and like Bill it was the quality of his work that initially caught my eye, not the medium he worked in. From a distance his work looked like regular steel, and not until you are up close to them can you tell the butts of the sculptures are made from spoons, and the hair is made from forks. At the festival he displayed human statues, measuring fifteen to twenty-five inches tall. I asked him if he had anything bigger, and he said he had two pieces in his home that were "quite large", one was a half-size rearing horse, and the other was a ten-foot tall mermaid, complete with a real tree stump. He had my attention, and I was very eager to make a road trip north.

Eric's work is definitely "fine art". His understanding of the human form rivals Rodin or Remington in perfection and beauty but I am not sure he will ever have the time, or inclination, to make another large piece, as he has enough orders for his small sculptures to keep him busy for years. Since I bought the horse and the mermaid, he has won several major show awards, including prizes at Miami's world-famous Art Basel contest. The Ripley horse is on display in Niagara Falls, the mermaid is a landmark key piece in Amsterdam.

Reese Moore and his two adult sons, Chris and Jesse, of Blue Springs, Florida, were a family I discovered a little closer to town, but who were still "rural" artists. I first saw their art on Reese's front lawn on a back road going towards a state park to see manatees. I did a serious double-take, thinking I was looking at a dinosaur skeleton garden ornament. Reese and his sons make fantastical dinosaurs, and motorcycles, out of cow bones, turtle shells, and gator skulls: quintessential rural Florida materials.

I bought the garden dinosaur, a six-foot tall, ten-foot long "moo-a-saurus", part T-rex, part Allosaurus, part Gorgosaurus, all cow, gator and deer; there isn't a real dinosaur bone in the entire realistic looking creature. One of the meanest things I ever did was challenge a smart aleck child dinosaur expert to identify my skeleton. He identified all the main dinosaurs it represented, but was confounded with no idea how so many characteristics could be found in one specimen. When I told him, it was a moo-a-saurus he went running to his books, but to no avail. I kept him in suspense for many minutes before I let him in on the secret. He was much more manageable the rest of the tour.

Reese only had a couple dinosaurs when I first discovered him, but a year later he showed up with a flatbed truck with three full-sized animal bone motorcycles at an event I was running in St. Augustine. The wheels were cow vertebrae, the seats, gator heads, the headlights, turtle shells, and the handlebars were cow horns, including one set of "Texas long horns". I bought all three, and later bought two more. Bikers and Goths alike love these bikes, and they do make for wonderful photo ops. With care they will support a full-size adult, and children absolutely love to sit on them.

I never visited Doug Powell in his home, but he lived in a fairly rural area when I first met him. By the time I retired Oviedo was becoming a suburb of Orlando. Doug is a two-trick pony. For the most part, he sticks to portraiture of recognizable celebrities. One of his styles is "pixilation" using computer keys. From a distance you see a clear distinct portrait (and the camera sees it even clearer than your eye), and up close you can tell everything you see is computer keys, white, black, or grey, cleverly arranged to spell out words associated with the portrait. For example, Frankenstein's portrait includes the words: "Boris Karloff", "Mary Shelley", "neck bolts", and "electricity". Typically, each of his portraits has at least a dozen hidden words. I bought several of these, including, Mr. Spock, Steve Jobs, John F. Kennedy, Ben Franklin, Abraham Lincoln, Princess Leia, and the aforementioned

Frankenstein.

Doug's other portraits are made from jigsaw puzzles, not complete puzzles, but random pieces assembled from dozens of puzzles he buys second-hand at church bazaars and garage sales. Doug pours thousands of pieces into a wheel barrel, and then looks for colors that match. None of the pieces interlock, they just look the same color. I think some people miss the uniqueness of these pieces not understanding how many thousands of pieces Doug goes through to make match-ups. In this style I acquired portraits of John Lennon, George Washington, George Burns, Judy Garland (as "Dorothy"), and my favorite, Lucille Ball. The colors are vibrant and eye popping, and every portrait features a well-hidden American flag, Doug's signature touch, in honor of his former career in the Navy.

In Orlando proper, I discovered and followed the growth of four different artists, one found at the Winter Park Art festival, who worked exclusively in wood, and three multi-media artists who found me, rather than vice versa.

Jeff Matter caught my attention at the Winter Park Art festival because his wood sculptures were truly beautiful, and some of them had movement. His largest, most intricate pieces, including working clocks, also had an unbelievable back-story: they were made from a very famous tree, called **The Senator. The Senator** was one of the oldest and largest cypress trees in the USA, until it was tragically burnt down by a careless drug addict. The tree was legendary in Central Florida and had a state park built around it to protect it. Unfortunately, to no avail. Though less than thirty minutes from my home, I regret I never saw it standing. I figured since it had been there for more than 3,000 years, it wasn't going anywhere soon, and, therefore, it could always wait "till next weekend". My mistake.

Jeff was one of a handful of wood sculptors allowed to salvage pieces from the fire with the proviso that they made art from the remnants. Jeff made clocks, and intricate puzzles that I call "whirligigs". Two of his best pieces were titled **"Hypnotic"** and **"Hypnotic Two"**. As museum displays they weren't ideal, as they required manual start-ups and, therefore, a lot of handling, but for visual appeal they were standouts. They are absolutely mesmerizing. Ripley's ended up automating them, but had to sacrifice some aesthetics to do so.

Jeff was an engineer by trade, so he understood motors and moving parts, but he was over sixty years old before he learned woodworking. Even his smallest and simplest pieces now sell for hundreds of dollars. Not bad for a second career.

Wilmer Lam was a college student studying fashion when he first walked into the Ripley office. The first pieces I bought from him were seven two-dimensional portraits of Hollywood celebrities, "painted" with cigarette ashes. Anytime Wilmer had a Ripley-worthy piece he would phone and ask for an appointment to bring it directly to the office, at his expense, with no assurance of a sale. I don't believe I ever turned him away though, and I ended up buying eight, three-dimensional sculptures. His skill, and his humorous sense of whimsy, were perfect for my taste, and Ripley's demands. Pieces bought, all larger than life, included a dog made out of blue denim shirts and pants; a dragon and a cougar made from white plastic cutlery; a wolf made from black licorice, and a woman's evening gown made from red licorice; dresses made out of tea bags, and coffee filters; and a six foot-long velociraptor made from pumpkin seeds, with corn kernel eyes. His understanding of anatomy and physiology, made his figures very lifelike regardless of the medium in use.

Buying exhibits made from food, especially if not framed under glass (but even then, subject to melting under display lights) was risky business. I had some bad experiences with jelly beans in the past, but Wilmer's licorice pieces were just too good to pass on. Ultimately their life span is limited.

Mateo Blanco is larger than life, both physically and metaphorically. He is another artist who found me by walking in off the street with two portraits: John Lennon and Michael Jackson made from dog hair (he would later do a Hendrix dog hair picture too). I'd be lying if I said I like these, but dog hair was a medium I could appreciate for its weirdness factor. Prior to meeting me and Ripley's, Mateo was only a part-time artist, still seeking a muse. He had once been both a

451

well known opera singer and a pop star vocalist in Colombia, South America. In Florida, he had quite a reputation as a singing chef in an upscale Italian restaurant. He once even sang for George H. Bush at the White House. Between 2012 and 2017, he made pieces for Ripley's made out of dog hair, coffee beans, peanuts, cupcake "beads", wool, sugar, pasta, and my favorite, chocolate. I regularly teased him — all 300 lbs. plus of him — that if it was edible, he could make something out of it.

Mateo is a great spokesman both for the Orlando art community, and the Hispanic community. In 2016, we traveled to his home country of Colombia together and he introduced me to marvelous indigenous traditional bead and basket craftsmen, an armless-legless painter who held her brushes in her teeth, and a woman whose late father owned a collection of paintings on pin heads. I bought sixty-seven of her seventy-three pins. Mateo sang to me at dinner every night we were in Colombia, everything from traditional folk songs, to opera, to Beatles classics. It was both a successful trip and a very memorable one.

I purchased at least one thing from Enrico Ramos while I was still living in Canada. He had walked into the odditorium in St. Augustine with a common house fly with twelve human faces painted on it. The paintings were done with a one-haired brush. Enrico specialized in miniature paintings on bugs: beetles, spiders, butterflies and house flies, but also did standard oil paintings of "The Last Supper", Elvis, Marilyn Monroe, and George Washington, in which dozens of related images were hidden in the larger portrait. I first personally met Enrico at a Mexican street festival in Orlando. I was in line to buy a burrito when my eight-year old son Curtis ran up to me, and excitedly pulled me out of line to come see a guy who painted on cockroaches. Enrico spoke no English, but I knew it had to be the same guy, there couldn't be two people in Florida who painted on bugs!

Enrico actually lived in Oaxaca, Mexico, but he had three sons that lived in Orlando, and so visited regularly. Over the years I bought a lot of things from him and his three sons, but for my money, his son Christiain is even more talented than the father. He

too paints on butterflies — wonderful, colorful reproductions of old masters but he also works with toothpaste, nail polish, seeds and beans, Cheetos, and especially candies: licorice, peppermints, jellies and
M&Ms. Even better than his "paintings", however, are
his three-dimensional full-size sculptures: Elvis, Pirates of the Caribbean's Captain Jack Sparrow, and Captain America, each painted and made from clay, and containing miniature related sculptures all over their
bodies (5); and a full-sized motorcycle made out of licorice and gummy bears and fish.

To purchase from the Ramos family, I needed a translator. I tended to use whatever bilingual Ripley employee
was available at any given time; they used Christian's
lovely wife Alyn. Over the years I taught them a little
English, and they taught me some Spanish: gracias, la
cucaracha, mariposas, murcielago, incredible, and "Aunque
no le crea".

71

One that Got Away #9 — John Zweifel
the Patriot, and His Wonderful Collection

I may have known about John Zweifel even before I started to work at Ripley's. His miniature White House is legendary, and one of the strongest salutes to America one can imagine. I met him in person in August 1993, on my third day of work after I moved to Orlando.

First and foremost, John is the ultimate patriot, I suspect more Republican than Democrat at election time, but a man who understands, and preaches the sanctity of the office of president in every conversation he has, no matter what party is in power. If you were to look up patriot in the dictionary, it might just have his picture beside the definition. His lifetime achievement, a forty-foot long "miniature" replica of the White House that he changes all the furnishings of with every new president, and seasonally decorates twice a year for July 4th and Christmas, is a testament to his talent, his patience, and his love of his country.

I can't with a straight face say John's White House ever "got away" from me, though at least once a year for twenty-five years, we would discuss:

(A) was it for sale? and (B) if so at what price?

Depending on how many Presidential Libraries he had advanced bookings for, or his health, sometimes the answer to (A) was "of course it is for sale", while other times it would be, "not yet, maybe in a couple more years". The answer to (B) when he gave one, was usually in the neighborhood of five million dollars, but quite often could change in a matter of minutes. It was never less than two million dollars, however, and if I without hesitation, said okay at two million, the price would rise again instantly. Safe to say, it was just a game. John never really wanted to sell the House, and likely never will.

The House is the best thing John has, but he also has a whole Presidential museum, and two warehouses of other stuff that was always on the selling block — or at least considered to be "for sale".

John probably had at least a dozen things I wanted to acquire, but we were seldom ever close on prices, and when we were, the deal was never consummated for one reason or another. His favorite ploy was trying to add something into the deal to make up for the difference I had negotiated him out of on the piece I wanted. As I said, it was more a game between John and I, than serious negotiations. As John got older he just liked to chew the fat every once in a while. He would often talk to me for a couple hours at a time.

The piece he had that I really wanted, was an authentic Charles Stratton -Tom Thumb owned carriage, made in England, and used by Tom when he visited with Queen Victoria in 1844.

In addition to being a presidential historian, John is a serious fan of the circus. Before I knew him, he had run a circus museum, and having grown up in Baraboo, Wisconsin, the summer home of the Ringling Brothers Circus, John had started collecting circus memorabilia in his youth. He had hundreds of circus pieces in storage, but Tom's carriage was always on display in his Presidential museum. It didn't really "belong", but it was simply too wonderful not to display.

On any given day the quoted price for the carriage ranged from $30, 000 to $300,000, depending if I wanted anything to go with it, say the oldest wooden carousel horse in the country, or a life casting of Abraham Lincoln's face and hands, or a replica miniature roller coaster, or a car used by Franklin Roosevelt, or another limo used in a movie about John F.

Kennedy's assassination. These were all things I wanted but buying more than that one at a time was beyond the pocket book. I may have on a whim offered him $300,000 for the carriage at one time, but $10,000 was my standard offer, plus I would pay the shipping — always an issue with John. His comeback was if I would take the Kennedy car for another $200,000 he would put the carriage in the backseat and drive them both to me — no extra charge. If I would throw in a wax figure of Donald Trump, he would throw in a Tom Thumb circus banner. The number of proposals was never ending. Around 2015 I mentally gave up. I started to believe he was more likely to leave the carriage to me in his will than to sell it to me.

John and I go back a long way, and I love him like a father, but I only ever closed one deal with him — he practically gave me a 1940s department store automated post office worker because we both felt it would be a great piece to display with entrants of a mail contest I was running (see Chapter 27). He regretted the deal almost instantly

— the price was cheap enough that I paid him cash on the spot preventing him from having time to ruminate on the price. For years in a friendly fake tears sort of way, he claimed I had cheated him.

I haven't seen John since November 2017, and I know his health is not good. I am sure that when he passes there will be one hell of an auction, or at least the garage sale of the century. I read recently of his selling of a few of his most prized circus possessions, several things I remember seeing and trying to buy — but no mention of the carriage. So maybe there is still hope it will one day be in a Ripley odditorium, with or without, a doll collection, or a working mechanical steamboat, complete with over 100-carved figurines, an FDR wheelchair, or even a completely furnished minia-ture White House.

John Zweifel, I salute you. God bless America, and you too.

72

The Really Small World of Willard Wigan

My absolute favorite Ripley exhibits are the really small pieces. Ripley's has drawers full of miniatures, about 120 of which are considered "micro-miniatures", because you can't see them without a microscope. These are the crème de la crème of artistic unbelievability. How they are done can only be imagined, and even after an explanation, they still demand to be seen in person, eye to scope, to fully comprehend.

I was first introduced to micro-miniatures at EXPO 86, the World's Fair in Vancouver, Canada, that Jimmy Pattison was the chairman and driving force behind. My wife and I were in Vancouver for a couple of hours of business to be followed by a few days of pleasure. As Jimmy was going to see me as part of the business portion of the trip I thought it wise to visit EXPO, if only briefly, before meeting him; I was sure he would ask me if I saw I see anything I liked, and I was right. He asked the question, and I had a real, honest answer: the micro-miniatures on display in the Russian pavilion.

I don't remember how many there were, but they were all created by one man — Nikolai Syadristy (1). They were displayed in large glass bubble domes attached to walls. The bubbles had microscope lenses inserted in the middle, so you could see the art properly, but also look at them outside the lenses to assure you that "seeing was believing". My two favorites were a rose inside a human hair, measuring 0.05mm in diameter, and a woman's brooch of a dragonfly that had a working watch with 130 parts for an eye. The watch (eye) was about this big: O.

As it just so happened, Jimmy was to entertain the entire Russian delegation on his yacht that night. Would my wife and I like to come for the ride and meet them? Maybe I would meet someone who would be able to help me buy a few pieces for Ripley's? I called my wife at the hotel and told her to be ready in thirty minutes. She thought I was joking, and almost said no thanks. I told her "No" was not an option. Less than an hour later we were cruising Vancouver harbor on an eighty-foot yacht with about fifty Russians, Jimmy, his assistant, Maureen Chant, EXPO's Jane Butler, the woman in charge of Public Relations, and a Canadian legendary television evangelist. The only Russian that spoke a word of English, was a hockey announcer; he had been the Russian commentator for the legendary 1972 Canada-Russian hockey tournament. After about a ten second conversation regarding the micro-miniatures, we talked about hockey the rest of the night. He informed me quite emphatically that Syadristy's works were considered national treasures in the Soviet Union, they had never been shown outside the country before, they were worth millions, and were not for sale at any price. Period. End of conversation. "How about that Paul Henderson guy?"

It was a wonderful evening of food and song (a Russian balladeer serenaded us with "Danny Boy" accompanied by Jimmy on the yacht's large organ), an evening like no other in my life, but from a business standpoint, a total non-event.

Later I wrote a few cursory letters trying to buy a couple of these masterpieces, but I never got very far. Luckily, however, Eduard Terkazarian, an Armenian-Russian living in California, somehow learned of my interest in the Syadristy micro miniatures. With the stealth and secrecy of a spy in a James Bond movie, he agreed to meet me in San Francisco, and offered me a few 'similar' works of art. Turns out he was a student of Syadristy's who had defected, and was now living incognito somewhere in "the Valley". His works though small and beautiful, were quite simple in comparison to Syadristy's, but they were also considerably cheaper. That day I bought three, a few years later, I bought three more. Five of the six have religious themes, including a portrait of Christ, a portrait of Mary, the Mother of God, a church, and Michelangelo's David, each about the size of a period (.)

Word got out very quickly that I had bought these, and within a couple days I bought some micro paintings by a Chinese artist (while dining on dim sum), and I had an appointment to meet Orville Elton, a man in Seattle who claimed to have a collection of over 30,000 miniatures; he was sure he had lots of things I would be interested in. He was more right than wrong, I ended up buying about 100 pieces from him, but there was only one micro miniature of significance.

That one piece, however, was very special.

On December 16, 1929, the first year the Ripley cartoon was nationally syndicated, Ripley drew a cartoon about Charles Baker, of Spokane Washington, who had engraved the Lord's Prayer onto the head of an ordinary hat pin. The incredible task cost him both his eyesight, and his sanity. This pin was displayed around the country for several years (2).

I can't verify who actually engraved the pin Orville showed me, but he claimed it to be a pin created by a jeweler in prison for forgery, named A. Schiller. The pin had been displayed by famed miniature collector Jules Charbneau at the Chicago Century of Progress World's Fair of 1933-1934, but had then mysteriously disappeared from the public eye. On a cold rainy November day in Seattle in 1989, I was looking at a treasure stored with a small monoscope in a shoe box that nobody had seen in fifty-five years. The pin has twelve lines of text, sixty-five words, 254 letters, and fourteen punctuation marks engraved on a space about this big: **O**.

I was blown away. It was quite simply the most amazing thing I had ever seen, never mind the provenance and back story. To this day it is one of my all-time favorite pieces, though its monetary value did decline in my estimate when I discovered there was more than one, and maybe as many as four different people who claimed to have carved Lord's Prayer pins. Though it is incredulous to believe that more than one of these amazing pins can exist, I personally have bought two (3), and seen a third, none of which are the Lundberg pin which is supposed to have been locked in a safe in 1917, and hasn't been shown to the public in the 102 years since. So strange as it seems, and as unexplainable as it is, it is safe to say there are at least four of these pins, and maybe more. The so-called Lundberg pin was offered to me several times for a price in the neighborhood of $1.5 million dollars considerably more than I paid for my first and second Lord's Prayer pins, combined.

I'm still emotionally attached to this pin, with its long journey to its Ripley home, but sometime around 2007-2008, I became aware of Willard Wigan, an artist of Jamaican descent, living in Birmingham, England, and I had to concede his micro-miniatures are even more amazing than the Prayer pins.

There are no words to describe Willard's work, neither their minuscule size, or their exquisite beauty. In his sixty-one years on earth, Willard has created close to 150 masterpieces all either on the heads of pins, or in the eyes of needles, and all but a couple cannot be seen with the naked eye. They are made from a variety of things, from precious metals to eyelashes. They are detailed and astonishingly accurate. Inspired both by ants, and the Biblical quotation:

"It is easier for a camel to go through the eye of a needle than for a rich man to enter the Kingdom of God." (Matthew 19:24),

Willard not only can put one camel in the eye of a needle, but throughout his career, has put three, then five, then seven, then nine camels in one needle eye! —

Though aware of the school of Russian micro-miniaturist led by Syadristy and Terkazarian, he is completely self-taught, and his work is very different from theirs in that he not only etches and sculpts, but he then with a one hair brush, paints his carvings.

I first heard about Willard when he sold a sculpture of the Beatles' **Yellow Submarine** inside the eye of a needle for one million dollars, at a London hospital cancer awareness charity event. Apparently, he had been working on micro-miniatures in the privacy of his mother's home since he was five years old, but made them for his mom and himself only; he had never sold one before. Based on this sale he soon had a manager who created a traveling show of several of Willard's works and toured them around England and parts of Europe. I was not by any means the first person to buy a Willard sculpture, as celebrities like Prince Charles (who made Willard a MBE-Member of the Most Excellent Order of the British Empire) and Elton John, soon had samples, but I was probably the first person to buy more than one.

I met Willard's manager in a hotel pub in Piccadilly Circus in 2010.

My intent was to buy Willard's eye of the needle sculpture of Hollywood icon Betty Boop. The sculpture features Betty in a red dress, with pearl earrings, a wrist watch, red shoes, a red garter, and her legendary eyelashes. The entire sculpture is smaller than the eye of a housefly, yet the details are as clear as day under the proper 400x magnification. Willard's manager, however, had brought more than thirty pieces for me to see, each in an individual small clear plastic case, all inside a fishing tackle box, inside a sports duffel bag. Each one he pulled out for viewing with a jeweler's loop, was more incredible than the last: Snow White and the Seven Dwarfs inside the eye of a needle; a gold Spanish galleon on the head of a pin; Marilyn Monroe on the world's smallest faceted diamond, set on the head of a pin; and Charles Chaplin balanced on a human eyelash, on the sharp pointed end of a needle, to name just a few.

It was pretty obvious I could never just buy one, and once I established they "were cheaper by the dozen" I worked my way up the negotiation ladder to eight, then ten, then twenty, then fifty, then to everything he currently had — ninety-seven in total. Discussions also included buying several microscopes that they currently had left over from their traveling show, as well as a couple hundred copies of two books that had been written about Willard. We also discussed bringing Willard to America to make a film about him and his surreal art. To that point in time it was the most money I had ever spent in one day, and all for a handful of pins not large enough to fill one of my pants' pockets.

The three days I spent with Willard in Orlando some months later were revelatory, real eye openers. First, I learned he couldn't read or write. Not only did I have to check him into his hotel, I had to order his food. I soon discovered his manager was really more of a handler, who did literally everything for him — but talk. Second, I learned all about ants. Every time we came across a colony of ants, no matter where we were, Willard would stop, get down on the ground face to face with them, and seemingly go into a trance-like meditative state. He was particularly enamored by Florida red army ants — the kind that bite. He had never seen or heard of red, or biting ants. He found out the hard way about their biting skills. Third, I learned to appreciate his amazing eye sight. Often compared by scientists to birds of prey, Willard's eyesight is superhuman. I know of nothing I can com- pare it to, but here are two examples of his ability:

From a distance of about six feet he could tell that one of his sculptures that I was holding in my hand was "not right". Now understand, I couldn't even see what it was I was holding. It was a piece he called **"Valentine Lunch"**. It was inspired by Audrey Hepburn in **Breakfast at Tiffanys**, and shows a couple seated at a table, laid with plates and cutlery, and a vase with a flower — all set on the head of a pin. I insisted he was bull-shitting me, there could be no way he could see anything from the distance he was standing from me. More insistently, he demanded I place the piece under a microscope for inspection. Upon doing so, we discovered a leg of the table was broken, and the table was in danger of falling off the pin. I kid you not.

We had brought Willard to Orlando for a press conference, and to make a short documentary film. As it turned out the film was to be the last Todd Day ever did for Ripley's, and it was never used (4), but we had fun shooting it, and we learned a lot about Willard in the process. For the film he and I sat opposite each other, and talked interview style. The cameras were shooting from the waist up only. Mid-sentence, Willard suddenly jumped up, and with arm and hand extended lunged forward nearly ten feet right off the stage. The director said "cut" and we all looked at Willard like he had lost his mind. "Willard you can't move out of the chair" we admonished him. He apologized and said: "Sorry, but I just had to get something I saw floating in the air".

As puzzled as could be, the crew collectively stared, and said "What thing?", assuming he was hallucinating. He then told us, that as he was sitting staring into the camera, he had seen a microscopic piece of "red" floating in the light of the camera. Still in disbelief, we mockingly asked, "Well did you get it?" He opened his hand, and sure enough there was a piece of red fluff about the size of a grain of sand in his palm. He then explained that much of the clothing on his carvings came from floating air fluff. I wondered if Betty Boop's dress was fluff. He said no, she was a painted figure, but the cape on the Superman pin-head figure I had bought was. We were suitably speechless, and in awe.

From the interview we learned that the most figures Willard had put inside a needles' eye was thirteen — a replica of Da Vinci's Last Supper, complete with table and place settings per the original painting (a piece Ripley's doesn't own), and that the single very smallest thing Willard had made to date was a doll, on a bed, in a room, of a four room doll house, inside the eye of a needle. Ripley's does own this piece.

I also learned two other things about Willard that I will never forget. Willard's art sells for thousands of dollars each, so Willard is quite wealthy. I wondered out loud what does a rich near sixty-year old who can't write his name, and until recently still lived with his mother, do with his money? Turns out Willard has two hobbies, one, is buying gold necklaces — he owns more than Isaac Hayes (think **Shaft** or Black Moses images) — and two, he likes to fly remote controlled aircraft.

The best thing I could do for Willard the whole time he was in Orlando, was drive him about thirty miles across town to a shop that Angela Johnson had discovered for him that had a new plane that he wanted to add to his collection that was not yet available in England. We called the shop, begged the owner to stay open a little late assuring him it would be worth his while, then drove like people possessed. By the time we got there, well past closing time, the owner was not too happy with us, but when I forked over nearly $500 for a toy plane, and a helicopter, he calmed down considerably. After three days of living with Willard, the last thing we did together, like two small school children, was fly planes in a parking lot. I've never seen a happier man.

I have only seen Willard once since then. We did however talk many times, and he made guest appearances in a couple of our odditoriums (including London where he proceeded to re-display all nine pieces that were there, claiming his eyes were better than our microscopes when it came to getting the sculptures into fo-

cus), but if I had to pick just one person to be the
most amazing I have ever met, or one exhibit to be the
most amazing I have ever bought, Willard would be the
hands-down winner. His work epitomizes the expressions:" Seeing is believing", and "Believe It or Not!

73

One that Got Away #10:
The Amazing Stephen Wiltshire

I met Stephen Wiltshire, autistic savant, and brilliant artist, the same day in 2008 I first viewed the art of Willard Wigan. Both men are amazing artists, both have Caribbean ancestors, and both are carefully guarded from people like me by well-meaning handlers. With Willard I made great headway, beneficial to both sides (see Chapter 72), but with Mr. Wiltshire I was blocked out totally with the door virtually slammed in my face. It certainly could have been worse, and I am grateful I did get to meet Stephen personally, but his manager did 95% of the talking, and I was never sure he really spoke for Stephen. He certainly didn't seem to have his best interests in mind, and I suspect I was summarily dismissed as a crass American by the somewhat reserved Brit without Stephen fully understanding the scope of my proposal and promises.

Prior to my meeting him, Stephen had actually been featured on our Dean Cain-Ripley television show, and in one of our books; I gathered he was unaware of these points. His gallery in the Royal Opera Arcade in London was actually quite close to our Piccadilly Circus odditorium, and I suspected I wasn't his first Ripley visitor. A few years later this was confirmed when I discovered one of his works that had been bought by one of the franchise owners of the location in a storage closet in the odditorium.

Stephen was only thirty-four when I met him, but he was already a very famous artist, and in 2006, had been made an MBE (Member of the Most Excellent Order of the British Empire) by the Queen for his cultural contribution to England's art community. It is nearly impossible to adequately describe the young man's artwork in words, it literally has to be seen to be believed. He has the unique ability to draw from memory entire cityscapes based on a single aerial flyby. For the Ripley television show, he had drawn Greater London after a short helicopter ride. In the years since, he has done similar drawings of Rome, New York, Paris, Venice, and dozens of other cities.

The pictures are often many feet long, and the detail is minute — right down to the number of windows on high rise buildings. He takes no notes, and no pictures, everything is drawn from memory, based usually on only a very brief viewing. Each drawing may have hundreds of buildings, and are always virtually perfect representations of the actual reality.

His gallery had many small pictures, typically of one specific building. I suspect these are what meet the popular price point for optimum sales, but when I asked the clerk about his larger works, I was immediately introduced to Stephen's handler/ manager. There apparently were a number of these larger works not on display in an upstairs room, but I was told in no uncertain terms that these sold for thousands of dollars. I'll admit this was more than I was hoping to pay, but I was miffed by the tone that suggested haughtily that I couldn't afford them, and would be wasting their time to get them out for showing. My feathers were ruffled, but my informing them that I was buying for a museum, and could afford whatever they may be asking, at least won me an audience with the master himself who was summoned by phone to come downstairs into the gallery. He was shy, downright timid, and said little. The most important thing I got out of him, is he would rather draw something new, than sell any of the pieces he currently had. I thought this was a little odd, and surmised he must like to ride in small planes. The price of the plane rental then becoming part of the sales price.

Their overall attitude towards Ripley's was not particularly promising; we weren't exactly the Royal Albert, and they made it clear that they didn't need us as much as they perceived we needed them. They even went so far as to give a considerably higher price than initially quoted, apparently the first price being for buying a piece, the higher price being that for displaying the piece in a commercial venue. I thought it was a joke. I don't know if it was my increased volume, crazed looks, or my general disdain, but Stephen started to uncontrollably tremble, seemingly in fear, and the meeting came to a very abrupt end.

Subsequent letters went unanswered, and I was never

privileged to acquire a Wiltshire original, but as noted earlier, less than two hours after our meeting I was
meeting Willard Wigand's handler, and making one of the
best deals of my career. I forgot Stephen pretty quickly, and of course had the last laugh when I discovered
we already had a significant piece of his art, albeit,
a print and not an original. I suspect that in the ten
years we were neighbors he was never allowed to darken
our doors.

I have never understood what went wrong that afternoon,
or for that matter the general disdain Londoners, and
many other Europeans, have for Ripley's. No matter what
we did in London we were never quite accepted, we had
no royal lineage. London was by far the biggest, and
actually one of the best, shows we ever had, and we
could have given a Wiltshire original the royal treatment. As the famed Red Rose tea commercials once said:
"Pity".

My Life with Marilyn Monroe:
Fame & Infamy

She was dead before I knew her. I was only six on August 5th, 1962. I can't say with any certainty when I first heard her name, or saw one of her films, but safe to say by my teen age years in the late six- ties, early seventies, I was spellbound by her beauty and sensuality. "**Some Like it Hot**", "**Niagara**", "**Bus Stop**", "**Gentlemen Prefer Blondes**", "**How to Marry a Millionaire**" and "**River of No Return**" all left strong impressions on a hormonal young boy. "**Some Like it Hot**" is still one of my all-time favorite films and the train sequence including Marilyn singing "**Running Wild**" is as exciting today as it was back in 1959.

It wasn't until October 27-28, 1999, however, that my love affair took full bloom.

Ten days earlier I had received a phone call from Jimmy Pattison, the owner of Ripley's. It was a hot summer afternoon in Winter Park, Florida, and I was sitting pool side in my backyard with a beer. He asked what I was doing. Politely I said not much, but I was sure to say I had just got home from church, so as not to sound like a complete lazy loaf on a Sunday afternoon. He then asked what was I doing on the 27th and 28th. I was a little dumbfounded not just by the question, but also by the fact that the big boss was calling me at home on a Sunday afternoon — the first and only time I recall this ever happening.

He said: "I want you to go to New York to help me buy dresses, clothing worn by Marilyn Monroe". A pretty hard offer to say no to. Jimmy had recently acquired the famous Frank Sinatra Rancho Mirage estate in Palm Springs, California, where Marilyn had stayed a few times, and reportedly had a liaison with President John F. Kennedy. It was his desire to decorate one of its haciendas with personal attire and property of Marilyn, items she might have traveled with for a retreat in the desert. At this point I knew nothing about the Monroe estate auction to be held by Christies Auction House in New York, and, therefore, had no idea what was to be sold. As I would soon learn, the answer was virtually everything she had that was left to her estate, and controlled by long-time friend, and acting coach, Lee Strasberg: furniture, clothing, jewelry, home décor items, books, film scripts — 576 lots in total, fifty-five to be sold Wednesday evening in a high-end gala like atmosphere, and 521 the next day. Jimmy wasn't interested in the glamour-side of Monroe, he wanted to capture the quiet life side. Once I got a catalog, I picked a few things that I thought would be reasonably priced and would work for Ripley's. Ultimately, I would be shopping for two different people, with two very different goals, and very different budgets.

The morning of the 27th I flew to New York and met with Jimmy at Christies. Jimmy already had a pre-selected shopping list, but we went inside, and hurriedly reviewed the presale exhibition. We then went across the street to an Irish Pub, and had a sandwich lunch (1). He showed me his list, and we added and subtracted from it based on the preview. It was only then that I learned he would not be attending the auction; I would be on my own for the evening gala. I had a shopping list, but with no prices. I had no clear understanding of how bad he wanted anything, nor if he wanted everything on the list. All I knew for sure was he wanted her Bible, her white baby grand piano, her West Coast Canadian Native Peoples' style sweater (made famous in George Barris', Malibu Beach, 1962 photo shoot), and maybe the infamous President Kennedy -Madison Square Garden, May 19th, 1962 "Happy Birthday" bejeweled gown — the predicted high point of the sale.

Of these four items, I got two, the Bible and the sweater. On both the other two I was the under-bidder. The piano had been estimated by Christies at $10,000 to 15,000, but everything was selling for ten times their estimates, and bids went up in increments of $10,000 up to $100,000, then by $20,000 up to $300,000, then by $50,000 up to $500,000, then by a $100,000 up to $2 million, and then by a half-million per bid after $2 million. This was unlike any auction   I had ever had a seat at. I had never bought anything for even a

$100,000 at this point in my career. I bid slow, and cautiously, up to $500,000 on the piano feeling this was the one thing Jimmy wanted most; if I was going to go high on anything I figured this was it. It was an instrument of real beauty, and I knew Jimmy played, so I thought this would be "personal" for him. When I bid $500,000 I was shaking, not knowing if getting it at that price would be good, or the end of my career. For a few moments I was running on high adrenalin and thought it was mine. The next bid was $600,000, and there was no one in the house still bidding. My breath was restored by a phone bid. I was more relieved than disappointed. The buyer was super star singer Mariah Carey, someone maybe with as much money as Jimmy. I was off the hook, and it was going to a good home. When the sweater came up thirty lots later, I had no trouble bidding, and won it for $150,000, a mere three times the auction house estimate.

"The" dress — there were several other dresses that evening — was the last lot of the night, lot #55. The lights went out, the curtains opened slowly, and there it was, center stage -9,000 rhinestones shimmering under the spotlights. Out of a magical ethereal mist came Marilyn's voice singing "Happy Birthday". It was pure Hollywood high drama, and pure Marilyn sex appeal. I knew my immediate boss, Bob Masterson, the president of Ripley's, loved the dress, and probably was okay with me bidding a few hundred thousand dollars (note there was no estimate price listed in the catalog which was a sure sign they were hoping for at least a half million dollars), and I also figured Jimmy was okay with that and a bit more. The bidding started at $200,000, but I didn't bid until it hit $500,000, at which point there were only a few bidders left, so I felt I might have a chance. It was suddenly mine at $1 million dollars. The crowd was loud and boisterous at each bid, and deathly silent in between. I definitely was holding my breath, and sweating. Another bid came in, I don't remember if they were in the house, or on the phone (there was no computer bidding back then). $1.1 million dollars, a number I couldn't fathom. I called it quits. The hammer came down and the room went crazy. I left quietly.

Out on the street, I bought a souvenir black and white Marilyn Monroe t-shirt to commemorate the event. It laid in a drawer for seventeen years before I ever wore it. Walking down the street I went to Mickey Mantle's famous restaurant on the Park, bought an over-priced dinner, and watched the Yankees in Game 3 of the World Series. (I later found out Jimmy had turned down tickets to the game, not knowing I was a big baseball fan who had never been to Yankee Stadium). I was nervous about how much I had spent – the most in a single day at that point in my fourteen-year buying career so I wasn't exactly celebrating, just watching a Yankees baseball game in a temple of the game.

The next morning Jimmy called me and asked how I had done. "What had we bought?" I ran through the list and he asked: "But no piano, no dress?" He clearly was disappointed about not getting the piano, and seemed surprised that I could just stop bidding. His attitude towards the dress was a little different: "I thought you wanted that for Ripley's", he said. I did, but I was not authorized to spend that kind of money.

At that point he said two things I would remember for the rest of my career:

1) "We play to win, not just to play"… and

2) "'Well we won't lose anything today!"

This second statement was said with a hint of aggressiveness. I now understood there was no budget, no limits, and "I want" means, "we get", so day two was going to be a lot less nerve racking than day one had been. He also let me know that he would attend at least part of the session. Based on the previous night's failures, I think he thought he needed to baby sit me. Regardless, I was grateful for his attendance, but I am sure he had no idea how long it would take to auction the remaining 521 lots.

We met at the auction house before the 10 am start, and nothing more was said about last night. Today's list was longer, but with much "cheaper" items, nothing that should be too troublesome. Unfortunately, I was wrong again.

I don't recall how long Jimmy stayed, but I would guess an hour at most. He was not one to sit still — and do nothing. Suddenly, without much warning, he was ready to leave. He pointed out he was really interested in Marilyn's traveling make-up case — think fishing tackle box with makeup inside — six snapshots of Monroe's dog

471

"Mad" (short for Mafia), which Frank Sinatra had given her as a present, and the dog's license tag.

The case was listed at $15,000; I paid $240,000. The dog pictures, the most inflated purchase I paid in my life, were listed at $800; I paid $200,000. The dog's license was listed at $1,200; I paid a whopping $55,000. Mad the dog in total cost me $255,000, and innumerable comments for the next nineteen years — the last from Jimmy himself on June 23, 2018, when I was about to buy him a Frank Sinatra painting. I asked him if there was a ceiling, and he hesitated, "no, but don't go crazy like with those dog pictures many years ago." Obviously, he remembered it as well as I did!

The auction didn't end until around 8 pm that night. With an eleven-hour numb bum, I left and walked down Broadway to Times Square, feeling pretty good about myself, especially when I saw on the news building marquee: "Ripley's buys $1.2 million dollars' worth of Monroe memorabilia". I was, however, not sure where I was going to stay that night — having missed my flight home by hours, and not having a hotel booked. As I searched the streets for a place that looked like I could afford to stay, I bought a bootleg "Yankees Sweep, win World Series" t-shirt even though Game 4 hadn't yet actually started. I found a place right on Broadway that cost more money than I had (I may have just spent $1.2 million of someone else's money, but I only had about $10 bucks cash, and a company credit card to my own name).

The hotel was far too depressing to sit in given the emotional high I was on, so I decided to go to Times Square and watch game four of the World Series on the Square's Jumbo Tron. With the Yankees up three games to none, and "Rocket" Roger Clemens on the mound, there were thousands of people gathered to watch and the atmosphere was electric. I couldn't have been happier — even though I have never been a Yankees fan. I don't remember the score, but the Rocket pitched the way his salary and the occasion demanded, the Yanks won, and all was right in the world, or in New York City at least. I went to bed knowing I had just had two of the most exciting days of my life.

The next morning was filled with mixed emotions, and

trepidation. Had I done good? Did Jimmy know how much I had spent? Knowing he had gone back to Vancouver yesterday, when was too early – or too late — to call him with a final report? Did I still have a job? I figured the people in my home office in Orlando should be okay to call, and perhaps that would give me a reading on the bigger picture. Bob was calm, but concerned: "Who was paying the $1.2 million, hopefully not Ripley's!". I assured him that my Ripley purchases were a small fraction of the total and he had no cause for concern. He suggested Jimmy would have been up by then, and I should not wait to call — so I did.

I didn't get through to Jimmy, however, and spoke with Maureen Chant, his executive assistant and trusted right hand. She was non-committal as to how I had done, but thanked me for doing it, and assured me Jimmy would call at some point later in the day. Figuring this bought me some time, I flew back to Orlando, and into the office late on a Friday afternoon. The call never came. What did that mean I wondered? The weekend went by, and still not a peep from Vancouver.

On Monday the silence was broken. Jimmy called early. He didn't congratulate me, but he didn't chew me out either. I surmised I had done just fine. To my surprise, he said he had calls from all over the world for the last three days to discuss his purchasing $1.2 million worth of Monroe memorabilia. He had literally been inundated by the press as to what he was going to do with the "stuff". His solution: keep a few things as originally planned (notably the Bible), but "give" all the rest to Ripley's. "Talk to Bob and see what he thinks". There were tax implications, but I was sure Bob would not be too concerned, and would accept the gift (I really didn't think Bob had a choice). Within a couple weeks we were the proud owners of a truck full of Marilyn clothing and artifacts. Now what do we do?

I was given the mission to try and buy some filler low hanging fruit Monroe items on eBay, or anywhere else I could find things to create a real show. I bought some Monroe hair, a lip print, and most significantly, a nylon stocking from her honeymoon night with Joe DiMaggio in 1954, but most of the additional things were trinkets, stuff any Monroe fan could have bought. Within a few months, however, we were ready to open a special traveling Monroe exhibit, advertising an inflated value of "over $2 million dollars' worth of Monroe artifacts and memorabilia". We did things big in those days. We hired two former Monroe photographers to do press, a NYC PR firm (Dan Klores Associates) to get us on **Larry King Live**, and other talk shows, and we had a Monroe look-alike contest with a $10,000 diamond necklace for a prize. We also let the contestants wear the Malibu sweater for photo ops. With all the hype, and wonderful displays and graphics by our then company museum design director Jimmy Doyle, the show couldn't help but to be a success in Hollywood (the first stop of the tour). The show however, sputtered with each of its successive stops: Orlando, Dallas and Atlantic City, and we were forced to pull the plug after just two years.

Monroe wasn't "dead", but the show was broken up, the best stuff going to Hollywood, then later London, then back to Hollywood, while the rest was spread individually throughout the Ripley odditorium chain.

For the next fourteen years I sporadically bought a few Monroe pieces, including things that resurfaced from the 1999 Christie's auction, but in general I tried to keep my personal love affair with Norma Jean in the far dark corners of my buying brain, until she burst out screaming louder than ever in the fall of 2016.

75

Marilyn — Part 2: My Finest 7 ½ Minutes, and the Subsequent 18 Months of Consequences, or "How Marilyn Brought Down Another Good Man".

Sometime in the late spring of 2016 I heard through the internet auction grapevine, that the Marilyn Monroe-JFK $1.1 million dollar "Happy Birthday Mr. President" dress was going to be auctioned by **Julien's Auctions** of Beverly Hills, California, in November. It had to be a dream. A once in a lifetime event, about to happen for a second time in my life! I was excited.

A month or so later I got the confirmation details: the dress would indeed be the highlight of the first night of a three-day Monroe auction in Los Angeles on November 17-18-19, and bidding on the dress would start at $1 million. Words cannot describe how excited I was. I told everyone I knew that would be interested, that I wanted this dress. Call it arrogance, call it vanity, call it megalomania, I wanted the dress more than I had ever wanted virtually anything else, and I was sure Jimmy Pattison would feel the same way.

When I was sure I had all my ducks in a row — having a prepared answer to any question I might be asked — I walked twenty-feet down the hall, and spoke to the president of Ripley's, my immediate boss. He dismissed it very quickly: we had enough Monroe things and nothing was worth a million dollars. Extremely deflated, but not beaten, I asked if it was okay if I contacted Jimmy who I was sure would feel different, and at very least, would let me give him a sales pitch.

For years I had a very unusual, almost father-son relationship with Jimmy, and an even closer mother-son relationship with Maureen, so I emailed Maureen requesting an audience with Jimmy. To my surprise he called back within a few minutes. He vividly recalled the day seventeen years ago when we didn't buy the dress, and more importantly, he almost instantly said: "Well we won't miss it this time."

He gave me explicit instructions to hire a conservator, and get a full report on the dress's condition. He also wanted weekly reports as to what people thought it might sell for, and he made it crystal clear I was to attend the auction in person, so clear the calendar. As it turned out, I did already have something on my calendar for the day before, something that I couldn't, or wouldn't, cancel. The two events together one in New York and one in Los Angeles, would make for a very memorable twenty-four hours.

I spread the word throughout the office that "we" were going to buy the dress. For the better part of four months I warned people, but to no avail. No one thought Jimmy would buy it. I seemingly understood Jimmy better than anyone; I knew he would not want to lose twice. With seventeen more years' experience, both at auctions, and with Jimmy, I was very confident I would be buying a very expensive dress on November 17.

Through contacts at Sudbury, Ontario's Science North Museum (see Chapters 26 & 31) I had no problem hiring Susan Maltby, a textile expert associated with Toronto's Royal Ontario Museum. Her subsequent report got the project green-lit, and as the date approached, both Jimmy's and my excitement bubbled like an erupting volcano.

I have already discussed my involvement with Robin Lung's film **"Finding Kukan'** (see Chapter 32), so I need not rehash it here, but on November 16th, the day before the auction, the film had its North American debut at the DOC-NYC Film Festival. My role in the film, both as a talking head, and a consulting researcher, were small parts in the overall work, but my pride in being involved was immeasurable, and there was no way in hell I was going to miss the film's debut. I decided my right-hand assistant Angela Johnson, and my wife Giliane both needed to attend both events with me. At least for a couple days we would be real coast to coast jet setters. We flew to New York on the morning of the 16th, saw the film in the afternoon, dined with Robin and her husband in the evening, then flew to LA the next morning.

We were like three giddy school kids talking about the

film and the dress, all the way to LA. We landed with just a couple hours to spare, and as soon as we were heading north in a rental car towards the city from the airport, I called Jimmy. He asked a familiar question: "What was the word on the street"? I said in New York people thought it might go for as high as $10 million. It was the first time I ever heard Jimmy gulp, and say nothing. I followed the silence with," but in LA they are saying around $5 million". He got his breath back, but said very firmly: "Well, we are not going to spend $5 million." Elation to deflation within a couple seconds. He made it clear he was hoping for something around $2 million, and I was not to bid over that without his approval. It was agreed that I would phone him while the auction was in progress.

I hung up, and hung my head down to the ground. I knew the dress would go for more than $2 million. I was really pissed. I had been planning this for months, and had just traveled 3,000 miles to buy the dress, but now I was just going to just be a miserable spectator. The ladies were silent and afraid to speak. They both knew how much this meant to me.

As always, LA freeway traffic was horrendous. I wanted to see the preview for the sale, which was not in the same building as the sale itself, so our hotel stops (Angela was not at the Roosevelt on Hollywood Blvd., where we were, but very close by) were super quick. No time to eat, and barely time for make-up.

The preview was gorgeous, elegant and sensual, but "the dress" was already gone. We did see a few other things we would be bidding on, but were disappointed not to have had a private moment with fashion history.

The auction itself was in a restaurant in Beverly Hills. The catalog cost $150 and the seats, seventy-five dollars each. Wine was eight dollars a glass. Not your neighborhood auction for sure. I knew not to bid on the dress until I had Jimmy on the phone, but there were a few lots related to the dress that were coming up before the dress that we would need for future display if we got the dress, so I started bidding. I got a couple items: an autographed ceramic panel (lot #75 $10,000), home film footage of Monroe in the dress singing (lot #76 — $10,000), a Bob Mackie original design painting of Monroe wearing the dress (lot #80 — $7,000), and a ticket to the Madison Square Garden event (lot #83 — $6,500). I did, however, hold back on a couple items that I figured would be useless without the dress.

With Angela and the paddle on my right, and Jimmy on the phone on my left ear, the bidding started on the dress, lot #84, the last item of the evening, opening at $1 million. The bids went up quickly by $100,000 to $2 million, at which price it was ours. It didn't stay there long though, hitting $2.5 before I had even told Jimmy it was ours. With some hesitation he said bid, and it was ours at $ 3 million. Like back in 1999, the room was pin-drop silent when no one was bidding, but exploded like a bomb when someone did. Again, it was ours only briefly. Explaining as loudly as I needed to be, that at $3.5 million, it wasn't ours, with more confidence than before — the killer instinct had surfaced — he said bid, and I did. It was now ours at $4 million. I was suddenly aware of the paparazzi, and the auction owner, Darren Julien, as well as Julien's #2 guy, Martin Nolan, just a few feet away from me staring me down. Up until this point the action had all taken place in under four minutes, and I had voted with my hand, unsure where the paddle

was, or even if Angela was still sitting beside me (and Giliane beside her). I was zoned in, only aware of the auctioneer, and Jimmy's voice in my ear.

The next three minutes, like a bad television commercial, were painful. The auctioneer told the whole history of the dress, explained whose bid it currently was, urged phone bidders to hurry up, and did everything in his power to get a raised bid…but all to no avail. The hammer came down at $4 million, and the place erupted. I am sure Jimmy couldn't hear me, but I heard him say good work, and that he was hanging up, going to bed, and would talk to me in the morning. When I looked up Angela was waving the paddle around for the whole room to see, and a cameraman was coming at me from one direction, and a woman dressed like Marilyn, from another. The Marilyn look-alike was an English actress named Suzie Kennedy (how ironic!), and her escort was the legendary dress designer Bob Mackie, who had been one of the tailors of the dress back in 1962.They expressed congratulations, and promised to talk again but were nearly pushed to the ground in the frenzy. Next up was a well-dressed woman who flung herself around my neck and kissed me (my wife looked on in shock), introducing herself as the president of the International Marilyn Monroe fan club. She literally cried as she said loudly for everyone to hear: "I am so glad Ripley's won the dress as now people like me will get to see it." How she knew I was from Ripley's I wasn't sure. (It turned out she had been sitting beside my wife and talking with her during the proceedings).

When I at last turned around, the cameras starting flashing, and the microphones were thrust forward from every angle. En-masse, we moved closer to the front stage and the dress, so everyone would have a sparkling backdrop. I spoke at length to a British film crew who it turned out were making a documentary film about Marilyn, starring Suzie Kennedy. (I would see this in England seven months later and was astounded just how much Suzie did look like Monroe, something I really didn't appreciate that evening). The interviews went on for more than an hour without a moment's pause. It would continue six hours later when Europe woke up, and before it was all over, Ripley's would have 2.5 billion press impressions, everyone from **Time** Magazine to **Rolling Stone** magazine, and every news station in between, from countries like, China, Australia, Singapore, South Africa, Italy, India, and my homeland, Canada. For now, however, we wanted to escape, celebrate, and eat — we hadn't had a thing in over fifteen hours.

We headed back to Hollywood Boulevard and the venerable Musso and Frank's Restaurant. Though long past its glory, this is still my favorite Hollywood restaurant; you can literally feel the presence of the hundreds of stars who have eaten there, including Frank Sinatra, and Marilyn Monroe. I can't remember what we ate, or what we drank, but we did do both, and probably talked way to loud trying to grasp just what had happened. My life would never be the same.

It was nearly 3 am before we were in bed, but the phone started ringing at 5 am. By 7 am Jimmy had phoned, and had already read that we had bought the Monroe-JFK Happy Birthday Mr. President dress for a world record $4.81 million dollars. He was confused. I am not sure he knew what we had paid, in terms of the hammer price, but he definitely hadn't considered the auction house commission of 22%, or the taxes. When I explained the $4.81 million and made it clear there would still be tax on top of that, he said, "So we did pay $5 million after all." I wasn't sure if this was spoken with humor, or disdain.

The next person to call was Jimmy's lawyer, Nick Demarais, who wanted to get it insured instantly. I calmed him a bit saying we had not actually taken possession of the dress (I hadn't slept with it!), and it would be awhile before we did. The auction house would not release it until it was fully paid for, and he and the accountants would have to decide in which state we would take possession of the dress to decrease state taxes (for example there would be no state taxes if in Oregon, 6% in Florida, or 8% in California). He was greatly relieved that this decision did not have to be made at that moment at 7 am.

The phone would continue to ring all day, lots of press, but also people with Marilyn things they now wanted to sell. I was as much a celebrity as I would ever be. One small problem for the moment though was we still had two more days of the auction, and the auction was starting at 10 am. So, we wolfed down breakfast in the hotel restaurant, and headed out for day two. I would buy a couple other nice pieces of clothing on that day, and then some photos on day three, but the commotion was still all about the dress, and would continue to be so for the next several months, right up until I retired in June of 2018.

For the next five months there was eerie silence from some people, and exuberant joy from others. The dress was flown to Orlando by FedEx aboard a private jet paid for by the auction house, then stored in a vault in the Ripley archives — affectionately known as Edward's closet. Conservator Susan Maltby visited a couple times, and recommended a cabinet maker. Designs were created, and an $80,000 display case, with GPS, lights, heat sensors, humidity control, and shatter proof glass was ordered. Our wax figure seamstress, Olga Irizarry, and her daughter Kathy, were commandeered to make a replica dress (they had to count all 9,000 jewels), and a model was hired to create a figure from. I was removed from the project, and the dress was no longer to be my concern — for better or for worse.

This would be the case for three months until in February, when Jimmy called, and said he wanted us to take the dress to his annual Partners in Pride (PIP) manager's conference in Toronto in mid-March. Suddenly the dress was again at least partially my responsibility, as the high priced custom case was not going to be ready until June. A phone call to my friend Norma Henry, formerly at Sudbury's Science North, but now working for a cabinet company, would save the day.

I didn't know until much later that Norma had been on vacation sitting in a geothermal hot pool in Iceland, when she took my call.

Norma and her company rescued us with service beyond the call of duty, even making adjustments on the spot when the Toronto hotel's elevator couldn't accommodate the case. Officially, the dress was now Brian Relic, our VP of Design and Development's problem, but as VP of Exhibits, people associated the dress with me personally, so I helped assemble the display, and for the next couple of days was the guardian and spokesperson for it. Needless to say, it caused quite a commotion, with the hotel staff, Jimmy's delegates, and any other hotel visitor that happened to pass by the display.

A big part of the annual Partners in Pride (PIP) conference was presentations by all of Jimmy's individual companies. For thirty-two years I had been the author, director and producer, of the Ripley presentation so it was a no-brainer for me to include the dress in our show. It really wasn't well woven into the presentation, but we ended with a grand reveal, and received "oohs and ahhs". As always, a "Q & A" followed. The first question went straight to the white elephant (dress) in the room. From the floor, an accountant asked: "How do you plan to make your ROIC (return on invested capital) on such an expensive acquisition?" To my joy, Jimmy, from the back of the room, said, he didn't care if he got his money back, this was about preserving, and most importantly, sharing, a unique unbelievable one-of-a-kind piece of American history with the world. I let out a huge sigh. I was validated. Thank God.

Before I could inhale again though, I heard him saying: "Edward go to the podium and tell the room the story of this dress." It wasn't the first time I had been asked to speak extemporaneously to this elite group, but it was certainly the longest, and most intense time in all the seventeen PIP's I attended. I told the story you have just read here, speaking clearly and quickly, but leaving out no details. The crowd was silent, but then applauded loudly. I felt like a conquering hero.

Later that evening every delegate got a chance to have both individual pictures and group pictures taken by the Pattison photographer Ron Sangha with the dress. My picture was taken several times including individual shots with Jimmy, and with Maureen Chant, who beamed with pride for me. It was my finest hour, but it was soon followed by my darkest ones.

The display case would stay in Toronto in case the dress had to return to Canada, which Jimmy was hinting loudly might happen. The dress was flown back to Orlando aboard our company jet. Needless to say, I wasn't with her anymore, she was Brian Relic's sole responsibility now that he had learned how to ship her, how to deal with customs, and how to assemble the display. He did have an adventure

— he was held up by customs, and he had to destroy the acid free special box we had made to carry her in — but the dress returned without much ceremony, and was put back in my closet for a few more months.

I had very little to do with her next adventure, but Jimmy still saw me as his connection go-to-guy, so I did work behind the scenes with his pilot and his drivers. Brian, however, had the real anguish being the one who physically had to move the dress. The dress now was to return to rural Western Canada for a week-long tour of grocery stores, moving first by jet, then by private truck. First stop was the small town of Luse, Saskatchewan where Jimmy was born (go ahead see if you can find it on a map!). Here, he and it, would be part of a fund raiser to help the town raise money to build a community swimming pool. People came to see the dress in this small town of less than 500 people from miles around. It made Luse famous for a day, with news stories on front pages across the country. From there, it traveled by truck with a team of armed guards, and employees, to **Save-On Foods** grocery stores, a chain that Jimmy owns and was expanding from their home base into Saskatchewan and Manitoba, probably two of the three least populated provinces of Canada.

I wasn't on the tour, so I can't comment too much. The press loved it, and Jimmy and the grocery store presidents were happy, so that was all that really mattered. The poor buggers who I worked the logistics with from Orlando, and who had to move it, pack it up and down, and even sleep with it, probably weren't very happy until the tour was finally over. After six unveilings the case was shipped to our aquarium in Toronto for future use, and the dress was once again flown by private jet home to Orlando.

With this big learning curve behind us, and the super-display case at last finally ready — and Jimmy telling us in no uncertain terms to get the dress on display — we were now ready to start her Ripley odditorium tour. I was only a small player in the circus, but as the MC-host at her premiere unveiling, in San Francisco, my role was still significant. I had very little to do with the newly expanded display design, which included nine other Monroe pieces from the Ripley collection, seven of them directly related to the birthday singing event at which the dress was worn in 1962. In fact, the designers virtually ignored every suggestion I made. It was clear the dress really was no longer my concern. I flew out to Seattle a week before the dress unveiling for another exhibit related event, and landed in San Francisco about eighteen hours before the morning press event at the odditorium. Gil was again with me, and we stayed within walking distance of the odditorium. I headed there almost right away, and was just a little shocked to see how ill prepared they were. It was quite a while before I found our press agent, but I knew I had to volunteer to be part of her set up crew that couldn't start work until at least 10 pm, or there would be no show at 8 am the next morning. It was a long night.

The next morning my worst nightmare came true. We had more staff than visitors, and half the visitors we had were our neighborhood wax museum competitors from down the street. The event was terrible. Our Monroe look-alike was good, but not good enough to save the day. If this was the best we could do, it was going to be a long time before we would make any money, never mind $5 million.

After six weeks of mediocre attendance in San Francisco, the manager quit, and the dress went to our odditorium in Grand Prairie, Texas. I had literally nothing to do with it there, but it did better than in San Francisco. It then was shipped to the Orlando odditorium. I was on vacation and had virtually nothing to do with its stay there either. Unfortunately, it was now Christmas time, publicity was hard to get and the dress left no real impression on the museum's attendance, or the press. The dress was then sent to St. Augustine, the company's oldest, and my favorite, location. I was once again asked to MC, and I was happy to accept knowing the local manager, Kim Kiff, would work a lot harder than either her San Francisco or Orlando counterparts had done. The event was a formal evening function, rather than a morning press conference, so I was confident if we didn't get the press, we would at least get real guests. I speech-ivied, we let certain people try on a real $30,000 Monroe sweater, and everyone got their picture taken with Heather Chaney, a Monroe look-alike (coincidentally Heather was the same woman who had won our Monroe look-alike contest back in Orlando in 2002). There also was a scavenger hunt throughout the museum, a giant birthday cake -our Monroe sang Happy Birthday in a sensuous breathy way to me-and even door prizes. A splendid time was had by all. At the debrief a few days later, it was determined that this was now the template for future dates.

A little more than a month before my retirement, I would have one more fling with my girl in Branson, Missouri. Branson was a Ripley location I had not been to in approximately twenty-five years. It was not exactly where I wanted my last company trip to be, but somehow it seemed appropriate that my last public gig would be with the dress that had come to be both my crowning glory and my swan song. I flew there with our Monroe look-alike, and we were met by our PR lady, Suzanne Smagala-Potts. We arrived at our hotel at about 11:30 pm. The town was as dead as the proverbial doornail.

The next morning, I was on my own while they did a television interview — historically my territory, but apparently no longer. I made good use of the time, visiting a movie and classic car museum where I bought a **Star Wars** "land speeder" craft, and a very famous art car shaped like a red high heel shoe. Suzanne and "Monroe" came to pick me up, and we did an impromptu photo shoot with "Marilyn", the high heel shoe car and a Batmobile (the car I had really hoped to buy, but wasn't given the okay on).

A few hours later "Marilyn" and I boarded a Ripley "duck", an amphibious armored vehicle that was part of a company Ripley's had just acquired a few weeks before. It was not quite a limousine, but we did make quite an entrance! The night went smoothly, copying everything we had done in St. Augustine. The crowd was a little smaller, but very into it. My speech was well received, and there was some comic electricity between 'Marilyn" and I, now that we knew each other a little better than we had in St. Augustine.

After everyone had gone home, I said an emotional goodnight and goodbye to "the dress". I didn't know for sure at that point, but I was thinking I may never see her again. She had been a major part of my life for sixteen months, and a memorable landmark in my career for eighteen years. Parting was such sweet sorrow. At the time of this writing I have told her story hundreds of times. The company is probably no closer to making any real money from her, but all over the world it is known that Ripley's owns it, and that I'm the guy who spent over $ 5 million dollars on a dress that didn't even fit me.

PS — The dress is designed for a woman with measurements 37-22-35, measurements not easily found these days.

76

One that Got Away #11 the Pigeon Cove, Massachusetts Paper House

To say something got away implies you had it in your grasp at one point, but when you go fishing there are at least three levels of "the big one that got away": the hook was never set, the line broke, or the fish got off by tossing the hook. Using this analogy, the Paper House of Pigeon Cove fits in category # 1 — the hook was never really set.

One of the Ripley cartoons about this unique building and its furnishings, was one of the first items I cataloged in the summer of 1978. The visual of the cartoon didn't really do it justice, but the caption caught my attention, and my imagination: an entire house, roof, walls and porch, and everything in it, is made of rolled up pages of newspapers. The paper piano actually can be played, the paper grandfather clock keeps good time, and the paper fireplace (think about this for a minute!) can really be used to burn wood. This has to be one of the most unbelievable Believe It or Not! achievements of all time.

The house was constructed by Elis Stenman, who read three papers a day, over a twenty-year period starting in 1922. Over 100,000 news-papers were used — mainly from nearby Boston, but papers from the capital of every state were used to make the clock, and if you look closely, there are some Irish newspapers sprinkled throughout the house that were donated by a relative. In places the papers are fifteen inches — 215 pages — thick. What had started as an engineer's test to see how strong paper was, ended up being a life-long obsession.

Over the years Ripley published a few stories on the house, and my interest in it never faded. So, imagine my glee when sometime in the late 1980s, I heard it was for sale. I had childlike visions of placing it on the grounds outdoors in St. Augustine, and letting people walk through it, much like we would do a few years later with a certain redwood tree log home (see Chapter 49). I imagined it would be tough to move, but this was not a game-changing problem, just a challenge. What I couldn't imagine was that the seller was not willing to let it leave the state of Massachusetts. It was only for sale under the condition that it remain exactly where it was, and that it continued to be open to the public to enjoy. This was not an option from my side of the fence. It, therefore, got away from me before I even set the hook.

It was not until July 2018, a month after I had retired from Ripley's, that I finally saw the Paper House of Pigeon Cove, Massachusetts, in person.

Through a simple twist of fate, and a random conversation, my wife and I learned that friends of ours, Karen and John Moran, originally from Lowell, Massachusetts, were going to be in Massachusetts at the same time we were going to be in nearby Newport, R.I. for a wedding. I had already planned to spend a day in Boston, but they said why don't we come spend some time with them in Lowell. I knew   of Lowell but wouldn't have been able to place it on a map in relationship to Boston, or Newport. I impulsively said sure, then scurried to the atlas to discover what I had just committed to.

A week later at their Florida home the Moran's asked what would   I like to do in Lowell. In between the initial conversation, and this meeting, I had done a little research, and confessed to them I would actually rather spend the day in nearby Salem (site of the first American witchcraft trials) than in Lowell. Without missing a heart-beat they said that was easy, we could make a day trip of it and see their first home in Gloucester too (built in 1818) and, "Oh, there is this weird little house in a nearby place called Pigeon Cove that you might be interested in". There may not be another person in the world that the words "Pigeon Cove, Mass." would mean anything to, but my eyes lit up.

"Not a house made entirely of paper, by any chance, I said cautiously.

"So, you know of it, they said in unison".

"Know of it?! I once tried to buy it!" They couldn't believe it.

A couple months later, on a lovely July day the four of us drove along the coast, saw Salem in the morning — the tour of Hawthorne's legendary House of Seven Gables is much more substantial than the local witch sites — lunched in Gloucester on the water, then wove our way through the rural country lanes of Pigeon Cove. It was immediately apparent why the house couldn't be moved: it was supported by a very big Cambrian Shield rock outcropping, and the outside looked a little worse for wear (it was nearly 100 years old at this point, and would never hold up to the abuse of a crane or fork-lift).

We paid a donation fee to go inside (it resides next to an occupied home, the owners of which act as "gatekeep-ers" for the Paper House), and our jaws hit the ground. Everything was perfect, chairs, book shelves, tables, the clock, the piano, the fireplace, they were all still there looking exactly like they had in Ripley's old photos. It's a thing of real beauty, and a testimony to man's creativity and ingenuity.

I emptied my pocket in the donation box, and smiled like a Cheshire cat. I couldn't have been happier. Like all big fish that get away, talking about it is almost better than catching the big one. It warms my heart to know this big fish is still in existence, and I believe its legend will continue to grow for generations to come. It should be a national monument.

The Best of the Rest

Reporters and interviewers almost always asked me what was my "favorite" exhibit, or what was the "strangest thing" I ever acquired. I didn't always say the same thing — depending on my mood, what the questioner seemed most interested in, or even just the flavor of the day. New purchases were always worth mentioning so that the reporter would get something new, and not just a rehash of something someone else had already mined. Typically, I would randomly select something on the spot. For many years I published an annual top ten, and Canada's **Maclean's Magazine** once published a definitive all time top ten, but it was probably already out of date by the time they printed it. What follows is a list of artifacts that might not make my top ten today, but certainly would appear in my top twenty, and are worth highlighting for one reason or another aside from just my liking them.

My Robert Ripley Faves

The first caveat I would establish if I were to make an authoritative list would be whether the list took in the entire collection, or was to be made up of just things I personally acquired. If I was to include Robert's contributions, he would receive the top three spots, no contest, plus one other, not too much further down the list:

1) Hananuma Masakichi

2) The Devil & The Damsel

3) A two-headed baby skeleton from 1894

4) A set of four wood carved and hand painted replicas of the temples of Beijing's Forbidden City and the Summer Palace.

Evidence is pretty clear regarding how fond Ripley was of the Masakichi statue, a wood carved self-portrait of the artist, made from thousands of dovetailed pieces of wood and adorned with the artist's own hair and fingernails, created as a gift to the woman he loved, believing he was dying from tuberculosis. Ripley only paid ten dollars for it in 1933 (along with a handful of Tibetan artifacts thrown in to close the deal), but it is insured for considerably more, and has been featured on Ripley radio shows, television shows, web broadcasts, and in more than a half-dozen odditorium locations. It is macabre, no doubt, but it is also beautiful, and the tragic story of the tubercular artist adds to its lasting appeal.

The Devil and the Damsel is a life-size fine art wood sculpture, featuring Mephistopheles on one side, and the Virgin Mary on the other, based on a scene from Goethe's play **Faust**. The viewer can only see one figure at a time from any given stand point. The piece dates from the early 18th century, and was found by Ripley in France in the 1920s, but maybe Italian in origin. Much to my amazement, an exact copy can be seen in a museum in South India. That there are two of these may devalue it monetarily, but the mystery behind the second one only increases their intrinsic value in my view.

Very little has ever been written, or said, about the two-headed baby skeleton. I have to conclude the PR people were always nervous about it, and literally ignored it. It was featured on a Dean Cain-TBS-television episode, and in a 1990s-era guidebook, but it has been in Australia out of the limelight for more than twenty years. The earliest photo of it is a 1950s era Ripley's Time Square black and white postcard. The postcard says the skeleton was from Philadelphia in 1894. There are no other details. The birth of a two-headed baby is an exceptional anomaly, that nothing is known about this specimen is almost more amazing than its existence. It is professionally articulated, and probably was used at some point as a medical study reference. Its large deep eye sockets are hauntingly disturbing. Philadelphia's **Mütter Museum** has other 19th century medical artifacts that may have the same effect on a viewer, but I have never seen anything to match the mesmerizing stare of this particular piece.

Beauty is in the eye of the beholder, and though I am sure everyone recognizes the colorful beauty of the Ripley Forbidden City buildings, the average person misses their true beauty — the workmanship in their construction. The four buildings in question are all hand carved perfect replicas of real buildings, each one containing thousands of small pieces, dovetailed together. There are no nails, or screws, and no glue. They are architectural wonders.

Ripley visited the Forbidden City and the Summer Palace twice, in 1923 and again in 1932. There are several pictures, and film footage of him outside the real buildings, the Temple of Heaven, The Audience Hall, the Hall of Dispelling Clouds (1), and The Temple of Seventy-Two Gables, but none are in color, or taken close enough to see the hidden details. The models are roughly five-feet square, small enough to get quite close to, yet big enough to inspect every inch of ornamentation. They were originally displayed in New York as early as 1940, then in St. Augustine from 1950 until 1989. Since that time, they have been dispersed to four different odditoriums, and have never been reunited. Individually they are magnificent, together, definitely worthy of a top ten designation.

Now with those out of the way, I am left with "my" best of the rest, a small group of exhibits that may not show up on anyone else's best of list, but that have a special place in my heart regardless of how anyone else might judge them.

Collections:

In forty years, I saw a lot of personal — unusual — collections, everything from potato chip bags to shrunken heads. More than once it was a widow, or a widower, showing me the collection of their recently deceased spouse. Even if, perhaps especially because, someone has lived in the same house as a rabid collector, it doesn't mean they were happy about it. My experience is that they can barely wait to get rid of the stuff and reclaim part of their house. Usually they will want some money, but they are much more interested in getting rid of the stuff, and not having to deal with it anymore. For example, a poor man living in a pink and red house, with over 3,000 things with pictures of Betty Boop on them, everything from his front door, to his curtains, to his dinnerware, to the rug on his floor. In terms of obsessive compulsiveness his wife would have been hard to beat. The collection represented more than thirty years of travel, souvenir shops, and their marriage. I thought the collection a real hoot, but I only bought about fifteen pieces, the best being a classic 1940s-style juke box featuring Betty on the front. Even if the owner could come to tolerate Betty's omnipresence, I am sure the color scheme of the house had to be driving him crazy. The whole house reminded me of a child's perfect cupcake, complete with sprinkles. I couldn't wait to escape.

At the opposite end of the collector spectrum are Tom Van Pelt of New Jersey and Warren Raymond of Maryland. Both these men have meticulously kept collections of Ripley memorabilia, all lovingly cared for, documented, preserved, and displayed with the pride equal to the best museum curators. I bought dozens of items from Warren over the years, including clothing worn by the smallest woman, Lucia Zaratte, and the tallest man, Robert Wadlow, but my favorite items were vintage Ripley's 1930s odditorium posters, advertising the human oddities to be seen inside, everything from fat ladies and giants, to a half-man, and a man who could blow up his stomach to epic proportions with a car tire pump. Despite being over eighty years old, the posters were all in mint condition. Warren's collection of circus sideshow performers, specifically half-man Johnny Eck, is the best in the world.

I only convinced Tom Van Pelt to part with one item from his collection but it was a game changer. I thought I was on good terms with Robert Ripley's only living relatives, but when they decided to sell things from their personal collection, they sold some things outright to Tom, then sold a few others via an auction house in Philadelphia that somehow flew under my radar. I only learned about the auction at the last minute, and was not able to personally bid. Tom got all the best stuff.

The treasure Tom sold to Ripley's was thirteen baseball outfits worn by Ripley's 1939 charity team. He literally had no room for them in his modest home, and under condition that they be displayed in New York City, he parted with them all at a very reasonable price. Baseball being my favorite sport, and the fact that Babe Ruth had worn one of these jerseys, makes them one of my pride and joy acquisitions. Yet, these were not the biggest treasures in Tom's Ripley collection.

Strange as it may seem, when I first contacted the government in the hopes of finding records pertaining to Ripley's overseas travels, they told me that they had no passport records for the world's most traveled man. Baffling, considering Ripley's own four Robert Ripley passports, and Tom must have a dozen others! Gorgeously displayed in a dining room glass corner cabinet, Tom has the papers — passports and visas — needed to make the definitive chart of Ripley's travels to a reported 201 countries. I may have drooled on them. Tom also has at least a dozen things associated with Ripley's office, and artifacts from the Mon Lei as well. His is not the largest Ripley collection, but it is the most important by far.

More Miniatures

Long before I found Tom Van Pelt in New Jersey, I found George Tabasco, another New Jersey collector-builder that had the perfect collection for the soon to open Atlantic City Ripley Odditorium: twenty-one tableaus of miniature furniture, that all together make up the rooms of a Baroque era chateau. Each "room", measuring two cubic feet, has dozens, sometimes hundreds, of pieces, everything from sofas and chandeliers, to books on shelves. Some of the pieces are store-bought plastic figurines, but the majority are hand carved wood. The entire collection had been displayed by Ripley's at the Steel Pier in Atlantic City in the 1950s, but had not publicly been shown in nearly fifty years. To display them, each individual room was inset in to the wall of the odditorium; together they take up more than 2.000 square feet of display space. Individually they are delicate and delightful. Together, they rival any doll house collection that can be found in any museum anywhere in the world, including the House on the Rock, in Wisconsin, or the Rijks in Amsterdam.

The pieces took George thirty years to build and collect. There are over 7000 miniature screws and forty gallons of adhesives holding it all together. The total weight is over 3,500 pounds, and the materials alone cost in excess of $100,000.

My love for miniatures is no secret, but in addition to the mini artifacts already mentioned elsewhere I need to mention Stan Richards of Pennsylvania, and Andrew Gawley of Meaford, Ontario, Canada (2).

Ripley had a real fascination with miniatures, especially rice writers. Stan Richards maybe the best rice writer of them all. His masterpiece, the Lord's Prayer written free-hand on a single grain of rice, is letter perfect — his opus — but he also did miniature scrimshaw etchings, and miniature wood carvings. Both he and Gawley, who Ripley had featured at the Chicago and Dallas odditoriums of 1934 and 1936, could carve intricate multi-linked chains out of single matchsticks and toothpicks. They are the best pieces of wood whittling in the Ripley collection.

My Definition of Insanity

One of the largest pieces in the Ripley collection, and incontestably the most complicated, is a twenty-six foot in circumference working Meccano — Erector set Ferris Wheel. It is the largest, **working** Meccano model in the world — it spins around, and it can even carry dolls in its carriages. It has over 30,000 pieces. I bought it sight unseen based on a newspaper story. It had been on display, in Chicago, at a toy convention, but it was about to be dismantled and shipped back to France. I asked the silly question, was it for sale? The young French team of builders were more than happy to not have to totally dismantle it and ship it back to France. The piece(s), and the team, went straight to St. Augustine, Florida, where it took four days to reassemble the wheel in the room with the greatest ceiling height in the Ripley odditorium chain. The wheel fit like a glove with just inches to spare in all directions. The wheel ran night and day, seven days a week for the next seventeen years.

Aside from its size, and the crazy number of pieces, part of the appeal of this piece for me is the fact that I could never make anything out of even the simplest Meccano sets. Growing up, they were my idea of hell and I was sure anyone who liked these demonic toys must be insane. Later I bought a giant Meccano lunar capsule from the same team, but it didn't have any moving parts.

I am not sure where the wheel's next home will be, but lights have now been added to it, and there has been talk of building some type of weather resistance protection so that it could be displayed outside. Currently there is still no other room in the Ripley world big enough to hold it.

The Sacred Buffalo

Scrimshaw, the etching into ivory or bone, is closely associated with 18th and 19th century New England whalers, but was practiced by the Inuit peoples of the Arctic long before then. The inspiration for the indigenous peoples of the Plains to take up the art form in the 19th and 20th centuries probably was influenced by both these sources.

James Durham, a Lakota Sioux, and a Vietnam veteran, is one of the biggest people I have ever met. Nearly seven-feet tall, his shoulders and chest were huge. At first glance I would have picked him as either a football player, or a wrestler. He had a prominent Roman-nose, long hair in a pony tail, and was a majestic and imposing figure. If his voice wasn't so soft and calming, his size and appearance would have scared me.

On different, separate occasions, James and his son had sweat lodge visions of a magnificent buffalo that talked to them in a strange language of sacred past times. James turned the visions into the largest piece of scrimshaw art in the world, a full-size buffalo skeleton, carved with the stories of the seven sacred rites of the Lakota: Chanunpa; the rite of Purification; Making of Relatives; the Keeping and Releasing of the Soul; Throwing of the Ball; Crying for a Vision; and the Sundance.

A long-time Ripley odditorium franchisee called me one morning from the University of Central Florida, about thirty miles from our office. He encouraged me to come out to the school to hear a lecture by a Sioux Indian.

He mentioned the art work, but was more taken with the speaker than the buffalo. I was apologetic; being a fan of all things Native American Indian I was interested, but I simply couldn't drop what I was doing.

Later that afternoon to my surprise, James himself called me and introduced himself. My associate had given him my number in the thought that I might want to buy the skeleton. The lecture series was over, but James was going to be in town for a couple days. He personally invited me to come see his buffalo. I couldn't say no. mounted on a huge carved wooden compass-like disc, representing the four winds, and the circle of life, the artwork was breathtaking. Along the wall of the room were framed detailed close-ups of various bones, and story-boards explaining their meanings. I was awestruck. I had never seen more detailed scrimshaw, and nothing even close in terms of the size. Every inch of the skeleton was engraved. Knowing there are over 25,000 etched lines on the legs alone, and 163 different spirit figures on the ribs, I estimated there were over a million markings on the complete skeleton. James assembled a team of carvers to complete his vision; in total it took seven years to complete. For a couple of years, until Miss Monroe came along into my life, it was the most expensive item in the collection; it still ranks in the top ten.

Over the next few weeks I saw James a lot, each time he pulled me further into the spiritual world of the Lakota Sioux, which was in general, way too deep for me to fathom. When I acknowledged my Catholic beliefs, he surprised me by saying he believed in Jesus too. Turned out he had been partially educated by missionaries, and his second biggest work was a scrimshawed crucifixion, depicting the life and death of Christ as told in the four Gospels, carved on a real human skeleton, hanging on a cross beautifully carved to match the buffalo's majestic base.

Buying, and displaying the Crucifixion was considerably more controversial than the buffalo, and until Ripley's came along, James had not publicly ever displayed it. I could never have displayed this in one of our smaller or more rural odditoriums. The Baptists in our corporate office wouldn't even look at it: too shocking, too disturbing, too blasphemous.

The etchings on each arm and each leg tell the life of Christ, as written by one of the Gospel writers: Matthew, Mark, Luke and John. The Crucifixion scene is front and center on the skull. The piece isn't as detailed as the buffalo — human bones being smaller and more fragile than buffalo bones, but I would still rank it as the number two scrimshaw work in the world. It hung in London for ten years without a single complaint, someone, however, did break a couple toe bones.

The Biggest Acquisition

For the company's entire 100-year history there have always been copy-cats, people who either unknowingly, or blatantly, tried to capitalize on Ripley's popularity by creating their own replicas of Ripley products, typically the Ripley cartoon, but also the Ripley museum concept as well. The most famous knock-off was during Ripley's lifetime, John Hix's **"Strange As It Seems"** cartoons, books, and a New York World's Fair museum. Others included, **"Now You Know"**, **"Amazing but True"**, **"Believe It or Don't"**, and **"It Happened in Canada."** The Ripley legal team fought these imposters diligently, so no surprise that when a museum in Majorca, Spain appeared on the radar, borrowing liberally from our architecture, our story-lines, and displaying duplicates of much of our most iconic exhibitory, the battle was fought to close them down as quickly as possible.

The case was quite ugly, and relationships, in some cases with long time associates, would never quite be the same again. The resolution was that the operators could stay in business, but had to sell everything to Ripley's that Ripley's wanted in order to distance the two companies from each other in content. Ripley's purchased almost the entire museum's collection of over 700 pieces.

The best pieces we got were a set of megalodon shark jaws, with over 300 real prehistoric teeth, a Chinese jade dragon boat bigger than any in our existing collection, two giant Patrick Acton matchstick models (see Chapter 55), and over sixty buildings made from toothpicks, called **"Toothpick City"**, made by Stan Munro of New York State. All five of these exhibits had been things I had once tried to buy, but had been seriously outbid on. I now knew who my buying nemesis was.

Toothpick City is unique in its vision and scale, if not in its quality. The workmanship pales compared to Patrick Acton's matchstick marvels, but Stan set out to build a replica of every major world-famous building. Since we acquired **Toothpick City**, which took over thirty years and a million toothpicks to assemble, and includes models of the Eiffel Tower, the Leaning Tower of Pisa, the Brooklyn Bridge, the Sydney Harbor Opera House, and Yankee Stadium, Stan has completed **Toothpick City II**. Nicknamed Temples and Towers, it contains well over 3.5 million toothpicks. Stan has already inspired dozens of other toothpick artists, and may not be finished yet.

Due to the legal nature of this acquisition, both the company's lawyer, Scott Line and the CFO, Darren Loblaw, were intricately involved in the transaction. They worked on this deal a lot harder and longer than I did. I did no negotiating, but behind the scenes, did the critical inventory and appraisals that determined the scope of the purchase, and I did get a trip out of the deal. Majorca is a beautiful island, and has the best olives I have ever eaten.

2010 with this acquisition was the last year that I ever acquired more than 1,000 new exhibits in a calendar year.

78

One that Got Away #12 — the Mon Lei

When Robert Ripley died in 1949, his brother and sister took a few personal things from his three homes, but the majority of his treasures were sold at public auction. One man, named John Arthur bought as many of the items as he could afford that he felt he could capitalize on. He did buy a couple rugs, and some furnishings, but for the most part these went elsewhere. He was more interested in shrunken heads, narwhal tusks, tribal masks and Oriental statuary. The most expensive lot of the week-long auction was Ripley's full size

— sixty-five-foot long authentic, (but not old), Chinese Junk, named the **Mon Lei** (loosely translated as "10,000 miles"). It cost Arthur $5,500.

Even then this was a paltry sum for a working yacht, but compared to other prices in the auction (a shrunken head went for ten dollars) it may have seemed like a king's ransom. For whatever reason, Arthur didn't install it at his first Ripley odditorium in St. Augustine, Florida, where it had often been docked between 1946-49, and in less than two years, he had turned around and sold it. The biggest fish in the Ripley collection got away for the first time. In 2016-2017 it got away a second time, not only breaking the line, but breaking my heart and will.

There are dozens of stories regarding the Mon Lei, some of them apocryphal, and some probably made up by Ripley himself. What I am sure of was that it was his very favorite possession, at least for the last three years of his life (1946-1949), when he regularly sailed it all around Long Island, NY, motored it to work from his island home in Mamaroneck to his office or apartment in Manhattan, took leisurely press excursions up the US Eastern Seaboard to Boston, and joy rides down the coast to his second home in Palm Beach, Florida. On one trip, he sailed it around Key West, and up the west side of Florida to Tampa. This is the furthest that he ever sailed it that I can vouch for.

The ship, however, definitely had been across the Pa-

cific Ocean and through the Panama Canal at some point
before Ripley owned it. Most likely the junk was barged
across the Pacific, rather than sailed. It was brought
to America for the 1939 San Francisco Golden Gate
World's Fair. Ripley had an odditorium at that fair, and
most likely saw and fell in love with the junk there.
Evidence suggests – contrary to contemporary literature
– that the ship was probably built in Hong Kong in 1938
specifically for the Fair. It is very unlikely that it
was pre-owned by pirates or warlords, but it was – and
still is to my knowledge — the only authentic Chinese
Junk in America.

What better ship could Ripley have imagined as his personal yacht?

It is unknown how the boat got to Baltimore in 1944,
whether it was sailed or towed, or whether Ripley already owned it, but once in Baltimore, Ripley took full
possession, and immediately started to convert it into
his personal luxury yacht. He added intricate paintings
and a dragon-like face to its bow, furnished it in the
finest silks and Oriental artifacts from his collection, redesigned its sails, and most significantly,
added a diesel engine. Ripley's favorite pastime was to
motor it in the opposite direction that the sails were
set, causing passersby to gasp in amazement. He would
give elaborate cocktail parties on board, and even
hosted a couple of weddings. Guests, especially his
confidant, Li Ling Ai, would often be dressed in gorgeous silk robes like an Oriental potentate. Ripley
himself wore a more traditional blue blazer and white
Captain's hat, and played the part of Admiral to the
hilt.

I first saw the boat in 1982 when Jack Palance was
filmed on it for the first Ripley-ABC television show.
After John Arthur had parted with it, it had been sold
one more time; the same owner had had it for almost
thirty years at this point. The sails had been changed
(westernized, and modernized), but otherwise the ship
was still pretty much like it had been when Ripley
owned it. The sale price was $2 million dollars. We did
not even make an offer.

I then saw the boat a second time, docked on Manhattan's Lower Westside, ten years later. It was still

owned by the same owner, but it had suffered an electrical fire below deck affecting the galley, the head, and the three sleeping areas. The damage was not extensive, but the boat couldn't be repaired as it had been. The owner was now willing to sell it for $1.2 million. We considered it, and entered negotiations, but didn't get too far. The price was firm, and we thought it too much. Recall the boat had once been worth less than $6,000.

I lost track of the Mon Lei for more than twenty years. In 2016, a Norwegian businessman-sailor, named Victor Samuelsen, living in Greenwich, Connecticut, cold-called me on behalf of the owner — still the same man – who was now wishing to sell it because maintenance costs were hurting him, and he was too old to sail the ship himself. Turns out it had not gone too far in twenty-years. It did visit Manhattan occasionally, rented for parties and weddings, but it was docked in Connecticut, and increasingly used less and less. It had a second fire and this time lost its pilot house, and some other deck details. It had, however, been repaired, and more restoration was underway. In a couple of months it would be as good as new. Asking price was now $1 million. I considered this in my ball-park.

I flew to Connecticut in May of 2016, met Victor, one of the most amiable people I've ever met, and saw the boat dry-docked. It was in rough shape, and I doubted it would be sea-worthy anytime soon, but it was still recognizable as the Mon Lei, and I loved it. Victor thought the boat would be ready by the end of the summer. He was over optimistic. For the next eighteen months I would frequently talk to Victor who had been promised a commission if he could sell the Mon Lei. He sent me progress reports and photos, and even offered to pilot the ship to Florida if I would buy it.

He was my sole contact. I did eventually meet the owner's son, but I never met, or talked directly, to the owner.

As the months went by, I whittled down the price, but I wouldn't commit a penny until the work was actually finally done. For months I regularly begged the Ripley brass to give me a firm price, a number I could say "take it or leave it", but no one but me was passionate about the boat, and the longer it took to repair, the more the initial luster and sheen fell away. I did everything that was asked of me: financial analytics, proposals for both land and water scenarios, with locations ranging from Atlantic City to Harbin, China, determine costs of storage and the price of new sails, etcetera, but all to no avail. Every doubt and obstacle were repeatedly thrown in my face, and I grew very discouraged. The party-line was "Where would we put it?" The mind set was "We can't. It won't fit", rather than "What if". Buzz Price, and Robert Ripley were probably both rolling over in their graves. The asking price was now only $300k; the work that had been done gratis, and the captain, were potential free bonuses. Victor even offered to pay out of his own pocket for the upcoming winter storage.

Somehow, the company still said no.

There were a dozen things that influenced my decision to retire, but the passing on the Mon Lei was very high on the list. I had struggled with corporate decisions before, but this one just didn't make sense to me, especially after eighteen months of negotiations, and a 90% discount in the price from when I first looked at the ship oh so many years earlier. The Mon Lei was what opened my eyes and made me realize I no longer agreed with either management's philosophy or direction. If owning the only Chinese Junk in America wasn't a believe it or not, not to mention that it had been owned by the company's founder, and that it was affordable, I was pretty sure I no longer knew what I should be shopping for. I had been giving it some thought for a couple years, but the decision to leave on my 40th anniversary, May 8, 2018, was pretty much cemented October 6, 2017.

After seeing the boat wrapped up for the winter, like a mummy going to its tomb, I asked Victor to drive Angela and I past Ripley's B.I.O.N. Island before dropping us off at the airport. Ripley's home was torn down in 1957, but the beautiful home now on the island was for sale (for around $5 million). It was a lovely autumn day with some colorful leaves already on the ground, but most still on the trees. We drove through the gate and introduced ourselves to the grounds keeper who allowed us a short walk around the property. I wistfully stared out at where the boat had once been docked, and noted how peaceful and serene the reflected forest scene in Ripley's harbor pond was. Angela took it all in with child-like excitement, it being her first time there, snapping photos a mile a minute. I looked on it with a tearful farewell, knowing it was marking the end of an era for me.

The owner's Plan B for the boat was to make it into a floating oyster bar, and the following spring he gutted "the head" and made some other necessary changes to it, then sailed it down the coast to Upper Manhattan. The restaurant-bar idea didn't work out though, and by late 2018 the boat was once again for sale. Victor appealed to me two or three more times, but I passed him over to Angela.

I would be happy if Ripley's could one day buy it. It would be a great kickoff to the post-Edward era of the Ripley's exhibit collection, and a huge feather in the company's cap, to catch the big one that broke my heart [1].

79

Space, the Final Frontier

I was never much interested in the NASA space program when I was growing up, and the grade school gymnasium events when the entire school assembled to watch space launches and landings on black and white televisions mounted on rolling metal stands, were pretty much lost on me; they were just times to chat with friends about important stuff, like hockey, music and girls. The fact that I do remember them, however, suggests they did leave some kind of imprint on my adolescent mind. To this day — nearly fifty years later — I certainly remember where I was at 4:17 pm (EST), July 21, 1969, when Apollo XI, the Eagle, landed on the surface of the moon (1). Based on fifty years worth of conversations, I am convinced I, and my family, were the only ones on Earth who were not in front of a television set that day. We heard the news on a small three-inch by six-inch transistor radio deep in the woods about twenty miles south-west of Huntsville, Ontario.

My mother loved to listen to baseball games on the radio and in the summers carried a small transistor radio with her just about everywhere, even to our small run-down fish camp-cottage. She literally forced my sisters out of the lake to listen to the broadcast. My mother sat on the front porch — two rickety wooden stairs — my father leaned against a tree, my sisters Janet and Jean, lounged in the near-by hammock, and I, sitting cross-legged on the ground, looked longingly the other way to the water. My mother cried the whole time, and in no uncertain terms told us how important this moment was: "Pay attention, or no one will be going in the water again all week!"

It took twenty-four and a half years for my light bulb to flicker.

I didn't literally sleep through the shuttle years, but even the tragedies didn't move me the way they should have. The only notable space pro-gram experience I had between 1969 and 1993 was sitting with a bunch of the Ripley team in Toronto at a local restaurant near the office mid-afternoon to see the shuttle piggy-backed on a cargo air-craft. I don't recall where it was going, or why Toronto was on the flight path, but it was front page news and the entire city stopped that afternoon for about ten minutes. If anything, I am afraid it had a negative effect on me; if the shuttle was "small" enough to be carried by an airplane, what was the big deal?

It took a behind the scenes tour of the Houston Space Center in 2015, when I got to see inside the International Space Station, and see the top of the Earth from the Space Station view, for the light bulb to reach maximum brightness (see Chapter 31).

On December 11, 1993, Sotheby's Auction House in New York City held the first ever Space auction, and Bob Masterson and I were there. The items sold that day were all from the Russian space program, as were the items in their second auction in March of 1996. In between those dates a few smaller history specialist auction houses started to sell a few pieces of American space objects, but it wasn't until the early 2000s did every auction house in the country pride itself on offering space artifacts for sale. From 1993 through 2018 Ripley's acquired everything from razors flown in space; to urine bags and space food; to souvenir program pins and patches; to full Russian space suits; to fragments of the only Bible to ever have been on the surface of the moon; to meteorites from the moon and Mars. We also discovered **Star Trek** and **Star Wars** memorabilia in a big way.

Sotheby's 1993 auction was truly historic. No one had ever sold space related items, aside from meteorites, before and no one knew if there was a market for the materials or not. Sotheby's got their answer immediately. The room was packed with people from all walks of life — Bob and I were sitting beside astronauts — and one of the very first items on the block, a slide rule used by Sergei Korolov, Russia's chief rocket engineer, and spacecraft designer, sold for $21,000. This was followed shortly after by a letter from Soviet leader Nikita Khrushchev to Yuri Gagarin, the first man to travel in outer space. It was estimated at $2,000, but sold for $66,000. Several other Gagarin items sold for more than ten times the estimates, culminating in a lot that was an official announcement from the Soviet government declaring Gagarin the first man to travel into space, estimated to fetch

$20,000, but realizing $354,000.

In total, Sotheby's collected a cool $6.8 million dollars for their three hours work. We were outbid on just about everything we were interested in, but did manage to get several hydro-survival suits and kits

items flown in space, but used on land after the cosmonauts returned to earth. (The Russians tended to land in the middle of Siberia with no pin-point accuracy, rather than in the water, so they were equipped with survival kits just in case they were stranded for any length of time).

The gem of the auction was the actual Vostok space capsule that Gagarin flew in in 1961. It may have been the only thing that didn't reach its estimate, but it still sold for $1.7 million dollars. Bob Masterson, a veteran Vietnam helicopter pilot, had his photo taken in it before the sale.

That first sale revolutionized the auction world. Suddenly baseball cards and fine art weren't the only things worth millions of dollars. Space, natural history, and pop culture auctions all flourished in the wake of Sotheby's unbridled success.

Bob was much more interested in "space" than I was, but we both had our eyes opened that day. It was clear that anything that had been in space, could be sold, and was of interest to someone; it was a market we had to explore further. At the auction we met Darryl Pitt, a meteorite broker, and the same day we bought our first meteorite.

Meteorites are not particularly visual, and it is very hard to get a big one. Price and rarity prevent the average person from even getting close to one, but Bob wanted one, and Darryl over the years proved to be the right guy for the job. He eventually found us several Gibeon iron meteorites over 500 pounds in weight, but our collection started with very small pieces associated with specific crashes, such as the giant Arizona crater and the Peekskill, New York meteorite that hit a car in October 1992. The single most unusual meteorite acquired was a small chunk of a Zagami, Africa, meteorite scientists determined came from Mars. We bought the piece Darryl had for a high, but fair, price. Timing is everything, and less than a month later, headlines around the world proclaimed scientists had determined there had been life on Mars. The value of our small rock went up over 1000% overnight. As per Bob's vision, we encapsulated it in the floor of the new museum in Hong Kong, with advertising that said come to Ripley's and "Stand on Mars" — marketing genius of the highest degree. Martian meteorites are the rarest stones on earth, with only a handful of samples having been found in Zagami, Africa, and the Antarctic. They are not sold too often, and when they are, it is by the gram, not the ounce or pound.

By the time of Sotheby's second Russian space auction on March 1, 1996, we were fully invested. We graduated from the smallest items, to clothing: space gloves, exercise suits, cold weather gear, and two full space suits, that three years earlier had been worth hundreds of thousands of dollars, but were now only the price of a very nice car. We also got the molded fiberglass seat liners from a number of capsules, exhibits that would let everyone understand just how crowded and uncomfortable the first capsules were. Wearing street clothes, I can last only about ten seconds in one of these seats; I can't fathom what they felt like to the cosmonauts fully dressed for space.

To the Moon

Much of the Russian space artifacts sold by Sotheby's belonged to the cosmonauts themselves. NASA's objects on the other hand were slow to come to sale. Technically, items associated with the space program are paid for with tax money, and, therefore, belong to "the American people", not to individuals. Based on the success of Sotheby's Russian auctions, the rules loosened in the 21st century and American Space items started to appear on the market. Buzz Aldrin in particular, seemed to have an endless supply of things to sell, and as "anniversaries" cropped up, space auctions became an annual event for most auction houses, with Sotheby's still leading the way.

Visual and generally affordable, I started collecting

flags that had been flown in space. Every astronaut on every mission seems to have taken at least one into the stratosphere in their PPK (personal preference kit). Astronauts could take just about anything with them, given that it fit inside a five by eight by two-inch bag, and the contents of these bags were theirs to sell as they pleased (2). Flags fold easily and small three by five-inch versions in particular, didn't take up much room. Astronauts didn't just carry the Stars and Stripes though, they carried flags from their home countries, like Japan, India, England, and Jamaica, as well as state flags, from California, and Texas. The most sought after are from Apollo missions, and the rarest of them all of course are the ones that have been flown to the moon and are autographed by the mission astronauts. Ripley's has at least one from every lunar mission.

Astronaut Edgar Mitchell flying on Apollo XIV was determined to take a Bible to the moon, but he couldn't find one that would fit in his PPK. His lab friends at NASA, however, came up with a solution using the latest in micro-technology developed in Houston, NASA, produced a complete King James' Bible measuring just two inches square, and as thin as a piece of paper. The medium was called microfilm.

Deeply religious, Mitchell decided to use this Bible to raise funds for missionary work. He chopped it up into thirty-two quarter inch fragments, and working with the world-renowned jewelers, Fabergé of Paris (and New York), had them encapsulated inside ornate gold, silver, ruby and amethyst encrusted eggs, built in the style of the famous Russian Czarina Fabergé eggs of the early 20th century. Ripley's now has four of these. They are the Crown Jewels of the Ripley space collection.

In the summer of 2017, Sotheby's had its first full "NASA" and property of Buzz Aldrin space auction. With the 50th anniversary of the moon landing on the near horizon, and the fact that it would coincide with the 100th anniversary of Ripley's Believe It or Not! I was determined to get some items associated with Apollo XI. By this time, I had personally met not just John Glenn, but two of the twelve men that have walked on the moon, Charles Conrad, and Neil Armstrong. I had a much greater understanding and appreciation of what the space program, and the moon landing of 1969 in particular, had meant to America in the 1960s. I foresaw a traveling exhibition that would remind America just how unbelievably courageous these men had been. Glenn and Armstrong, I now understood, were real heroes, and Armstrong's steps were now seen to me as being as important as Columbus' voyage to America five hundred years earlier. That said, meeting Armstrong was not as thrilling as meeting Glenn, in fact he disappointed me. When I asked Armstrong, what went through his mind as he stared out the capsule window into space — expecting an epic definition of the universe, or seeing the face of God — he talked about worrying about nuts and bolts and heat shields. Once an engineer, always an engineer.

That July day in 2017 was one of the rare times I got almost everything I was after. The highest prices were achieved on Armstrong's Apollo XI mission patch, autographed by Armstrong, Aldrin and Michael Collins, with a letter of authenticity from Collins, and a large flattened geographical map of the moon's surface autographed by all the astronauts that had walked on its surface (signed where they had walked), as well as the astronauts that had orbited the moon, but not landed — the unsung heroes of the Apollo space pro-gram. The first part of my space mission was complete.

In a Galaxy Far, Far Away

Both my elder sister and my wife are **Star Trek** fans. For the most part I have managed to keep an arm's length away from their geekdom, but the original 1967 television show did have some effect on my pop culture sensibilities. Leonard Nimoy, the show's Mr. Spock, had after all been a Ripley company spokesman in the 1970s [3]. **Star Wars** on the other hand was never even on my radar until 2011 when I bought some life-size statues in Thailand of the brands' main characters that were made from recycled car parts. I of course bought them because they were made from car parts, not because of whom they portrayed. That day I learned just how passionate the **Star Wars** fan base was — including my associate Angela Johnson. From that point on, with her guidance, I made a conscious effort to hunt for **Star Wars** memorabilia.

Art work based on **Star Wars** characters was not too hard to find, and in addition to car parts statues, we were soon able to find sculptures made from chalk, staples, computer wires, and computer keys. We even acquired a replica Darth Vader helmet made from shells in the style of New Guinea clay-covered ancestor heads. Finding actual film related pieces, however, was more difficult, and considerably more expensive. At the end of 2016 we obtained a Carrie Fisher autographed personal script and her used "director's" chair, and I saw millennials engaged in our collection like I had never seen before. I didn't understand it — and still don't – but I certainly couldn't argue with it, or ignore it.

The chair was followed by the purchase of Luke's light saber from the first and second (sic-fourth and fifth) films in the summer of 2017. I almost stopped twice during the bidding, but devil-eye looks from Angela told me there was no quitting allowed in space wars. The press and office employee reactions, were over the moon. Based on first impressions, I am forced to say it is the most popular artifact I ever bought. It physically is just a tube of metal, a part from an old camera, but it has mojo, an aura, that can't be explained, or fathomed. People shake and go speechless in its company, and the lucky ones who have touched it, joke about never washing their hands again. The saber, the chair, the script, a used C3PO helmet, and a cement hand print of Chewbacca's, with a hair lock and autographed photo, were on display within months of the acquisition and receiving enthusiastic response wherever they went.

With a substantial collection of both real and make-believe space items, I envisioned a combination "real" space and "Hollywood" space traveling show for the company's 100th anniversary starting in December 2018, and to be celebrated for a full year in 2019. Whether the vision will come to fruition remains to be seen, but in the last month of my Ripley career, I shifted into warp speed, and went out in a blazing nova. I bought two **Star Wars** land speeders, complete with a flock of Ewoks, and two R2-D2 robots, one a shelf model, the other the most extant movie-used version in existence a conglomerate of several models that post the films, was used regularly in Disney theme parks. (I bought this less than two weeks before I retired, from an auction house in Texas, from my phone, while in a moving car traveling home to Orlando, from New Orleans).

Finally, eight days after I had actually left the building, with Angela's help, and her permission, I was called in to make my last official acquisition: Hans Solo's, **Return of the Jedi DL-44 Blaster**. The blaster is not quite as iconic as Luke's light saber, but one thing Angela taught me well was that there are team Luke followers, and team Hans' followers. I had now appeased both. Reuniting the two weapons gave Ripley's the two most talked about and revered weapons in film history. I have pride in having returned the universe to its proper equilibrium. What the company does with them is a sequel to be directed by some other adventurer. For my part, I'm done.

80

Epilogue

I first visited Santa Rosa, California, the birthplace of Robert Ripley, in September 1983. My mission was to visit the **Church of One Tree** for the Ripley-Jack Palance television show. The church was legendary: Robert Ripley's father had helped build it in the 1880's; his mother had attended services there regularly in the 1990's and early teens; Norbert Pearlorth claimed his knowledge of it had helped him get his job with Ripley in 1923; it had been featured in the cartoon twice (1939 & 1957); and since 1972 it had housed the Robert Ripley Memorial Museum, a joint venture between Ripley International (the company name prior to Ripley Entertainment Inc.), and the city of Santa Rosa. In 1983, there was only two, maybe three, Ripley employees who had ever visited Santa Rosa, and by 1985, two of them were retired. I asked the question then that I still ask myself today: "So just how important to Ripley's is Ripley?"

I may be wrong, but I believe the answer is "crucial", just like Walt to Disneyland, Colonel Sanders to Kentucky Fried Chicken, or Babe Ruth to baseball. You can't have a meaningful present, or any chance of a purposeful future, without an understanding and appreciation for the past. Robert's been dead seventy years, and there have been hundreds of employees since that have added their piece to the puzzle, but Rip is, and always will be, the cornerstone from which the empire stands on. Me, and all the others, are just random bricks added to the foundation. At age sixty-three I have outlived Ripley, and I even worked with the company longer than he did, but without his trail blazing chutzpah, everything else would be "sound and fury, signifying nothing."

The Church of One Tree was glorious, with a central stained-glass window behind the altar featuring a giant redwood tree, a depiction of the original source for not just the existing church, but also for the rector's home (the second building burnt down in the 1960s). The displays, however, were pretty low key and had been virtually ignored. The two-headed cow was missing hair, and all the photos were faded.

I am not sure why I didn't go looking for Robert's gravestone on that visit, or why it took me another thirty years to get back to Santa Rosa to find the hallowed spot, roughly five miles from the church site. It was unfortunate the church was closed that February day in 2013, and we couldn't get in, but at the cemetery, my small party consisting of my wife, Giliane, Ian Iljas, the manager of the nearby Ripley's San Francisco Odditorium, and my assistant Angela Johnson, were met with open arms as celebrities, direct links with the past, and one of the town's trilogy of famous sons (1). The director even had a pre-printed map pointing visitors directly to the site, appropriately situated in the "Odd Fellow's" designated section. We took pictures and reverently left flowers. Rip was the past, I was the present, and Angela was the possible future. A large circle of adventures and joys had come full circle for me.

The tombstone is simple. Robert is buried under the same stone as his mother and father. Under his name: Robert L., and his dates (1890-1949), seemingly as an afterthought, in cursive trademark script style, are the words **Believe It or Not! Ripley** — lest we forget who started it all one hundred years ago with a simple drawing and a catchy phrase (2).

Notes

Chapter 3

1) At various times in my career, I actually had both desks in my office. My dear friend John Corcoran at one point had them both refinished for me, and I loved them. No one else wanted such a small desk, so until my last office was finally at bursting point, I cherished them both like twins, unsure which one was really more significant than the other. The second desk since about 2010 has been used by our warehouse manager. I am not sure if he knows its significance.

Chapter 4

1) As this story tells, I owe my forty-year Ripley career to Noreen Crawford. Coincidentally, it was her and her older sister, Kathleen, that hooked me up with my wife Giliane, four years prior to this event. I owe her an awful lot.

2) Rita Copperthwaite was her married name. Later in her career she would revert to her maiden name of "Copping" to distinguish herself from her brother-in law, Derek Copperthwaite who was the number two man with Ripley's at the time when I was hired.

Chapter 5

1) Terry Hull whom I loved would never reappear in my life. He was a tall burly genius with tools. He made me a set of glass and wood book shelves that I would cherish for the next forty years. When I retired, I took them home with me. They truly were the defining part of my office for years. Jimmy Doyle would never fully disappear from Ripley's, resurfacing in a big way three years later, and then again about fifteen years later as an employee once again in our design department.

2) Claudia would never let Alec forget this momentous occasion and I would retell it myself in a eulogy I gave for Alec at the Toronto Is-land Yacht Club in 2013. As for the book, it is still around somewhere in my house.

I gave it to my son when he was a young kid, and he loved it. I like to think it was one of the books that made him into a lifelong nature lover, and I thank Alec for that.

Chapter 6

1) During a review of this chapter my wife pointed out that I autographed copies of the company's latest book, **Ripley's Book of Chance,** for over thirty minutes, during which time she was given a personal behind the scenes tour of the kitchen — which she considered the highpoint of the evening!

2) Singer Marie Osmond in what was probably her first career move from performing with her brother Donnie, to trying to make it on her own, would host in the aborted half-fourth season. She was better than Holly, but still not as good as Catherine. Of the three it was of course she who would be the one that would become a megastar with incarnations, from diet spokesperson, to talk show host, to Las Vegas headliner. She may have sold a few million records along the way too. I often wonder if she ever thinks of her brief sojourn into the odd back in 1985.

Chapter 7

1) Earlier subject books included **"Animals"** from the mid-50s and **"World Religions"** (early 60s) and the most obscure of all Ripley's books, **"A Catholic's Believe It or Not!",** published by Dell circa 1962.

2) Bland is still one of my all-time favorite singers. Patrick, his wife Mary, and my wife, would see him together live at the Colonial Tavern on Yonge Street in Toronto a couple times. We also drank red wine together in Patrick's home and listened to the album **"Here's the Man"** over and over.

Chapter 8

1) When ABC moved the show in season four from Sunday night to Thursday night, it was seen as a bad omen. We had been competitive versus the ratings powerhouse **"60**

Minutes" for three years, but their sacrificing us to the time slot opposite **"The Bill Cosby Show"** suggested that the end was in sight. The Cosby show would be a ratings monster for the next eight years. It ate us alive.

2) We would eventually learn that John was contractually committed to stay only two years. After about two and half, he left Ripley's and went to work side by side with Jimmy in Vancouver. He left the Pattison Group, and severed any remaining professional connection to Ripley's after about another two and half years (circa 1991).

3) There were eight Ripley's Believe It or Not! museums when Jimmy bought us. New Orleans would be number nine, and there would be two franchises, Las Vegas, and Newport, Oregon, added within another year.

4) "I" never actually worked totally alone. We had company exhibit acquisition contests in which all employees, company – wide, were expected to contribute under my guidance, and from 1994 through 2004 I had an assistant buyer named John Turner, based out of England. John worked on commission, but could not buy anything without mine or Bob Masterson's approval. John definitely was a big reason why the 1990s were our most prolific years. Before his first retirement in 1994 he had been a Ripley odditorium manager in Blackpool, England and St. Augustine, Florida, for a total of twenty-two years.

Chapter 9

1) John indeed didn't stick around too long. He stayed two years per a contractual part of the sale deal, but left early in 1988. Working out of the Pattison Group corporate offices in Vancouver, he was still physically around for a couple more years, but in practice he was gone in 1988 from Ripley's after twelve years at the helm.

2) In order, at Pattison Group events, I later met: Presidents, Ronald Reagan, Jimmy Carter, George H. Bush, Bill Clinton, and President George W, Bush. Other Pattison Group meeting celebrities included Al Gore, Colin Powell, John Glenn, Neil Armstrong, and Margaret

Thatcher.

3) Jimmy subsequently donated the car to a transportation museum in Victoria, British Columbia, who regularly loaned it to other museums, including the Rock N' Roll Hall of Fame in Cleveland, Ohio, gradually making back some of the purchase price. When a first major cleanup and restoration of the car took place in 1988, a small roll of film was found inside the back seat. The film was a home movie believed to have been made by John Lennon. The film was eventually sold for a very pretty penny. The car now belongs to the Royal British Columbia Museum.

Chapter 10

1) "Over twenty-five hundred" is a "conservative" estimate based on seventy items a year for thirty years and a few handfuls for fifteen years before that. It might be more, it might be less — but the total is definitely more items than were acquired from any one other single source, and thus the reason Mr. Lissauer deserves this chapter of his own.

2) During my first three or four years I met with Lissauer in the company of others, first Jimmy Doyle, then Rita Copperthwaite, then Bob Masterson, before I was to deal with him on my own starting in 1985.

Chapter 11

1) This approximation was calculated by multiplying 365 days a year, by fifty-two years, times an average of four items per day, minus 20%. I suspect the actual number is probably higher, not lower.

Chapter 12

1) The Ripley cartoon is available every day electronically, but somehow, it's not the same as looking at it in print. I simply can't get into it online.

Chapter 14

1) Ripley's Amazing Sharks; Ripley's Whales & Dolphins;

Ripley's Big, Weird & Dangerous Fish; and Ripley's Coral Colony Creatures were published. The fifth book about commercial fishing and conservation was 95% finished, but never published, and the sixth book, about North American freshwater species, was started but only about 30% ever completed.

2) Scholastic titles published in 2004 that look exactly like my fish books, except with soft covers, include Ripley's Big Cats, Ripley's Incredible Insects and Ripley's Cold-Blooded Creatures. These are perfect samples of "imitation is the best form of flattery".

3) Photos of the exterior of the building, taken later that January at sunrise from a 100' tall crane ("cherry picker") with a bit of snow on the ground, were widely circulated that year and were amongst the best glamor shots ever taken of any Ripley facility.

4) The book eventually came out in 2003 under the title "Walt's Revolution".

4) Corena appears elsewhere in this book. She is the wife of Kevin Ricks and daughter of Norm Rollingson. Together the three of them are franchisees of the Ripley odditorium in Wisconsin Dells, Wisconsin, and the former Ripley's Jackson Hole venue as well. Samples of her sculpture, mosaics, paintings, and fabric artwork, can be seen throughout the town of Wisconsin Dells.

Chapter 15

1) True story, I met him in Penticton, British Columbia in 1995, and it was one of the first things out of his mouth. We had our picture taken together, two opposite side profiles, and one straight-on. The contrast in the beard is very self-evident.

2) Over the next decade the beard would morph from brown and red, to brown and white (still cut perfectly in half), to all white, without me ever giving it a color touch-up or shaving it to accentuate the color mix. I did occasionally tell people it was how I got my job, and for the real inquisitives I would direct them to an existing cartoon from the early 1930s of another man inflicted with the same unusual skin-pigment defect.

3) In the Iron Maiden episode Steve tried to put me inside this medieval torture device. Todd added some grizzly sound effects and some ultra close-ups that made the viewer wonder did I actually get inside? I didn't.

For the Babe Ruth spot, I actually wore the Babe's 1939 Ripley baseball team uniform. Throughout the filming Steve randomly threw a baseball at me to tell me to "lighten up". I ignored them until the very end when I decided to bat at one with my clipboard. I not only hit it, but the ball traveled high and bounced off a metal shelf. In the aired version it sounds like I hit a home run into the bleachers; Steve can be heard laughing in the background.

3) The statues indeed did come from the West Coast of Africa, and they were bought from an African, named Muhammed Keita, but Mr. Keita sold them to me out of the back of a truck in a parking lot in Orlando, Florida. I personally didn't set foot in Africa until 2016.

4) When Geist announced his retirement in September 2018, after 31 years on the show, CBS included this segment in their official retirement video on television and on the web.

5) I loved this cartoon and considered it my fate. It in turn may have been inspired by a Warner Brothers Porky Pig cartoon from the 1940s in which a wolf character drinks gasoline and blows himself up in order to impress Porky and get on Porky's show. Porky is very impressed and says to the wolf. "You're hired." As a spirit (angel or devil, your choice), the wolf says "trouble is I can only do it once".

Curtis was 14, we were on my I-95 Ripley book road trip (July 23, 1998). That morning my daughter, Celeste, age 12, was pulled out of the outdoor concert audience (Gloria Estefan) and interviewed on **Good Morning America.** She was bragging all day. Around 5 pm the family was walking down Broadway in front of the Ed Sullivan Theatre and we heard a voice, seemingly coming out of a telephone pole. It was Dave. Curtis ran towards the pole, and proceeded to get soaked with water from above. We all watched Dave that night from the hotel room, and sure enough there was Curtis looking very wet, but also very happy. For years both my kids thought anytime you go to New York you would get on television.

Chapter 16

1) Until 2010, the Ripley newspaper cartoon appeared in black and white six days of the week and in color only once (typically in Sunday papers). In addition, the Ripley archives actually had no color cartoons on file past the early 1970s.Therefore, the selection of color material was always greatly limited. We did produce one very nice all color cartoon book in England in the late 1980s, but it had very limited distribution and was only available in America in Ripley odditorium gift shops. Suffice to say it is a real rarity today. Starting in 2010, the newspaper cartoons, drawn by John Graziano have been released in color all seven days of the week.

Chapter 17

1) Names have been purposely omitted in this chapter to protect the not so-innocent.

2) I had been to Australia twice before, in 1988 and again in 1994.

Chapter 19

1) Tim Horton was a real person — not just the name of a very popular Canadian donut store chain. He played defense for the Toronto Maple Leafs during my childhood and later for the rival Buffalo Sabers. He was the last of the great defensive defense men, a player of the muscular-power skating style defense men played before the Boston Bruins' Bobby Orr redefined the position in the early 1970s.

2) Not long after the end of his only season (2008) with the Vipers, Odum committed suicide. He had a horrible season and the publicity the trade generated — not to mention Ripley's part in promoting the bats — was too much for him.

Chapter 20

1) Hank's real name being Henry, this was a wonderful tribute to the legend. As Aaron approached Ruth's home run record during the 1973 season, fans often shouted

"Oh Henry" when he hit a home run. Some fans even threw Oh Henry chocolate bars on the field.

2) A couple years earlier, I bought a number seventeen of fifty-six, 1941 commemorative autographed Joe DiMaggio bat. It was my favorite, and most significant, baseball purchase.

3) I actually got the news of my mother's death, in 2014, while in a minor league Cardinals baseball park in Peoria, Illinois. Many of my best memories of her are linked to baseball.

4) In 1985 I had been on the riverboat, Natchez, docked in New Orleans, but as that boat had drastically been remodeled in 1975, it didn't feel legitimate to me at the time. The tour passed the Battle of New Orleans battlefield, but didn't go much farther down the river, and really was just an excuse for a nice Creole dinner on the water.

5) The crowd of 167,227 in attendance on May 7, 2016 was the second largest ever recorded in their 144 year old history.

6) For the record, they gave Angela her own bat too, but I suspect it doesn't quite mean as much to her as it does to me.

Chapter 22

1) The Wild Magnolias led by Big Chief Bo Dollis, and the Yellow Pochohantas, led by Big Chief Tootie Montana. The Wild Magnolias re-leased seminal albums of classic New Orleans music in the 1970s, and are considered legendary. Ripley's was miles ahead of the curve.

2) I didn't have a prom, and I wore a tailored suit to my wedding, and in 1985 I was only twenty-nine. From this experience, however, I would grow to like a tux and would be sure to wear one at least once a year. B.B King once famously remarked that New Orleans is the only place you can wear a tux any hour of the day and no one will comment, but somehow, I always get asked "Do you work here?". I must really look like either a musician or a waiter.

3) There were some big events in Asia, in the 1990's, most notably, in Korea, but I wasn't involved in these productions, and not at any of them to give first hand commentary.

4) This odditorium was a franchise, so Steve wasn't just spending Ripley's money.

5) London was also a franchise; it operated for nine years before closing in 2016.

6) Chronologically it happened a few months before London, but I have switched the order here as strictly speaking, it was not a Ripley museum opening, and, therefore, considerably different.

7) Steve had done special VIP gifts of replica shrunken heads for the New York opening too, but here the crowd was caught totally by surprise, the effect was electric.

Chapter 23

1) Olga for over twenty years has been Ripley's, and Louis Tussaud's Wax Works, chief costume designer. An extremely talented and creative woman, she could make anything from royal capes and dresses, to a tuxedo made out of salmon skins. A sequined vest was mere child's play for her.

Chapter 24

1) The real highlight for me of this entire tour, I confess, had nothing to do with selling books, and occurred on my one night off in New York. By coincidence, at dinner I met actor Alan Alda of M.A.S.H television fame, and later the same evening, at an appearance of the legendary guitarist Les Paul at the Iridium nightclub, actor John Lithgow, who was appearing as **Don Quixote de la Mancha** on Broadway. It was Paul's 87th birthday, and he was dynamite.

2) I would have preferred to go trout fishing, or cave exploring on my day off, but the WETA tour gave me real bragging rights back in Orlando, and the sound studio portion of the tour featuring Jackson's **King Kong** was

truly unforgettable.

3) I knew before hand where the statues were, but in finding them, I found two other art studios doing very similar work. Over the next seven years, I would buy more than fifty car part sculptures from these rural Thai artisans.

Chapter 25

1) Commander Tom started airing in 1965, when I was 9. The host's full name was Tom Jolls. He had started as a weatherman, but doubled as the host of a kid's after school show that ran from 3:30 to 5pm five days a week. The show always had cartoons, but it also featured classic black and white movie serials from the 1940s, like **Superman** and **Flash Gordon**. He was corny, but great. I loved the show, and watched it religiously for at least seven years.

2) I am aware that divers today can last underwater more than twenty minutes, but these involve inhaling pure oxygen beforehand, and typically some downward vertical movement. Our guys literally just jumped in the water, and sat on the bottom of the tank for as long as they could. The sharks and rays were meant to look dangerous, but the divers were never in any danger, the rays were barb-less and the bonnet-head sharks, though related to the fierce hammerhead, are non-aggressive and are generally passive.

Chapter 26

1) Earlier Ripley's had done a "traditional Pepper's Ghost" film utilizing a full-sized actor as a small two-feet tall leprechaun. It was Anton Gosley who was convinced if you had big enough mirrors anything could be projected, including a moving five-foot, ten-inch tall Mr. Ripley.

2) Under my direction, and my Native Peoples-era fanaticism, Ripley's created a wax figure display of this ritual and featured it in several odditoriums throughout the 1990s and well into the next decade.

3) Though it was the first filmed, the segment didn't

523

air until the 5th episode.

4) At the time of writing, Kevin still does Scottish Highland games and the occasional charity truck pull, but I think his wife and two grandchildren have convinced him to "slow down". For the record, his daughter, and his wife, are also extremely fit individuals, and happen to be world-class beach volleyball players.

5) Years later while filming two other stunt men, Jim Stilianos and "Lucky, the Pain Proof Man", in our warehouse in Orlando, I added stepping on a man's face while he laid in glass, and smashing concrete blocks set on a man's stomach while they laid on a bed of nails, to my list of credentials. Tough jobs, but someone had to do them! Jim also did the human blockhead nail stunt described earlier in this chapter, and juggled bowling balls and M&M candies at the same time (think about that for a moment). He also juggled fire sticks. One flaming torch got away from him, and caused a near panic, as we rushed to put it out before our warehouse caught fire!

6) Stein's boat was a well-used second-hand model. Though equipped with modern conveniences, it was much heavier than modern aluminum and fiberglass models. Stein was actually overtaken by another rower, Laval St. Germain, in a lighter, faster, boat during his trip. St. Germain who has also scaled Mt. Everest, holds the honor of being the fastest person to row solo across the Atlantic. He was forty-nine years old and completed the 4,500 km trip in fifty-three days.

7) Stein's goal was St Mary's, Isles of Sicily. This is where Harboand Samuelsen first came ashore. After a brief rest they got back in their boat and rowed to Le Havre, France, thus the reference to France in Jerry Bryant's ballad.

Chapter 27

1) As a family member, Celeste was not eligible to win anything in the contest, but in year two she sent me a foam replica ice cream sandwich. The address was written in white letters directly on the brown "chocolate". I now had cake and ice cream too — what a birthday! The

next year — my 60th birthday (the contest was long over) she sent me two large fake Pepto-Bismol pink cookies— complete with sprinkles. I was afraid to ask what the pink icing was made of.

Chapter 28

1) For my first meeting, in 1984, in Acapulco, Mexico, there had been only seventeen people. It grew very little during the 1980s, but by the 1990s, as many as ten new people were coming each year. It peaked at about 115 people around 2015, and currently is back around 100.

2) I love Ed and Laura Wideman, and their sons. The kids were all small when this trip occurred, so I have withheld their names to protect the guilty. One other day on this trip I bravely took all three of them on a submarine ride, which they liked much better than the road to Hana. A "thank you" drawing they gave me stayed on my fridge for years, and is probably still in a file someplace, hidden but not forgotten.

Chapter 29

1) In 2012 he would sell back Panama City to the corporate company, and end his long-troubled history with Ripley's. Earlier he had already sold back Key West and Ocean City. Bill is still a doer and a dreamer, and I suspect not finished with the attraction business quite yet.

2) I drove from Orlando with my wife in tow. We met my daughter in New Orleans the first night, and our friends from England, Anne Marshall and Chris Seaber, would join us three days later. The Brits had never been to Nawlins before, so to them all seemed "fine". Celeste had been to the city twice before, but both times as a child. She didn't really have any memories to compare to, but she could tell I was playing tour guide, rather than tourist, and that a great deal of the city's magic had been blown way off shore never to return for me.

3) This chapter was written October 11, 2018, the day after Hurricane Michael devastated Panama City Beach and the Florida Panhandle. A new ghost, but the same horror. This chapter is dedicated to all the people who were

affected by either of these two catastrophic storms Katrina and Michael.

Chapter 30

1) I had the foresight to take my good shoes off, and put my phone inside one before I went into the water, but without knowing my phone was in one of the shoes, my shoes were thrown in after me for me to fetch. Ripley "hazing" at its worst. I was without a phone and direct contact to my wife for the next three days.

2) We had not seen Queenie since we took her to Myrtle Beach, South Carolina exactly twenty years before, but in the interim, we had been in regular written communication. She lived in a Catholic senior's home. She did not own a phone, or a television, and did her ablutions in a communal bathroom. Her privacy wall was a drape like in a Western hospital, yet she was happy. A true follower of Christ.

3) The wax museum was ours but it contained only second-hand wax figures from all over the world, the majority from a previous Louis Tussaud's museum we had recently closed in Copenhagen, Denmark.

4) At the crack of dawn everyone in the city goes to the river — Mother Ganga — and performs sun salutations, bathes, and takes home enough holy water for the day's needs. In the evening, giant fires are lit, songs sung, candles set a float on the river, and prayers recited to say goodnight to the Holy Mother of all life. Both are must see grand spectacles, and both have been occurring every day for over 5,000 years. Varanasi is not only the holiest city in India, it may also be the oldest continuously inhabited city in the world, dating back in time to at least 3,000 BC., centuries before the making of the pyramids of Egypt.

5) For me, even more baffling than the funerals on the ghats (steep stone staircases), was the wild cricket games played on them. One misstep and it would be a fall of several feet onto hard cement, then straight into the river. I watched intently like I understood what was going on, but politely declined an invitation to play.

6) Less than a month after we rode this train and I had my middle of the night rendezvous with the bathroom, I read in a newspaper that a woman had given birth in the dark through the hole while squatting to do her business. The baby fell right through to the ground. The mother was able to stop the train, and the baby was recovered, miraculously untouched by the wheels of the train.

7) Puchkas are round golf ball-sized hollow shells that you pour chick pea and tamarind sauce into and try to eat in one bite without the juice squirting all over your face and clothes. A perennial favorite of my wife's, she did not eat them on the train, but they were the first meal she had when we arrived on Park Street in her old Kolkata neighborhood.

Chapter 31

1) Angela and I were shown the original Apollo-era control room, which has been left virtually intact, and the new control room. Entering this new room at a specific time we were able to witness a conversation with astronauts inside the International Space Station. It was a once in a lifetime, make your heart pound like a hammer moment. Seeing the top of the Earth, and a bright green glow above it, which we were told was the Northern Lights as seen from space, was a sight I will never forget. It gave me chills. It was the first time I ever grasped the magnitude and importance of space travel.

Chapter 32

1) Ripley had a heart attack on live television during the filming of his 13th episode, May 23, 1949. He died three days later in the hospital. Li Ling Ai was the last person he saw and talked to. She became one of several guest hosts the show had in 1949, until a permanent host was found – Robert St. John — who would continue the show for two more full seasons 1950-51.

Chapter 33

1) This chapter, and most of this book was typed while sitting in a Nigerian beaded throne, one of my most prized possessions, presented to me by the Keita family.

2) Leopards are the fifth of the big game animals. I didn't see any of these, but in addition to elephants, rhinos, lions and water buffaloes, I did see ostriches, zebras, wildebeests and several kinds of antelope. I also sampled many kinds of game at various meals.

Chapter 34

1) In the 2016 season I was out of town when **The Fireball Run** crew actually filmed in St. Augustine, Florida, but I selected the exhibits that were shown, and I was filmed as a clue reader on the episode. In the 2018 season, in addition to the Burlington sequence, I did a commercial that was filmed in our warehouse summarizing Ripley's involvement with the show. I loved working with J. Sanchez, and hope there will be another opportunity in my future. Of all the producers I have worked with, he may be the guy I most saw eye-to-eye with.

Chapter 35

1) Two original Ripley drawings, one from 1939 and one from circa 1915, and a matchstick violin were given away as retirement presents to worthy influential employees, but nothing else was ever **sold.**

2) Except for once, when I was forced to sing karaoke with him, and he chose the hardest song in the book: "Unchained Melody"!

Chapter 38

1) Robert spent the last couple years of his life promoting the shoe company that made his custom giant shoes. Over the years I bought several of these size thirty-nine shoes, including a two-toned pair. I also acquired his baby shoes (normal sized), lots of photos, printed memorabilia, film footage, and a three-piece blue pin-striped wool suit containing enough material to make four or five regular sized suits. A wax figure, or robotic statue of Wadlow, is displayed in virtually

every Ripley odditorium.

2) Drew no doubt had real concept drawings back in San Antonio, but while out on a rousing night on the town in St. Augustine — porch drinks at Scarlett O'Hara's — he realized he had not brought them to Florida for his next morning presentation. That night, in his hotel room he redrew them from memory on cocktail napkins. The following morning, his presentation amazed everyone, including his boss Bill Phillips.

3) Atlantic City features a two-man construction crew on the roof who appear to have dropped a huge globe through the front of the building. The cracked building is just a fake façade but because it can be seen for quite a distance from either direction on the boardwalk, it surprises people, and to this day, first time visitors ask if the people on the roof are real. The illusion is uncanny.

4) There is one other odditorium I should at least mention. Our second franchised location was in the Four Queens Hotel in Las Vegas (1986-1993). They had a huge budget, and brought a lot of glitz to the product. Overall it was an old style museum, with only one real special room, but that room, a thirty-foot high cave filled with some of the greatest villains of history, would get my vote for the all-time single best Ripley odditorium gallery. It was cold, dark, damp, creepy, and because of the big budget, very realistic. The only thing that was missing was bats. It was designed and built by Jimmy Doyle, a former Ripley in-house designer who used the success of this building to launch a rewarding Las Vegas design business. Several years later, he moved to Florida, and led our in-house design team for a second term.

Chapter 39

1) There is a sixth one that I could include here, but other than meeting a wonderful man named Steve Gordon, our truck driver from St. Augustine, there wasn't too much I wish to remember about my first trip to Gatlinburg, Tennessee in November 1985. The racism this man confronted in this town, both obvious, and not so obvious, shaped my negative feelings towards East Ten-

nessee for life.

2) The company was up for sale, and would be bought by the Jim Pat-Tyson Group of Vancouver, Canada, less than six months later.

3) Estes Park is over 7,500', nearly one mile, high in elevation. Breathing in this town was hard enough never mind trying to move a metal safe by hand down eighty-year-old worn wooden stairs. Norm would frequently get a nose bleed just by venturing to the top of the building.

4) The real name was the Bull and Finch, but nobody called it that.

5) This storm was called the 'storm of the century", and it was the first time in seventeen years Ocean City had been cut off from the mainland. I had seen worse storms in Toronto, but I had never been hounded, or stranded for six days by one.

6) As in Estes Park, Norm Deska, the company controller at the time, was also on this trip for the first couple days to handle any big money made from the sale, and to sign the legal papers required for the sale of the property. Somehow, he failed to check-out properly, and I was charged for five nights for his room that had been used only two nights.

7) The giant shark was the center piece for a gallery on Sharks and Rodney Fox, an Australian spear fisherman man who had survived the attack of a Great White shark. The shark grabbed him by the side of his stomach and swam with him in its jaws. To escape he pounded at its face with his left arm. He miraculously survived, receiving 463 stitches. A shark tooth remained embedded in the top of his hand.

In 1999   I had the pleasure of meeting Rodney and his wife Kay   for a dinner in Orlando. My family joined us as my son was a big fan of Rodney's and was very interested in sharks. Shaking hands with Rodney he felt and saw the outline of the embedded tooth and screamed with excitement. It was a wonderful evening that Curtis has never forgotten.

8) It is worth noting that prior to building Jackson

Hole, Norm had built the successful Ripley franchised odditorium in Wisconsin Dells, Wisconsin (1990), which at the time of this writing is now in its 28th year of operation, and is still the most unique of all Ripley locations. When he finally retired to become a full-time missionary, Norm sold the Wisconsin location to Kevin and Corena, which they continue to operate.

9) In 2014 there were rumblings of my demise, but I was still needed for a significant television special that would air in January 2015. Once that project was completed, I was living on the edge of thin ice. It, however, took considerably longer for the ice to break than I would have bet in September 2015. At the time I really thought this might be my last big trip, and certainly my last odditorium closing, which it proved to be.

10) Angela was my longest running assistant (2010-2018), and was still with Ripley's after I retired in June of 2018. In July of 2018 she led the closing of a temporary Ripley exhibition at the Memphis Zoo. I assume skills learned out west in 2015 came in handy.

11) To be totally honest, seeing a Ripley warehouse manager named Mel(vin) Calloway drive a big truck in the small narrow streets of Key West, during the closing of that odditorium in 2003 was almost as beautiful, but he unfortunately did "nick" one building on Duval Street.

12) Since I didn't end up leaving the company that year, I managed to see Wyoming and Kevin and Corena again, but not Norm or Heather. The last I heard they were doing missionary work in Yugoslavia (Croatia). God continues to bless them.

Chapter 40

1) The white alligators of Louisiana are the most famous leucistic animals on the planet. To the average person they look like albino gators, but look closely and you will see they do not have the trademark pink eyes of albinism, but rather Paul Newman-like piercing blue eyes. Like white tigers, all white gators can be traced back to one mutant adult. The first nest of white gators was found in Louisiana in the 1970s.

Chapter 41

1) The Niagara Falls History Museum owned a forty-five-foot long humpback whale skeleton, once owned by P.T. Barnum. It was the first, and oldest whale skeleton display in the world. I would learn much more about it ten years later in 1999.

2) These, and one of the most bizarre exhibits in the entire Ripley collection: the complete **Moby Dick** novel typed on six rolls of toilet paper!

Chapter 42

1) Torontonian Bill Jamieson, an independent scholar and collector put forth his theory after substantial research, but initially was mocked by everyone, including myself. It simply seemed absurd that Ramses could be in Canada, and no one know it. Bill's borrowing a considerable amount of money to acquire the museum's entire collection in 1999, then the subsequent selling of bits and pieces of it, including the Ramses mummy, led to his wealth, and elevated status amongst collectors all over the world. Ramses returned home to Egypt with great fanfare in 2003, and Bill became a Canadian legend.

2) Three other dime museums mummies in the Ripley collection are more animal than human, and were created in the mid-1920s post the discovery of King Tut's Tomb. Though claiming to be real Egyptian mummies thousands of years old, they were "brand new" and made near Boston.

3) In ancient Egypt, the goddess Bast, the goddess of protection and the daughter of Ra, was represented by a cat. Cat mummies were often buried with the pharaohs and entire cemeteries dedicated to Bast, filled with hundreds of cat mummies, have been excavated.

Chapter 43

1) After reviewing this chapter, collector and friend Warren Raymond told me that "Atta Boy" had belonged to

a Californian named Sam Houston (not the famous Sam Houston), whose family had it buried. I have no reason to doubt him, but I still hope more details might arise.

Chapter 44

1) Ripley's has clay-over-modeled skulls from at least four South Sea Islands: New Guinea, New Ireland, New Britain, and the New Hebrides.

2) Collectively the head hunters of the Philippines are known linguistically as the Igorot. Amongst the six tribes that make up the Igorot, only two, the Bontoc and the Ifugao are known to have been headhunters. The Catholic Church was fairly successful in converting the native peoples of the Philippines early on, and though there is lots of evidence of head hunting, there is little evidence of actual cannibalism. I am no expert on the distinction between the two, but suspect that people actively collecting heads, probably ate human flesh too.

3) Ripley met headhunters in Taiwan in 1923, and self-proclaimed Fijian cannibals in 1932, but seemingly these societies did not keep the skulls of those they ate. For much of the 18th and 19th centuries, the Fijian islands were called "the Cannibal Islands". Sailors were afraid to land on them, and the natives openly boasted of how many people they had eaten (one chief claimed to have eaten 932 "long pigs" — the local term for human flesh). From Fiji, Ripley brought back ceremonial forks used exclusively to eat human flesh.

4) There is a lot of controversy over these shrunken bodies. Reportedly they were created by a German doctor who spent some years amongst the Shuar. Two are male, one a Negro, the other allegedly a Spanish sea captain. The other two, are Shuar women. Bill Jamieson owned one of the female specimens, and openly had it on the market for several years with an asking price of $100,000. Unlike the other three, it did not have legs or arms causing some people to believe it may have been from a different source than the other three. It was not in very good shape when I saw it in New York City in 2007. It was not offered in his estate auction held by Wad-

dington's Auction in Toronto in 2014, but it reportedly was sold privately in Europe around the same time.

5) Ripley's is occasionally criticized for being too dark, literally and figuratively, but very rarely does anyone point out a specific exhibit to complain about. The Christian martyr head and an Indian scalp being exceptions. Believe it or not, the loudest, and most vitriolic display complaint in my 40 years of service was over a topless wax figure of Cleopatra. We silenced the anger by putting a chain and jeweled bra on her.

Chapter 45

1) The prices quoted are more or less accurate. The difference is, that in buying the carcass, the risk was all mine. If it hasn't been frozen solid, or it wasn't frozen quick enough, or if it thaws in trans-port, the carcass may spoil and be useless when it arrives at the taxidermist. If the seller opts to get it mounted locally, and I would say this happened about 10% of the time, more often with a multi-limbed creature than one with two-heads, he takes all the risk. If his local taxidermist does a crappy job, I didn't buy it, and he is back looking for a buyer, but now with money already invested. Taxidermy prices, like everything else, went up each year, and today $5,000 won't likely get the job done. On occasion, if someone got a good job done, but spent more than he should have, I would give them a little lagniappe at the end so that he went away a satisfied customer. There was always the hope he would call me again with another animal in the future.

2) The two-headed peacock was acquired already mounted, reportedly from a game farm. It was cheap — -a good sign that it was not real, but I couldn't take the chance. It looks magnificent, but was proven after the purchase to be fake.

3) The elephant is my single favorite exhibit I ever bought. Sometimes I wish I had mounted the entire animal, but the head alone is ten-foot by ten-foot, weighs nearly 1,500 lbs., and cost more than an arm and a leg — pun intended.

Chapter 47

1) Ripley's owns a poster size chart that I purchased in Spain that list the traits of each individual type of wolpertinger. I am pretty sure they are all listed as evil forest spirits. I suspect fairies and elves are their good guy opposites.

Chapter 48

1) Hairballs are created by animals licking each other, or themselves, to obtain salt. The cow has a multiple chambered stomach, so the hair is exposed to gastric juices that shape it, and dump it in a far chamber from whence it can't be regurgitated; it can only be removed by butchering the cow. The older the cow, the bigger the balls might be. A cow can have several of these balls in its stomach at the same time. Remind me never to be a butcher, or to visit an abattoir.

Chapter 49

1) I was a big fan of Indian lore long before I discovered Grey Owl, but for a few years he was my biggest hero. I grew my hair long, and wore a fringed buckskin jacket and moccasins to high school my first three years (9th to 11th grades). If my mother would have let me, I would have loved to have had a pet beaver in our basement.

2) As will be explained a bit later, my third redwood purchase involved six pieces of the same tree, but here I am counting it as just one acquisition.

3) It is worth noting that the church Robert Ripley's mother Lillie Belle attended, in Santa Rosa, California, was built from one single redwood tree. For twenty-eight years (1970-1998) it housed a Memorial Museum to Robert Ripley. Today, it is still standing, and can be rented for weddings, but it does not host regular church services. It features a lovely stained glass window image of a redwood tree over the altar. Robert Ripley's dad Isaac, was one of the lumberjack-carpenters who built it in the 1890s.

Chapter 50

1) Counting tree growth rings to calculate a tree's age is called"dendro chronology". It is a legitimate "science", but requires a skilled eye and a lot of patience. Chuck was the Ripley man for the job.

2) Chuck also led me to numerous giant petrified logs from New Mexico that are in the Ripley collection. Some of these weigh over a 1,000 pounds, and are big enough to sit on, or use as end tables.

3) Chuck retired in 1984. In 1988 in his honor, the company named a trophy given out annually to the odditorium staff that contributes the most towards the company's exhibit acquisition program. To date San Francisco, led by employees initially hired by Chuck, has won it more times than any other location.

Chapter 51

1) A few years later I managed to buy one of these types, but initially I went looking for the full metal plate armor type.

2) Following popular trends was always an important part of my job, both for cartoon content, and museum exhibits. Early in my career, under the direction of Norm Deska, Ripley's bought the rights to a casting of the actual Great White shark the film **"Jaws"** was based on; he also bought the fishing gear it was caught on. Sharks, like dinosaurs, are perennial favorites with younger museum visitors, and a subject I would revisit many times in my buying career.

3) Eventually, Bob went back to the hotel, but not until he had driven me to the Filmore West to see Chicago Blues legend, Otis Rush. This was my one and only ever visit to the Filmore. There was a double bill with Rush and the Godfather of British Blues, John Mayall. Mayall had already finished before I got there, but I did see a good ninety-minute set by Otis.

4) This sentence has been kept as it was written, but Bob Masterson who was one of my fact checkers for this book in 2018, after reading this chapter called me from

the Houston airport chuckling. On the phone he told me the actual story, told here for the first time: Bob had tried every possible "smooth-talking" way to get the gun aboard, but no one would give approval. Standing in a boarding line, fearing he was defeated, he was approached by the plane's pilot. The pilot had overheard his plea, and more importantly, had heard on the news the previous evening of Bob and I buying the pistol. He volunteered to personally get the derringer on the plane, took it from Bob and walked through the staff line, avoiding the passenger metal detector line-up. At the end of the flight in Orlando, he returned the gun to Bob.

5) Parts of this story have been told many times before, often with factual errors regarding dates. I apologize for any previous mistakes and incongruences, but go on record here, acknowledging this as the full and correct version of this important tale. The name of the diplomat's son has been withheld by request.

Chapter 52

1) Bob worked in St. Augustine from 1974-77. He recalls the stone still being there at the end of 1976, but by the time I came along six years later, people thought I was dreaming, or insane.

2) Another very baffling thing about rai is that because of their size and weight, even when used in a trade, they stayed on the property of the original owner. Oral histories were passed down from generation to generation so owners could be traced, but the "coins" themselves never moved.

Chapter 53

1) Though often called "mouth gags" there is speculation, based on size and especially shape, that the mouth was not the only place a "pear of agony" may have been thrust by a zealous torturer.

2) It is quite possible that "I have seen it all", but there were two things I wouldn't even consider to allow myself to acquire during my career, lampshades made from

the human skin of Jews murdered in German concentration camps, and a Ku Klux Klan robe. After listening to a lecture in 2018 by Darryl Davis, author of **"Klandestine Relationships"**, and an advocate of peace through open dialog, I now believe that even these two items should be openly displayed not necessarily in a Ripley odditorium — but somewhere appropriate, "lest we forget". It is important to remember that the objects of hate are in themselves just symbols, the evil is in the people that used them.

Chapter 54

1) The assault had happened in the Fall of 1999, but Michael was still seeing doctors, weekly, almost twenty months later.

Chapter 55

1) For the sake of this chapter I will consider things like the Spanish Armada which has over 250 individual model ships, as just one "display". If I were to count every single model as "one", the total number would be well in excess of 500.

2) Patrick Acton, described in detail elsewhere in this chapter, has lovingly repaired Reg's Rolls at least three times, but notes Reg's English matches are a little different than standard American ones. A discerning eye, therefore, can see the repaired areas no matter how good Patrick's repair work was.

3) See Footnote #1. Len's Spanish Armada was the largest of his multi-pieced displays, but he also had an entire history of navigation with about fifty pieces, a Cowboy-Western town with about the same number, and a World War I dog fight battle scene with about twenty individual Fokker and Sopwith Camel planes.

4) Of all the small to mid-size matchstick models I've seen, or acquired, this one is the best. The motion of the horse and its muscle tones are perfectly captured. The variety of shapes, from triangles to circles, makes this a marvel of realistic sculpture.

Chapter 56

1) Stollery's was a Toronto institution. It was on that busy street corner for over 114 years before closing in 2014.

2) The engine for the carriage was hidden in a wood carved trousseau chest mounted to the back of the carriage, behind the driver. We took delivery of the carriage without its engine.

3) More than twenty years later I read a newspaper story about a carriage museum in Ocala, Florida, going out of business. Angela Johnson and I took a short road trip, and not only discovered a wonderful museum collection of antique carriages, but also the woman who had lent us her horses, and the man who had driven our pumpkin carriage nearly twenty years before. Both remembered the day with big smiles; she owned the carriage museum, and he worked there. Small world.

Chapter 57

1) I believe the owner eventually sold it two years later to the same car museum that bought the Mansfield car. Reportedly each car was sold for $8,000 which must have been a magic minimum number to the seller.

2) Including, but not limited to, medical equipment used in his autopsy and a newspaper photo of the autopsy that would make your hair curl. It is definitely the most grotesque photo I know of. Presumably, it was taken and distributed by the press to show Oswald as more monster than human.

Chapter 58

1) Our famous giant "string" ball is actually composed of nylon cord, there is no real 'string", or binder twine in its construction. The distinction is somewhat semantic, but it does matter to some people mainly residents of Cawker City, Kansas, and Darwin, Minnesota. More on this later in the chapter.

2) In addition to the big balls to be discussed here, Ripley's does own several "smaller" string balls and

one or two rubber band balls too, the smallest of which is basketball-size.

3) The show was officially canceled after this episode, but more shows were in fact aired several months later as a "summer replacement" program, until the network could find a new full-time replacement.

4) The giant plastic bag ball owned by Ripley's, and also inspired by the same television episode at the time of writing is still in the Ripley warehouse, and has never been displayed. Luckily, it was donated and virtually no money was invested in it.

5) Lyle's ball was the world's biggest barbed wire ball for many years, but J. C. Payne, discussed later in this chapter, after finishing the world's biggest string ball, went on to build a barbed wire ball almost twice as big as Lyle's. A vanity project to be sure.

Chapter 60

1) The "Buddhas" are actually representations of a female bodhisattiva known as Guanyin, goddess of Mercy and Compassion. The statues do not literally have 1,000 arms, more like 100, but each arm, has a unique delicately carved hand. Weighing nearly a ton each, they are masterpieces of jade carving, considerably more intricate than the ships, the chariot or the coins.

2) I had first learned about this ancient device, in my first-year college Chinese History class. It is a vase-shaped bronze urn with dragons, and/ or frogs, mounted to it, that spit balls when the urn was jostled. If the balls came shooting out all at once, it was believed to be a sure sign of underground earthquakes. I had seen one years before in Toronto as part of a government sponsored, traveling Chinese cultural exhibition. I didn't realize at the time that it was and exceedingly rare, one of only two or three then known to exist. At the fair I did meet a group who advertised a brass, gold and ruby version in their brochure. It had to be made to order and would take six months to complete. The price? -$25,000.

3) I was introduced to the other two items at the same traveling exhibition.

540

4) I was never quite sure how old Jack was, but he looked ancient, and had some significant health problems. He knew that neither his wife, or his son, loved his collection like he did. He would have liked to get a fair market value, but he was more interested in making sure the collection would not disappear. Jack dreamed of it being housed in a museum for the world to appreciate. I cringe to think that the big pieces are still in storage waiting for a natural disaster or theft.

Chapter 61

1) The Generals and David have both been thoroughly cleaned from tip to toe by the Chicago staff more than once now, and they also did repair work with great care and patience to St. Augustine's Chinese jade dragon boat that received violent treatment from a moving team.

2)

Chapter 62

1) In the first paragraph alone there are at least three clues that should have alerted me to the hoax. Rosa says there were lots of wax museums in Indiana during the 1930s-1940s and his parents visited them as many as twenty times a year. The first wax museums didn't really start to appear in America until the late 1950s (Ripley's Louis Tussaud's wax museum, in Niagara Falls, Canada, opened in 1957 and is often quoted as being the first authentic European – style wax museum in North America) around the same time that the birth of Interstate Highways made the possibility of family road trip vacations an annual event. Almost no one randomly traveled to see man-made attractions during the depth of the 1930s depression — even if they did own a car — and there were never "quite a few" wax museums in the "Hoosier State".

Chapter 68

1) The OMG Car has several ornamental roosters on it, some large flowers, and is painted in bold big stripes. Most of the decorations are on the roof. It is actually quite tame compared to other art cars, but as seen in

the film, it was not much liked by officers of the law.

2) I didn't know it when we first met, but Harrod is the son of Les Blank, a maker of blues music documentary films that I absolutely love. Through Harrod I would later get to meet his father who gifted me with DVDs of his best films. They are more precious to me than gold.

Chapter 69

1) I would later buy a gold coin covered limousine and a two-story high gold coin covered double-decker English bus from the Burkitts, as well as several portraits made of Swarovski crystals, including one of Louis Armstrong, and one of Marilyn Monroe. Ken was a grand English showman in the tradition of P. T. Barnum and Robert Ripley.

Chapter 70

1) For more than twenty-five years, all of the two-dimensional flat wall art, and some three-dimensional pieces too, both in the Ripley offices and all Ripley's odditoriums around the world, were framed by Mike Van Der Leest & Rudy Wright of **Framing of Central Florida**. Together these two gentlemen probably did as much to create the look of Ripley odditoriums as any one of the company's designers.

2) This mural is made of 3,000 postcards, each depicting one of a 110 different paintings by Van Gogh, and assembled, they create a depiction of Van Gogh's very famous "Self-Portrait". This picture was done as a Van Gogh centennial project long before "computer digitization" was a possibility. It was a forefather of a whole genre, which became popular circa 2010, and inspired David Alvarez of Washington State, who made giant murals of Ray Charles, Jimi Hendrix, Marilyn Monroe and Humphrey Bogart, that are also in the Ripley collection. His Ray Charles is made from post-it notes, Hendrix is made from playing cards, Monroe from dice, and Bogart from dominoes.

3) Years later I bought four marvelous paper pieces, two

aboriginals, a Vietnam soldier, and Brad Pitt as seen in the film "Troy", made by a husband and wife team, Allan and Patty Eckman of South Dakota. There is no comparison regarding quality, the work of the Eckman's being much more refined and detailed, but Schiavone's work, especially his Pieta and his thirteen figure Da Vinci's Last Supper, are still exemplary works of folk art. Schiavone made wedding dresses for a living. The Eckman's are professional artists.

4) The only other piece that may have been better, or at least as good, was a pencil sketch of a World War I military troop. It was over thirty-feet long by ten-feet high, and was based on a two-inch by three-inch photo. I believe it was the last piece to win $500,000 before the prize money was decreased.

5) Elvis is covered in over fifty figurines representing the history of rock n' roll music; Jack Sparrow has real sea shells and seaweed as well as toy fish; and Captain America has dozens of sculpted heroes and villains, including a large fierce "Wolverine" clawing his way out of the Captain's back in a scene reminiscent of the birth of "Rosemary's Baby".

Chapter 72

1) I still own a 'souvenir" descriptive book about Syadristy and his art that I bought at the Fair. It shows forty-two pieces, but I am sure there were no more than ten or twelve actually on display, and may-be even fewer.

2) It is possible that Ripley got at least some of the facts wrong on this one, as another pin by another Spokane resident, Godfrey Lundberg, had first been shown at the Panama Exposition World's Fair in San Francisco in 1915, and a pin created by A. Schiller had been displayed at the Chicago World's Fair in 1893. There is considerable debate that Baker may have purloined a pin carved by Lundberg rather than carved one of his own.

3) Legend or myth, concerning A. Schiller you decide, says that when he was found dead in his California jail cell, guards found seven pins in his possession, but upon inspection, only one was perfect. I believe the second pin I acquired may be one of Schiller's "mistakes",

but it might also be the Baker pin Ripley wrote about in 1929.

4) A couple of years later Ripley's sent a different film crew to Birmingham and made a very different style film that would be shown wherever they displayed any of Willard's art.

Chapter 74

1) I know for sure Maureen Chant, Jimmy's right hand administrative assistant, did not attend the auction itself. She may have joined us for the viewing, and I do believe she was at the pub lunch creating the shopping list as Jimmy talked strategies. For years Jimmy and Maureen were inseparable, and virtually all my contacts with Jimmy involved Maureen at some level. I respected her authority and always appreciated her playing "middle woman" in my buying adventures with Jimmy.

Chapter 77

1) Note Ripley never called it this, using instead the more colloquial British name, The Hall of Victory.

2) If the minuscule size of Gwawley's work isn't amazing enough, con-sider he had no hands, and his carvings were done with artificial limbs of his own making.

Chapter 78

1) As of May 8, 2019, it has been rumored that Ripley's has in fact closed a deal to acquire the Mon Lei, but the details have not been released.

Chapter 79

1) Neil Armstrong didn't walk down the ladder and into the lunar dust and history for all eternity until six hours later. I suspect I didn't hear his "One small step…" speech until the next day, though I am sure my mother was still sitting with her radio to her ear at 10:17pm inside our small cabin.

2) For a real good understanding of the things that have the things that have been carried into space by astronauts, visit the Houston Space Center museum. Ripley's has restricted its interest to flags and "Bibles", but they have on display everything from plush children's toys, to religious relics, to jewelry and clothing.

3) Nimoy did a promotional commercial for Ripley's **"World of the Unexplained"** in 1975, and his face was on all the print ads. The museum had a large **Star Trek** exhibit including wax figures of the central characters, and a very stereotypical round flying saucer. Ripley's even sold tribbles in the gift shops.

Chapter 80

1) I don't think the people of Santa Rosa have ever forgotten Robert Ripley, but he is now eclipsed by the shadow of Charles Schulz (note Schulz was not born in Santa Rosa, but moved there in 1969), and perhaps even Luther Burbank, the world's famous horticulturist, a true native son.

2) I have reason to believe, but have never been able to confirm, that this epitaph was added by Alec Rigby between 1970 and 1972, perhaps as part of the opening celebrations of the Memorial Museum.

Acknowledgements:

Thanks to everyone I worked with at Ripley's for forty years, especially:

Alec, John and Bob who had faith in me; Jimmy and Jim who allowed me to continuously grow; and to my long line of assistants: Sheila, Rachel, Jan, Kathy, Kim, Margaret, Angela A., Lisa, Aida, Viviana, Anthony, and Angela J., who patiently, and lovingly guided me.

Thanks to Sidney Kirkpatrick and Drew Hunter for convincing me to write this book.

Thanks to Akiko Currie for proofing the manuscript with a fine-toothed comb and saving me from a thousand embarrassments, and thanks to all my friends and associates – you know who you are – that reviewed specific manuscript chapters, and offered much needed encouragements.

Thanks to Angela Johnson and Lifetouch Portraits for their original photos, and Barry Anderson, Drew Hunter and Wendy Westbury for their original drawings.

Special thanks to Robert Goforth, Angela Johnson, and Bob Masterson who did editorial fact checking during the manuscript's development.

Thanks also to all the people I bought exhibits from that contributed so much to my life, and to Ripley's collection.

And, thanks especially to my children, Curtis and Celeste, and my wife, Giliane, for their encouragement, faith, dedication and love. This book is for them.

43703679R00307

Printed in Poland
by Amazon Fulfillment
Poland Sp. z o.o., Wrocław